I0034486

EUL VERLAG

SCHRIFTEN ZU KOOPERATIONS- UND MEDIENSYSTEMEN

Herausgegeben von Prof. Dr. Volker Wulf, Siegen, Prof. Dr. Jörg Haake, Hagen, Prof. Dr. Thomas Herrmann, Bochum, Prof. Dr. Helmut Krcmar, München, Prof. Dr. Johann Schlichter, München, Prof. Dr. Gerhard Schwabe, Zürich, und Prof. Dr.-Ing. Jürgen Ziegler, Duisburg

Band 23
Ralf Reichwald, Helmut Krcmar und Michael Nippa (Hrsg.)
Hybride Wertschöpfung – Konzepte, Methoden und Kompetenzen für die Preis- und Vertragsgestaltung
Lohmar – Köln 2009 ◆ 420 S. ◆ € 67,- (D) ◆ ISBN 978-3-89936-855-0

Band 24
Jan Marco Leimeister, Helmut Krcmar, Martin Halle und Kathrin Möslein (Hrsg.)
Hybride Wertschöpfung in der Gesundheitsförderung – Ergebnisse des Verbundprojekts „Systematisches Design zur Integration von Produkt und Dienstleistung in der Gesundheitswirtschaft" (SPRINT)
Lohmar – Köln 2010 ◆ 272 S. ◆ € 58,- (D) ◆ ISBN 978-3-89936-914-4

Band 25
Zoulfa El Jerroudi
Eine interaktive Vorgehensweise für den Vergleich und die Integration von Ontologien
Lohmar – Köln 2010 ◆ 200 S. ◆ € 49,- (D) ◆ ISBN 978-3-89936-916-8

Band 26
Carsten Ritterskamp
Informationstechnische Unterstützung der Handhabung von Unterbrechungen in der Multiprojekt-Wissensarbeit
Lohmar – Köln 2010 ◆ 296 S. ◆ € 59,- (D) ◆ ISBN 978-3-89936-941-0

Band 27
Christian Dörner
Tailoring Software Infrastructures – Integration of End-User Development and Service-Oriented Architectures
Lohmar – Köln 2010 ◆ 188 S. ◆ € 48,- (D) ◆ ISBN 978-3-89936-947-2

JOSEF EUL VERLAG

Schriften zu Kooperations- und Mediensystemen · Band 27

Herausgegeben von Prof. Dr. Volker Wulf, Siegen, Prof. Dr. Jörg Haake, Hagen, Prof. Dr. Thomas Herrmann, Bochum, Prof. Dr. Helmut Krcmar, München, Prof. Dr. Johann Schlichter, München, Prof. Dr. Gerhard Schwabe, Zürich, und Prof. Dr.-Ing. Jürgen Ziegler, Duisburg

Dr. Christian Dörner

Tailoring Software Infrastructures

Integration of End-User Development and Service-Oriented Architectures

With a Foreword by Prof. Dr. Volker Wulf, University of Siegen

EUL VERLAG

Bibliografische Information der Deutschen Nationalbibliothek

Die Deutsche Nationalbibliothek verzeichnet diese Publikation
in der Deutschen Nationalbibliografie; detaillierte bibliografische
Daten sind im Internet über <http://dnb.d-nb.de> abrufbar.

Dissertation, Universität Siegen, 2009

ISBN 978-3-89936-947-2
1. Auflage Juli 2010

© JOSEF EUL VERLAG GmbH, Lohmar – Köln, 2010
Alle Rechte vorbehalten

Umschlaggestaltung: Luzia Sassen
© Cover-Abbildung: Benjamin Helsper

JOSEF EUL VERLAG GmbH
Brandsberg 6
53797 Lohmar
Tel.: 0 22 05 / 90 10 6-6
Fax: 0 22 05 / 90 10 6-88
E-Mail: info@eul-verlag.de
http://www.eul-verlag.de

Bei der Herstellung unserer Bücher möchten wir die Umwelt schonen. Dieses
Buch ist daher auf säurefreiem, 100% chlorfrei gebleichtem, alterungsbestän-
digem Papier nach DIN 6738 gedruckt.

"The human mind is our fundamental resource."

John F. Kennedy

for Eva

Foreword

Dynamic and differentiated markets demand a high flexibility from organisations regarding their business processes as well as their working practices. To be able to be responsive to changing environmental impacts, organisations depend on adaptable software infrastructures. However, these infrastructures do frequently not offer the necessary flexibility to adapt applications at runtime.

Current research in the field of Information Systems investigates into opportunities to effectively adapt software applications. There are numerous approaches and tools for modelling business processes which are often part of Enterprise Resource Planning (ERP) systems. However, these tools are not jet sufficiently oriented towards the demands and needs of end users. Approaches that support end users in orchestrating software services are still missing. Christian Dörner's PhD thesis deals with the question of how the adaptation of service-based software infrastructures can be supported.

Approaching this issue in an appropriate manner increases the opportunities of organisations and reduces their dependency on software service providers and technical advisers. Focusing on end users requires research on the appropriation of new technologies in organisations. Challenges exist in the field of user-oriented service documentation and the search for services as well as in terms of reusing adapted artefacts. Such a research agenda can only be approached if research is embedded into the organisational practice following an approach which covers three phases: empirical pre-study, design of innovative technology, and its empirical evaluation.

Especially the first two phases are excellently worked out in this book. The analysis of current research is very extensive and shows that Christian has dealt intensively with different traditions of science as well as existing approaches for the problem he investigates. Christian became acquainted with segments of Information Systems, Software Engineering, and Human Computer Interaction (especially in the fields of End User Development, Service-Oriented Architectures, and Business Process Management) to support his elaborated approach.

The empirical studies evaluating the appropriation of ERP systems in medium-sized organisations are important findings presented in this book. The investigation of the actual usage of ERP systems in organisations occurs in a profound manner – in terms of the problems expressed with regard to the given ERP systems as well as with the description of practices to circumvent these problems. The process modelling environment was appropriately designed based on the results of the empirical pre-study. The scientific attraction of this concept is the successful consolidation of a multiplicity of difficult design decisions.

Christian had to balance between the power of the adaptation mechanisms and the ability of end users to appropriate these mechanisms. The concept of enhancing service-oriented software architectures can be considered innovative as it integrates usage-oriented metadata into this architecture in a transparent manner and allows end users to modify this data. The resulting modelling application has been sophisticatedly implemented which is also reflected by its publication in form of two open source projects and its usage in the evaluation study.

The results of the evaluation study are interesting as they deliver detailed insights into the usefulness and usability of the approach. However, the evaluation of the developed solutions in a real organisation would have been desirable, but as service-oriented infrastructures were not available in the researched firms at that time, it was impossible to conduct such a study.

In conclusion, the book provides very interesting findings dealing with an important field of research for the German software industry. Remarkable are also the numerous publications which arose in the context of this work, involving some high-quality, internationally recognised papers. In addition, this thesis has just recently been awarded with the "Förderpreis des Fachbereichs Wirtschaftswissenschaften, Wirtschaftsinformatik und Wirtschaftsrecht" of the University of Siegen.

I hope the reader may gain many interesting insights by reading this book.

Siegen, July 2010   Volker Wulf

Acknowledgements

This thesis describes my research activities between April 2006 and March 2009 at the University of Siegen. Most of these activities were carried out as part of the EUDISMES project that was funded by the *Bundesministerium für Bildung und Forschung (BMBF)*. First, I would like to thank *Prof. Dr. Volker Wulf* for supervising me and supporting my ideas. I would also like to thank *Jun.-Prof. Dr. Volkmar Pipek* for discussing different topics of my thesis with me, managing the EUDISMES project, and agreeing to act as my second examiner.

In addition, I would like to thank some other colleagues. First of all, I thank *Dr. Fahri Yetim* for his constructive criticism and valuable feedback during our work on various papers. Likewise, I would like to thank *Michael Veith* for his inspiring ideas and the work we did together in the field of end-user development. I am also equally grateful to *Kai Schubert*, with whom I discussed earlier versions of my thesis. Furthermore I thank *Sebastian Draxler* for our discussions about 'end users' and his generous help on Eclipse. Last but not least I would like to thank *Torben Wiedenhöfer* for his work and guidance on the evaluation studies.

Many students have contributed to the thesis either through their diploma theses or their work in several student projects. I would like to thank *Björn Borggräfe* for his excellent work on PaSeMod. I am also very grateful to *Frank Paczynski* for his implementation of the first version of SiSO and *Thorsten Theelen* for the redesign of SiSO's search system. *Farid Ahmadov, Rashid Bakirov, Parviz Karimov, Thorsten Theelen* and *Eldar Mammadli* have also contributed to the development of SiSO by features as part of their student project. *Moritz Weber, Benedikt Ley, Mirko Heinbuch, Markus Hofmann* and *Min Wang* successfully implemented EUSOP in another student project. I was particularly grateful for the discussions about the implementation of EUSOP I had with *Moritz Weber*.

I am very grateful to the people who contributed to the participatory design workshop and were essential to its success: *Claudia Müller, Michael Veith, Sebastian Draxler, Frank Paczynski* and *Michel Claussmann*. I thank *Dr. Markus Rohde, Mirko Heinbuch, Torben Wiedenhöfer* and *Björn Borggräfe* for helping me to set up the online survey. I also like to thank the whole EUDISMES team and all employees of the participating firms who made it possible to conduct the pre- and evaluation studies.

Several people helped me to put my work down on paper. First of all, I would like to thank *Susanne Leitterstorf* who has done a marvellous editing of the text to make it more concise and coherent. In addition, *Seth Hulse* and *Theresa Dörner* provided corrections to earlier versions of the text. I thank *Benjamin Helsper* for designing the figure on the book's cover. I would also like to thank *Michael Veith* for his comments on my presentation of the research design as well as *Dr. Markus Rohde* for his valuable feedback on my description of the empirical studies.

Finally, I thank all my friends and my family. They supported me throughout my work on this thesis and understood that I did not spend as much time with them as I would have liked.

Pittsburgh, July 2010   Christian Dörner

Table of Contents

Table of Figures

Table of Tables

Chapter 1

"The Windows-powered PC enabled millions of individuals, for the first time ever, to become authors of their own content in digital form, which meant that content could be shared far and wide. [...] Suddenly ordinary people could get the benefit of computing without being programmers."

Friedman, 2006, p. 55

1.   Introduction

Software that used to be constructed monolithically is now more flexibly designed with reusable building blocks (Mocan et al., 2006) that facilitate the adaptation of software during its life cycle. Such adaptations can accommodate continuous changes in software requirements, driven by, for example, novel applications, different user groups, changes in legislation, and improvements in machine vehicles (Brooks, 1987).

The need for such adaptations should be taken into account at the stage of identifying the requirements of a proposed new piece of software (Henderson and Kyng, 1991). It is practically impossible to fully identify the requirements of a software product in advance given the range of possible applications and the divergent needs of different user groups. It is easier to adapt a software product to particular uses within a defined scope (Stiemerling et al., 1997).

My research focuses on the development of software that can be adapted by end users. I discuss the design and evaluation of a business process modelling environment for end users in small and medium enterprises which enables them to adapt software infrastructures by themselves.

1.1.   Motivation

Today's non-tayloristic working environment calls for increased flexibility in work practices and dynamic IT systems in support of these practices. Taylorism (Kieser and Ebers, 2006) is no longer the dominant model of organisational development (Wulf, 1994) as organisations aim to adapt more flexibly to environmental changes (Kahler, 1995; Paetau, 1994; Stiemerling, 2000; Wulf and Rohde, 1995). Adaptations are driven, for instance, by changes to formal organisational constructs, individual work practices, and external factors such as changes in legislation and technology. These adaptations allow firms to differentiate themselves from rivals and to gain a competitive advantage by dynamically addressing customer needs (Carr, 2004; Gurram et al., 2008). Therefore, adaptability is now considered to be an important characteristic of software systems (Bowen et al., 2002; Sprott, 2000; Won, 2004).

Modern Enterprise Resource Planning (ERP) systems are at the centre of organisations' software infrastructures[1]. They usually provide a variety of different customisation options, facilitating, to a limited extent, their adaptation to the changing requirements of individual organisations. Organisations tend to be process-oriented (Melão and Pidd, 2000) and can usefully be described as sets of business processes[2]. However, such descriptions are limited in terms of covering every detail of an organisation's work practice. Nevertheless, the adaptation and optimisation of business processes are commonly used approaches to improve the efficiency of organisations, and also have the potential to provide an enhanced adaptability.

However, the adaptation of business processes was not well supported by standard enterprise software in the past because it was difficult to change business processes within these systems (Markus et al., 2000). Moreover, the integration of third party and legacy systems into busi-

---

[1] The *New Oxford American Dictionary* (McKean, E. *The new Oxford American dictionary* Oxford University Press, Oxford, UK, 2005.) defines an *infrastructure* as a basic physical and organisational structure, which is needed for the operation of an enterprise.

[2] A business process is a sequence of activities which transforms particular inputs into an output of value for the organisation (Legner, C., and Wende, K. "The Challenges of Inter-organizational Business Process Design - a Research Agenda," Proceedings of the ECIS '07, University of St. Gallen, (St. Gallen, Switzerland, 2007), pp. 1643 - 1654.).

ness processes or ERP systems, if necessary, added significantly to the time and resources needed to implement changes within an organisation. This is a significant concern since many organisations have back-office systems which are a patchwork of 50 or more databases, one or more ERP and office systems, and hundreds of separate legacy systems connected by poorly documented, customised business processes (Rettig, 2007).

Business process modelling tools address these issues. Crucially, they allow the (re-)composition of implemented business processes. On a technical level, business processes are usually implemented as workflows,[3] which are executed by a workflow engine. Modern workflow management systems[4] can handle workflows that are part of complex 'grown' software infrastructures. Such workflow management systems are often underpinned by Service Oriented Architectures (SOAs), which facilitate the integration of legacy systems in firms' software infrastructures. In fact, SOAs helped workflow management systems to achieve an industrial breakthrough (Brahe, 2007; Brahe and Schmidt, 2007).

SOAs are software architectures, consisting of reusable building blocks, i.e. services, which can be arranged in different ways to provide particular functionalities. They are often implemented by the Web service technology, which provides a high degree of interoperability, facilitating the dynamic publication, discovery and aggregation of Web services. SOAs enable organisations to create innovative business processes (Chung et al., 2003) and enhance the efficiency of process modelling (Deboeser, 2008; Henn, 2007; Spierling, 2008) since they permit a comparatively easy integration of legacy systems into business processes.

Whilst very useful, business process modelling attracted some criticism. Business processes are formal organisational constructs used for the coordination of (work) activities (Schmidt, 1997). There is a discrepancy between such formal constructs and actual work practices (Suchman, 1987). Business processes do not capture all aspects of work practices (Faustmann, 2000). They are good for describing how work should be done, but do not necessarily reflect how work is actually done (Suchman, 1982).

To address this issue, I propose that business users of the organisations should be able to create formal constructs themselves. They possess the domain knowledge required for making business process modelling effective and efficient. They can use such business processes for describing work practices in advance to determine work practices, but also afterwards to (semi-) automate existing work practices.

This means that it is best if business users model their own business processes and workflows (cf. Agostini and Michelis, 2000) in the use context to describe sequential work practices (e.g. creation of new bank account). These workflows can then be executed automatically, requiring only basic data input from users (e.g. the name and address of a customer). This shift of power into business users' hands increases flexibility as the temporal and spatial distance between the construction and application of workflows is reduced (Agostini and Michelis, 2000; Orlikowski, 1992) and lowers the total cost of ownership of ERP systems (Beringer, 2004; Wulf and Jarke, 2004).

The involvement of business users, i.e. end users, in the development activities of computer systems is nowadays quite common and in many ways beneficial (Lieberman et al., 2006).

---

[3] A workflow is a technical implementation of a business process, in whole or part. A workflow passes information from one participant (e.g. person, system) to another for action, according to a set of rules (Fischer, L. *Workflow Handbook 2001* Future Strategies, Lighthouse Point, FL, 2000.).

[4] A workflow management system is a system that defines, creates and manages the execution of workflows. It interacts with the workflow participants and invokes IT tools and applications where required (Ibid.).

End users are already engaged in many programming-like activities (Blackwell, 2002). It has even been reported that end-user programming has become the most common form of programming (Boehm et al., 2000). Scaffidi et al. estimated the number of end-user programmers would be 13 million by the year 2012 in the United States of America, compared to 3 million professional programmers (Scaffidi et al., 2005).

However, enabling end users to develop and modify software systems does not automatically mean that they are in charge of creating good system designs (Burnett et al., 2004; Fischer and Girgensohn, 1990). Design environments for end users should have innovative user interfaces, such as paper-based interfaces or multi-device interfaces. These interfaces should hide the technical complexities of the underlying architecture by using metaphors that are understandable for end users (Wulf et al., 2008).

1.2. Research Objective

End users should be involved in business process and workflow modelling since they have the necessary domain knowledge for creating precise models. While models cannot be expected to capture every conceivable real life situation (Faustmann, 2000), end users' contributions can significantly reduce the gap between formal organisational constructs and their computational manifestations. Therefore, the technology used should support the redesign of business processes as a constitutive part of everyday work (Agostini and Michelis, 2000; Divitini and Simone, 2000). The recent shift of ERP systems' architectures to service-orientation leads to a convergence between formal constructs (business processes) and their computational manifestations (workflows).

This convergence allows the tailoring, i.e. adaptation of ERP systems, by manipulating business processes and thereby changing workflows. There is already a large body of research on the development of business process modelling and workflow tools. However, most of this research does not focus on end users as a target group.

I explore what form business modelling environments should take from the perspective of end users and provide an answer to the following more abstract research question:

How can service-oriented architectures be used to support the tailorability of software infrastructures by end users?

1.3. Research Design

My work follows the tradition of interpretive research (cf. Orlikowski and Baroudi, 1991; Ulrich, 1994), which aims to understand the context of an information system and how this context influences the system and is influenced by the system (Walsham, 1993). As interpretive research does not predefine variables, it focuses on the full complexity of human sense making in a particular situation (Kaplan and Maxwell, 1994).

Addressing the research question requires engagement with existing research in the fields of Computer Supported Cooperative Work (CSCW), End-User Development (EUD), Human-Computer Interaction (HCI), Business Process Management (BPM) and Service Oriented Architectures (SOAs). I adopt the perspective of end users. Small and medium enterprises (SMEs) are selected as the application domain since they require very flexible software infrastructures. It is particularly challenging to design tailorable software infrastructures for SMEs for two main reasons. First, they have fewer resources than large companies (Dörner and Rohde, 2009) and require affordable IT solutions. Second, they are usually less diversified than larger companies, requiring them to quickly react to changing business and market requirements.

The design and use of IT artefacts cannot be clearly separated from each other. This calls for the cooperation with users during the design of new IT artefacts (Rohde et al., 2009). Therefore, I have chosen a research design that is similar to action research (cf. Baskerville and Wood-Harper, 1996). It combines empirical pre-studies and evaluation studies to embed research in practice and follows a three-phased process (Myers et al., 2004; Pane and Myers, 2006; Wulf, 2009):

1. Analysis of the state-of-the-art in EUD, SOA, BPM, and some other subsequent and adjacent research fields, including the identification of gaps in the literature. Empirical study of the application domain to understand the domain in detail and to identify existing problems.

2. User-centred development of the business process modelling environment which involves end users from the application domain. The design is based on the requirements that have been deduced from the results of the previous step, i.e. the identified gaps in research as well as the results of the empirical study.

3. Evaluation of the developed system by end users from the application domain.

1.4. Contribution

My research question has an interdisciplinary character, allowing me to contribute to the existing body of research in different fields (EUD, SOA and CSCW). In essence, I design new technology support tools for a user-centred business process modelling approach consisting of two steps:

1. The creation of process models on sheets of paper, which is supported by a paper-based sketching tool, called PaSeMod (Paper-based, Service-oriented Modelling). PaSeMod enables end users to create such sketches and transforms them into electronic representations.

2. The transformation of the previously created sketches into workflow models consisting of Web services. The workflow tool SiSO (Simple Service Orchestration) supports this transformation. It provides end users with easy search and modelling mechanisms as well as extended documentation functions for Web services.

The involvement of users in business process modelling reduces the distance between the users and system designers. End users become less dependent on externals, e.g. consultants, which increases the efficiency of enterprises due to a closer alignment of business and IT and faster reaction times to market changes. The focus on software infrastructures instead of standalone enterprise systems blurs system boundaries and allows users to address overlapping problems which involve different systems. Providing two modelling mechanisms, a paper-based and a screen-based mechanism, has the advantage that user groups with different skills sets can participate in the modelling process.

Component-based architectures are usually used for the development of EUD tools (Wulf et al., 2008). I aim to transfer the 'tailoring by composition' mechanism (cf. Teege, 2000) to the next generation of adaptable technologies, i.e. SOAs. This extends current approaches and contributes to research on EUD as designers are enabled to construct flexible EUD tools based on these architectures. One example of such EUD tools is SiSO. It allows end users to adapt software by orchestrating Web services, i.e. by creating workflow models. This contribution is a step towards realising the vision of Klann et al., who predicted that service composition would become an activity of end users in the future (Klann et al., 2006).

In relation to SOAs, I contribute to the existing body of research with the development of a platform called EUSOP (End User Service Orchestration Platform). EUSOP enhances the metadata structures of SOAs by providing extended facilities to store usage-related metadata, such as such as tags, user comments, ratings, and examples. It is stored in the WSDL (Web Service Definition Language) files of the Web services and the UDDI (Universal Description Discovery and Integration) directory. EUSOP helps to make Web services more comprehensible for end users. In addition, EUSOP provides features which support the implementation of workflow modelling environments. My research also contributes an advanced UDDI search system which includes service names, function names, tags and community-generated, usage-related metadata and provides personalisation mechanisms to improve the quality of search results. In contrast to most semantic Web service approaches, the developed concepts aim to assist users when searching and selecting Web services instead of automating these tasks.

In the field of CSCW, I focus on a specific example of collaborative innovation in workplace infrastructures. I address concerns about the discrepancy between formal constructs (business processes and workflows) and actual work practice. My work demonstrates how end users could be enabled to describe their sequential work practices by using formal constructs. Their involvement improves the precision of the formal descriptions. The workflows that are created can (partially) be automatically executed to save time spent on repetitive tasks, reduce the delay between business process and workflow changes, and improve decision support as information becomes available more quickly.

1.5. Structure

This document is structured as follows:

Chapter 2 provides an overview of the research in End-User Development (EUD), Service Oriented Architectures (SOAs), and Business Process Management (BPM). I define the target group of end users for the developed system, provide a classification of existing EUD approaches and discuss the level and scope of the tailoring mechanism used in the new business process modelling environment. I also discuss EUD design principles for the implementation of adaptable systems, present the implementation options for SOAs, compare them with component-based architectures, and provide information about Web service retrieval. The existing problems with enterprise-resource-planning systems and process design tools are covered as well. Finally, I introduce paper-based user interfaces and mashup tools.

In Chapter 3, I discuss the methodology used in my study. I also describe the application domain of small and medium enterprises in which I am interested and provide a characterisation of the participating enterprises and employees.

Chapter 4 is a summary of the empirical pre-study which was conducted to explore the application domain and to identify relevant problems of the domain. The study consisted of four parts: an interview study with users from the application domain, a scenario analysis, an online survey, and an interview study with Danske Bank. In addition, I describe the business process modelling process, which should be supported by the business process modelling environment as well as additional requirements for its design.

Chapter 5 sets out the design and implementation of the business process modelling environment, consisting of three different EUD tools: EUSOP, SiSO and PaSeMod. I present the limiting assumptions and requirements of the design of the business process modelling environment. Afterwards, I discuss the results of a participatory design workshop forming part of the design process and describe the interface design, interaction concept, and software architecture of the different EUD tools.

In chapter 6, I present the results of the evaluation of two EUD tools, SiSO and PaSeMod, focusing mainly on their usability and usefulness in the application domain. EUSOP is evaluated implicitly as it is a substantial part of SiSO. In addition, I describe the redesign of SiSO based on the results of the evaluation and present the evaluation results of SiSO's new search system.

In Chapter 7 I present my conclusions. I discuss the results of my research, highlighting its main findings as well as acknowledging its limitations and identifying the scope for further research.

Chapter 2

"In sum, we started in the 1980s with people being able to use PCs to author their own content in digital form, which they printed out on paper and then exchanged with others by hand or surface mail and eventually e-mail. Then we went to people being able to churn out digital content on their PCs, which they transmitted around the Internet, thanks to standardized protocols, collaborating with anyone anywhere. And finally, today, we have reached a point in work flow that machines are talking to other machines over the Internet using standardized protocols, with no humans involved at all."

Friedman, 2006, p. 83

2.   Literature Review

In this chapter, I review recent research on end-user development (section 2.1), service-oriented architectures (section 2.2), enterprise-resource-planning systems and business process management (section 2.3). In addition, it includes research in the fields of paper-based user interfaces (section 2.4) as well as Mashup and composition tools (section 2.5). I also identify gaps in this body of research (section 2.6) which I aim to address.

2.1.   End-User Development

This section explores research in the field of End-User Development (EUD). In section 2.1.1, I define the term EUD. In section 2.1.2, I characterise the target group of end users in the context of this work. Section 2.1.3 provides a classification and a detailed overview of existing EUD approaches. In section 2.1.4 I discuss the level and scope of the tailoring mechanism used in the newly designed business process modelling environment. Section 2.1.5 presents four related systems that use such a tailoring mechanism. Section 2.1.6 focuses on collaborative tailoring, which is considered to be an important factor for successful EUD systems. In section 2.1.7, I examine the pros and cons of EUD and discuss EUD design principles for the implementation of adaptable systems.

2.1.1.   Definition

Although the term end-user development emerged only a couple of years ago, its main idea of enabling end users to adapt/create software is rather old. It dates back to the time when non-programmers started to create BASIC programs on their PCs, referred to as *end-user programming (EUP)*, and continued in the 1970s with fourth generation languages (Burnett, 2009; Sutcliffe and Mahandjiev, 2004). During the 1980s the development of applications by end users became a key research and management concern. It became known as *end-user computing (EUC)*, involving a variety of research fields. EUC is defined as *"[...] the adoption and use of information technology by personnel outside the information systems department to DEVELOP software applications in support of organizational tasks."* (Brancheau and Brown, 1993, p. 439) Later, the term *(end-user) tailoring (EUT)* evolved from the previous research efforts, referring to the change of stable aspects of an artefact (Henderson and Kyng, 1991). More recently the term *End-User Software Engineering (EUSE)* emerged. It is very similar to EUD and addresses issues of software quality by looking beyond the 'create' part of software development (Burnett et al., 2004).

Today, applications are customisable and extendable (Powell and Moore, 2002) and the development of applications by end users is widespread. End users create numerous programs (Burnett, 2009) in at least two fields: scientific computing and business computing (Brancheau and Brown, 1993). Changing the term from end-user programming via computing to tailoring and finally to development as well as software engineering indicates that today end users do some form of programming in the wider sense (Repenning and Ioannidou, 2006).

The most common definition of EUD is the working definition by Lieberman et al.: *"End-User Development can be defined as a set of methods, techniques, and tools that allow users of software systems, who are acting as non-professional software developers, at some point to create, modify or extend a software artefact."* (Lieberman et al., 2006, p. 10)

This definition tries to cover the broad spectrum of EUD approaches published in the same book. As a result, the definition is not very precise, especially in terms of the user group, the adaptation power of the approaches and the point at which EUD takes place in the design process, i.e. the life cycle of a software system. I will discuss the life cycle of a software system in this section and take up the other issues in subsequent sections.

Design processes are usually split into design time (development of the system) and use time (using the system in the application domain) (Fischer et al., 2004a). EUD can be characterised as a kind of meta-design, providing a design for designers for creating 'open' systems that can be modified at use time by their users (Fischer and Giaccardi, 2006; Fischer and Scharff, 2000).

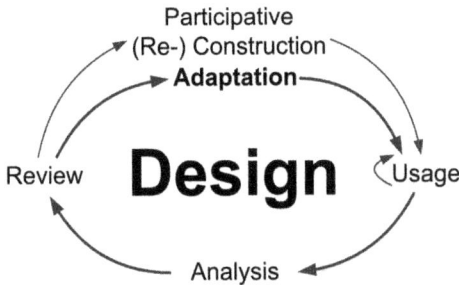

Figure 1: Design Process (taken from Oberquelle, 1994, p. 43)

Figure 1 depicts the common design process of a software system, showing how the adaptation, i.e. EUD, is embedded in this process. Adaptation is a continuous process during the use time of a system and not just a single step. It is important to emphasise that adaptation differs from the (re-)construction and maintenance cycles of systems as it has a different scope and is performed by different actors, i.e. the users of the system instead of designers. However, Dittrich et al. argued that adaptation could be interleaved with system maintenance and re-design (Dittrich et al., 2006). Fischer proposed the SER (Seeding, Evolutionary Growth, and Reseeding) model, essentially a process model for evolutionary systems, which is of interest in this context (Fischer, 1998; Fischer et al., 2001). In SER, designers create a *seed* that is an 'underdesigned' version of the system implemented in the application domain. Users of the application domain use and change/extend the system in accordance with their needs which leads to an evolutionary *growth of the system*. Once this evolution has lead to a substantially different version of the system, designers use this version for creating a new *seed* that is *reseeded* in the application domain to restart the whole process.

2.1.2. End Users

The term *end user* remained rather unclear in the above discussion of end-user development. In this section, I aim to clarify its meaning. It covers a variety of different types of users: *"Professional programmers and domain professionals define the endpoints of a continuum of computer users."* (Fischer, 2009, p. 5) Around the year 1990, several researches attempted to identify subgroups within this user continuum. They used users' varying levels of expertise to form the groups. I briefly introduce the classification of users by Nardi and Miller (Nardi and Miller, 1991), which is similar to that by Mackay (1990) and MacLean et al. (1990). They define the following subgroups of users:

- *End Users* have little or no programming education and a lack of intrinsic interest in computers.

- *Local Developers* are domain experts, but no professional programmers.

- *Professionals* have much broader and deeper knowledge of computing than local developers.

Users can move between the different subgroups by acquiring additional expertise. Members of the group of *end users* can for instance 'move' to the group of *local developers* by acquiring additional knowledge about computers and programming (MacLean et al., 1990).

Åsand and Mørch (2006) extended this early classification by adding a fourth group, referred to as *super users,* which is in between Nardi and Miller's groups of end users and local developers. Super users are defined as *"[...] advanced end-users who have accumulated considerable expertise in local (in house) development and tailoring. They provide help and guidance to other users and they train these users to participate in end-user development activities."* (Mørch and Mehandjiev, 2000, p. 76) The important characteristics of super users are their domain expertise and their computer know-how.

Super users have been referred to by different terms, like *prosumers* (Tapscott and Williams, 2006) and *professional amateurs* (Leadbeater and Miller, 2004), who are a mixture of consumers and producers, and participate in system development, for instance by adapting systems to their needs (Fischer, 2009). Other terms, like *boundary spanners* (Volkoff et al., 2002) and *gurus* (Gantt and Nardi, 1992) have been used as well (Andersen and Mørch, 2009).

Super users are usually not in charge of changing business processes. However, as adaptation mechanisms increasingly move into the 'direction' of end users, I consider super users as the target group for my envisaged business process modelling environment. Super users have been considered to be the best candidates for tailoring since they have domain expertise and computer know-how (Mørch and Mehandjiev, 2000). In contrast, software vendors, external consultants, or in-house development teams are not involved in the execution of business processes. Accordingly, they do not share the work practices and would find it very difficult to design appropriate (software) solutions (Wulf and Jarke, 2004).

2.1.3. EUD Approaches

Having defined the group of end users, I will now provide an overview of the existing adaptation approaches in the field of end-user development. EUD covers a broad variety of tailoring mechanisms, ranging from simple customisation options like changing parameters to more complex features like writing code (Sutcliffe and Mahandjiev, 2004). In a recent paper we provided an overview of research on EUD and classified the existing approaches according to the dimensions *complexity* and *adaptation power* (Spahn et al., 2008b).

Complexity 'measures' the technical knowledge which is needed by an end user in order to use a tailoring mechanism, i.e. an EUD approach. Referring to the discussion about end-user classifications in the previous section, we used the older, three-fold classification of Nardi and Miller (1991).

The spectrum of tailoring mechanisms was classified in several ways. One of the most common classifications is based on Henderson and Kyng's three ways of changing behaviour (Henderson and Kyng, 1991). It divides the spectrum of tailoring mechanisms into three tailoring levels (Mørch, 1997; Oberquelle, 1994):

1. *Customisation* allows users to select among a set of predefined configuration options. An example of customisation would be the setting of parameters in an application by users.

2. *Integration* links predefined components. Components can be linked within one application or between different applications. Linking is often supported by scripting or composition languages and often needs 'glue code' for connecting components, leading to a certain kind of extension (depending on the amount of 'glue') (Teege, 2000).

3. *Extension* refers to mechanisms which add new program code to an application, such as the programming of a new component.

Adaptation power measures how much power an EUD approach (i.e. an adaptation mechanism) has by using these three levels of tailoring.

EUD Approaches				**Supportive EUD Approaches**
Complexity / **Adaptation Power**	**Customisation**	**Integration**	**Extension**	
Programmers			Programming	**Testing:** Question-based testing; WYSIWYT; Integrity checks; Exploration environments
Local Developers		Component swapping at runtime; Separated tailoring interfaces	Natural Programming; Scripting	
Non-Programmers	Interface customisation; Parameterisation	Programming by demonstration (PBD); Accountants paradigm; Integrated tailoring interfaces		**Community aspects:** Configuration files **Appropriation support**

Table 1: Classification of EUD Approaches (taken from Spahn et al., 2008b, p. 486)

Table 1 divides EUD approaches into two groups, depending on whether they are stand-alone and are directly used for adaptations or used for supporting other EUD approaches. The complexity and adaptation power of the supportive approaches must correspond to those of the supported EUD approach in order to be useful. In the following paragraphs I briefly present some examples for different approaches.

Interface customisation is a comparatively simple approach, which can be found in many software applications. It allows users to change e.g. themes, skins, the applications' 'look and feel' and its toolbars.

Parameterisation can be achieved for example by providing an option menu, enabling users to adjust certain settings like security options in a Web browser. One popular research prototype is the *Buttons* system, consisting of on-screen buttons which allow users to execute a particular action when a button is pressed (MacLean et al., 1990). Buttons implement a parameterisation mechanism, i.e. functions for influencing a button's functionality by setting parameters.

Programming by demonstration (PBD), also referred to as Programming by Example (PBE), is a more advanced EUD approach. It enables users to 'demonstrate' algorithms 'to' the computer, by using it in a 'normal way'. The computer tracks and records all actions of the user and allows him to modify and re-execute this chain of actions later on. A popular example for a PBD approach is a macro recorder, empowering users to record actions in form of macros used for the automation of recurring tasks. The books *Watch What I Do: Programming by Demonstration* (Cypher, 1993) and *Your Wish Is My Command: Programming by Example* (Lieberman, 2001) provide a broad overview of the existing research in this field.

The **accountants paradigm** is a powerful but fuzzy EUD approach which improves the handling and cognitive perception of information. It relies on the observation that people can understand tabular representations of data with comparative ease and offers formulae for manipulating this data. Spreadsheet applications utilise this paradigm as an interaction model with the users.

Integrated tailoring interfaces combine the design time and use time user interfaces of an application seamlessly. Spreadsheet applications are, once more, a good example because they integrate these two views. Users can 'switch' from use time to design time by clicking the 'edit' button of a particular cell, change the formula, and switch back to the runtime perspective.

Component swapping at runtime, also referred to as 'tailoring by composition', is probably the most interesting EUD approach in the context of this research. It enables designers to create systems that can be tailored by composing pre-defined building blocks (e.g. components, services). The composition of building blocks can be changed by adding or removing blocks, which allows users to tailor the system at use time. An example of such a system is the Fre-Evolve platform (Stiemerling, 2000) that will be described in detail in section 2.1.5.1.

Separated tailoring interfaces have in contrast to 'integrated tailoring interfaces' clearly separated design time and use time interfaces. This approach is often used in more complex versions of adaptable systems since it allows the construction of more powerful and specialised adaptation functions (Dittrich et al., 2006).

Natural programming aims to create programming languages and environments which are more 'natural' for end users. Such languages are mentally close to the way users think about their tasks, trying to enable them to express their ideas in the same way as they think about them. HANDS is a system for children which follows this EUD approach, allowing children to create interactive graphical programs by playing an electronic card game (Myers et al., 2004).

Scripting languages are another widespread EUD approach. They are less complex than programming languages since they do not require strong typing, but they are limited in terms of adaptation power. One example is the utilisation of Visual Basic for Applications (VBA) to program extensions for Microsoft Excel.

The supportive EUD approaches involve testing approaches, community aspects and appropriation support.

Testing approaches address quality-related issues of programs created by end users (Burnett et al., 2004). One popular approach is called question-based testing, which allows users to ask questions in order to debug their code. Myers et al. (2004) developed a system called WhyLine, which is based on this approach and allows users to ask 'why did' and 'why didn't' questions. Another approach is characterised by the metaphor 'What You See Is What You Test (WYSIWYT)'. Burnett et al. (2004) used it to construct a testing system of the same name which allows end users to test spreadsheets incrementally by validating cell values. Enabling end users to do integrity checks is another approach which can help users to verify created compositions. Such checks facilitate the identification of semantic errors in compositions (Won, 2004). Exploration environments enable end users of a system to experiment safely with its functionality and to test adaptations without damaging the system or influencing the work of other users (Wulf, 2000; Wulf, 2001).

Community aspects involve for example the handling of configuration files. Such files are used for storing and exchanging adaptations supporting user communities to perform their adaptations collaboratively. The FreEvolve platform allows users to store their individual adaptations in configuration files which are accessible by all users via a central repository.

Appropriation support "*[...] covers all measures to support appropriation activities as creative and collaborative processes of user-user interaction to fit a technology into an application field.*" (Pipek, 2005, p. 33) It covers for instance articulation support, decision support, observation support and explanation support. These functions afford also changes in usages. These changes do not require tailoring in a technological sense. Concrete tools in this context could be for example a forum system or a help system (Pipek and Syrjänen, 2006; Pipek and Wulf, 2009; Wulf et al., 2008).

This section provided an overview of EUD approaches. However, I focused only on a subset of the existing approaches. The interested reader can find a more comprehensive survey in the two available books on end-user development (Lieberman et al., 2006; Pipek et al., 2009).

2.1.4. Level and Scope of the Tailoring Mechanism

This section elaborates on the EUD approach which will be used in the envisaged business process modelling environment. Considering the previous description of 'tailoring by composition', this approach seems to fit very well with the idea of developing a business process modelling environment for super users. Teege (2000) applied the classification of different tailoring levels (see section 2.1.3) to component-based systems and introduced a second dimension describing the affected unit, as shown in Table 2.

Level	Affected unit		
	Component	Application	
		(Many components)	(Infrastructure)
Customisation	(a)	(b)	(c)
Integration	(d)	(e)	
Extension	(g)	(h)	(i)

Table 2: Scope of Component-based Tailoring Mechanisms (taken from Teege, 2000, p. 104)

A component is defined as "*[...] unit of composition with contractually specified interfaces and explicit context dependencies only. A software component can be deployed independently and is subject to composition by third parties.*" (Szyperski, 2002, p. 41). Therefore components and services are quite similar (see section 2.2.3 for a detailed discussion) allowing me to use Teege's classification to describe and characterise the kind of tailoring mechanism that will be used in the business process modelling environment.

The creation of process models follows the same basic idea as the 'tailoring by composition' mechanism since tailoring is done by arranging activities, i.e. services in a process model. Applying this definition to the classification given above, 'tailoring by composition' falls into category *(e)* because it connects predefined building blocks in a procedural flow (cf.

Oberquelle, 1994). The *affected unit* is an *infrastructure*[5], which uses different services of different applications provided by a SOA. Considering software infrastructures rather than single applications is important since today's dynamic environments have many interdependencies, making it necessary to use various tools for performing a certain task (Pipek and Kahler, 2006).

Tailoring by composition can only be used in systems that can be decomposed into parts (here Web services) and features (here functions of Web services) (Teege, 2000; Won et al., 2006). Features are described in some programming language (here WSDL as interface description of a Web service) and need a composition language (here BPEL) for linking (Teege, 2000).

2.1.5. Related Systems

The above characterisation of the level and scope of the 'tailoring by composition' mechanism allowed the identification of related systems which used the same mechanism to provide adaptability. In this section I present four such systems: FreEvolve, TailorBPEL, ECHOES and Oval.

2.1.5.1. FreEvolve

FreEvolve (Stiemerling, 2000; Won et al., 2006; Wulf et al., 2008) is a distributed client-server system which enables end users to tailor component-based applications. FreEvolve supports the tailoring of any system that uses the FLEXIBEANS (Stiemerling, 2000) component model, which allows the manipulation of the component structure of applications during use time. As FLEXIBEANS is an extension of the Java Beans component model, it is limited to components written in Java.

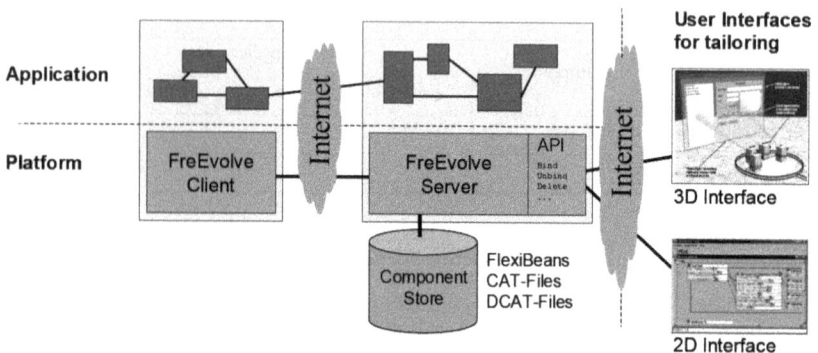

Figure 2: Schematic Overview of FreEvolve (taken from Won et al., 2006, p.130)

Figure 2 presents a schematic overview of FreEvolve. FreEvolve uses a server to store the available components and their component composition descriptions, called CAT (Compo-

---

[5] The infrastructure definition, used in this work, matches Teege's definition of 'many components'. His definition of an infrastructure refers to a technical framework like a SOA.

nent Architecture for Tailoring) or DCAT (Distributed Component Architecture for Tailoring) in the case of distributed systems. The FreEvolve server has an API which can be used for tailoring the application, i.e. the stored component compositions. The API supports different types of user interfaces, including both 2D and 3D interfaces, as shown in the figure. The CAT and DCAT files represent differently tailored versions of the application. The different users of the system can easily share these files as they are stored on the server.

The composition mechanism of FreEvolve can be characterised as a structural variant of the 'tailoring by composition' mechanism. It allows the declaration of bindings between components, but makes no assumptions about how and when operations of the constituent components are executed (Alda et al., 2007). This is the main difference to workflow systems, which also take the execution order of 'components' into account.

2.1.5.2. TailorBPEL

The design of TailorBPEL drew on experience with component-based tailoring systems, such as FreEvolve (Alda et al., 2007). The target group of the system are users who have the need to tailor a particular BPEL (Business Process Execution Language) process to their personal needs. TailorBPEL has a multi-tier architecture for the generation of personalised, BPEL-based workflows consisting of the following tiers (see Figure 3): provider tier, orchestration tier, portal tier and client tier.

The *provider tier* contains Web services offered by any provider which are registered in a UDDI (Universal Description Discovery and Integration) directory.

The *orchestration tier* contains a runtime engine for deploying personalised BPEL processes. The templates of such processes are duplicated and can be personalised to meet the requirements of a particular user. This can be achieved by using the system's tailoring component. The orchestration tier also offers a consistency management component, which provides basic integrity checks and thereby helps users to validate the tailored BPEL processes.

The *portal tier* implements the presentation logic of the system, which can be used by different clients to access the orchestration server. The main functionality of this tier is provided by the portal server, which is built upon various standard technologies, such as Sun's *servlet* technology. The personalisation component allows users to create personalised views on the system.

The *client tier* contains all client applications. The use of Web-based technologies in the portal tier favours the usage of *portlets* running in a Web browser, making it difficult to implement other clients on top of the portal tier.

2.1.5.3. ECHOES

ECHOES (Easily CHangable OfficE Systems) is a general-purpose architecture for end-user development systems. It was for example used to implement tailorable workflow applications. In contrast to standard workflow applications, non-programmers can control it in terms of functionality and structure through the tailoring interface (Mørch and Mehandjiev, 2000). The system was implemented in Smalltalk-80 and allows the creation of different views of the underlying application at different levels of abstraction: information flow, service definition, organisational structure, information taxonomy, and information appearance description. To illustrate, Figure 4 presents a screenshot of the information flow view.

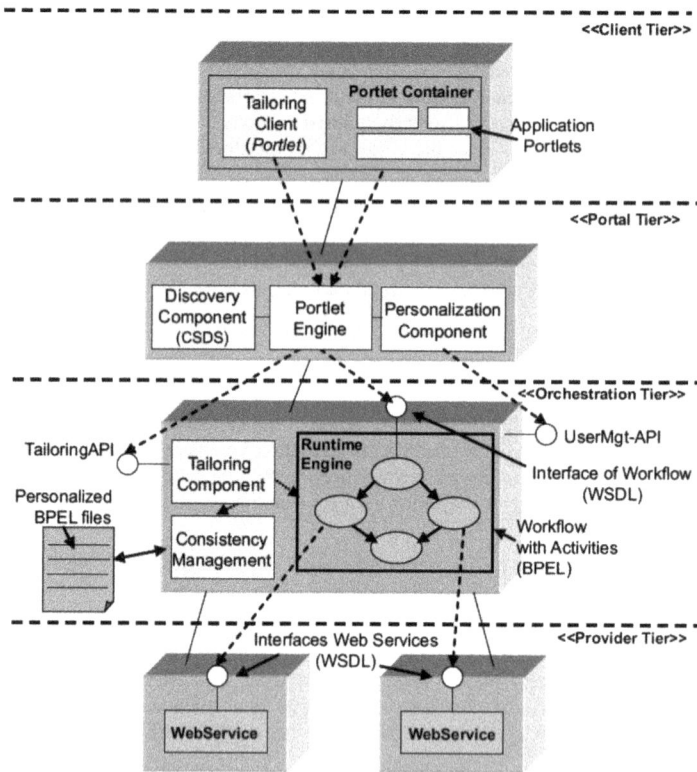

Figure 3: Architecture of TailorBPEL (taken from Alda et al., 2007, p. 247)

The information flow is based on the dataflow paradigm. The figure shows the flow of information and control messages between the different activities that constitute the application. An activity is performed by a human being and usually concerns information processing. Activities are visualised as rounded rectangles. Behind a particular activity rectangle, a number of other rectangles may be stacked which represent the people who perform the activity. Arrows connecting the source and the target of the message represent the message flows (cf. Mehandjiev and Bottaci, 1996). Alongside the flow of forms, the system shows the responsibility of people for particular activities in the workflow.

2.1.5.4. Oval

Oval is an acronym for *objects*, *views*, *agents* and *links* and is characterised as a 'radically tailorable' tool for CSCW. It can be considered as an improved version of Malone's *Object Lens* system (Malone et al., 1995).

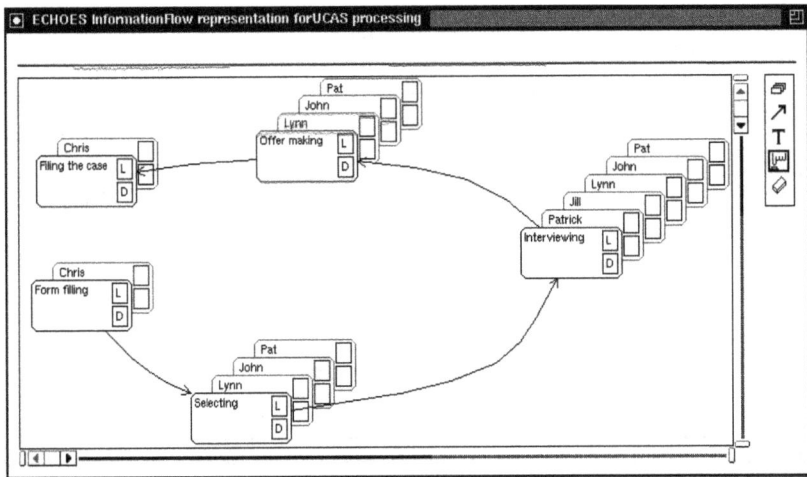

Figure 4: The Information Flow View of ECHOES (taken from Mehandjiev, 1997, p. 126)

Oval is one of the older, path-breaking tailorable systems which make use of four building blocks:

- Semi-structured *objects*, representing things in the world, like people, tasks and messages.

- User-customisable *views* summarise collections of objects and allow users to edit individual objects.

- Rule-based *agents* perform active tasks for people automatically. Agents can be triggered by events like the arrival of new mail or a pre-defined time.

- *Links* represent relationships or connections between objects. One example could be links from one object to another to represent a relationship between messages and their replies.

Oval offers six levels of user modifications: defining object types, adding fields to objects, selecting views, specifying parameters for a given view, creating new agents and inserting new links. Figure 5 is an example network view, which shows the relationship between different objects.

Oval also implements several ways for sharing collections of objects. Users can share those collections by mailing them, storing them in databases or sharing them as files. These features make Oval one of the most important systems for the development of tailorable systems which use the 'tailoring by composition' mechanism. Oval demonstrated that *"objects, views, agents, and links provide a kind of elementary tailoring language for user interfaces to information management and cooperative work applications."* (Malone et al., 1995, p. 200)

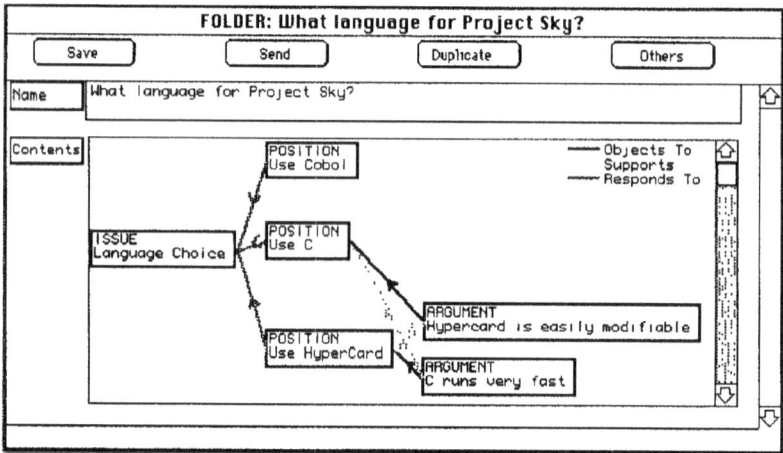

```
┌─────────────────────────────────────────────────────────────────┐
│                 FOLDER: What language for Project Sky?            │
│   ( Save )        ( Send )      ( Duplicate )      ( Others )     │
│ ┌──────┐ ┌───────────────────────────────────────────────────┐   │
│ │ Name │ │ What language for Project Sky?                     │   │
│ └──────┘ └───────────────────────────────────────────────────┘   │
│ ┌────────┐                                                        │
│ │Contents│   POSITION              ── Objects To                  │
│ └────────┘   Use Cobol             ── Supports                    │
│                                    ── Responds To                 │
│              ISSUE      POSITION                                  │
│              Language Choice  Use C                               │
│                                                                   │
│                                ARGUMENT                           │
│                                Hypercard is easily modifiable     │
│                  POSITION                                         │
│                  Use HyperCard   ARGUMENT                         │
│                                  C runs very fast                 │
└─────────────────────────────────────────────────────────────────┘
```

Figure 5: Network View of Oval (taken from Malone et al., 1995, p. 189)

2.1.6. Collaborative Tailoring

This section focuses on the collaboration of users who jointly tailor applications. Collaboration is considered to be an important factor for making EUD successful (Gantt and Nardi, 1992; Mackay, 1990; Pipek and Kahler, 2006; Wulf, 1999).

Collaboration became an important success factor for software in general. Recently it was driven by the success stories about the so-called 'Web 2.0 technologies', which supported the collaborative creation of artefacts. One of the most popular examples remains Wikipedia, which has contributors from around the world (Fischer, 2009). The Web 2.0 has led to a fundamental shift from the consumer culture to a culture of participation (von Hippel, 2005). Other good examples of collaboration in a different context are open source projects (Ye and Fischer, 2007). While usually only a small number of people contributes content, it should be kept in mind that even a tiny percentage of a large base is a substantial number of people with a potentially wide range of interests (Anderson, 2006).

The culture of participation has been of interest to EUD research for a long time. Gantt and Nardi (1992) argued that cooperation between users increases the number of solutions available to each of them because users can learn from each other and share solutions. Mackay explored collaboration patterns of users, showing that the sharing of artefacts allows users to take advantage of each other's work. Another strong argument for collaboration is that *"complex design problems require more knowledge than any single person can possess, and the knowledge relevant to a problem is often distributed among all stakeholders thus providing the foundation for social creativity."* (Fischer et al., 2004b, p. 335).

Collaboration can involve different user groups (Eriksson and Dittrich, 2007). Following the classification of Kahler (2001), there are four levels of collaboration: cooperation between tailoring users, cooperation between tailors and users, cooperation between tailors and software developers and the organisational recognition and coordination of tailoring efforts.

2.1.7. Assessment

In previous sections, I explored various aspects of EUD. In this section, I briefly discuss the advantages and disadvantages of EUD and describe the design principles for adaptable systems.

"Technologies are products of their time and organisational context, and will reflect the knowledge, materials, interests, and conditions at a given locus in history." (Orlikowski, 1992, p. 421) Orlikowski's proposition of the dynamic nature of technology provides the foundation for the two main arguments for EUD: requirements of software systems cannot be captured completely during design time (Brooks, 1987; Fischer et al., 2004b; Nardi, 1993; Oberquelle, 1994) and they change frequently during use time (Brooks, 1987; Fischer et al., 2004a; Mørch and Mehandjiev, 2000; Oberquelle, 1994; Stiemerling, 2000).

Capturing requirements of software systems during the design time of a system is a complex and cumbersome task since there are usually many different stakeholders with (very) different requirements (Germonprez et al., 2007). Consider for example the requirements a secretary and a scientist may have in terms of using a word processor. The secretary might be interested in an efficient creation of letters while the scientist might be interested in creating references. In addition, there are often 'cultural' issues, i.e. communication problems between designers and users of the system, which make it difficult to design appropriate solutions (Gallivan and Keil, 2003; Taylor-Cummings, 1998).

The dynamic nature of the organisational context in which software systems are embedded requires frequent adaptations to changing requirements. Adaptations may need to be made for several reasons. First, users' requirements may change, e.g. a manager may like to have new reports which cannot be created with the existing system (Henderson and Kyng, 1991). Second, the organisation might want to increase its efficiency by optimising work processes, with implications for software systems. Third, the organisation may have to respond to 'external' factors, e.g. changes in legal requirements (Wulf et al., 1999). Fourth, applications may be updated or replaced, leading to changes in APIs. Finally, organisations and software systems must be adapted to environmental changes to stay competitive (Kawalek and Leonard, 1996). If domain professionals, i.e. end users, can respond to such changing requirements without relying on professional developers, systems will evolve in response to real needs (Fischer, 2009).

Another argument for EUD are ill-defined and wicked problems (Rittel and Webber, 1984) which cannot be delegated to professional developers (neither during design nor use time). As end users know such problems best, they should be able to adapt systems without the assistance of professional developers (Fischer, 2009).

However, it remains unclear whether these advantages of EUD outweigh the following disadvantages. Tailoring can increase the complexity of systems by adding idiosyncratic material (Gantt and Nardi, 1992; Paetau, 1994). Furthermore, tailored systems may be error-prone (Harrison, 2004; Panko, 1998), which may put data at risk (Gantt and Nardi, 1992). Designers of tailorable systems must make sure that it is possible to re-establish the state of the system at an earlier point in time (Henderson and Kyng, 1991). Another argument against EUD is that end users probably have to spend a lot of time on tailoring because they need to familiarise themselves with the interfaces of the tailoring mechanisms (Henderson and Kyng, 1991) and they also have to manage systems instead of doing their work (Gantt and Nardi, 1992).

There is a considerable body of literature on the nature of design principles for adaptable systems. They can relate to different levels of abstraction, including process models, high level design principles and the ways in which specific functions should be implemented. The most important high-level design principles can be referred to by the acronym TAILOR: Testing, Architecture, Interface, Learning, cOllaboration, Representation.

Testing: The tailorable system should provide the functionality for testing the adaptations created (Eriksson and Dittrich, 2007). In particular, the system should make it difficult or impossible to commit syntactic errors and allow the definition of decomposable test units (Repenning and Ioannidou, 2006).

Architecture: The tailorable system should have an architecture that supports re-designing the software application during use time (Wulf et al., 2008). It should have components which allow splitting, substitution and the integration of legacy systems (Germonprez et al., 2007). The system should initially be 'underdesigned', so that it can evolve over time (Fischer et al., 1994).

Interface: The tailorable system should have an interface which reveals its potential for unanticipated use to the tailor (Eriksson and Dittrich, 2007). It should use end-user-oriented concepts (e.g. point and click, hyper linking) (Germonprez et al., 2007; Wulf et al., 2008) and provide multiple views (Repenning and Ioannidou, 2006).

Learning: The tailorable system should facilitate the learning of the tailoring mechanisms by supporting tailoring on different levels of complexity (Won et al., 2006; Wulf et al., 2008) and by allowing incremental development (Repenning and Ioannidou, 2006).

COllaboration: The tailorable system should support collaborative tailoring (Pipek and Kahler, 2006; Won et al., 2006; Wulf et al., 2008), e.g. by providing users with a shared repository (Golombek, 2000; Kahler, 2001) for exchanging their tailored artefacts.

Representation: The tailorable system should use a programming language, i.e. an adaptation mechanism, which is closely connected to users' mental model (Pane and Myers, 2006). It should make a clear distinction between definition, execution and tailoring (Eriksson and Dittrich, 2007) but should provide a strong congruency between architectural and interface concepts (Wulf et al., 2008).

In summary, software systems should be considered intrinsically evolutionary (Kawalek and Leonard, 1996), as *"it is impossible to design systems which are appropriate for all users and all situations"* (MacLean et al., 1990, p. 175). This evolution can be supported by EUD since end users know their problems best. It is true that tailored systems may be error-prone and users may spend a lot of time for tailoring. However, EUD research has produced several design principles that allowed the implementation of mechanisms to correct errors and approaches that facilitate tailoring (cf. Burnett, 2009; Burnett et al., 2004).

2.2. Service Oriented Architectures

This section focuses on aspects of Service Oriented Architectures (SOA) which are relevant to this research. In section 2.2.1, I define the term SOA and present the basic concepts. Section 2.2.2 focuses on the implementation options. In section 2.2.3, I compare SOA with component-based architectures. In section 2.2.4, I discuss Web service retrieval and description. Section 2.2.5 concludes with a discussion of the pros and cons of SOAs.

2.2.1. Definition

The W3C defines a Service Oriented Architecture as *"[...] a set of components that can be invoked and whose interface descriptions can be published and discovered. A web service is a specific instance of a component that has a public interface defined and described in XML and that other systems can discover and use by passing messages transported via existing Internet protocols."* (Gold et al., 2004, p. 72)

SOAs were originally developed in the telecommunication industry but have been used more widely in the last couple of years (Adamopoulos, 2006). Delivering 'software-as-a-service' relaxes the constraints imposed by traditional software construction, use and ownership models (Turner et al., 2003). SOAs support the creation of distributed applications in a heterogeneous environment by using the Web service technology. Their objective is to enable developers to write applications that are independent of specific services. Instead, developers should provide abstract descriptions of the required functionalities and applications should select and integrate instantiations of these descriptions, i.e. services, on the fly (Verheecke et al., 2006).

The next section discusses options for implementing SOAs.

2.2.2. Implementation Options

According to the definition provided, the term SOA is not a synonym for a stack of XML protocols and standards. The fundamental core of the SOA concept defines an architectural solution for a specific design problem in a given context. The central objective of SOAs is to reduce dependencies between 'software islands' by balancing the following factors (Stal, 2006): distribution, heterogeneity, dynamics, transparency and process-orientation.

The SOAP-based variant of the Web service technology is currently the most common implementation variant of SOAs (Stal, 2006). The technology uses the XML standards SOAP (Simple Object Access Protocol), WSDL (Web Service Definition Language) and UDDI (Universal Description Discovery and Integration).

A Web service offers reusable functionality which is contractually defined in a service description containing some combination of syntactic, semantic, and behavioural information (Cervantes and Hall, 2005). Web services are self-contained, self-describing, modular software entities that can be published, located and invoked across the Web and *"[...] can be combined with other web services to maintain business transactions workflows."* (Adamopoulos, 2006, p. 260) This definition of Web services should not be mixed up with another, rather generic definition: *"In the most literal sense, a Web service is any service provided over the Web, which by inference might include common gateway interfaces (CGIs), HTML forms, Practical Extraction and Report Language (PERL), Java Scripts, and the like."* (Ma, 2005, p. 14)

Figure 6 depicts the so-called *Web service triangle,* which underlies the architecture of SOAP-based Web services. Service consumers invoke Web services provided by the service providers to consume the services' functionality. This is done by exchanging data via the SOAP protocol. Service providers can register their services in an UDDI directory, where service consumers can locate them. WSDL files are used for the description of the service interfaces in a human-readable way.

The interested reader might want to have a look at Bartonitz's description of the history of SOA-related standards, such as WPDL, Wf-XML, BPMN, BPML, BPEL, UDDI and SOAP (Bartonitz, 2006). It should be noted that the literature on SOAs uses three similar terms for defining connections between services: *composition, orchestration* and *choreography.*

Service Broker

UDDI

search
WSDL
SOAP

publish
WSDL
SOAP

Legend:
action
data format
exchange protocol

data exchange
XML
SOAP

Service Consumer   Service Provider

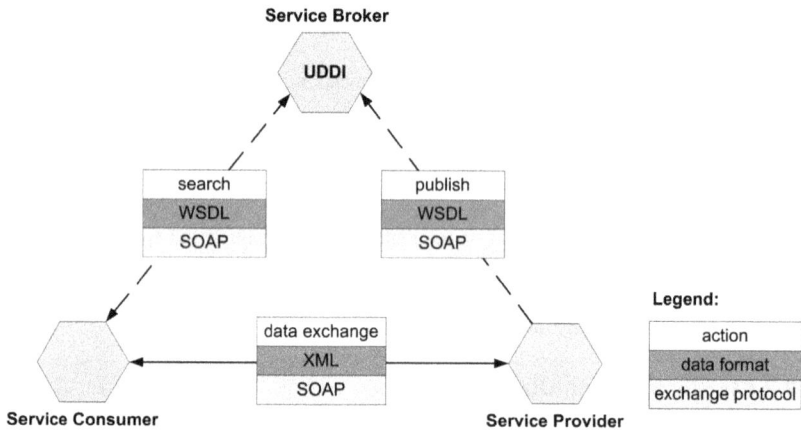

Figure 6: Web Service Triangle

Service *composition* is the incorporation of different services into an application. These services perform any function while the application itself plays the role of the service requester. The application controls the service composition and can be written in any programming language or a composition language like BPEL (Cervantes and Hall, 2005).

In a service *orchestration,* a parent process service controls the composition of the participating services. The service *choreography* is more collaborative than an orchestration. Each member involved in the choreography describes its part in the interaction (Peltz, 2003). Unlike an orchestration, a choreography is based on messages which are exchanged between services and does not implement a specific meta-process, executed by a single party (Alda et al., 2007).

While SOAP-based Web services are popular, they are not the only technologies for the implementation of SOAs. Another important implementation concept for SOA is REST (Representational State Transfer). The term REST was defined by Roy Fielding and originally had nothing to do with Web services. In his research, Fielding explored architectural concepts of Web-based applications and developed REST on the basis of his analysis of the architecture of the World Wide Web (Mintert, 2005). REST is based on the HTTP methods GET, POST, PUT, DELETE (Shi, 2006). The REST standard offers less functionality than SOAP (Mintert, 2005) and is therefore usually not used in the enterprise context.

Henceforth, my use of the term SOA always relates to the SOAP-based implementation of Web services.

2.2.3. SOA vs. Component-based Architectures

In this section, I compare and contrast SOAs with component-based architectures. A simple form of a SOA is merely a client-server architecture in a new variation (Ma, 2005). System designers have long tried to replace proprietary inter-process communication by abstract, well-defined, and ubiquitously invokable services. Therefore, SOAs are considered to be slightly overhyped. Popular RCP toolkits from the late 1980s to early 1990s (e.g. Sun's *Open Network Computing* or the open software foundation's *Distributed Computing Environment* were already 'oriented around services'. Object oriented systems like COM, CORBA and EJB had similar aims as SOAs (Vinoski, 2005). Hence, *"the ideas underlying web services are hardly new."* (Ma, 2005, p. 14).

However, the Web service technology gained much interest and matured. To prove this claim, I explore the advantages and disadvantages of Web services by comparing the 'old' component-based architectures with the 'new' service-oriented forms. Like components, Web services represent functionality that can easily be reused without knowing how the service is implemented. In addition, Web services are vendor-, platform-, and language-independent (Adamopoulos, 2006) and may therefore be better placed to achieve universal interoperability than other middleware technologies (Pasley, 2005). SOAs differ from today's component-based architectures in the following respects (Feurer, 2007):

Component-based Architectures	SOAs
Build to last	Build to change
Tight integration	Loose horizontal integration
Code-oriented development	Process-oriented composition
Technical complexity of the IT infrastructure	Interoperable architecture for business and IT

Table 3: Comparison of Today's Software Architectures with SOAs (according to Feurer, 2007, p. 9)

Despite these differences, SOAs and component-based architectures share a common development model. In both cases building blocks are developed and composed to provide certain functionalities. However, SOAs involve aspects like the dynamic discovery of services which are not explicitly considered in component-based architectures. Cervantes et al. (2005) draw an even more detailed picture of the differences between components and services:

	Component Orientation	Service Orientation
Development Model	Assembly based on available building blocks	Assembly based on abstract service descriptions; integration occurs prior or during execution
Building Block Concept	External view and implementation are not always separated; components are packaged to support independent delivery and deployment	Separation of description (WSDL) and implementation; packaging does not matter as service providers create service objects
Composition	Dynamic availability is not important; use of structural architecture description	Dynamic availability; composition becomes concrete during execution; use of executable process descriptions
Execution Environment	Instance creation by client	Instance creation by service provider

Table 4: Differences between Component and Service Orientation (according to Cervantes and Hall, 2005, p. 11)

In summary, SOAs are 'built to change', providing an interoperable architecture for business and IT. SOAs unite both perspectives by shifting the focus of the IT on processes instead of applications or systems. SOAs have a dynamic character since compositions only become concrete during their execution. Using executable process descriptions consisting of services provides a process perspective on applications instead of an object or component-oriented perspective (Wulf et al., 2008). The SOA concept also aims to integrate all systems of a software infrastructure instead of replacing them. While the technical advantages of SOAs are rather small, they make an important difference by shifting the design philosophy of systems towards process-orientation.

2.2.4. Service Description and Retrieval

The description and retrieval of services are important functions of SOAs. However, they are supported only to a certain extent by the concepts of UDDI and WSDL. Therefore, many research efforts aim at improving these concepts. Prominent amongst these is research on semantic Web services, which seeks to capture the main properties of services and provides advanced semantic search functions. I will briefly explore this research field and describe technologies which bridge the gap between the concepts people use and the data formats computers manipulate (Sirin et al., 2004).

The idea of creating semantic Web services is based on the semantic Web which extends the WWW by an additional layer of metadata, allowing programs to obtain the semantic meaning of the content (Berners-Lee et al., 2001). XML-based languages are used to ensure that the representation of the information is computer- and human readable. The semantic structure of data is often expressed by using the so-called Resource Description Framework (RDF). Objects are described in RDF by using a triple of URIs expressing relations to other Web resources. The first URI references a subject, the second a property of the subject, and the third a value of this property.

Information resources often use different terms to refer to the same subjects, properties and values. Therefore, the semantic Web uses so-called *ontologies* to uniquely identify relations between the concepts. Ontologies are defined as information resources which contain the formal representation of a set of concepts within a particular domain. They use classes of objects, attributes and relations between these concepts to describe relations (Berners-Lee et al., 2001). Ontologies are stored as directed graphs which express semantic relations that create a hierarchy between elements. Ontologies are often used for the extension of search engines, improving their keyword-based matching algorithms by retrieving semantically similar results.

The Web Ontology Language (OWL) can for example be used for creating ontologies. One example of a public available ontology is WordNet[6], a large lexical database of English. Words are grouped into sets of cognitive synonyms, called *synsets*, each expressing a distinct concept. These synsets are interlinked by conceptual-semantic and lexical relations to create a network of meaningfully related words.

The semantic Web is sometimes used as a basis for the implementation of agents, i.e. programs that execute tasks automatically and use the available Web resources. The number of Web services is constantly growing, but semantic descriptions for searching and the implementation of agents are often inadequate. Therefore, researchers began to transfer the ideas of

---

[6] http://wordnet.princeton.edu

the semantic Web to the Web service technology to support an automated search, selection, execution and composition of Web services (Burstein et al., 2005).

There are different approaches for connecting the Web service technology with the semantic Web. The principle is always the same. The existing service descriptions located in WSDL and UDDI are supplemented by additional semantic descriptions. These semantic descriptions refer to ontologies which contain information about the concepts used by a service like operation names, attributes and quality aspects.

One example is the method of Paolucci et al. (Paolucci et al., 2002). They use a service profile, based on OWL-S[7] for the semantic description of a service. OWL-S profiles are used to connect the different attributes of a service with ontologies, which define all relevant concepts of the domain. These service profiles are created by the services providers and deployed to a matching engine, which is the core of the semantic search function of the system. The service profiles are also used for the creation of UDDI entries. Some fields of the service profiles, like service and provider names, can be mapped directly onto the equivalent UDDI fields while others have to be stored in UDDI t-models. Using concepts that conform to the UDDI standard has the advantage of using the semantic search together with the UDDI search, thus avoiding the need for an additional service repository. A search request is a semantic description of the functionality represented by an OWL-S profile. This abstract service description is compared with the existing services by the matching engine using a specific ontology. The search results include all services which match the semantic description of the functionality to a predefined extent. The items contain UDDI keys allowing requests for additional information from the UDDI repository.

Kawamura et al. (2005) presented a similar system. Service profiles are described by the Web Service Semantic Profile (WSSP), which is inspired by OWL-S. The profile fields in this system are used for the semantic description of WSDL fields instead of UDDI fields. Each WSDL field has a link in WSSP that relates to the corresponding concept in a specific ontology. In addition, the system uses various filters, like text filters, to improve the quality of search results (Kawamura et al., 2005).

However, according to Abramowicz et al. (2006), more work needs to be done to include more information about non-functional features of Web services in their descriptions. One important issue in this context is the quality that is provided by a service, referred to as Quality of Service (QoS). QoS relates to criteria like the maximum costs of using a service, the availability of a service and the execution time of a service. Such criteria depend on the type and function of a service and have to be determined by a community which is familiar with the domain (Bianchini et al., 2006). What is interesting about this idea is the extension of Web service descriptions facilitating the implementation of advanced search algorithms.

2.2.5. Assessment

SOAs address the issue of software inflexibility arising during maintenance and evolution since they facilitate the realisation of the necessary changes (Gold et al., 2004; Ma, 2005). Thereby, SOAs increase the responsiveness of organisations to changing market requirements. The traditional division between business and IT gives way to a holistic view of the

---

[7] OWL-S is a set of OWL (Web Ontology Language for Web services) ontologies supporting the rich description of Web services for the semantic Web. OWL-S is the follow-up standard of DAML-S, which was based on DAML-OIL (Sirin, E., Parsia, B., and Hendler, J. "Filtering and Selecting Semantic Web Services with Interactive Composition Techniques", *IEEE Intelligent Systems* (19:4) 2004, pp. 42 - 49.).

organisations' processes. Services become common building blocks for the functional approach of business departments and the object oriented approach of IT departments.

Every organisation faces the challenge of integrating diverse IT systems. The interoperability of SOAs helps to address this issue by allowing the creation of complex processes across different departments and different organisations (Brahe, 2007). Using BPM tools avoids the 'hard-coding' of business processes and shifts tailoring from programming to assembling (van der Aalst et al., 2003b). Using BPM on top of SOA assists with the integration of legacy systems in business processes, which can improve productivity (Brahe and Schmidt, 2007).

The main disadvantages of SOAs are related to their *complexity*, the *retrieval* of services and the *description* of services.

SOA standards have a high technical complexity (Hoyer et al., 2008). The number of SOA-related specifications has grown rapidly from 2000 to 2006 (Mocan et al., 2006) and these specifications are still changing rapidly (Brahe, 2007; Brahe and Schmidt, 2007; Ma, 2005; Stal, 2006). Nevertheless, SOAP, WSDL and UDDI have evolved to de facto standards supported by W3C and OASIS.

While the interoperability and standardisation of SOAs is an advantage, *"[...] software does not work as Legos do."* (Rettig, 2007, p. 26) Software code is more like fractals with no universal connections. This may help to explain why only 6% of the companies have made it into later stages of SOA implementations (Rettig, 2007). In addition, SOA adds additional layers of code. If processes fail due to problems below the process layer, software engineers will need to deal with those layers (Rettig, 2007). This can take time and delay adjustment to change (Hoyer et al., 2008).

Web service retrieval is only inadequately supported by Web service marketplaces, which only have very basic mechanisms for helping users to choose the most suitable Web services. Marketplaces must take non-functional parameters into account as they matter to customers (Abramowicz et al., 2006).

UDDI's keyword-based search function frequently returns no results because of a mismatch between the concepts used by the providers and those used by the clients (Aguilera et al., 2007). In addition, UDDI sometimes fails to recognise similarities and differences between Web service capabilities (Kawamura et al., 2005). Thus, UDDI's main limitation is the lack of semantic service descriptions, such as the name of a service provider, the service's location, or the business classification, which limits the search to keywords (Turner et al., 2003). Public UDDI directories have been shut down since their complexity was considered to be too high for end users. This can be related to the fact that UDDI is more driven by its primary members than by the feedback from end users (Chang, 2006).

WSDL describes a service only in terms of data types, methods, message format, transport protocol and its end-point (Turner et al., 2003). Additional service descriptions are sometimes incomplete or incorrect and often lack the up-to-date information required for an effective retrieval of services (Hoyer et al., 2008). Service providers may only include a few non-functional parameters in the service description, like some quality of service values (Abramowicz et al., 2006). Usability breakdowns may be caused by the API design itself, client-side Web service tools or an inadequate documentation (Beaton et al., 2008). The most common errors are:

- Specification errors, resulting from wrong names
- Structural errors, as no example code exists
- Default errors, as users are unsure if they needed to provide specific values

According to the Web 2.0 philosophy, end users could contribute comments, descriptions, tags or other information to improve the services' documentation (Hoyer et al., 2008). However, this is difficult since the documentation facilities of WSDL and UDDI have been designed for services providers rather than end users.

Research on semantic Web services provides improved search algorithms and systems which are based on additional semantic metadata. Such semantic search systems usually aim to automate the search, selection and execution of Web services and processes. One of the main problems is that the quality of the search results delivered depends on the ontologies used, which contain information about the used concepts of a service, such as operation names, attributes and quality criteria. Since ontologies can have multiple interpretations and are not always sufficient to capture the richness of the problem domain (Alvarez et al., 2007; Linn, 2003), they cannot be complete solutions.

Considering both pros and cons, SOAs are a suitable technical basis for the implementation of adaptable systems. However, it is essential to make the technology usable for end users by overcoming the shortcomings discussed.

2.3.   ERP Systems and Business Process Management

In this section, I first provide a brief introduction to Enterprise Resource Planning (ERP) systems, including a description of existing problems with these systems (section 2.3.1). I then give an overview of Business Process Management (BPM), including the description of existing problems with business process design tools (section 2.3.2). Finally, I discuss related systems (section 2.3.3).

2.3.1. Enterprise Resource Planning Systems

ERP systems are defined as "[...] software packages composed of several modules, such as human resources, sales, finance and production, providing cross-organisation integration of data through embedded business processes." (Esteves and Pastor, 2001, p. 2)

ERP was an inside-out process, starting from inventory control systems and expanding to today's complex systems, which consist of many modules like sales and order management, financial management, and supply chain management (Kumar and Hillegersberg, 2000). The history of ERP systems dates back to management information systems in 1969, when Blumenthal proposed an integrated architecture for organisational information systems. The first generation of ERP systems appeared later in the production industry.

ERP systems became popular in the 1990s. Only 10% of the European industrial companies had an ERP system in 1990, compared to 45% in 2000 (Kumar and Hillegersberg, 2000). In the end of the 1990s the ERP market had a crisis, leading to its consolidation, which left SAP and Oracle as the two big players. Today, ERP systems are considered to be amongst the largest existing applications (Sprott, 2000). ERP systems were traditionally constructed monolithically (Gurram et al., 2008), but due to the specific requirements of organisations they usually have to be customised. This need for customisations led to the construction of ERP systems on top of flexible software architectures, like SOAs. However, despite some improvements in recent years, ERP systems remain inflexible in some respects, with a hierarchical top-down structure (Pfeiffer et al., 2008).

A study of Markus et al. (2000) identified common ERP problems. Although the study is several years old, its findings remain relevant today as ERP systems usually have long update cycles. It shows that ERP systems have limited functionality and fail to provide 'complete' solutions for information processing. One of the most severe problems is the lack of support for unusual business processes. Customers, i.e. users have adopted a range of approaches to deal with this issue (Markus et al., 2000):

- Leaving some processes un-automated
- Adopting manual workarounds
- Adopting specialised 'bolt-on' packages designed by independent software vendors to work with a particular ERP system
- Integrating multiple enterprise packages in a best-of-breed solution
- Integrating the ERP packages with the organisation's legacy systems
- Building new custom modules to work with the ERP system
- Modifying ERP package code

Markus et al. (2000) also point out that ERP systems often lack decision support functions because they were originally designed for transaction processing. This lack of decision support either lets users struggle with vendors' facilities for creating reports or forces them to use Excel for reporting.

ERP vendors have addressed the lack of support for unusual business processes in several ways. One solution is the development and integration of business process modelling tools which allow customers to change and create business processes in their ERP system. The next section describes the core concepts of such tools.

2.3.2. Business Process Management

This section provides an overview of research on business process management. It helps to start with some basic definitions of a business process, a workflow, business process management and workflow management systems:

A *business process* is a sequence of activities which transforms particular inputs into an output of value to the customer (Legner and Wende, 2007). Business processes can be implemented technically as workflows, for instance on top of a SOA (Brahe, 2007).

According to the workflow management coalition a *workflow* is: *"the automation of a business process, in whole or part, during which documents, information or tasks are passed from one participant to another for action, according to a set of procedural rules."* (Fischer, 2000, p. 15). In the context of this work, workflows are compositions of existing computer programs, i.e. Web services, used for the automation of business processes (e.g. processes which transfer data between different programs).

"Business Process Management (BPM) includes methods, techniques, and tools to support the design, enactment, management, and analysis of operational business processes." (van der Aalst et al., 2003b, p. 1). The term BPM is often used interchangeably with workflow management (Brahe and Schmidt, 2007). However, in fact BPM is an extension of classical workflow management systems and approaches (van der Aalst et al., 2003b).

The workflow management coalition defines a *workflow management system* as *"a system that defines, creates and manages the execution of workflows through the use of software, running on one or more workflow engines, which is able to interpret the process definition, interact with workflow participants and, where required, invoke the use of IT tools and applications."* (Fischer, 2000, p. 16)

Having defined these terms, I will now explain how business process modelling can be performed in a service-oriented environment. Figure 7 gives an overview of the architecture of such an environment.

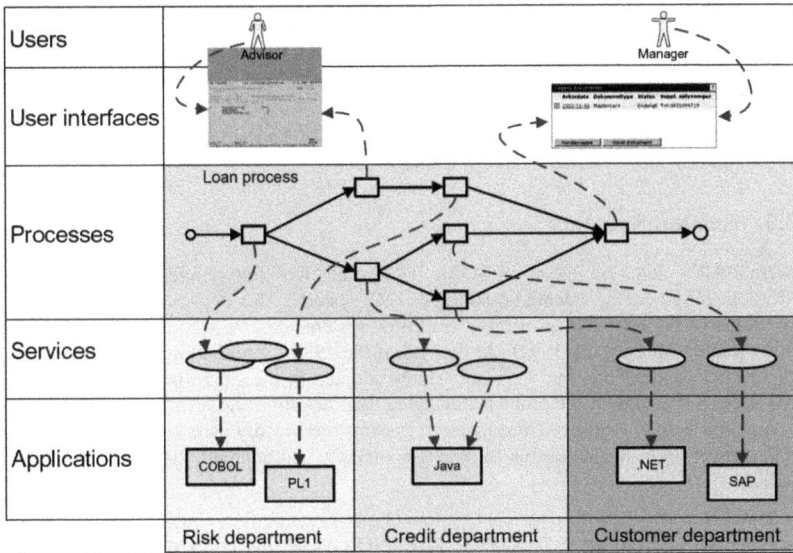

Figure 7: Architectural Overview of BPM in SOA (taken from Brahe and Schmidt, 2007, p. 250)

The *applications* layer contains all applications of the enterprises' software infrastructure, written in various languages. These applications provide a set of functions that have to be 'exposed' as services to be accessible within the SOA and are part of the *services* layer. The SOA concept itself has no high-level rules that determine when Web services should be accessed and which data should be used. Process languages like the Business Process Execution Language (BPEL) address this issue and belong to the *processes* layer. On top of this layer is the *user interfaces* layer, which contains graphical representations for the interaction with the process. This layer also includes process modelling tools which enable users to create new processes, i.e. workflows, by using the available services.

Modelling a workflow usually starts with the retrieval of services. According to Zhou et al. (2005) it can be divided into two phases. In the first phase, a service requester searches for services by using functional information, i.e. information about the services' functions, their input and output parameters as well as their preconditions and effects. In the second phase, the service requester has to select the most appropriate service from the results achieved in the first phase. For this purpose, the service requester uses non-functional information, i.e. information about the services' quality, service level agreements, management statements, security policies and pricing information (cf. Zhou et al., 2005). The services thus selected are then used for the orchestration of a workflow model. The process model produces an output, but has no graphical user interface which would allow users to interact with the workflow. A user interface should therefore be generated automatically or implemented by a programmer.

An important part of the architecture shown in Figure 7 is the *processes* layer. Processes are usually implemented by using a modelling language. BPEL has evolved to a de-facto standard for Web service orchestration in service-oriented environments. It superseded its predecessors XLANG, WSFL and BPML (van der Aalst et al., 2003b). It expresses the event sequence and collaboration logic of business processes while the underlying Web services provide the functionality (Pasley, 2005). A WSDL file describes the public entry and exit points of a BPEL process (Peltz, 2003). Hierarchical processes can be created because BPEL processes can be used as 'services' in other BPEL processes. Since BPEL is very technical and complex, it is usually generated from BPMN (Business Process Modelling Notation) descriptions, which have a business-oriented modelling notation.

BPM is supported by a variety of professional tools developed by various ERP vendors. The next section provides a market overview of these tools.

2.3.3. Related Systems

Modern ERP systems are based on SOAs. As a result, workflow management systems, i.e. BPM tools, have become essential modules of ERP systems. This evolution took considerable time. Some of the earlier interoperable workflow systems date back to the beginning of the 1990s (Medina-Mora et al., 1992). At the end of the 1990s, workflow management systems became broadly available, but were not widely adopted in the enterprise context (Leymann and Roller, 2000). One of the problems delaying their adoption was a lack of support for legacy systems. Today, workflow management systems are broadly used in the enterprise context. However, they are not usable for end users (Brahe and Schmidt, 2007; van der Aalst et al., 2003b).

The MILANO workflow management system is one example for an advanced research prototype and was developed as part of the MILANO CSCW platform (Agostini et al., 1997). This system is thought to be very flexible in comparison with current workflow management systems, making it easy to change workflows. The interaction modes support users' cooperation by supporting their articulation work. However, the prototype does not have a design environment which allows end users without programming skills to create workflows (cf. Agostini and Michelis, 2000).

Readers might be interested in the study of van der Aalst et al. (2003) of 15 commercial workflow management systems (van der Aalst et al., 2003a). They characterise the systems in terms of their expressive power, stating whether they support the creation of complex workflow constructs. Figure 8 provides a recent overview of the market for BPM tools, differentiating them in terms of *current offering*, i.e. functionality, *strategy*, i.e. costs, strategic alliances and customer references, and *market presence, i.e.* the installed base, new customers, and the delivery footprint. The figure shows that Software AG, IBM, TIBCO, Vitria, Oracle, SAP, and Cordys are the market leaders providing solutions that are strong in all areas of functionality. I briefly introduce the SAP solution as one example of the market-leading tools.

SAP introduced its business process management component NetWeaver BPM, a part of its NetWeaver Composition Environment, at the end of 2008 (Volmering, 2009). It is based on the SAP NetWeaver platform, which provides connectivity to other applications (Eisele et al., 2007). The NetWeaver Composition Environment provides a unified Eclipse environment for composing services, business objects, user interfaces, etc. (Silver, 2009).

NetWeaver BPM supports a model-driven approach and provides an integrated design and runtime environment that enhances collaboration between business and IT. It consists of the following components (Silver, 2009):

- The *Process Composer*: A BPMN-based modelling tool, which is part of the NetWeaver Composition Environment (see Figure 9 for a screenshot);

- The *Process Server*: A JEE-based runtime engine;

- The *Process Desk*: A process runtime environment within the NetWeaver Portal.

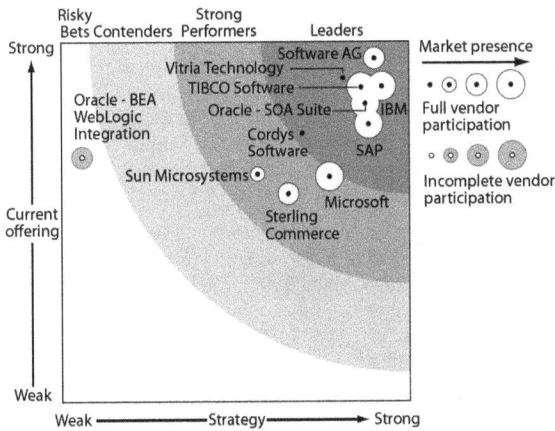

Figure 8: Market overview, Business Process Management Suites (taken from Vollmer, 2008)

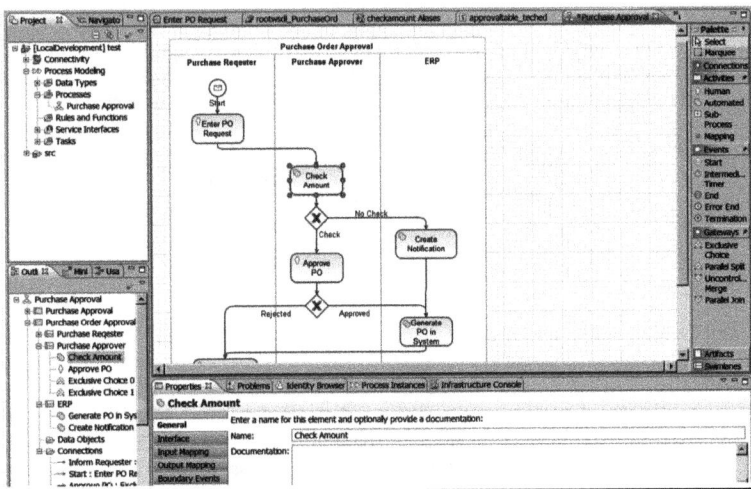

Figure 9: SAP Process Composer, the Design Tool of NetWeaver BPM (taken from Silver, 2009)

2.4. Paper-based User Interfaces

Using pen and paper for the 'conservation' of information has a long tradition, making it a 'natural' medium for most people. The interaction with computers is quite different, relying in many cases on the WIMP (windows, icons, menus, pointers) metaphor. In most cases, the keyboard and the mouse are used as the standard input devices.

WIMP does not support all creative processes very well since using keyboard and mouse interrupts these processes quite often (Tian et al., 2008). Therefore, tangible concepts, based for example on pen and paper, have become popular over the last years (Iacucci et al., 2003). The nature of such concepts allows users to concentrate on the content instead of the interaction with the computer (Subrahmonia and Zimmerman, 2003).

Paper-based user interfaces (PBUI) allow a 'natural' interaction with the computer and support the linking of physical and digital artefacts. The objective of PBUIs is not just to digitalise paper-based work routines but also to combine the advantages of both worlds (Tian et al., 2008). In *The Myth of the Paperless Office*, Sellen and Harper argue that paper will remain important in the office, especially as a temporary medium and increasingly in combination with electronic tools (Sellen and Harper, 2002).

Paper has different affordances than today's computer systems. Paper is tangible, movable and transportable and can be annotated. It also supports uninterrupted creativity and sketching and has low usage requirements (Oviatt, 2006), making it interesting for creative and collaborative settings. Users often start with creating sketches on sheets of paper when they create models or designs (Landay and Myers, 2001). However, this kind of creativity is usually not supported by modern software systems.

The 'informal' character of pen and paper allows mental models to be sketched quickly and effortlessly (Nakagawa et al., 1993). Pen and paper approaches, in form of paper mock-ups, have proven effective for the creation of interface designs since they enable users to 'play' with the computer (Bødker et al., 2004). Other advantages of paper are its ubiquity (Wellner, 1993) and its comparatively low costs (Yeh et al., 2006).

PBUIs allow the development of systems which enrich the existing paper-based work practice with digital content and facilitate the development of systems for specific new application fields. Examples include the processing of digitalised information and the design of interactive applications which allow a constant monitoring of sketches via a connected computer. In addition, location-aware PBUIs allow the design of systems which have 'affordances' that exceed the ones of paper-based work practices. Such systems could support for instance the creation of digital relations between different sheets of paper. Furthermore, the sheets of paper could be categorised in different types with distinct semantics.

However, paper also imposes some restrictions (Sellen and Harper, 2002). In terms of PBUIs, interaction-related problems are the most important ones since paper is a non-interactive medium. The main problems are:

- The static nature of paper,
- The lack of feedback (beyond the strokes created),
- The difficulty of changing or removing sketches once created.

It is also challenging to design the interaction concept for PBUIs, which must have sufficient power and incorporate the paper-based interaction concept (Liao et al., 2005). The design of PBUIs requires a detailed analysis of the 'affordances' of interactive paper and its digital representation so that they can be effectively combined. As interaction is related to the social backgrounds and the work context of people (Sellen and Harper, 2002), it is necessary to gain a precise understanding of existing work practices in the application domain. Table 5 summarises the opportunities and challenges presented by PBUIs.

Opportunities	Challenges
Advantages of paper in informal and collaborative scenarios	Combining the digital and physical worlds to optimally exploit their different 'affordances'
High degree of user acceptance	Lack of dynamic feedback
Enrichment of existing work practice	Difficulty of changing sketches
Online and offline access to paper	Integration in work practice
New use possibilities through location-awareness, i.e. differentiation of type and area of a paper on which the pen is currently used	Design of a suitable interaction concept

Table 5: Opportunities and Challenges presented by PBUIs

Several studies in the field of HCI show that users like to use pen and paper for the creation of sketches, transferring them later to the computer (Damm et al., 2000; Landay and Myers, 1995; Yeh et al., 2006). This reflects some of the advantages of paper-based sketches over computer-based design and modelling tools. Computer-based modelling tools limit the modelling to a set of pre-defined elements (Chen et al., 2003) in a fixed modelling area which cannot be extended easily.

The inherently unfinished character of sketches leads to an increased focus of discussions on the 'content' rather than the 'design' of sketches (Black, 1990). In addition, it is more likely that (inexperienced) users contribute to sketches rather than to perfectly drawn models (Winograd, 1995).

Many PBUI approaches focus on the creation of sketches used in the context of computer-aided design (CAD) or interface design. The system ModelCraft enables users to model 3D objects by using interactive paper. The models created can be annotated with descriptions regarding the behaviour and changes of the model. A CAD program uses these annotations and applies them to the digital representation (Song et al., 2006). Another system, called Fly Pentop[8], is a learning tool for children, enabling them to model paper interfaces for games and learning applications. Children can use pre-printed interfaces, which can be extended by self-created elements, or they can design new interfaces from scratch.

So far, no specific tools which support the modelling of diagrams have been developed. There are only general-purpose sketching systems supporting collaborative brainstorming. An example of such a system is Diamond's Edge. Users sit together at a table that has an interactive digital display. Each user has a private interactive block for creating sketches. These sketches can be transferred to the display of the table for further collaborative processing (Bernstein et al., 2006).

Closely related to research on PBUIs is research on electronic sketching systems based on *low-fidelity* visualisations. These systems are usually implemented on top of electronic white-

---

[8] See http://www.flypentop.com

board systems and tablet PC technologies. Various studies explore how sketching functionalities can enrich modelling tools and how tools can be designed which allow users to sketch user interfaces. The focus of these approaches is on the design of input concepts, the recognition of gestures as well as the visualisation and formalisation of sketched prototypes. Electronic sketching systems are referred to as 'informal' design tools since they support the ambiguity and informality of sketches (Yeung et al., 2007). In contrast to PBUIs, they support direct feedback, but lack some of the advantages of paper, such as low costs, tangibility and mobility. Electronic sketching systems are usually used by professional developers to enrich UML models.

One of the oldest electronic sketching systems is called Knight. It enables users to model UML class diagrams collaboratively on a large electronic whiteboard. The interaction with the system is realised by gestures which can be drawn with a pen. Knight uses *compound gestures* and *eager recognition* for making the interaction with the system as intuitive as possible. *Compound gestures* are combinations of spatial and temporal gestures for the creation of elements. These gestures are recognised during their creation by the *eager recognition* concept, allowing the system to provide direct feedback. Users can sketch combinations of informal and formal elements. In addition, the system provides a special *freehand mode* for the creation of annotations. Formal elements which are recognised by Knight are replaced by computer-generated representations (Damm et al., 2000).

SUMLOW is another electronic whiteboard system supporting the collaborative creation of different UML diagrams (class, use case and sequence diagrams). Unlike in Knight, the recognised formal elements are not replaced by computer-generated representations. Furthermore, the system follows a *lazy recognition* approach, which formalises the elements progressively (Chen et al., 2003).

Donaldson and Williamson present a prototypical approach for sketching UML activity diagrams (Donaldson and Williamson, 2005). Their system, called MaramaSketch, is an extension of the meta-diagram tool Marama[9].

2.5.   Mashup and other Composition Tools

This section explores some additional composition tools. Of particular interest are the so-called mashup tools since they are often used for similar tasks as BPM tools, i.e. for composing data or services.

Mashups have become very popular over the last three years. In September 2006, the Website *ProgrammableWeb.com* listed 1019 mashups (Wong and Hong, 2007). By April 2009, the number had more than tripled to 3826. Mashups combine existing content and services from multiple Websites to create new applications which were not envisaged by the Web site designers (Hoyer et al., 2008; Lin et al., 2009; Wong and Hong, 2007). There are many different mashup tools, like Karma, Sifter, Solvent, Potluck, Marmite, Intel MashMaker, Yahoo Pipes, and Serena Business Mashups. Below, I will briefly introduce the four last-mentioned tools.

Marmite enables end users to combine existing Web content and services. Its architecture is based on dataflows which are similar to Unix pipes. Marmite's key features are (Wong and Hong, 2007):

---

[9] See https://wiki.auckland.ac.nz/display/csidst/Welcome

- Support for the extraction of content of Web pages (e.g. names, addresses, dates)
- Processing of data flows (e.g. filtering values or adding metadata)
- Integration of different data sources (e.g. from databases, Web pages or services)
- Directing the output to a variety of sinks (e.g. databases, map services, Web pages)

Figure 9 shows an example of a mashup created with Marmite. The mashup searches all addresses in Pennsylvania in a specified set of Websites and displays them on Yahoo Maps.

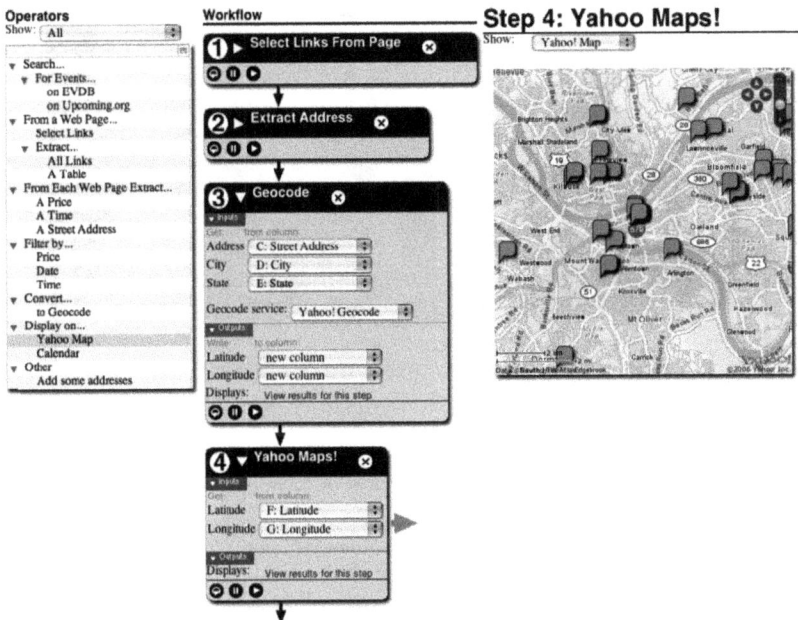

Figure 10: Marmite (taken from Wong and Hong, 2007, p. 1442)

Intel's *MashMaker*, shown in Figure 11, enables end users to create their own mashups based on data and queries produced by other users and by remote sites. It borrows ideas from various tools, including word processors (editing unstructured data), Web browsers (browsing information) and spreadsheets (mixing computed values with data). MashMaker is designed around the following key principles (Ennals et al., 2007):

- An un-typed tree data model which has no constraints on the form of the tree
- A mixture of data and queries enabling users to enhance their view of data by adding computed nodes based on the 'surrounding' data
- A sharing of queries with other users in the form of widgets, i.e. small applications
- An 'overlaid' editing of live data, allowing data to be updated while preserving user edits

- An example-driven query construction based on interactive data exploration, enabling users to formulate queries by interactive data browsing and exploration

- A collaborative exploration of data enhanced by automatically suggested widgets that have been applied to similar data inside the users' social network

Figure 11: Intel MashMaker (taken from http://mashmaker.intel.com/web/)

Yahoo Pipes is probably the most advanced mashup tool for end users available on the Web. It offers predefined building blocks, i.e. functions and data sources, which can be connected with each other to integrate, manipulate and visualise data. These compositions are referred to as *pipes* and are similar to the pipes used in Unix. Figure 12 shows the modelling interface of Yahoo Pipes. On the left side are the different building blocks. The centre of the window displays the modelling area, which follows the box & wire metaphor. In this metaphor, boxes, i.e. building blocks, are wired with each other. At the bottom of the window is an area that shows the (intermediate) results of the created pipes and can be used for debugging. Yahoo Pipes supports various formats for the presentation of the results, such as RSS, widgets or Google maps. Pipes can also be shared with other users by publishing them on the Yahoo Pipes Website.

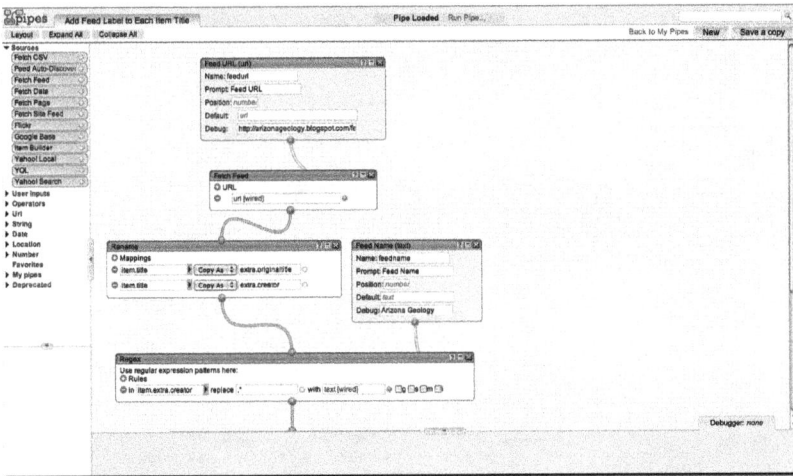

Figure 12: Yahoo Pipes (taken from http://pipes.yahoo.com/pipes/)

Serena Business Mashups, depicted in Figure 13, is somewhat different from the other mashup tools since it is designed for the enterprise context. It enables business analysts, i.e. super users, to create processes without the help of programmers by providing an easily accessible Web interface.serena Business Mashups was launched in December 2007 and aims to automate business processes of relatively low complexity. The mashups created can be wrapped as Adobe Flash or Microsoft Silverlight objects as well as RSS feeds and Google gadgets. Technically, Serena Business Mashups takes advantage of SOAP-based Web services and BPEL, hiding the complexity of these technologies from users.

A number of composition tools other than mashup tools are also of interest. One of them is an early-stage research prototype called *Koala*. The system enables users to capture, share, automate and personalise business processes on the Web. It uses a programming-by-demonstration concept, called *sloppy programming*, which produces pseudo-natural language scripts. These scripts are automatically stored for sharing in a wiki system (Little et al., 2007).

Vegemite extends the Koala system and enables users to collect and process data across multiple Websites. Users have to 'demonstrate' in the system how the columns of the table-based visualisation are filled. Vegemite's architecture consists of two parts: the *VegeTables* for storing data and the *Koala engine* for recording and playing back actions (Lin et al., 2009).

Apple's *Automator* (see Figure 14) is another popular composition tool and is part of the Mac OS X operation system. It provides end users with functionalities for creating workflows by chaining a series of operations. The operations available depend on the applications installed. However, processes have a limited complexity since the operations have exactly one input- and one output-port.

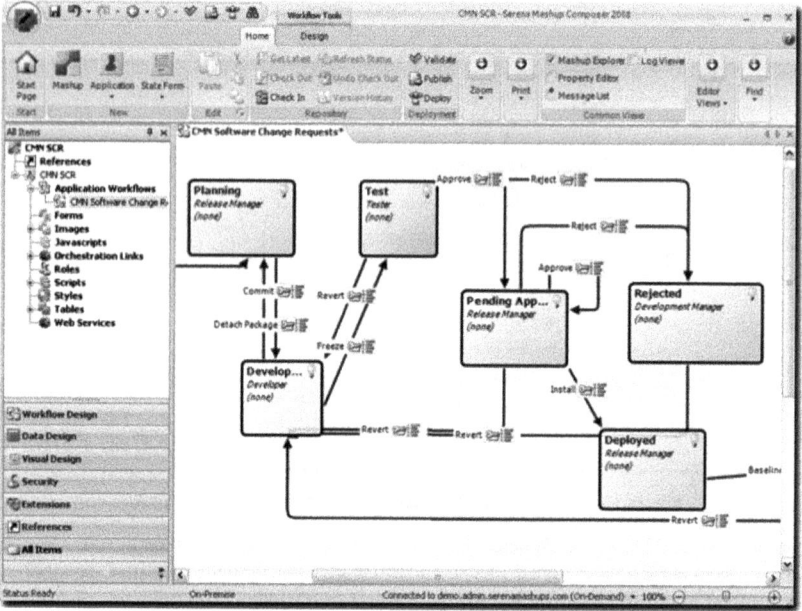

Figure 13: Serena Business Mashups (taken from http://www.serena.com/)

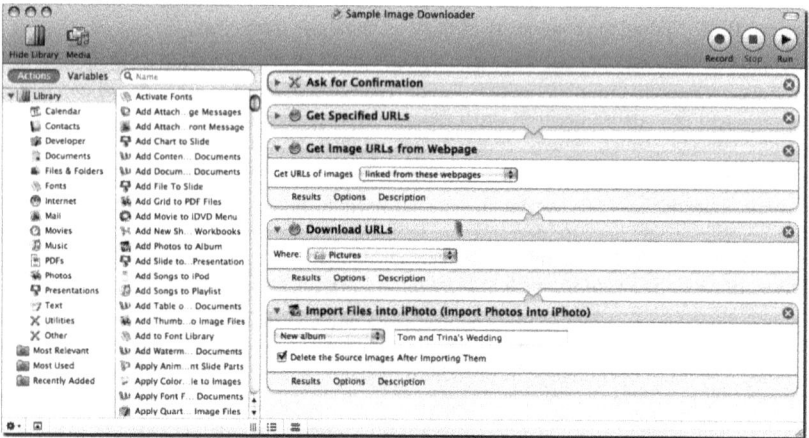

Figure 14: Apple's Automator (according to http://automator.us/examples-05.html)

2.6.   Concluding Remarks

In this section I summarise my review and formulate the research questions I aim to address.

My review of research on EUD covered many different tailoring approaches of varying complexity. Most of the EUD tools presented, including FreEvolve, ECHOES and Oval, were designed for component-based architectures. The more recently developed system TailorBPEL was designed to enable users to tailor BPEL processes. TailorBPEL is therefore an interesting platform for the implementation of workflow modelling tools. However, its aim is to support the personalisation of existing BPEL processes rather than the modelling of new processes. TailorBPEL does not address the disadvantages of SOA related to its complexity, the retrieval of services and the description of services. In addition, TailorBPEL does not provide extended functionalities for the implementation of workflow modelling tools which can be used by end users.

EUD research has generated considerable design knowledge. I have presented a set of important EUD design principles, referred to by the acronym TAILOR. These principles inspired the design of the business process modelling environment presented in chapter 5.

The review of literature on SOAs showed that service-orientation adds a process perspective to applications, extending the prevalent component-oriented perspective (Wulf et al., 2008). Despite the rather small technical advantages of SOAs, this extension shifts the design philosophy of systems to processes, uniting the views of business and IT. Due to this shift in the design philosophy, BPM tools have become important tools for the (re-)design of systems. However, existing BPM tools remain difficult to use for end users (Brahe and Schmidt, 2007; van der Aalst et al., 2003b).

SAP NetWeaver BPM was presented as an example of one of the leading BPM tools. While this solution is quite powerful and offers all data and services required for modelling a business process, it has not been designed to be used by end users. BPM tools, designed for professional process designers, are significantly different from tools designed for end users since tools for end users must especially address the 'cognitive distance' between using and designing an application (Malone et al., 1995). They should follow a *"low threshold, no ceiling"* (Papert, 1980) philosophy, enabling end users with low technical skills to address their issues without getting a computer science education first (Repenning and Ioannidou, 2006).

My discussion of paper-based user interfaces (PBUI) showed that sketching tools could support creative design and modelling processes since users often start such processes by creating sketches which must be digitalised later on. The informal character of PBUIs does not limit the creativity of users since it permits the creation of elements which are not part of a set of pre-defined notation elements. In addition, PBUIs support uninterrupted creativity, have a low cognitive 'workload' (Oviatt, 2006) and comparatively low costs (Yeh et al., 2006).

The mashup tools I described help end users to create service compositions by providing appropriate modelling mechanisms. Schroth and Janner (2007) compared Web 2.0 technologies like mashup tools with SOAs and identified the differences and similarities set out in Table 6.

Serena's Business Mashup tool tries to combine the advantages of 'both worlds'. It uses a visualisation that simplifies the modelling process for end users and uses reliable enterprise SOA technologies like SOAP Web services and BPEL. However, the system was developed in parallel to this work and offers no advanced end-user-specific functionalities in terms of service search and service documentation, which were identified as important shortcomings of SOAs from an end-user perspective.

Similarities	Differences
Reusing and composing existing resources	SOA requires an expert whereas Web 2.0 is self-managed
Collaboration and coupling of remote resources	Web 2.0 is about presentation and user interface integration whereas SOA deployments are abstract and less visible to users
Principle of agility	Web 2.0 deals with human-readable content (e.g. text, pictures) whereas SOA connects business functionality on a machine-to-machine level

Table 6: Similarities and Differences between SOAs and Web 2.0 Techniques (according to Schroth and Janner, 2007)

In summary, EUD research mainly offers component-based tailoring tools, which are not usable in service-oriented environments. In contrast, mashup tools are usable by end users, but fail to support enterprise requirements since they aim at connecting human-readable content, like texts, instead of SOAP-based Web services provided by different enterprise systems. BPM research offers a broad spectrum of professional modelling tools for connecting services of different enterprise systems. Nevertheless these tools are not intended to be used by end users. In addition, they do not provide mechanisms like paper-based user interfaces to foster creativity.

Therefore, it is worth trying to implement a new kind of business process modelling environment which combines the best concepts of each research field.

2.6.1. Gaps in current Research

In this section I discuss which research gaps should be addressed by the design of the business process modelling environment.

In terms of EUD, the tailoring of heterogeneous software infrastructures still poses a major challenge for research on tailorable systems (Eriksson and Dittrich, 2007; Pipek and Kahler, 2006). The introduction of SOAs in the EUD discourse will address this challenge. SOAs facilitate the implementation of tailoring tools for heterogeneous software infrastructures since they can integrate the different technologies by using common interfaces, described in XML. Another challenge is the transfer of the 'tailoring by composition' mechanism to SOAs, which has so far only been used as a tailoring mechanism in component-based systems (Wulf et al., 2008).

SOAs were designed to be adaptive, i.e. automatically adapting, but not adaptable, i.e. changeable by end users. In addition, the focus of SOAs on machine-to-machine interaction makes them difficult to use for end users (Schroth and Janner, 2007). Two of the most severe problems in this context are inadequate service descriptions from an end-user perspective and the limitation of UDDI's search mechanism to keywords.

Proper and up-to-date service descriptions within the WSDL files of services are important for search mechanisms, like the ones of UDDI (Hoyer et al., 2008). However, service descriptions may be incomplete or incorrect. Some service providers only include a few non-functional parameters (e.g. different quality of service values) in the descriptions (Abramowicz et al., 2006). Usability problems of service APIs may result from specification errors, i.e. the use of wrong names, structural errors, i.e. failing to provide example code, and default errors, i.e.

failing to provide default values for the parameters. The limitation of service descriptions to functional metadata is the most severe issue from an end-user perspective. End users need additional information about the usage of services to understand them and to be able to use them in their work contexts. Considering the Web 2.0 philosophy, end users could improve current service descriptions by contributing additional (usage) information (Hoyer et al., 2008).

UDDI's keyword search either returns no results, as there is no relation between the concepts used by service providers and those used by clients (Aguilera et al., 2007; Kawamura et al., 2005), or it returns a number of services, making the selection time-consuming (Liu et al., 2007). Choosing appropriate services would be much easier if users could take non-functional parameters and usage information into account. In addition, UDDI is thought to be generally too complex for end users (Wu and Chang, 2006).

Research on semantic Web services tries to overcome theses issues by providing improved search algorithms and systems which are based on additional semantic metadata, i.e. service descriptions. Such semantic search systems usually aim at automating the search, selection and execution of Web services and workflows instead of supporting users in these tasks. However, the quality of the search results depends on the ontologies used. This is because ontologies contain global information about the functionality and concepts used by a service, including operation names, attributes and quality criteria. Unfortunately, ontologies can have multiple interpretations in different domains and are not always sufficient to capture the richness of the problem domain (Alvarez et al., 2007; Linn, 2003). Therefore, semantic search systems are an incomplete solution for overcoming the limitations of UDDI's keyword search.

In terms of BPM, the combination of BPEL and SOA increases the flexibility of workflow design. Despite this achievement *"[...] we are far from a situation where ordinary workers are able to define and compose their own local computational workflows."* (Brahe and Schmidt, 2007, p. 257) One reason is the professional skills required for using composition tools, including knowledge about XML, BPEL, design-time IDEs and runtime middleware, which cannot be acquired easily by end users (Liu et al., 2007).

The development of paper-based user interfaces (PBUI) could reduce the skill levels required for modelling since such interfaces use a well-known interaction concept, i.e. pen and paper, and encourage the creativity of users thanks to the unrestricted informal character of paper. However, PBUIs lack a dynamic feedback since paper is not interactive. So far, no specific PBUI applications have been made available which support the creation of process models.

In light of the gaps in research I identified, I can now formulate the main question guiding my research:

"How can Service Oriented Architectures be used to support the tailorability of software infrastructures by end users?"

This question is detailed by the following sub-questions:

- How can 'tailoring by composition' be realised in service-oriented systems?
- How can effective UDDI search functions, usable by end users, be realised?

Chapter 3

"A computer system embodies a model of another system in the 'real world', e.g., in the simple case of a payroll system, a model of the wage calculation system (tariffs etc.) and the staff of the company (names, positions, account numbers etc.)."

Schmidt, 1991, p.9

3.   Research Design and Application Domain

In section 3.1 of this chapter, I provide an overview of different research methodologies[10] that could be used for addressing the research questions I am interested in (see section 2.6.1). I then describe my own research design, which combines different research methods[11]. In section 3.2 I discuss the application domain of small and medium enterprises (SME).

3.1.   Research Methodologies and Research Design

A number of research methodologies could be used to address the research questions raised. The methodologies must involve end users in my research since it is embedded in the application domain. Several user-centred methodologies have been reviewed, for example, by (David et al., 1999; Palvia et al., 2003; Palvia et al., 2004; Wulf, 2009). Drawing on their work, I briefly describe the research methods which are most relevant for addressing my research question while closely involving end users: *ethnography, case studies, participatory design, surveys, action research*, and *design science* (section 3.1.1 to 3.1.6). I then present my research design in section 3.1.7.

3.1.1.   Ethnography

The roots of ethnographic research are in social and cultural anthropology. Following the groundbreaking work of Suchman (1987), ethnography has become widely accepted as qualitative research methodology in Information Systems, Human-Computer Interaction and Computer Supported Cooperative Work (Myers, 1997; Randall et al., 2007). Ethnographic researchers aim to gain insights into a domain and the existing work practices in the domain by collaborating with people from the application domain (Myers, 1999; Wilde and Hess, 2007).

Many researchers, like Bloomberg (e.g. Blomberg et al., 1993), Crabtree (e.g. Crabtree, 2004), Dourish (e.g. Dourish, 2006), Harper (e.g. Harper et al., 1989) Heath and Luff (e.g. Heath and Luff, 1992), Hughes, Randall and Shapiro (e.g. Hughes et al., 1994; Hughes et al., 1992) have contributed to research on the role of ethnography in design processes. Some have developed methods which 'inform' system design by ethnography with a view to better meeting users' needs. However, ethnography should not just be used to generate a *"bullet list of design implications"* since it provides deep insights into an organisation and offers *"[...] models for thinking about those settings and the work that goes on there."* (Dourish, 2006, p. 549) Randall et al. point out: *"Systems are used within populated environments that are, whatever 'technological' characteristics they may have, 'social' in character and thus the intent to design distributed and shared systems means that this social dimension has to be taken into account."* (Randall et al., 2007, p. 3)

Popular qualitative ethnographic research methods are for example open and semi-structured interviews. Semi-structured interviews allow researchers to grasp the subjective views of the interviewees. This approach facilitates the comparison of the different interviews and allows

---

[10] A methodology is defined as a set of guidelines to assist in generating results. It consists of various methods or techniques which are not all used every time (Mingers, J. "Combining IS Research Methods: Towards a Pluralist Methodology", *Information Systems Research* (12:3) 2001, pp. 240 - 259.).

[11] Methods are basic research activities. They are generally well-defined sequences of operations (Ibid.).

exploring specific topics (Kvale, 1996). The design of the interview guidelines followed accepted criteria (Merton and Kendall, 1946):

- Non-directivity (no manipulation of the interviewee)
- Elaboration of the interviewee's subjective meaning of the interview topics
- Capturing different facets of the interview topic
- Emotional profoundness of the interview statements and situations

Ethnographic research methods use different designs:

- *Case studies[12]* focus on a single enterprise to gather rich descriptions of the existing work practice for example by conducting observations.
- *Cross-sectional* studies use data gathered from multiple enterprises, for example by conducting interviews or questionnaires.
- *Time-series* analysis uses data like documents and protocols on one or more enterprises over a defined time period (cf. David et al., 1999).

Ethnographic research presents some practical challenges. First of all, one needs to have access to a sufficient number of organisations to collect data. These organisations often have little to gain from the research. The data then needs to be captured, coded and analysed in a way that can be replicated to provide evidence (David et al., 1999). In addition, the results of ethnographic studies can provide requirements for system design, but it is rather difficult to use them to design.

The data collected will be qualitative rather than quantitative. Qualitative data often takes the form of texts gathered by observations, interviews or documents, but can also consist in still or moving images (Strauss and Corbin, 1998). Qualitative data usually needs to be 'processed' before it can be analysed which is always achieved by creating transcripts. Afterwards, the transcripts can be analysed in three different ways (Miles and Huberman, 1994, p. 8):

- *Interpretivism:* The existing data is read/watched over and over again to capture the 'essence' of an account, which is supposed to remain stable across changes in a person's life. The aim is to achieve a 'practical understanding' of meanings and actions. Interpretivists insist that they are more 'detached' from their objects of study than their informants. However, interpretivists are also affected by what they observe in the field. This makes it difficult to separate their contributions from the 'real' information when encoding or decoding words from their informants.
- *Social anthropology:* Researchers maintain extended contact with a given community, participating directly or indirectly in local activities. They often use audio- and videotapes, films and structured observations to gather data. The data analysis tends to be descriptive and aims to capture behavioural regularities in everyday situations.
- *Collaborative social research:* Researchers and local actors collaborate in performing a field experiment, e.g. an organisational change process, often following an *action research* methodology (see section 3.1.5).

---

[12] Since the term *case study* has multiple meanings, it should not be noted that the term refers in this case to a unit of analysis (e.g. a particular organisation) and not to the description of a research method.

3.1.2. Case Studies

Case studies serve to explore contemporary complex phenomena within their natural context, especially when the boundaries between phenomenon and context are blurred (Yin, 2008). Their focus is on a small number of participants who are studied in depth. The validity of an extrapolation from one or more such individual cases is achieved by the plausibility and cogency of the logical reasoning used for the description of results as well as by drawing conclusions from these results (cf. Walsham, 1993).

The design philosophy of case studies can be behaviouristic, examining theses objectively, or constructivistic aiming to interpret behavioural patterns of the participants within their constructed realities (Wilde and Hess, 2007). The former position is advocated by Yin (2008), the latter by Walsham (1993).

3.1.3. Participatory Design

Participatory Design (PD) is a set of theories, practices, and studies which integrate end users as full participants in design processes. PD is an extraordinary diverse field having no single theory or paradigm of study. The idea is always to bring together researchers and practitioners, be it in the context of software design or other institutional settings (Muller, 2003).

PD began as part of the Scandinavian workplace democracy movement in the 1970s. It was used in research projects on user participation in systems development which were done in cooperation between labour unions and other parties, including software developers (Ehn and Kyng, 1987). The projects developed an *action research* approach (see section 3.1.5) which fostered the cooperation between researchers and the workers participating in the research.

The aim of PD is that the participating workers (and not only the researchers) get something (e.g. new systems, optimised work practices) out of the project (Bødker, 1996). The involvement of people in the design processes of software applications can be achieved, for example, by conducting design workshops that use mock-up and prototyping techniques to simulate (future) work situations.

The simulation of work situations gives access to peoples' subconscious knowledge which is hardly accessible by other methods. Workshops can be recorded (audio and/or video) to carefully analyse verbal and other reactions from workers. This can help researchers to identify problems, related to break downs and changes in use practices. They can be discussed and evaluated in early stages being used as input for the design process (Kyng, 1994).

An interesting concept in this context is PICTIVE (Plastic Interface for Collaborative Technology Initiative through Video Exploration) (Muller, 1991; Muller, 1992). Designers create so-called 'plastic icons', i.e. mock-ups of the envisioned system, based on their knowledge about the application domain and existing work practices. These mock-ups are discussed in a design workshop to inform the design process.

3.1.4. Surveys

Surveys are a quantitative research method allowing researchers to ask predefined questions to a sample population. Surveys are often used for information gathering, the exploration of new areas or the refinement of established theories. They can be conducted face-to-face, via telephone, mail or in a Web-based form since they are always structured. Fowler (2002) proposes several criteria for the development of the used questionnaire:

- *Focus group discussions*
- *Drafting Questions*
- *Critical Systematic Review*
- *Cognitive laboratory interviews*
- *Putting questions into a survey instrument*
- *Pre-testing an interview schedule*

Using surveys for large-scale exploratory studies is rather difficult since it requires the coding of a large number of responses to open-ended questions. Therefore, surveys are often used to supplement and direct ethnographic research (cf. David et al., 1999).

3.1.5. Action Research

Action research is a qualitative research methodology conducted by groups of researchers and practitioners who solve a practical problem together within a mutually acceptable ethical framework (Wilde and Hess, 2007). The collaboration can help practitioners to achieve practical improvements while assisting researchers in their scientific inquiries (Rapoport, 1970). The collaborative aspect of action research combined with its aim to enlarge the body of knowledge distinguishes it from applied social science which aims 'simply' at the application of scientific knowledge (Myers, 1997).

Action research assumes that complex social systems, interacting with information technologies, cannot be studied easily, e.g. by observations. Such systems can only be understood as whole entities. They can be studied best by observing the effects of changes which were introduced to these systems (Baskerville and Wood-Harper, 1996).

The different forms of action research can be distinguished by four main characteristics: the process model (iterative, reflective, linear), the structure (rigorous, fluid), the involvement of researchers in the field (collaborative, facilitative, expert), and the objectives of the study (e.g. organisational development, system design) (cf. Baskerville, 1999, p. 10).

In practice, action research is often a *cyclic process* consisting of the following steps (Susman and Evered, 1978, p. 588):

1. *Diagnosing:* Analysis of the problems in the application domain
2. *Action Planning:* Collaborative planning of changes
3. *Action Taking:* Collaborative execution of planned changes
4. *Evaluating:* Analysis, if changes were successful and to which extend
5. *Specifying Learning:* Reflection on the results (independent of the success) being used to improve the process in future iterations

3.1.6. Design Science

The design science paradigm[13] allows researchers to perform normative studies. Its roots are in engineering and the sciences of the artificial (Simon, 1996). It is basically a problem-

---

[13] A *paradigm* is a construct which specifies a general set of philosophical assumptions. It has for example an ontological perspective (what is assumed to exist), an epistemological perspective (the nature of valid knowledge), an ethical perspective (what is valued or considered right), and a methodological perspective

solving paradigm which enables researchers to evaluate theories or prove that new system designs are feasible. Design science seeks to create innovations and products through which the analysis, construction, and use of information systems can be effectively and efficiently accomplished (Hevner et al., 2004). It focuses on 'real world' problems which must be properly conceptualised and represented in order to construct appropriate solutions, i.e. artefacts, which must be implemented and evaluated on their efficacy and efficiency by using appropriate criteria.

March and Smith (1995) proposed a research framework for design science following the two dimensions *research activities* and *research output*. The research activities consist of two basic actions, *build* (does it work?) and *evaluate* (how well does it work?). Apart from these basic activities, it is important to determine why and how the artefact worked or did not work within its environment. This could be achieved by applying natural science methods to the artefacts to theorise and justify the theories about those artefacts. The generated research outputs are four types of artefacts: *constructs, models, methods,* and *implementations. Constructs* form the vocabulary of a domain. *Models* are sets of propositions or statements expressing relationships among constructs. *Methods* are collections of steps, e.g. in form of an algorithm or guideline, used to perform a task. They are based on a set of underlying constructs and a representation of the solution space in form of a model. *Implementations* are instantiations of an artefact in its environment operationalising constructs, models, and methods (cf. March and Smith, 1995).

Design science research takes a lot of efforts. Researchers need to have an in-depth understanding the problem and the technologies available for addressing it (David et al., 1999), gained perhaps by means of one of the above mentioned research methods. Once an artefact has been constructed to solve it, a complex evaluation process begins to assess the efficacy and efficiency of the solution as well as providing an understanding of how and why it works or why not.

The design science approach proposed by Hevner et al. (2004) has recently been criticised in terms of its limited epistemological and ontological perspective. Design science research should have a stronger focus on the embedment of IT artefacts in social practices of organisations (Rohde et al., 2009).

3.1.7. Research Design

My research follows the tradition of interpretive research (cf. Orlikowski and Baroudi, 1991; Ulrich, 1994). *"Interpretive researchers start out with the assumption that access to reality (given or socially constructed) is only through social constructions such as language, consciousness and shared meanings."* (Myers, 1997, p. 242) Interpretive studies explore the context of an information system and how the context influences the system and is influenced by the system (Walsham, 1993). Since interpretive research does not predefine variables, it focuses on the full complexity of human sense making in the particular situation (Kaplan and Maxwell, 1994). Interpretive research usually involves empirical studies to create an understanding of the context, i.e. application domain.

Natural science, in a broad sense of the word, includes research in social and behavioural domains trying to understand and explain reality. In contrast, *design science,* i.e. 'artificial science' including architecture, engineering and urban planning, tries to create things that

(Mingers, J. "Combining IS Research Methods: Towards a Pluralist Methodology", *Information Systems Research* (12:3) 2001, pp. 240 - 259.).

serve practical purposes (March and Smith, 1995). Since design science focuses on real world problems which must be solved followed by an evaluation of the efficacy and efficiency of the solution. In opposition to the previously argued use of design science for *normative studies*, Niehaves argues that *"design science research is not only a positivist domain."* (Niehaves, 2007, p. 11.) Following his argumentation, design science seems to be an appropriate choice for my research design at first sight.

However, the design and use of IT artefacts are inseparably interwoven making it necessary to have a strong focus on the organisational perspective in the design process, e.g. by involving users (Rohde et al., 2009). Wulf claims that the design science paradigm fails to provide such a strong focus because it does not provide clear guidance in terms of considering work practices and the evaluation of long-term effects of IT artefacts in social systems (Wulf, 2009). He favours an interpretive research design that has a different epistemological and ontological perspective in which 'reality' is socially constructed. This makes his approach similar to action research. It combines empirical pre- and evaluation studies to embed research in practice. He suggests proceeding in three stages:

Stage 1: Empirical pre-studies of the domain to describe social practices and the usage of existing tools in detail.

Stage 2: A context-oriented design process for producing an artefact, with documentation of the interaction between changes in social practices and the design of the artefact.

Stage 3: A long-term study to evaluate the implementation-, appropriation- and redesign processes of the created artefact in the application domain (Wulf, 2009).

Wulf's three-phased research design is similar to the *natural programming design process* proposed by Myers and Pane in the domain of computer science (Myers et al., 2004; Pane and Myers, 2006). The *natural programming design process* has four stages: identification of the target audience and domain, understanding the target audience, designing a new system and evaluation of the system.

As my research straddles the fields of information systems and computer science, I combine elements of Wulf's and Myers' & Pane's research designs. Figure 15 gives an overview of my proposed research design. The research methods used in each of the three proposed research phases are discussed in detail below.

Phase I: The objectives of the first phase are the exploration of the application domain and the review of existing research. My review of research in the field has already been presented in the previous chapter. This helped to understand existing technologies and to identify the scope for further research. The exploration of the application domain has two objectives. First, I want to better understand the application domain by describing social practices and the use of existing tools. Second, I identify problems in the application domain.

I address the objective through a combination of qualitative and quantitative research methods to do justice to the richness and complexity of social practices in the application domain (David et al., 1999; Davison et al., 2008). I use semi-structured interviews as ethnographic method since it enables me to gather rich descriptions of the participants' existing work practices and problems while keeping my efforts limited. The results of the interviews are used for the creation of hypotheses which are tested in a quantitative online survey. In addition, the survey is used for the exploration of new areas which have not been covered by the interviews. Online surveys allow the involvement of a larger number of users while having the advantage that they require only limited personal effort from the researchers.

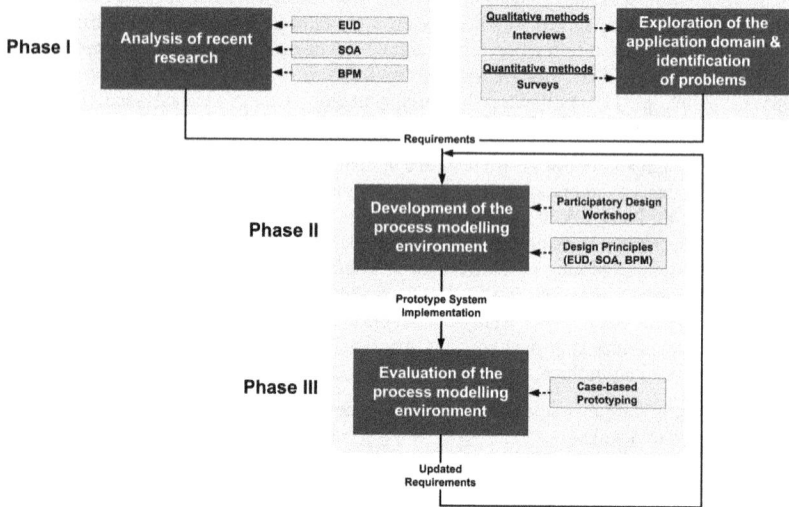

Figure 15: Research Design

The reflection of the empirically identified problems and the literature lead to the formulation of requirements for the business process modelling environment.

Phase II: The objective of the second phase is the development of the business process modelling environment in line with my requirements and the design principles identified in my review of research in the field. However, the research methods used in phase I do not produce results that can easily be used for the design of the environment. Therefore, I adopt a user-centred approach, involving a participatory design workshop as method. Participatory design workshops allow the simulation of work situations and provide access to peoples' subconscious knowledge. In addition, the workshop allows me to discuss and evaluate design ideas in early stages of the design process.

Phase III: The objective of the third phase is the evaluation of the business process modelling environment. It follows a case-based prototyping approach in combination with semi-structured interviews. I have chosen a case-based prototyping approach to align the evaluation with the application domain and to involve users closely. Using semi-structured interviews allows addressing the usefulness of the system beyond technical and graphical design. The business process modelling environment is an innovative system and cannot easily be implemented in the participating enterprises without further technical and organisational adjustments. Therefore, I evaluate the system in a laboratory setting, using exploratory methods to obtain feedback from users of the application domain.

The research design does not address the requirements of Myers' and Pane's second step as well as Wulf's third phase properly. Myers and Pane perform a detailed analysis of the language and thinking of users of the domain to develop a 'natural' programming language (Myers et al., 2004). However, as this is not in my focus I do not cover this step in my research design. Covering Wulf's third phase properly would have required an analysis of the business process modelling environment in the application domain in a long-term study

(Wulf, 2009). Such a study would have required the introduction of the environment in the participating enterprises. As this was not possible at this time, a follow-up study could use an action research approach to observe the effects of the introduction of the environment in terms of the implementation-, appropriation- and redesign processes.

3.2. Application Domain

In this section I describe the application domain of SMEs. Five German enterprises[14] partici-pated in the empirical study, the participatory design workshop and in the evaluation studies. All five enterprises were partners of the EUDISMES[15] research project. The five firms were taken from different industries. Table 7 provides information about their essential characteristics.

	SME A	SME B	SME C	SME D	SME E
Sector	Software	Industry	Industry	Industry	Const. trade
Business	Financial software	Luggage, especially satchels	Automotive systems	Construction of claddings, floorings, etc.	Construction of roofs
Turnover	Approx. 70 million €	Approx. 40 million €	Approx. 20 million €	Approx. 2,5 million €	Approx. 2 million €
Employees	Approx. 500	155	120	12	26

Table 7: Characteristics of the participating SMEs

The medium-sized firms (> 50 employees) in the sample mainly used SAP R/3 (version 4.6c), Microsoft Office and specific software for their particular sector as enterprise software. They also customised their SAP systems and used some individual software applications, such as extensions of the SAP systems or archival systems. The two small enterprises used mainly specific solutions for their sector (e.g. WinDach, HWS) and Microsoft Office as enterprise software. All five enterprises used for example individual Excel sheets which can also be con-sidered as a kind of adaptation.

The organisational hierarchy was rather flat in all firms in the sample. The main levels were: managing director, various department managers, in some cases group managers, and then the remaining employees. The managing directors were in charge of the corporate planning being supported by the department managers.

Most of the employees worked with computers on a daily basis for several hours. In general, employees of the medium-sized firms had greater experience with computers than employees of the small firms. All firms had some *local experts* who had profound knowledge of a par-ticular application such as Excel. The medium-sized firms also relied on SAP key users[16].

---

[14] The number of participating firms was increased for the online survey which is part of the second phase and is described in the next chapter.

[15] http://www.eudismes.org/

[16] SAP key users are experienced computer users who had specific trainings on SAP. They have similar characteristics as the group of users which was referred to as super users.

SAP key users, IT departments and external consultants are responsible for the software and hardware configuration in medium-sized firms. SAP key users and the IT departments solve standard problems while the more complex problems are delegated to consultants. The department managers tended to have the formal role of SAP key users or the informal role of local experts. Therefore, they are referred to by the term *super user* which was defined in section 2.1.2.

Adaptations of the software infrastructure have the potential to facilitate the work and to meet new business requirements. When a new adaptation is considered, firms tend to carry out a cost-benefit analysis to check if the costs are lower than the expected benefits (cf. Blackwell, 2002).

My research design closely involves users of the application domain. Table 8 characterises the users of the five firms who participated in the different phases, while Table 9 shows which person participated in which phase(s).

Participant #	Profession	SME
1	Manager IT department	SME A
2	Purchaser	
3	Product manager	
4	Employee support department	
5	Accountant	
6	Product manager	
7	Managing director	SME B
8	Manager IT department	
9	Manager purchasing department	
10	Accountant	
11	Manager accounting department	
12	Manager human resources department	SME B
13	Employee human resources department	
14	Salesman (in-house)	
15	Assistant manager of sales department	
16	Manager IT department	SME C
17	Controller	
18	Product calculation	
19	Manager sales department	
20	Controller	

Participant #	Profession	SME
21	Managing director	
22	Assistant manager	SME D
23	Secretary	
24	Draftsman	
25	Managing director	
26	Secretary	SME E
27	Craftsman	

Table 8: Characterisation of Participating Employees and SMEs

Phase	Study	Participants
I	Ethnographic study	All, except 5, 6, 15, 20
	Survey	
II	Participatory Design Workshop	8, 9, 15
III	Evaluation SiSO	5, 6, 8, 9, 18, 20
	Evaluation PaSeMod	8, 9

Table 9: Relation between Studies and Participants

Chapter 4

"In the early days of computing (Globalization 2.0), you worked in the office. There was a big mainframe computer, and you literally had to walk over and get the people running the mainframe to extract or input information for you. It was like an oracle. Then, thanks to the PC and the Internet, e-mail, the laptop, the browser, and the client server, I could access form my own screen all sorts of data and information being stored on the network."

Friedman, 2006, p. 196

4.   Empirical Pre-Study of the Domain

This chapter describes the empirical pre-study which was used to explore the application domain of SMEs and identify existing problems. The results contextualised the research gaps identified in chapter 2 and helped to specify further requirements for the business process modelling environment.

The pre-study uses a pluralist research approach, combining both qualitative and quantitative research methods in a sequential order (cf. Mingers, 2001). The quantitative research covers a large number of subjects while the qualitative research provides in depth-knowledge about a small number of subjects (David et al., 1999; Davison et al., 2008). Figure 16 provides an overview of the structure of the pre-study.

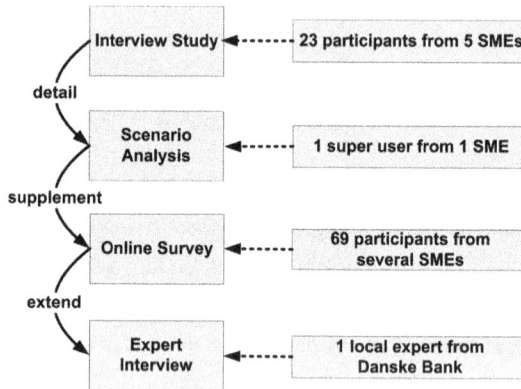

Figure 16: Design and Structure of the Pre-Study

The first step was a qualitative interview study with 23 users from 5 SMEs (for details see Table 7) to explore the domain and to identify existing problems (see section 4.1).

In the second step, the analysis of a scenario added detail to the results of the interview study (see section 4.2). In the scenario a super user (participant no. 9 in Table 8) struggled with the calculation of order quantities being part of the firm's order process.

In the third step, I set up an online survey to explore the application domain from a quantitative perspective, focusing particularly on users' familiarity with business process modelling. The results of this step supplemented the results of the previous steps with additional data. 69 users from several SMEs participated in the survey, which is described in section 4.3.

The users who participated in the previous steps were employed by SMEs which did not have a service-oriented software infrastructure. In step four (section 4.4), I therefore studied Danske Bank, one of Europe's SOA pioneers, by conducting an expert interview with an employee of the workflow department. I gathered information about the service-oriented development process of Danske Bank and identified challenges for the development of the business process modelling environment

Section 4.5 concludes by describing the *process development process* which should be supported by the business process modelling environment.

4.1. Qualitative Exploration of the Domain: An Interview Study

In the interview study I explored the domain and the problems faced by users. This is important since domain knowledge is thought to play a major role in system design (Fischer et al., 2001; Rohde et al., 2009). I have partially published the results of the study in three different papers (Dörner et al., 2009; Dörner et al., 2007; Dörner and Rohde, 2009). Here I will focus on those results which are relevant in the context of the work by providing answers to these questions:

- What are the participants' software-related problems?
- How are these problems addressed?

4.1.1. Research Method and Setting

We[17] used qualitative research methods, i.e. semi-structured interviews (cf. Myers, 2009; Strauss and Corbin, 1998), for the study (see section 3.1.1). Five SMEs participated. We had two sessions with each of them. In the first session, we discussed the internal organisational structures of the firms. The interview partners of this session were managing directors as well as managers of the IT departments (participants no. 1, 7, 8, 16, 21, 25 in Table 8). In the second interview session, we covered a number of topics: the interviewees' work practices, existing problems, strategies to solve these problems, and their demand and experiences for/with adaptations. All groups of employees (participants no. 2, 3, 4, 8, 9, 10, 11, 12, 13, 14, 17, 18, 19, 22, 23, 24, 26, 27 in Table 8) participated in the second interview session.

By using qualitative interviews it is possible to achieve very detailed and profound insights into the working field of the participants. All interviews were conducted at the firms' sites to keep the de-contextualization of participants from their workspaces as low as possible. As mentioned before, the interviews were done in two sessions.

The first session focused on organisational topics. We used two different interview guidelines (see appendix A 1.1, A 1.2) to be responsive to the differences between the small firms (< 50 employees) and the medium-sized firms. Three interviewers conducted the interviews, which lasted between 80 and 120 minutes each. The interviews were recorded with a digital voice-recorder and transcribed later on. The insights from these interviews were used for the identification of relevant interview partners for the second interview session. This time we used only one interview guideline (see appendix A 1.3) since we questioned the participants about their work practices and did not expect big differences between the answers of small and medium-sized firms' employees. Two interviewers conducted the interviews, which lasted between 45 and 90 minutes each. Again, the interviews were recorded with a digital voice-recorder and transcribed later on.

4.1.2. Results

The analysis of the interviews was based on qualitative techniques (Miles and Huberman, 1994). Well-trained researchers at my department transcribed all interviews in abbreviated form, reflecting the main arguments. We compared all interviews of each firm with each other and structured and consolidated them according to the questions of the respective interview

---

[17] In the following I use the pronoun *we* since the study was done together with some colleagues who worked with me in the EUDISMES project.

guideline. Afterwards, we analysed them in a workshop by interpreting the transcripts and marking important statements. This allowed us to identify categories of answers which were used for sorting the statements into these ex-post categories.

The results of the first interview session have already been presented in section 3.2 when introducing the application domain. The two most important ex-post categories emerging from the second interview session are *problem types* and *problem solving strategies*.

4.1.2.1. Problem Types

The term *problem types* refers to all kinds of problems that end users face with their software. Some problems like navigation problems or the accessibility of functions were related to the usability of software. Users had particular trouble with their SAP systems because they were not always able to find the functions they searched for:

"The SAP menu contains a data tree from which different sub trees can be opened. If I didn't know which transaction I need, and I had to search for it, I would be lost."[18]

In addition, participants mentioned that the graphical user interfaces of SAP do not always meet their expectations:

"What I don't like about SAP is the diverse design of the user interfaces. They do not follow a common design guideline. [...] You learn that you have to click the 'check-symbol' which means 'enter'. But there is also a 'clock with check-symbol' which doesn't let one get ahead. [...] Sometimes the 'check-symbol' is located at the top left and sometimes it is more centred. [...] I think the work was done by different developers."

Many participants had experienced problems with the integrated help systems of their software. They thought that the content of these systems was written by experts for experts rather than for ordinary users:

"I don't want to say anything about that [the help system]. [...] There is probably nothing in it that is comprehensible. The system is probably only written by experts for experts."

Many participants had particular problems with the limited functionality of the software. One participant described his problems with a program used for the creation of quotes. The system, called HWS, is an optimised standard software product for his sector. However, the program did not provide the necessary functionality for his calculations. It did not permit to determine the needed amount of raw material required for performing the job. Therefore, he used Excel for his calculations, while his colleague used HWS to manage and print the quotes. Since it was impossible to exchange data between HWS and Excel, both colleagues used printouts for the data exchange:

"When I get the prices I open my Excel template and start typing the whole text of the quote – if I have enough time. [...] The problem is that this text is not automatically available in the HWS system. Therefore, it has to be completely retyped. [...] We have to type it at least twice. It would be nice if we had some kind of program for the HWS system which is directly connected with my Excel template."

Many SAP users described problems related to the data analysis, i.e. decision support functions of the SAP system. One participant struggled with the collection of data that was used to perform credit limit checks:

---

[18] I have translated all comments of the participants from German to English.

"There are often problems when I want to compare things. I sometimes have the problem that I have to access four or five things [different SAP user interfaces] in order to get the things [data] I need; [...] for example, checking annually our customers credit limit. I need 'master data' and data from SD and some data from financial accounting and I don't get them by pressing a button."

Another participant was not able to create a production plan in the SAP system since this functionality was not available and tailoring was very difficult. As a result, she collected the necessary data within the SAP system and exported it into an Excel spreadsheet to be able to create the plan:

"[...] We would like to have a production list directly out of SAP to avoid exporting it to Excel. Our current solution is quite complicated. I have to create a template within SAP which contains only the information that I need from the list to keep the file small. Then I have to export it [to Excel]. Then I have to sort the data and insert them into a pivot table. This pivot table has to be edited to make the user interface understandable for people working in the production department. [...] We have to work together with a consultant to solve this issue in SAP. [...] It would be great if we could make it by ourselves [and without the consultant]. [...] I have to create such a list twice a week. [...] Each time I need approximately one hour to create it [with Excel]. [...] A small thing would help us, but SAP doesn't support it. [...] It has to be programmed."

The analysis of these examples reveals three main problems: First, the functionality of software is often limited. This can lead, for example, to a lack of interoperability between applications of the software infrastructure, such as data exchange problems between SAP and Excel (cf. section 2.3). Participants had to navigate through multiple often inconsistently designed screens (cf. Markus et al., 2000) to gather the required data manually. Second, there is a lack of tools that would allow end-user developers to (semi-)automate the creation of reports and other calculations. Third, external experts, e.g. consultants, are often the only persons who can adapt the software infrastructure, with the result that firms can become very dependent on them.

4.1.2.2. Problem Solving Strategies

In this section, I set out how participants address problems with their software infrastructure. Figure 17 gives an overview of problem-solving strategies identified in the interviews. There are many different ways to get from the topmost event in the diagram to one of those events at the end of the process. Participants' approach to problem solving tends to be 'problem driven', i.e. they select their 'help resources' in accordance with the problem and not as a result of their personal preferences.

Users do not always find a solution to their problem. The following three unsuccessful outcomes are distinguished in the diagram:

1. *Problem was not solved:* The user is not able to solve the problem but keeps looking for a solution or a workaround.

2. *Problem 'accepted':* The user ignores the problem permanently and does not want to create a workaround or solve it anymore.

3. *Workaround created:* The user created a workaround for the problem but keeps looking for a better solution.

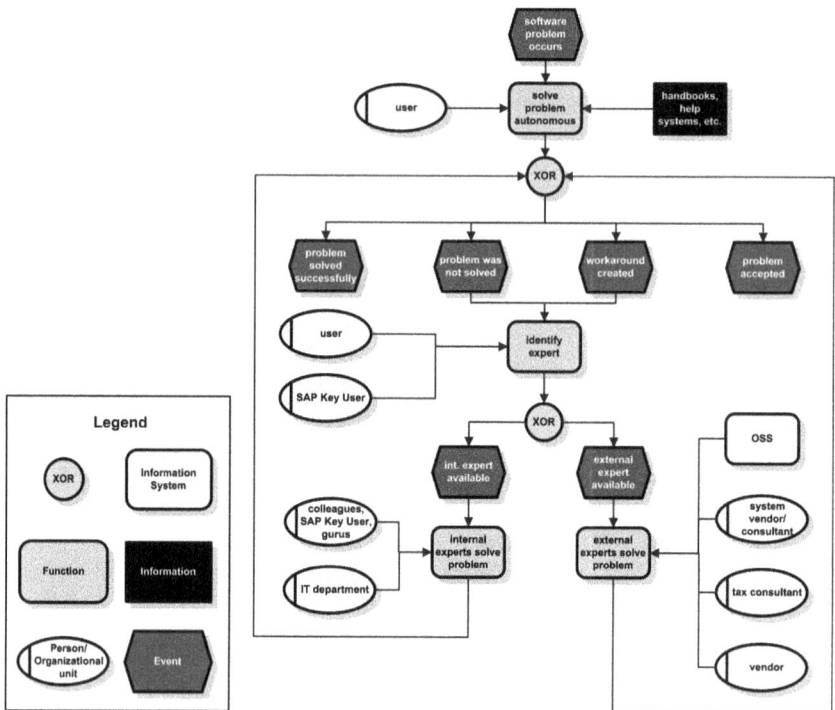

Figure 17: Problem Solving Strategies of Users (according to Dörner et al., 2007)

The third strategy is very popular. It often happens that people create their own structures (e.g. Excel sheets for analysing data) over years to process those cases which do not match the standardised structures of the ERP system (Pfeiffer et al., 2008). This can be partly explained by the fact that ERP systems sometimes seem to have an unfamiliar task execution strategy forcing users to adopt inefficient procedures (Costabile et al., 2006). An example for such inefficient procedures is the creation of workarounds in Excel which usually cause additional work (Pfeiffer et al., 2008). A participant described this issue in the following way:

"Statistics [...] my colleague wanted to know the daily overrun of each employee in his department during the last month; [...] now it would be wonderful if we were able to transfer this into an Excel file; no Mrs. X has to type each number herself."

Here are two illustrative examples of the problem-solving strategies used by participants in the interview study:

Example 1: Karen[19] tries to solve her problem of creating a report within the SAP system. She starts by using the internal help system. After one hour of searching and browsing the help system she gives up, wondering whether anyone else could help her to solve the problem. Preferably, this should be one of her colleagues since the firm would otherwise have to pay for external support. Maybe her colleague John could help. He is the SAP key user of

---

[19] I have anonymized all names.

her department and knows a lot about the SAP system. She calls John and tries to solve the problem together with him by using the various customisation options of the system. After a while John concludes that it is useless to continue trying. Neither he, nor any other SAP key user or colleague of the IT department could easily solve the problem. Therefore, only an external expert could help. John wonders whether it would be better to create an OSS (Online Support System) ticket in the SAP system or to ask Mr. White, a consultant. He comes to the conclusion that asking Mr. White is more likely to resolve the problem quickly. Therefore John writes him an email. Mr. White explains in his reply how the report could be created in the SAP system.

Example 2: Margaret wants to give a quote to a customer. After she has entered 64 positions of the quote, the system refuses to offer her further input fields for the remaining positions. She tries to work out a solution without using handbooks and the system's help system because she does not like them. After a while she decides to call the hotline of the software vendor because she is the only user of the system in the whole firm and none of her colleagues could help her. Calling the hotline leads to no solution. Mr. Black, an employee of the software vendor, told her that the number of positions of a quote would be increased in the next version of the software.

These two examples describe participants' strategies of solving software-related problems quite well. However, they lack a detailed description of participants' tailoring activities. We distinguished three groups of participants in our analysis according to their perceptions of tailoring a software. The first group was not familiar with the term and had never tailored their systems. Most of them even considered the tailoring of systems to be insignificant. Although the second group was familiar with the term, they had not tailored their systems by themselves. Members of the third group had already tailored systems by themselves.

Tailoring either occurs when a person encounters a breakdown or a mismatch between the information system and his needs (Germonprez et al., 2007) or when new tasks arise which could be better supported by a tailored application (Wulf and Golombek, 2001). This was confirmed and detailed by our analysis in several ways. Some participants thought that tailoring systems by themselves is essential and more efficient than delegating adaptations to others:

"[...] I do it because it has to be. If I were to delegate it, it would be necessary to explain exactly what needs do be done. [...] They [requirements] often emerge during the design of a table or a project. [...] Therefore, doing it by myself is probably easier than delegating it."

Other participants thought that spending time on tailoring pays off in the long run since it leads to significant improvements in work processes:

"[The participant tailors systems...] to make it [the work] easier. [...] As I mentioned previously in terms of the calculation program [...] I wanted to save the time in which I write everything and do the calculations with a calculator; now I have much more time to calculate and think about it; therefore I have done it [an Excel sheet used for his calculations]."

Some participants noted that changes in legislation, the introduction of new software, and the evolving business needs lead to adaptations:

"[...] We have to do some changes when the tax legislation changes. [...] Sometimes it could be easier; [...] there are these 'hints' – as SAP calls them – which must be installed to do all necessary changes of the program, but we had to adapt the system anyway a thousand times."

"[...] Well I think that [adaptations] will happen again and again. We have now a new business model for one of our products; therefore we have to adapt the Navision system. [...] Sometimes the management has a new requirement which must be implemented."

We also identified cases in which the available tailoring options were not powerful enough to solve participants' problems. Therefore, participants wanted to have more powerful adaptation options and more control (cf. Markus et al., 2000). The following statements are representative:

"[...] It is no problem to calculate it [expenses for travelling]. We use the SAP screen of the '1% method' and put it in a way that it uses the right value for the calculation of taxes – but this is not correct. There must be a possibility to enter the costs and the other relevant factors for the calculation. [...] But the consultant could not do it in different way."

"[...] But then the year turns and we have changes of the legislation; then there are patches for the software which are installed; but we can't do it ourselves. We always have a consultant who does it. [...] The problem is that we don't know what the new patches contain [...]."

The results of the study revealed several problems that were related to the limited functionality of software. Examples were data exchange problems between SAP and Excel requiring a manual gathering of data within the SAP system followed by an analysis in Excel. Such mismatches between the software infrastructure and participants' requirements lead to the need of tailoring, However, the available tailoring options were not always powerful enough to address participants' problems sufficiently leading to the need of implementing more powerful tailoring tools for end users.

4.2.   Typical Problems of Super Users: A Scenario

This section describes my analysis of a specific super user scenario. The aim was to understand a particular but in many ways representative work situation. This was necessary because super users are in focus of my research and the group of people who participated in the interview study was divers. Department managers often have the same characteristics as super users since they have domain knowledge and are often involved in customising.

The scenario was identified in one of our interviews with SME employees and was refined in several iterations together with the interviewee (participant no. 9, SME B, in Table 8). The interviewee was the manager of a purchasing department and the scenario involves the calculation of order quantities using data from different systems (internal and external). The analysis of the scenario was used to add detail to the results of the previous section for the subgroup of super users. I focused on the questions:

- What are typical problems of super users?
- Which approaches could possibly be used to solve these problems?

4.2.1.   Research Method and Scenario Description

I explored the scenario in several iterations in collaboration with the department manager via email and phone. The scenario focuses on the purchasing process of SME B, as set out in Figure 18. My description emphasises only its most important aspects.

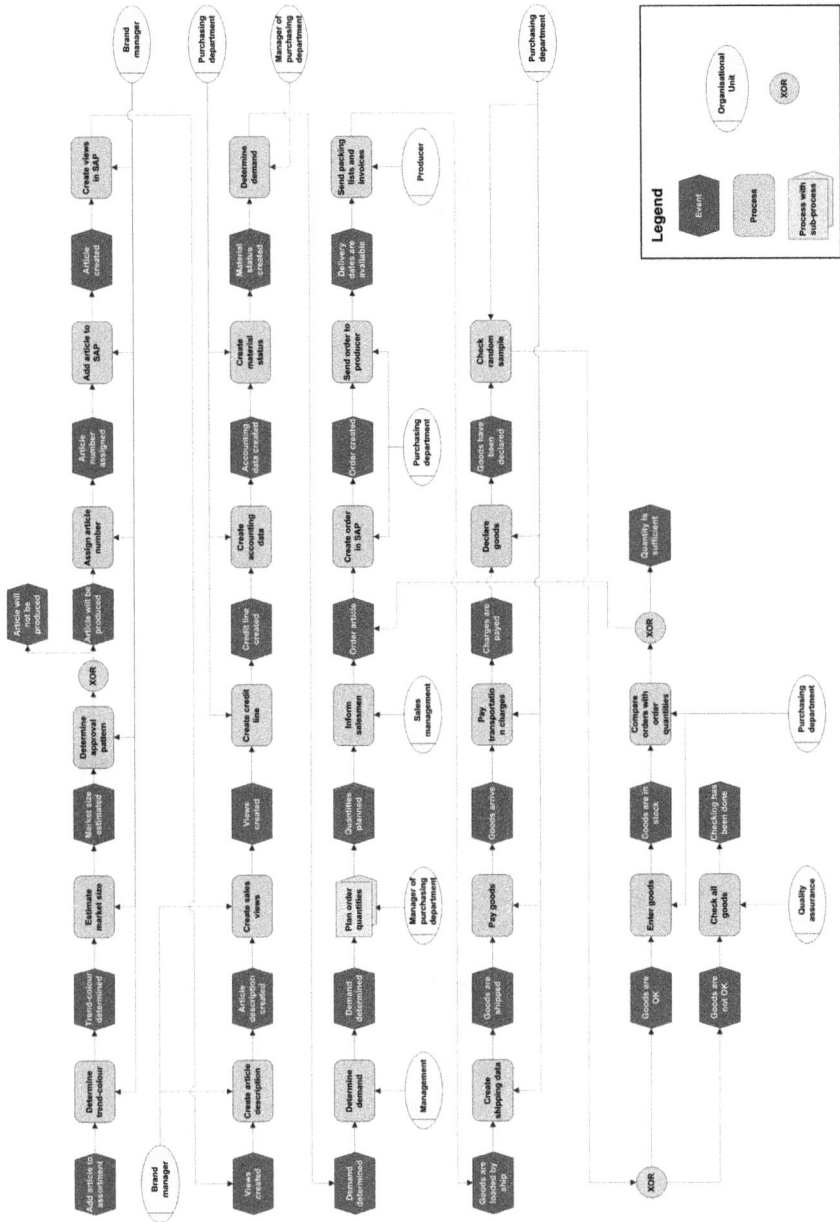

Figure 18: Purchasing Process of SME B

As shown in the diagram, the brand manager has to estimate the market size for a particular article using, for example, marketing instruments for the identification of market trends (e.g. colours). If the market is large enough, the article will be produced. If that is the case, he has to assign an article number to the article and add it to the SAP system in which he has to create appropriate views. The sales department, the management and the purchasing department have to determine the demand.

Afterwards, the manager of the purchasing department has to plan the order quantities. All articles (different kinds of luggage) are subject to seasonal fluctuations in demand which moreover varies across colours. To illustrate, a red bag might reach higher sales volumes in summer than in the rest of the year. Each article number contains a colour code which is not modelled as separate entity in the SAP system. This makes it difficult to distinguish between the different colours of a particular article within in the SAP system. In other words, the process of planning the purchase quantities of articles of different colours is currently not well supported by the SAP system.

After planning the order quantities, the order process is initiated. Since the production is outsourced to a firm located in the Far East, it usually takes three to four months until the ordered goods arrive. The goods are paid while they are shipped. On arrival they have to be declared and checked. If the goods are not adequate it is necessary to initiate a new order process. In any case, the amount of the newly arrived goods must be sufficient to cover the demand. If this is not the case, a new order process has to be initiated as well. As mentioned before, the main problem in the process is the planning of the order quantities, which is not well supported by the SAP system. The manager of the purchasing department has to translate the estimated sales volumes for a group of articles given to him by management into quantities of individual articles of different colours. She will rely heavily on sales experiences of the previous months and years to predict likely future requirements. She uses an Excel sheet with the following structure to plan the order quantities for different articles:

October 2007						November 2007	
Article number	Opening stock	Planned sales	Planned order quantities	Planned order quantities 2	Estimated stock	Article number	...
253101	500	1000	500	800	0	...	...
...	...	...	...	...	...	...	...

Table 10: Illustration of the Excel Sheet which is used for Planning Order Quantities in SME B

The most important column of the table is the column *planned order quantities 2*. This column is used to 'check' how changes of the order quantities affect the *estimated stock* of the subsequent months to gain a 'feeling' for these effects. Stock keeping ties up cash flow, but means that potential demand from customers can be met without delay. The column helps to determine the quantities of future orders required to respond to potential future demand. The SAP system does not have any support for this specific process since it contains only actual data which cannot be changed by users.

The table was furthermore set up in such a way that it creates a time series data. The data of the month October is followed by the data of the month November and so on. This allows the department manager to plan order quantities over a long time and to monitor the estimated stock over this period. The SAP system contains data on the annual planned quantities of classes of goods. This does not meet the needs of the department manager because the order quantities must be precise in terms of particular articles and particular colours.

The planning process is complicated further because production data and stock quantities of the producer in the Far East are not readily available. The department manager has to make a phone call or write an email to obtain the most recent data. An additional order could lead to an excess or lack of raw materials (e.g. threads, fabric, locks, rivets) in the warehouses of the producer. An excess of raw materials causes storage costs; a shortage of raw materials leads to delays in production. Some raw materials are used for different products leading to interdependencies. There is no IT support to manage these interdependencies properly since only some part lists are managed in an Excel sheet.

4.2.2. Analysis

The scenario illustrates the planning of order quantities of a department manager, which does not match the standardised structures of the ERP system. Therefore, the department manager created a workaround using Excel which is used as support tool and allows 'playing' with the available data. The scenario confirms the previous results, showing that today's software infrastructures do not provide enough flexibility to address all problems faced by users without further tailoring.

The basic underlying problems of the scenario are a limited functionality[20], a lack of decision support and a lack of process support (cf. Markus et al., 2000). The super user's workaround is rather inefficient due to the considerable amount of manual work involved in copying and pasting data.

Composition tools, such as the business process modelling tools presented in section 2.3.3, could be used to replace the Excel workaround with a more efficient solution: a semi-automatic workflow. Such workflows perfectly match the requirements of the planning process:

- Order planning is a recurrent task which is used by the super user for monitoring the estimated stock.
- Order planning involves data from different internal sources, i.e. different SAP modules and Excel (e.g. part lists).
- Order planning involves data from external sources, i.e. production data and stock quantities of the producer.
- Order planning involves decision logic.

In this section I presented a representative work situation of a super user, i.e. a department manager. My analysis of the scenario confirmed that today's software infrastructures do not provide enough flexibility to address all problems faced by users without further tailoring. The most important problems in this context were a limited functionality, a lack of decision support, and a lack of process support.

---

[20] It should be noted that some of the missing functionalities would probably have been available in later versions of the used software. However, the firm did not consider to update its software, especially the SAP system, as it would have been too expensive.

4.3. Quantitative Exploration of the Domain: A Survey

In this section, I describe a survey used to explore the domain from a different perspective to supplement the previous results with quantitative data, gathered from a large number of users. I used the survey to test two hypotheses: The first one is that software infrastructures do not provide enough functionality to support all tasks of users leading to the need of tailoring. The second one is that end users, especially super users, have sufficient knowledge about business process modelling, making it tangible for them to use a business process modelling environment.

Both hypotheses are examined by answering the following four questions:

1. What do respondents think about the tailoring of systems?

2. Why would respondents tailor systems by themselves and why not?

3. How familiar are respondents with business process modelling?

4. What modelling techniques did the respondents use?

First I discuss the design of the survey including the sampling method, the questionnaire design, and its implementation. Afterwards I present its results.

4.3.1. Survey Design

I developed the survey questionnaire as follows (see section 3.1.4):

1. *Focus group discussions:* I discussed the results of the interview study and the scenario analysis with several researchers in my group. The discussion lead to the identification of the four questions listed above which guided the survey design.

2. *Drafting Questions:* I created a draft of the questions for the questionnaire.

3. *Critical Systematic Review:* A colleague of mine, who is experienced in survey research, reviewed this draft.

4. *Cognitive laboratory interviews:* Several members of my research group volunteered to check the revised questions for comprehensibility.

5. *Putting questions into a survey instrument:* I transferred all questions to an online survey tool in which I designed the questionnaire.

6. *Pre-testing an interview schedule:* Again, several members of my research group volunteered to validate the questionnaire, checking its technical soundness, performance, and the question skipping patterns.

The questionnaire contained a total of 41 questions. 23 of these were closed question and 18 open-ended questions in which the participants had at least one option to enter free text.

I chose a self-administered procedure, i.e. an online survey, as the implementation form. Computer-based surveys have the advantage that they require only limited personal effort from the researchers, which helps to contain costs. Another reason for using a computer-based survey was the fact that the questionnaire (see appendix A 2.1) involved complex question skipping patterns, which would have been difficult to implement in any other way.

I am aware that including open-ended questions in self-administered surveys can be problematic. Responses are often not of sufficient quality to be statistically useful. I therefore analysed responses to these questions using qualitative methods. (cf. Floyd J. Fowler, 2002).

I used a simple sampling method, referred to as *nonprobability sampling*. This method does not require the calculation of the probability of drawing any particular sample. Instead, I limited the sample to the five SMEs that participated in the previous steps (see Table 7) plus some other SMEs to which we had good contacts. The sample consisted of 200 people who were contacted via email. They received information about the purpose of the survey and some basic instructions for using the survey tool. After six weeks I sent a follow-up email to increase the response rate.

4.3.2. Results

The questions were analysed either quantitatively or qualitatively depending on their type. I analysed all closed questions quantitatively to identify the percentage of respondents giving particular responses while I analysed the open-ended questions qualitatively to capture the 'range of respondents' answers[21]. Such a strategy is acceptable in terms of my interpretative research philosophy since *"[...] the use of quantitative data need not imply the acceptance of a positivist, objectivist epistemology. Rather, such data can (and should) be interpreted in the light of relevant social meanings, and their production as a social construction."* (Mingers, 2001, p. 247)

After removing incomplete and invalid records from the data set, 69 replies remained, corresponding to a response rate of 34.5%. The median duration for completing the questionnaire was approximately eleven minutes. 55% of the participants were male, while 45% were female. 44% of them were between 20 and 30 years old, 30% between 31 and 40 years, 22% between 41 and 50 years and only 6% were over 50 years old. 53% of the participants had worked for more than five years at their firms, 35% for one to five years and 12% for less than one year.

73% of respondents said that sometimes certain functionalities were not available within their software or that it was cumbersome to perform certain tasks, 17% did not feel a need for tailoring and 10% 'did not know'. Of the 73% of respondents adversely affected by a lack of functionality, 16% experienced it more than once a week, 32% at least once a week, 32% at least once a month, 16% less than once a month and 4% 'did not know'.

Participants named various reasons for the lack of functionalities. Some said that software vendors had implemented the software inadequately. Others said that their programs did not work properly together, their requirements changed frequently and their software had too many inappropriate functions instead of useful ones.

Participants reported that they solve problems in most cases by themselves or with the help of colleagues. In other cases, they rely on external help, i.e. consultants as well as solutions found on the Internet. In response to the question if the adaptation of software could help them to solve problems, 70% answered 'yes' while 30% answered 'no'. The participants who answered 'yes' cited the following reasons: adaptations improve efficiency by reducing the time needed to complete a task and by helping to avoid the creation of workarounds. The participants who answered 'no' identified the following reasons: creating adaptations takes too much effort, the software cannot be adapted properly, adaptations are too expensive, and the problems are too specific and do not recur.

68% of the participants would like to adapt their systems by themselves while 18% would not and 14% 'did not know'. Respondents thought that self-created adaptations were useful be-

---

[21] I have translated all free text answers from German to English.

cause they could save costs, reduce the length of the adaptation process, and increase their flexibility. However, some respondents also identified insufficient knowledge and experience as an obstacle for making adaptations as well as expressing concern about compatibility problems resulting from poor adaptations.

Asked about their experiences of describing or modelling business processes, 56% of the participants said they were familiar with it. 40% had not made any such experiences and 4% 'did not know'. Participants were also asked if they had already been involved in describing or developing business processes. 46% have already been involved, while 45% have not and 9% 'did not know'. Those who had not been involved in describing or modelling processes were asked who was responsible for this in their organisations and identified mainly quality managers, the IT department and department managers.

In terms of the used modelling technique, 46% of the participants said that processes were described in a text document, 18% said processes were described in a table and 31% said that processes were described as diagrams. 5% 'did not know'. 38% of the participants said they used software for such process descriptions, while 28% said they did not and 34% of them 'did not know'. Those who said they used software named Microsoft Visio, Excel, Word and SAP as support tools for creating process models.

Participants were asked if they knew business processes in which other departments of their firm or even other firms were involved to get a feeling for the complexity of the business processes of the firms. 70% knew processes in which other departments were involved, while only 35% knew processes in which other firms were involved.

The results of the survey are consistent with both hypotheses. They show that participants frequently experience a lack of functionality of their software infrastructures. This makes it necessary to tailor these infrastructures to overcome the existing problems. Most of the participants would like to do the tailoring themselves since it enhances flexibility and efficiency. Approximately half of the respondents had experience with business process modelling. Processes are described in most cases in text documents or in diagrams, but specific support tools are unavailable. The findings indicate that it would be useful to develop the proposed business process modelling environment.

4.4.   Identification of Challenges: Business Process Modelling at Danske Bank

The previously studied SMEs made no use of specific business process modelling tools that are usable in service-oriented environments. In order to identify challenges for developing such tools it was necessary to extend the previous studies.

Cases for studying service-oriented ERP systems are very rare (cf. Krafzig et al., 2005) because only 6% of the enterprises have made it into later stages of SOA implementation (Rettig, 2007). Since I could not find a SME which made it into a later stage of SOA implementation, I had to extend my search to large companies. There is an interesting study by Brahe and Schmidt (2007) of Danske Bank, which is one of the SOA pioneers in Europe.

However, the published material (Brahe, 2007; Brahe and Schmidt, 2007) of the study did not contain enough details about Danske Bank's service-oriented development process and lacked a detailed description of challenges for the implementation of a business process modelling environment. Therefore, we[22] supplemented the study to gather the required information

---

[22] In the following I use the pronoun *we* since the study was done together with Björn Borggräfe.

(Borggräfe, 2008). The analysis of the development process is of particular interest because it allowed us to understand which tasks should be supported and which requirements should be met by the envisaged business process modelling environment. In addition, it provides detailed information about the users involved. The following two questions were the focus of our study:

- Which users are involved in the service-oriented development process and how does it work?

- Which challenges arise in a service-oriented environment that should be addressed by the design of the envisaged business process modelling environment?

The following section introduces Danske Bank. In section 4.4.2, I describe the service-oriented development process of Danske Bank. Section 4.4.3 presents challenges for system design which should be addressed by the envisaged business process modelling environment.

4.4.1. A Brief Description of Danske Bank

Danske Bank, founded in 1871, is one of the largest financial institutions in northern Europe. Today, it employs approximately 20.000 people, offering a variety of services in banking, mortgage, credit, insurance, etc. Danske Bank has grown through acquisitions, leading to back-office systems which are patchwork systems. Therefore, it switched its IT to a service-oriented architecture in 2001 and became one of Europe's SOA pioneers. Danske Bank's SOA consists of several thousand service operations. BPM is supported by an IBM solution and the processes are implemented in BPEL. One example for a business process is the creation of financial products, e.g. accounts or credit cards. The workflow integrates more than ten different systems and has about 30 sub-workflows with approximately 200 service invocations or human tasks (cf. Brahe, 2007).

4.4.2. The Service-oriented Development Process of Danske Bank

Our interest was particularly on the service-oriented development process of Danske Bank. We decided to explore an information-rich case that manifests this process intensely (Miles and Huberman, 1994). Based on the results of Brahe, we explored the practice of the service-oriented development process of Danske Bank in cooperation with a local expert. The expert was a solution architect, being employed at Danske Bank for three years. He worked in the workflow department which was part of the IT department. His main task was the development support and specification of workflows from an organisational perspective, i.e. he defines requirements for the definition of solutions. We used a guideline (see appendix A 1.4) for our study which was done via phone, lasted approximately 90 minutes and was recorded with a digital voice-recorder. We transcribed it in abbreviated form. Its analysis was based on qualitative techniques (Miles and Huberman, 1994).

Today, Danske Bank has approximately 80 workflow models. They consist of activities that are wired with other activities in a specific sequence. Activities can be separated into automatic, manual and user experienced ones[23]. Workflows are orchestrated by using a repository which contains approximately 2000 services. The service-oriented development process of Danske Bank consists of four main parts:

---

[23] User experienced activities are manual activities which are supported by a system.

1. *The process part:* a business process model is created and then transferred into a workflow description

2. *The functionality part:* specifies which services are needed for 1., including all services which must be implemented

3. *The user interface part:* the graphical user interfaces for 1. are implemented

4. *The data part:* the data model, i.e. database schema for 1. is implemented

Since the development of business processes is of particular interest for my research, I will concentrate on part one, which will be referred to as the *business process development process.* Table 11 shows the different groups involved in the development process.

User Group, Danske Bank	User Group, (Åsand and Mørch, 2006)	Description
Employee, business department	User	Regular user; sometimes involved in the requirements analysis
Business Analyst (BA)	Super User	Representative of a business department
Solution Architect (SA)	Local Developer	Technician; has knowledge in a specific business domain
Process Developer (PD)	Professional Developer	Programmer; responsible for the implementation of workflows

Table 11: Classification of User Groups at Danske Bank

The business process development process has two main stages: the creation of a business process model and the transfer of this model into a workflow description. These stages can be described further:

Analysis phase: In this phase, a logical model, i.e. a business process model, is created. It starts with the definition of the 'current scenario' and the 'future scenario'. These are process sketches which are used for the identification of requirements. This work is carried out by a SA, a BA and some users. Afterwards, the 'future scenario' is transformed into a solution process flow (SPF) which is a process description from a business perspective. A SPF is a sequence of activities and connections and always relates to a business event. Activities are further described as system use cases. The definition of the SPF and the system use cases are done by a BA and a SA. The last step of this phase is the error handling on the business layer, i.e. the handling of logical problems in the SPF. A SA is in charge of this work.

Specification phase: In this phase, a technical model, i.e. a workflow, is created based on the SPF. The phase starts with the transformation of the SPF into a technical model, i.e. a BPEL model which uses new and existing services. The transformation is informed by the system use cases. The BPEL process must be precise and includes the linkage of services to the different activities of the logical process model. Initially, the SPF is transformed only partly based on its cost-/usage relation. The transformation is continued iteratively until the BPEL model is perfect. The last step is the error handling on the technical layer that addresses exceptions in the BPEL process. A PD is responsible for both steps, the transformation of the SPF and the exception handling.

4.4.3. Open Issues: Challenges for System Design

In this section I present the challenges for system design, i.e. the requirements that should be met by the proposed business process modelling environment.

Brahe (2007) identified several challenges. He reports communication problems between the various user groups. Since the SPFs were sometimes too imprecise, the PDs had to talk to both the SAs and the users to get more detailed information for the implementation of the workflows. Problems intrinsic to the Web services used further complicated the implementation. Services often had inadequate documentation or no documentation at all. The services also had the wrong granularity. Many service interfaces had up to 100 input parameters, making it difficult to locate the target parameters. Service names were often chosen according to their system name instead of their functionality.

As a result, SAs and PDs have to acquire knowledge of many technologies if they want to develop workflows. Brahe (2007) therefore recommends the design of support tools to facilitate the transformation of the solution model into the workflow.

The analysis of our interview extended Brahe's results by identifying additional challenges for the design of the proposed business process modelling environment. Danske Bank tries to enable BAs to model processes by themselves:

"The solution architect's role is to be a – what do we call it – a coach, or a reviewer and guider, but the developers and the business developers [business analysts] should be able to understand and to some degree model processes themselves [...]."

Currently the modelling of SPFs is done with IBM Websphere Business Modeller, while Microsoft Word is used for the system use cases. The Business Modeller's modelling area has a restricted size, which can be problematic in case of cooperative problem solutions:

"[...] It might help if you had a big drawing board where you did it [the modelling], so you could do it together."[24]

As mentioned above, the main disadvantage of the *business process development process* is the transformation of the SPF into a workflow (Brahe, 2007). An important part of this transformation is the manual transfer of the SPF to Websphere:

"[...] The main disadvantage that we have today – when we do it [the modelling] – is that you do it by a screen or you draw it and then you put it down and enter it in Websphere Business Modeller."

Another problem relates to searching for services by navigating through a service map. This is problematic in case the user does not know exactly what he is looking for:

"[...] There we have something called – in Danske Bank we call it – 'service map' and that is where we start. [...] So it is easy if you know: 'Well I have to do this and it belongs to this business area.' Then it's much easier locating the right service."

Our interview partner also noted instances of inadequate service documentation:

"[...] What we have acknowledged is that even though we have a lot of these services, some have been good at documenting them others have been bad so that we do call [...] the one who developed the service and ask: 'How do we use it?' And that takes a lot of time."

---

[24] It should be noted that slight changes have been made to some interview statements correcting the grammar.

In view of these challenges, I propose to support the *business process development process* as follows:

- *Analysis phase*

    o The restrictions of the screen should be overcome to facilitate collaborative modelling.

    o Simplified tools should enable business analysis to model business processes on their own.

- *Specification phase*

    o The transformation of the business process model into the workflow model, including its manual transfer to Websphere, should be supported.

    o There should be a search function for services. Currently, users must use a map that relates business areas to services.

    o Services should have proper names and descriptions should be improved to compensate for inadequate documentation.

    o Services should have the right granularity.

In summary, the technology currently available requires ongoing intervention by highly trained technical specialists. This suggests that specific support tools should be designed for business analysts, i.e. super users, to enable them to create local workflows.

4.5. Discussion

In this chapter, I identified a number of problems in the application domain. Users of SMEs often struggle with problems that are related to the limited functionality of software infrastructures. Common problems included difficulties with data exchange between different applications, a poor decision support, and a lack of process support for individual business processes.

Users expressed their wish to deal with these problems themselves. However, the limited tailoring functions of the applications often did not enable them to do so. Therefore, many problems could only be solved by external consultants who were often too expensive to commission. Users tried to deal with this situation by creating workarounds in Excel, a tool most of them were familiar with.

These workarounds were in many cases inefficient, because they required considerable manual work, such as copying and pasting of data from SAP to Excel. A (semi-)automation of these workarounds would be feasible since they often have a workflow-like character. However, as inadequate tools are often used to create business process models it is necessary to implement a proper business process modelling environment. Super users are the target group for this environment because they have the requisite business skills and technical knowledge. They tend to be local experts with in-depth knowledge of a particular program. In addition, they are often experienced in modelling business processes.

The study of Danske Bank showed that service-oriented architectures provide the necessary flexibility for the implementation of dynamic business processes. By analysing the *service-oriented development process* of Danske Bank, I was able to identify several challenges which should be addressed by the design of the proposed business process modelling environment. One challenge is to facilitate the transformation of the business process model into the workflow model which demands extensive technical and domain knowledge. The service search and description should also be further improved to make it easier for users to find the right services

Considering the problems just discussed and challenges in a larger context, super users of the organisations should be enabled to tailor their software infrastructures. Enabling super users to tailor applications by using 'business process modelling' as an adaptation mechanism has several benefits but also several disadvantages (see Table 12).

Benefits	Disadvantages
Reduced dependence on externals, such as IT consultants	High complexity; super users need probably trainings on process definition and modelling
Increased efficiency, due to: - faster reaction times to changes - a reduction of reappearing manual tasks	Increased workload of super users, since they are responsible for the automation of processes
Bridging the gap between business and IT, i.e. the definition of business process models and their implementation as workflows.	Technologies are evolving fast, making it difficult to stay up to date

Table 12: Benefits and Disadvantages of Business Process Modelling by Super Users

The study of Danske Bank provided details about its *service-oriented process development process* which should be used as basis for the design of the envisaged business process modelling environment:

Analysis Phase: This phase involves the definition of the 'current situation' and the desired 'future situation' for a specific business event. One or more business analysts and users from one or more departments should create these definitions. The outcome of this phase is a solution model which describes the future situation from a business perspective in form of a business process.

Specification Phase: This phase involves the transformation of the solution model into a technical workflow model. Business analysts, probably collaborating with the IT department, should be able to do this transformation.

In conclusion, the empirical studies provided valuable insights into the application domain. The analysis of the results helped to identify challenges that should be addressed by the design of the envisaged business process modelling environment. Enabling super users to address their software-related problems themselves reduces their dependency on externals. It increases the efficiency of the organisation by speeding up adjustments to market changes and automating recurrent manual tasks. That said, the business process modelling environment must have a low technical threshold since users do a cost-benefit analysis (Blackwell, 2002) to check if the value of adaptations is worth the effort of creating them (Fischer et al., 2002).

The identified challenges lead to the following questions which detail my main research question, identified in section 2.6.1:

- How can non-functional descriptions be integrated in WSDL and UDDI?
- How can process sketches be created and transferred to a computer?
- How can the professional skill levels required for using BPM tools be reduced?

Chapter 5

"Software construction is a creative process. Sound methodology can empower and liberate the creative mind; it cannot inflame or inspire the drudge."

Brooks, 1987, p. 18

5.   System Design and Implementation

This chapter presents the design and implementation of the proposed business process modelling environment which consists of three EUD tools: PaSeMod (Paper-based, Service-oriented Modelling), EUSOP (End-User Service Orchestration Platform) and SiSO (Simple
Service Orchestration). In section 5.1, I set out the limiting assumptions for the design of the
business process modelling environment. In section 5.2, I specify the requirements for the
environment. These requirements have been informed by my analysis of the limitations of the
technology currently available (see chapter 2) and the software-related challenges faced by
users of SMEs, as discussed in chapter 4. In section 5.3, I present the results of a participatory
design workshop. The aim of the workshop was to refine the requirements by seeking feedback from super users at an early stage of the design process. In section 5.4, I give an overview of the business process modelling environment. In section 5.5, I describe the three EUD
tools I designed in detail. Finally, in section 5.6, I explain how the requirements have been
implemented.

5.1.   Limiting Assumptions for the Design

In this section I discuss the limiting assumptions for the design of the business process modelling environment. These can be grouped into technical and organisational assumptions.

Technical assumptions: I assume that all services which are registered in the business process
modelling environment are either available on the Web or self-created. There are three reasons for this decision. First, the Web offers a large number of public available services (Liu et
al., 2007). Second, the SAP systems of the studied SMEs were not service-oriented. Third,
open source ERP systems, like Compiere[25], ADempiere[26], and OpenBravo[27] did not provide
appropriate service interfaces when the system was designed.

The granularity of services remains unchanged since the average number of operations per
WSDL file is less than 20 for most domains (Liu et al., 2008). I assume that services provide
the necessary flexibility and that they operate at a level which is intelligible to users. The interested reader can find a discussion of service/component granularity in (Feurer, ; Stevens et
al., 2006).

Issues related to the hierarchy of process models are not covered. For simplicity, I assume that
the processes created by users cannot be reused as 'services'. Technically, of course, BPEL
processes are compatible with the WSDL standard, making it possible to reuse processes as
sub-processes (Peltz, 2003). In addition, I do not go into issues related to error handling, performance, and security. The system does only check the created business process and
workflow models on a syntactic basis.

Organisational assumptions: I focus only on the business process modelling part of the process development process. Issues related to functionality (implementation of appropriate services), user interfaces (implementation of graphical user interfaces for the interaction with the
services), and data (canonical data model for syntactic and semantic data types) are not covered.

---

[25] http://www.compiere.com/

[26] http://www.adempiere.com/

[27] http://www.openbravo.com/

The use time perspective is partially covered. The business process modelling environment has a 'design-in-use' perspective which covers the modelling of business processes and workflows during use time, but disregards any aspects related to the execution of workflows during use time. I assume that someone else (e.g. ERP system vendors) provides appropriate user interfaces for this purpose. The services available in the environment are pre-selected by the IT department and cannot be changed by 'normal' users. The IT department is also responsible for improving the service descriptions created by the service providers, which are frequently inadequate (cf. Hoyer et al., 2008).

In addition, I do not consider issues related to service level agreements, the education of users, governance, and administration. The business process models created by users arise on a personal level rather than on an organisational level. Therefore, these models have a rather low complexity.

5.2.   Requirements Analysis

My specification of the preliminary requirements for the business process modelling environment was based on my review of research in the field and the challenges identified in the pre-study. I also consider the design principles described in section 2.1.7. Table 13 presents the requirements identified. The column *description* provides a short description of the requirement and states its priority, indicated by the verbs *must* and *should*. The column *basis* shows the source of the requirement, which can either be the *pre-study* (see chapter 3) or a particular *reference* (see chapter 2). The column *layer* distinguishes three design levels: *architecture*, *interface*, and *procedure*. The column *systems* shows by which system the requirement will be implemented.

#	Description	Basis	Layer	Systems
1	The system must use a programming language, i.e. an adaptation mechanism, which is closely connected to users' mental model.	(Pane and Myers, 2006)	Procedure	SiSO & PaSeMod
2	The system must provide an easy search function for Web services to overcome the limitation of UDDI's keyword search.	Pre-study & (Turner et al., 2003)	Architecture	EUSOP
3	The system must provide an improved information structure in the WSDL files and the UDDI for the description of Web services.	Pre-study & (Schroth and Janner, 2007)	Architecture	EUSOP
4	The system must support the collaboration of users, e.g. by providing mechanisms for sharing artefacts and documentation.	Pre-study & (Pipek and Kahler, 2006)	Procedure	EUSOP
5	The system must have an architecture that supports the (re-)design of workflows during use time.	(Wulf et al., 2008)	Architecture	EUSOP

#	Description	Basis	Layer	Systems
6	The technical skill requirements for using the system should be as low as possible.	Pre-study & (Blackwell, 2002; Klann et al., 2006)	Procedure	SiSO & PaSeMod
7	The system's user interface should be designed by using end-user-oriented concepts (e.g. point and click, hyper linking).	(Germonprez et al., 2007; Wulf et al., 2008)	Interface	SiSO & PaSeMod
8	The system should reduce the transformation gap between the business process model and the workflow model as much as possible.	Pre-study	Procedure	SiSO
9	The system should use a minimalistic design for the elements of the modelling notation and should be easy to distinguish.	(Green and Petre, 1996)	Interface	SiSO & PaSeMod
10	The system should clearly separate the process view, the search view, and the description of activities.	Pre-study & (Eriksson and Dittrich, 2007)	Interface	SiSO
11	The system should use a technology to overcome the restrictions of the screen.	Pre-study	Architecture	PaSeMod
12	The sketches created should be transformed automatically into a digital model, which can then be processed by a computer.	Pre-study & (Damm et al., 2000; Dittrich et al., 2006)	Architecture	PaSeMod
13	The system should facilitate the learning of tailoring mechanisms by supporting tailoring on different levels of complexity.	(Won et al., 2006)	Procedure	SiSO & PaSeMod
14	The system should be fault tolerant, allowing users to correct inputs and business process and workflow models.	(Damm et al., 2000)	Procedure	SiSO & PaSeMod
15	The system should make it difficult for users to commit syntactic errors.	(Repenning and Ioannidou, 2006)	Procedure	SiSO & PaSeMod

Table 13: Preliminary Specification of the Requirements for the Business Process Modelling Environment

The following section presents the results of a participatory design workshop which involved super users from the application domain at an early stage of the design process.

5.3. Involving Users in Design: A Participatory Design Workshop

The objective of the workshop was the refinement of the requirements presented in Table 13. The workshop was conducted at an early stage of the design process to allow users to influence the system design. The results of the workshop have already been partially published in several theses and papers (Borggräfe, 2008; Borggräfe et al., 2008; Paczynski, 2008; Spahn et al., 2008a).

The main focus of the workshop was the refinement of the requirements number one and nine involving the adaptation mechanism and the design of the modelling elements. User interfaces, including the adaptation mechanism, should *"speak the user's language"* (Nielsen, 1993, p. 126). In general, there are no ideal notations for any programming situation, but only designs that are more or less adequate for the activities (Blackwell, 2002). In the case of the proposed business process modelling environment, high-level building blocks (services) could enable end users to create new things (processes) by composing domain-specific entities (Beringer, 2004).

I have presented several composition tools in chapter 2. OVAL, ECHOES and FreEvolve (see section 2.1.5) incorporate some basic ideas for the design of composition tools, especially in terms of the composition metaphor used, which can be characterised in all cases as an instantiation of the *box & wire* metaphor. Box & wire is a rather simple metaphor consisting of building blocks (here process activities or service functions) that can be connected with each other by means of (directed) wires. Instantiations of the box & wire metaphor have become popular in the design of mashup tools like Yahoo Pipes and Serena Business Mashups (see section 2.5).

Due to its popularity, the box & wire metaphor has been chosen as composition metaphor for the business process modelling environment. However, despite its popularity, it was unclear whether the metaphor was suitable for end- and super users who should use it for modelling business processes and workflows. Therefore, the participatory design workshop was used to evaluate its appropriateness in this context. The workshop was supposed to provide answers to these questions:

- Is the box & wire metaphor a suitable composition metaphor for the design of the adaptation mechanism of the business process modelling environment?
- What are the key design criteria for the modelling elements used?

5.3.1. Research Method and Setting

The design workshop was based on the PICTIVE concept (see section 3.1.3 for a discussion). Following this concept, designers created mock-ups of the envisaged system on the basis of their knowledge about the application domain and the existing work practices. These mock-ups were discussed in the workshop to evaluate the questions of interest. Design workshops create an 'in-between' region which contains attributes of the environments of both participating groups, i.e. software designers and participants of the application domain. The workshop was documented on several media, video and audio recordings, pictures, and notes, as well as the 'workspace' created.

Three users from one SME (participants no. 8, 9, 15 in Table 8) participated in the workshop. Participants 9 and 15 could clearly be characterised as super users. They were the manager of the purchasing department and the assistant manager of the sales department and had advanced skills in Excel. Participant 8 was the manager of the IT department, making it difficult to classify him as a super user. However, he had a business background instead of a computer science background and performed similar programming and customisation tasks as the two other participants. Therefore, I classified him as an advanced super user. All participants lacked experience with designing business processes, but were familiar with the customisation of the firm's SAP system.

Six researchers, i.e. two designers, two moderators, and two ethnographers, attended and headed the workshop. It took place in a seminar room at my university. The three participants sat at a round table in front of the following materials: Papers of different formats, Post-its[®], differently coloured pens, and the 'workspace'. This 'workspace' consisted of a huge sheet of paper (1m x 1.4m) which participants were asked to use for the creation of the business process model. In addition, a blackboard and a smart board were available in the room.

The workshop lasted approximately six hours and was divided into a morning session and an afternoon session. The morning session started with the discussion and analysis of several scenarios from the work context of the participants. One scenario was selected for use in the workshop.

This scenario dealt with the 'planning of order quantities', which was part of the purchasing process described in section 4.2. The scenario reappeared because the super user (participant no. 9 in Table 8) was again amongst the participants. The scenario had to be simplified a bit to make it understandable for the others. It made the participants' work practice transparent and comprehensible for the researchers. The scenario was also used as basis for the introduction of the business process modelling concept. The introduction involved a collaborative defini-tion of the terms 'service', 'service function', 'data source', and 'query' to ensure a common understanding of these terms.

Figure 19: Setting of the Participatory Design Workshop

In the afternoon session of the workshop, the participants were asked to describe the scenario in form of a business process by using self created activities and services. They could use the following design elements: boxes, i.e. small pieces of paper (#1 in Figure 19) which could be arranged on the work space (#2 in Figure 19), and wires, i.e. pen strokes between the boxes. The boxes could be labelled to specify an activity or their function and had input and output ports which could also be labelled with different data (#1 in Figure 19).

5.3.2. Results

I carried out a qualitative analysis of the materials collected, i.e. the video and audio recordings, observers' notes, and the workspace as shown on the left side of Figure 20. The analysis helped to understand how users intuitively used the modelling elements of the box & wire metaphor and what syntax and semantics seemed to be natural for them. The right side of Figure 20 shows the most important elements of the workspace, translated into English.

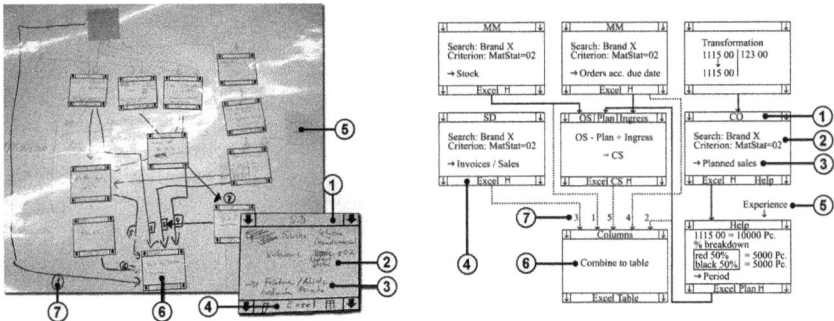

Figure 20: Workspace of the Participatory Design Workshop; Left Side: a Photo Right Side: an Illustration of the most important Elements (following Spahn et al., 2008a, p. 490)

At the beginning of the design process participants discussed how the boxes should be specified, i.e. what they should be used for. They agreed to introduce several boxes to retrieve specific sub-sets of data from particular SAP modules[28]. They annotated these boxes with the corresponding names of the SAP modules (#1). If necessary, the centre of the boxes was labelled by the participants with a selection criterion (#2) to get a subset of the data available in the SAP module. They also added a short explanation of the data that should flow out of a box (#3). Participants labelled the output ports of the boxes (#4) with the desired output format of the data, like an 'Excel spreadsheet'. They connected some output ports to the input port of a special calculation box, depicted in the centre (right side of the figure). They had labelled its input ports with the abbreviated names of the data that should be delivered by the other boxes. The centre of the box contained the formula that they used for the calculation. They connected one of the boxes' input ports to a pink coloured Post-it® labelled with 'experience' (#5). Participants wanted to express in this way that the planning process requires personal 'experience':

"It [a certain column of the spreadsheet] is filled each year with new data [...] to converge the value. [...] It not only includes the sales volume but also an estimate. [...] It is possible that we might say black becomes the new trend colour. [...] I would consider this to be expe-

---

[28] The participants labelled several boxes as SAP modules or Excel spreadsheets, which suggests they wanted to use them either as data sources or sinks and not as 'resources' to get a specific business process activity done.

rience [...] including trend predictions and estimations by the marketing department. [...] It
[experience] is a human factor which can't be automated." [29]

Participants connected the output ports of all relevant boxes to the input port of a box labelled
'combine in table' (#6), which they used to display the result of the process in form of a table.
They had coloured the wires ending in the input ports red and had them annotated with numbers to create an order of the columns (#7): *"Couldn't we sort this by using red arrows? We*
could use them to direct it [the different output values] this way."

By analysing the materials collected, particularly the workspace, I was able to obtain the following results. The discussion of the different scenarios in the morning session showed again
that there is a lack of functionality of software and that the data transfer between different
applications of the software infrastructure is difficult. This was usually addressed by a manual
transfer of data between the applications and the creation of workarounds in Excel which can
be inefficient (see section 4.1.2).

Participants tried to map the business process modelling concepts to the well-known concepts
of their work practice. In particular, they tried to relate everything to the Excel spreadsheet
which was used as a workaround in the chosen scenario and sketched the spreadsheet on a
sheet of paper. They used the created boxes as a kind of 'improved data import artefact' for
this Excel spreadsheet. However, using time- and event-related constructs matched well with
the concept behind business processes. This became clear when the participants created a
'watcher' box for the automation of the process created. The 'watcher' was supposed to execute the process at the end of each month to update the data automatically:

"Shouldn't we define it [the overwriting of the existing values] as service? [...] It would even
be possible to define a date, like October 31st. [...] It [the watcher] must have an 'eye' and
watch it [the time] and change the data at the right moment."

The successful creation of the business process by using pen and paper mock-ups showed that
sketching systems based on this set of design elements have the potential to fulfil requirement
eleven, overcoming the restrictions of the screen. In addition, sketching systems support the
creation of informal elements like comments, explanations and sketches on the workspace.
The participants sketched for example an Excel spreadsheet to visualise their 'goal'. They
also made use of different colours for the wires to express secondary notations, i.e. a logical
typing of the wires. Green wires were used for standard connections between the boxes while
red wires were annotated with numbers expressing the order of columns of the 'combine to
table' box. A black wire was used to integrate the 'watcher' box.

However, participants used the boxes inconsistently. In some boxes, the description of functions and the description of the output were placed in the centre; in others they were separated. One box did not even contain a description of the output. This inconsistent use is acceptable at an early and creative stage of the process modelling process. However, the
participants' use of the boxes and their, orientation on Excel concepts suggests that it would
probably be good to educate participants in business process modelling before they use such
modelling tools.

In addition, the business process model created showed that the box & wire metaphor is an
appropriate composition metaphor for the business process modelling environment. Participants had no significant problems during the creation process. A pen and paper approach was

---

[29] I have translated all comments from German to English.

helpful during the creative stage of the process modelling process since it allowed the use of informal annotations.

I identified the following design criteria for the modelling elements. The simple design of the boxes, with a separation of input, functionality, and output, was adequate. Boxes were used for various purposes, e.g. as data sources, data sinks, manual inputs, and calculations, which is consistent with the business process concept. The participants did not introduce any gateway elements like logical AND, OR and XOR. The process was modelled sequentially and the decision logic was introduced in form of different formulas within the boxes, like in the case of the 'watcher', which should be activated automatically on a regular base.

I used the results of the workshop to refine some of the preliminary requirements in Table 13 as follows:

#	Description	Evidence
1	The system must use a programming language, i.e. an adaptation mechanism, based on a box & wire metaphor, which it is closely connected to users' mental model.	PD Workshop & (Pane and Myers, 2006)
9	The system should use a minimalistic design for the elements of the modelling notation, similar to those used in the PD workshop. In particular, the elements should be easy to understand and to distinguish.	PD Workshop & (Green and Petre, 1996)
16	The system must support informal annotations.	PD Workshop
17	The system must have a semi-formal modelling notation to encourage creativity in early design phases.	PD Workshop

Table 14: Refinement of the Requirements for the Business Process Modelling Environment

5.4. System Overview

In section 4.5 I described the process modelling process which should be supported by the business process modelling environment. In this section I present the design and implementation of the environment. It consists of two EUD tools, PaSeMod and SiSO, which were designed for the two phases of the modelling process:

Analysis Phase (Business Process Creation): This phase involves the definition of a solution model which describes the 'future situation' from a business perspective in form of a business process. Business users, i.e. employees of one or several departments, create this business process. They should be able to describe a process even if they have only little experience with business process modelling. Therefore, the theoretical model should be easy to learn and provide a simple representation. Since this phase requires a lot of creativity, the business process is sketched on a (huge) sheet of paper. The sketches involve different kinds of elements, i.e. formal elements like activities and informal elements like comments and notes. The EUD tool PaSeMod, which enables end users to sketch business processes on paper with an electronic pen, supports this phase. The created sketches are transformed automatically into an electronic representation.

Specification Phase (Workflow Creation): This phase involves the transformation of the business process created in the analysis phase into a technical model, i.e. a workflow model. A super user creates a workflow based on the semi-formal (electronic) business process. The activities of the business process must be mapped to services registered within the system. Professional software developers have to create additional services if the services available are inappropriate. The EUD tool SiSO, which enables super users to orchestrate workflows by using Web services, supports this phase. These workflows can be transformed into BPEL models which can run on a workflow engine.

Figure 21 gives a high-level schematic overview of the business process modelling environment showing the connections between the different EUD tools.

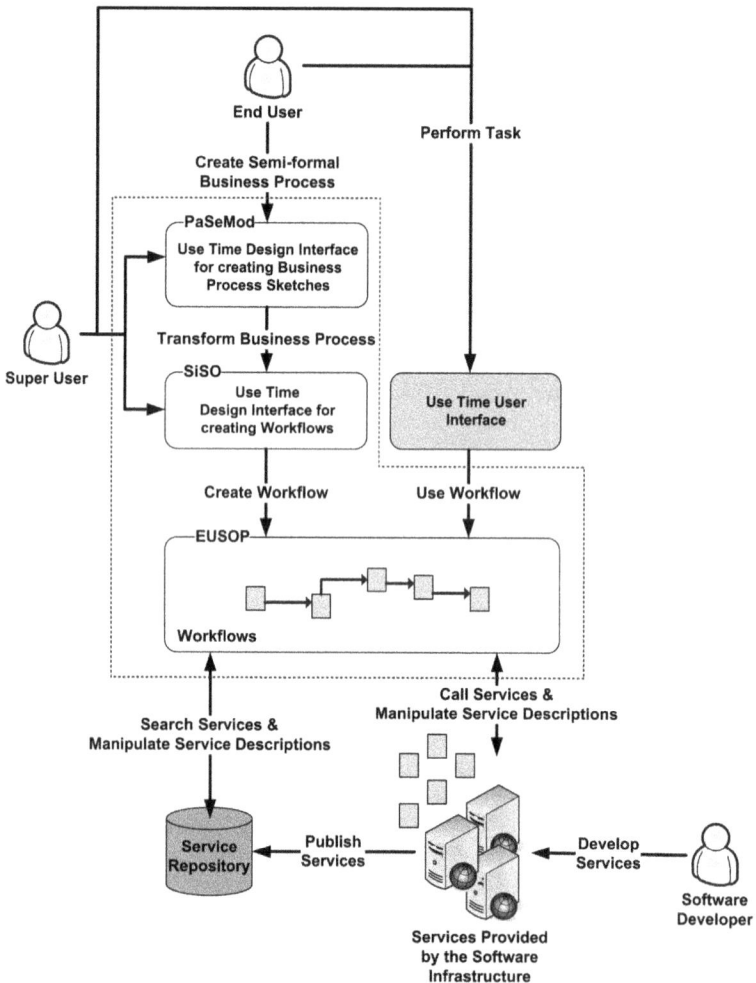

Figure 21: Schematic Overview of the Business Process Modelling Environment

The business process modelling environment consists of three EUD tools (PaSeMod, SiSO, EUSOP) which are placed within in the area enclosed by the red-dotted line. PaSeMod supports the *analysis phase* of the modelling process while SiSO supports the *specification phase*. The third tool, EUSOP, is a platform that extends SOAs in terms of user collaboration. It provides low-level functionalities for managing usage-related metadata in the services' descriptions and provides functionalities for connecting to the service repository and searching for services.

The tailoring process can be split into two steps (Hummes and Merialdo, 2000): the design-time customisation of new components within visual development environments and the insertion of components into the running application. The main advantage of this two-step tailoring process is to shorten the development cycles.

The business process modelling environment provides appropriate tailoring interfaces for end users and super users. Professionals, e.g. software developers and consultants, identify suitable domains and develop services for those domains. End users create sketches of business process models from a business perspective by using PaSeMod. Super users are application assemblers who either transform business process sketches into workflows or create new workflows from scratch by using SiSO. They can select domain-specific services and orchestrate them into workflows. Super users and end users can employ these workflows to perform their daily tasks by using the use time user interface.

The left side of Figure 22 gives an overview of the general workflow management system architecture proposed by Medina-Mora et al. (1992). The right side shows how this architecture is instantiated in case of the business process modelling environment.

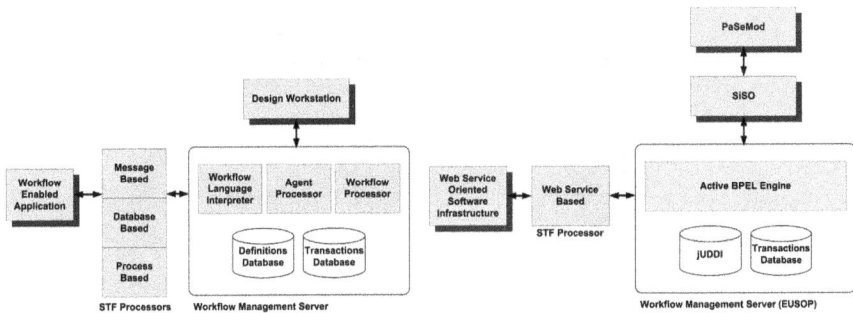

Figure 22: Left Side: Workflow Management System Architecture (following Medina-Mora et al., 1992, p. 286); Right Side: Architecture of the Business Process Modelling Environment

The business process modelling environment supports all *(workflow) applications* of the software infrastructure and all external applications which provide a Web service interface. These Web services serve as message-based *STF (Standard Transaction Format) processor*. The *workflow management server* is part of EUSOP and was constructed by using open source technology. The ActiveBPEL Engine[30] serves as *workflow processor, transactions database* and *agent processor*. Apache Axis2[31] is used as *workflow language interpreter*,

---

[30] http://www.activevos.com/community-open-source.php

[31] http://ws.apache.org/axis2/

Apache Tomcat[32] serves as application server and Apache jUDDI[33] is used as *definitions database*. The *design workstation* is the focus of my research since it is used to generate, modify and maintain workflow definitions. It consists of PaSeMod, SiSO as well as some parts of EUSOP.

5.5. Design and Implementation of the EUD tools

The previous section gave an overview of the business process modelling environment consisting of the three EUD tools PaSeMod, EUSOP, and SiSO. In the subsequent sections, I describe each tool in detail.

5.5.1. PaSeMod: A Paper-Based Business Process Sketching Tool

PaSeMod (Paper-based, Service-oriented Modelling) was developed by Björn Borggräfe, who provided a detailed description of the system (Borggräfe, 2008). In this section, I focus only on the features of PaSeMod which are relevant to my research. Figure 23 outlines the basic concept underlying the system. This concept consists of three parts, the *interaction concept*, *input processing* and the *feedback concept*.

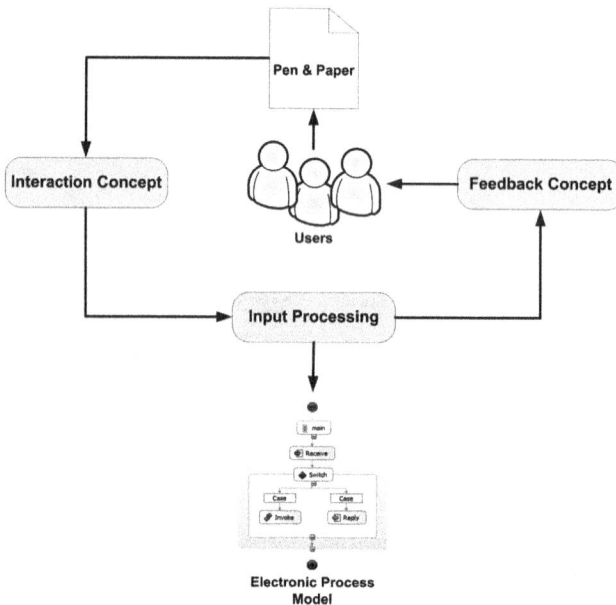

Figure 23: Basic Concept of PaSeMod

---

[32] http://tomcat.apache.org/

[33] http://ws.apache.org/juddi/

PaSeMod gave users the option of using electronic pens and one or more sheets of paper to interact with the system. The *interaction concept* involved the design of the user interface, which included the design of the used papers and the design of the input facilities, i.e. the different modes of the electronic pens. The pens then sent the input, i.e. the drawn strokes, to a computer for further processing. The strokes are processed in two different ways. First, they are used for the creation of an electronic model, which can then be processed by other applications. Second, the strokes are analysed for the creation of dynamic feedback. The *feedback concept* involved the design of this feedback. The concept included a visual electronic representation of the sketched model and audio feedback to inform the users if their pen strokes were recognised or not.

In the subsequent sections, I describe the interaction and feedback concept in detail. I then discuss the *input processing* together with the implementation of the system.

5.5.1.1. Interaction Concept

Figure 24 illustrates PaSeMod's interaction concept.

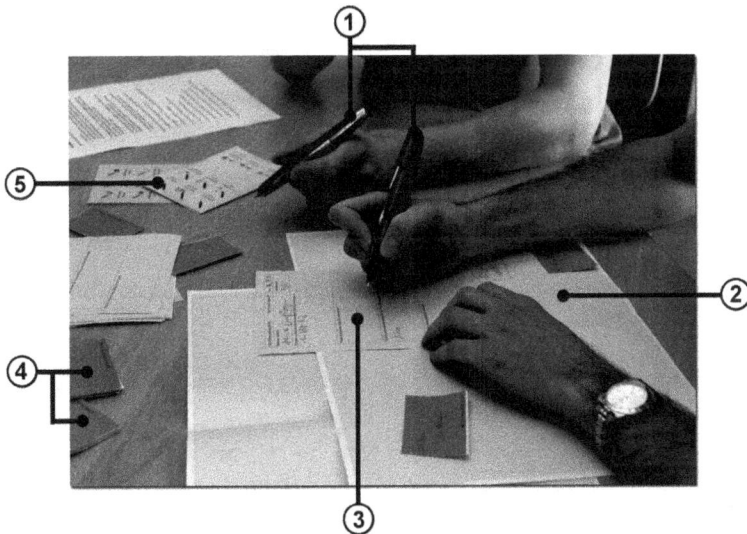

Figure 24: PaSeMod's Interaction Concept

The basic elements of the concept are the electronic pens (#1) and the process paper(s) (#2). Each user gets an own pen to participate in the modelling process. Process papers can be of different sizes. Groups of users can share large sheets of paper (> DIN A3) for collaborative work. Activity papers (#3) are used for a structured description of the activities of a process to others. The activity papers are designed as structured questionnaires which 'guide' users to create precise descriptions. Users have two options for creating process sketches. They can either sketch them on the process paper or stick Post-its® (#4) on the process paper and connect them with each other by pen strokes. Action cards (#5) are used for two purposes, as illustrated in Figure 25. They allow the selection of pen modes on the front side and show the process notation on the backside. Thereby, they aim to replicate some of the functionality of graphical user interfaces like function- and tool bars, which are not available in paper-based user interfaces.

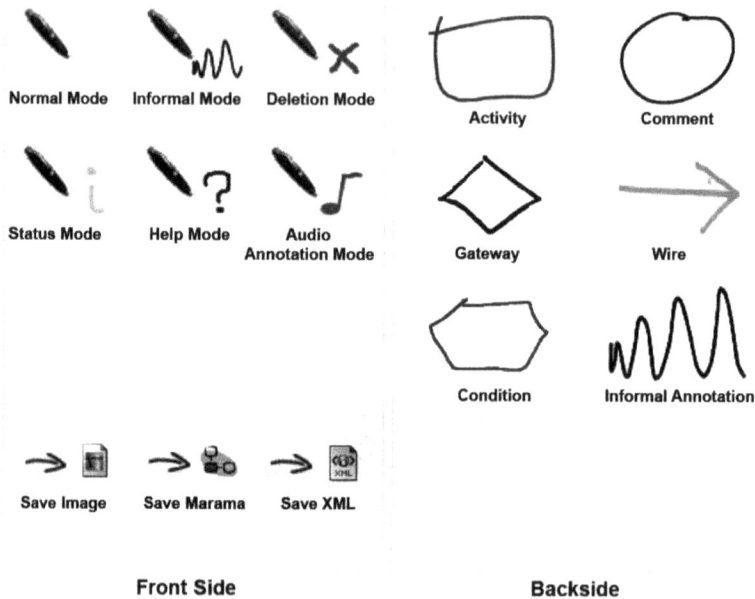

| Front Side | Backside |

Figure 25: PaSeMod's Action Card (according to Borggräfe, 2008, p. 78)

One of the key aspects of the interaction concept is that the system distinguishes between formal and informal elements. This makes it easier for users to keep focused on the modelling task since they do not have to switch between the different pen modes. Nevertheless, there are specific pen modes that have to be selected explicitly by the users:

- *Normal mode:* The system tries to recognise formal process elements and automatically distinguishes between formal and informal elements.

- *Informal mode:* The system does not try to recognise formal process elements. All elements are created as informal elements.

- *Deletion mode:* This allows users to 'delete' formal elements from the electronic process model by crossing them out in the paper model.

- *Status mode:* This allows users to check the 'status' of process elements. They can check for example whether an element was recognised as formal and what kind of formal element it is.

- *Help mode:* This allows users to open a context-based help function.

- *Audio annotation mode: This* allows users to record information which cannot easily be expressed by sketches.

Users can select between those pen modes by tipping the pen on the symbols. In addition, the action card allows them to save the electronic process models created in various formats: image files, Marama files (see section 2.4), and XML files.

Changing models is usually rather complicated because the strokes cannot be removed from the paper once drawn. The option of creating business process models by using Post-its® increases users' ability to adjust and amend process models. The Post-its® have two different colours: blue and red. The former is used for *comment elements* while the latter is used for *activity elements*. However, the problem of inconsistencies between the paper model and the electronic model cannot be solved completely by using Post-its®. This is because the strokes which connect the Post-its® with each other remain on the process paper when Post-its® are (re-)moved.

The modelling notation has a minimalistic design consisting of five elements (see Figure 26), *activities, comments, gateways, conditions*, and *wires* for connecting the other elements with each other. The shapes and colours of these elements have clearly distinguishable shapes and colours, making them easy to understand, differentiate, learn and sketch. These elements are sufficient for sketching simple business process models.

Activity   Comment   Gateway   Wire   Condition

Figure 26: Modelling Elements of PaSeMod (according to Borggräfe, 2008, p. 75)

5.5.1.2. Feedback Concept

The feedback concept involves the design of a dynamic feedback that supplements the basic 'feedback' of paper. The pen can be used for providing feedback, for instance by using differently coloured LEDs or vibration. In addition, a computer can provide visual and audio feedback. Pen-based feedback mechanisms have the advantage of providing individual feedback for each pen/user while computer-based feedback mechanisms are suitable for the whole group of users.

The feedback concept has the objective of presenting the current status of the model, the status of the system, and the recognition status of elements. In addition, it should support the appropriation of the system, i.e. it should help users to get comfortable with the system. It should provide the following information:

- Confirmation whether or not the input was recognised as formal element
- Confirmation if the different notation elements were connected appropriately
- Displaying the current pen mode and confirmation if the mode was changed
- Confirmation of other actions, e.g. the deletion of elements
- Displaying if an action was invalid
- Displaying the current status of the model

We considered combining a pen-based feedback with a computer-based feedback in PaSeMod's' feedback concept. This would have the advantages that actions of users could be confirmed by individual feedback and information would visible for all users without being obtrusive. If implemented, the pen could indicate if a formal element was recognised or if the pen mode was changed by different kinds of vibrations in combination with flashing a LED in different colours. In addition, the pen could confirm a successful connection of elements by a specific vibration and a glowing LED. Information, such as the current pen mode and the current status of the model should be provided via a rich medium like a graphical representation on a computer screen.

However, unfortunately, it was not possible to implement a pen-based feedback because the pen[34] used did not provide an API for controlling its vibration or its LEDs. Therefore, we instead combined a visual with an audio feedback controlled and presented by a computer. This was also used to provide individual feedback. Figure 27 is a screenshot of the graphical user interface of PaSeMod, which is used for the visual feedback. Window no. 1 shows the process sketch in form of an electronic model. The red rectangles have been recognised as activities by the system, the blue ellipses as comments, and the green strokes as connecting wires. The windows on the right side (#2, #3) provide an individual feedback for each of the connected pens (here two pens). They show the active pen mode and the last element that has been recognised (in case of #3 it was an activity).

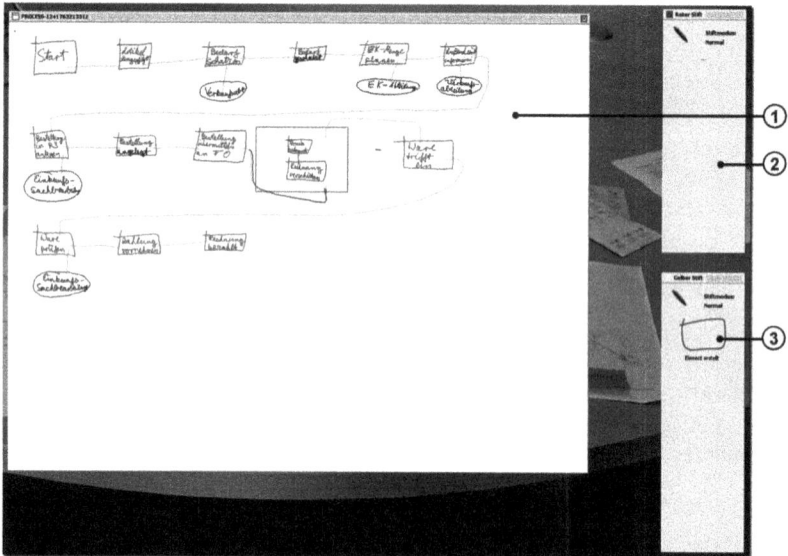

Figure 27: PaSeMod's Graphical User Interface

5.5.1.3. Architecture

Figure 28 gives an overview of the architecture of PaSeMod. It has seven main components, the *pen server*, the *ink manager*, the *recognition engine*, the *feedback manager*, the *process manager*, the *paper manager*, and the *persistence manager*.

---

[34] We used the Nokia SU-1B.

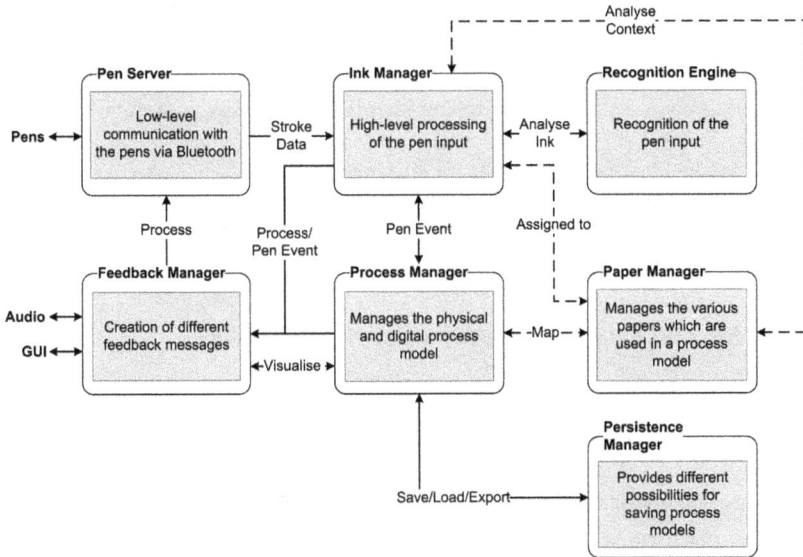

Figure 28: PaSeMod's Architecture (according to Borggräfe, 2008, p. 87)

Let me give you an example of how the system processes a pen stroke. A user creates a stroke by using one of the connected pens. The data is transmitted via Bluetooth to the computer which runs the *pen server*. The pen server is responsible for the management of pens and the communication with them. Since PaSeMod uses the Anoto[35] technology, the pen server has to transform the input of the pens into Anoto coordinates.

These coordinates are passed to the *ink manager,* which processes them at a high level and analyses their context. The context is determined by the paper type, the pen, and the selected pen mode. In addition, the ink manager differentiates between regions on the paper, processes formal elements, creates relations between different papers, connects formal elements and handles the events that have been triggered by using the action cards.

The ink manager uses the *paper manager* to determine the paper type: process paper, activity paper, action card, Post-it®. The paper manager also manages the different regions on the papers and allows the ink manager to determine on which paper and in which region a pen stroke has been created. If the stroke was created on a process paper, the ink manager calls the *recognition engine* to determine whether or not the stroke is a formal element. The recognition engine provides different recognition functions for processing the stroke data depending on the context provided by the ink manager.

The result, i.e. the recognised element, is passed from the ink manager to the *process manager,* which adds the element to the digital model. The process manger manages the physical

---

[35] The Anoto technology consists of a paper on which a specific dot pattern has been printed and a digital pen like the Nokia SU-1B. The pen scans the pattern printed on the paper with an integrated camera. The pattern allows the unique identification of 60 million square meters of paper.

and the digital model and keeps them consistent. If the physical model is changed, it checks the pen events created to determine the changes. These changes are mapped on the digital process model by relating physical regions on the paper to the digital representations of process elements. The mapping is important since it is needed for the determination of the relation between different elements. One example for the relation between elements would be the deletion of an activity element, which requires users to create a stroke element inside this element.

Afterwards, the process manager calls the *feedback manager* which creates feedback messages for the incoming events. The feedback can either be a message displayed by the GUI or an audio message created by the text-to-speech engine. The *persistence manager* is called explicitly by using one of the 'save functions' on the action cards. It provides different options for saving the process models as image files, Marama models, or XML files.

5.5.2. EUSOP: Extending SOAs for User Cooperation

EUSOP (End-User Service Orchestration Platform) extends SOAs to make them 'usable' for end users. In this section, I describe the main features of EUSOP. A more detailed discussion of platform can be found in (Hofmann et al., 2008). EUSOP's design incorporates two main features:

1. The improvement of the information infrastructure of SOAs.

2. An improved API for accessing this information as well as improved functions for service composition.

SOAs provide two different options for storing functional metadata about the available services: the services' interface descriptions (WSDL files) and the service repository (UDDI).

Service providers enter various metadata into the UDDI which provides three different 'pages' for this data: white, yellow and green pages. They contain for instance information about the service provider, industrial categorisations based on standard taxonomies, and technical information about the provided services. EUSOP is capable of extending these metadata by adding usage-related information, such as tags, tag clouds, user comments, ratings, related services, and examples, to name a few. In contrast to the conventional UDDI concept, these usage-related metadata must be created by the users of the system and not by the service providers as they do not have the necessary domain knowledge. This feature should increase the quality of the available metadata and facilitate the creation of an understanding and the selection of suitable services. As services may have different meanings in different use contexts, they can be registered in different UDDI directories, permitting the creation of community-generated, domain specific service documentations. The additional usage-related metadata is also important for the improvement of the quality of UDDI's search results since end users are not only interested in the functionality of a service.

WSDL files are the interface descriptions for Web services containing technical elements such as namespaces, functions provided, the message format, parameters, and data types. They can also contain *comment elements* for each of those technical elements. However, the comment elements are usually used in a similar way as the comments used for the documentation of source code. They are often incomplete, incorrect or even inadequate and contain often no usage information. In addition, the comments are usually useless for end users since professionals created them for professionals. EUSOP should improve the service documentation thanks to additional usage-related metadata, similar to the one proposed for the UDDI, and allow end users to create and modify it. Storing similar metadata in UDDI and WSDL seems to create an unnecessary redundancy, but guarantees that services remain self-contained and self-describing while making use of UDDI's search functions.

The second functionality offered by EUSOP is its API for service composition. The API provides software developers with basic functionalities for the development of graphical Web service composition tools without having to deal with low-level architectural layers. The API provides a universal composition model that supports currently the generation BPEL descriptions.

Figure 29 provides an overview of EUSOP's architecture. As already mentioned, EUSOP makes use of different open source solutions, i.e. Apache Tomcat, Apache Axis2, Apache jUDDI and the Active BPEL Engine. EUSOP has been released on Sourceforge[36] under GPL[37] in spring 2009.

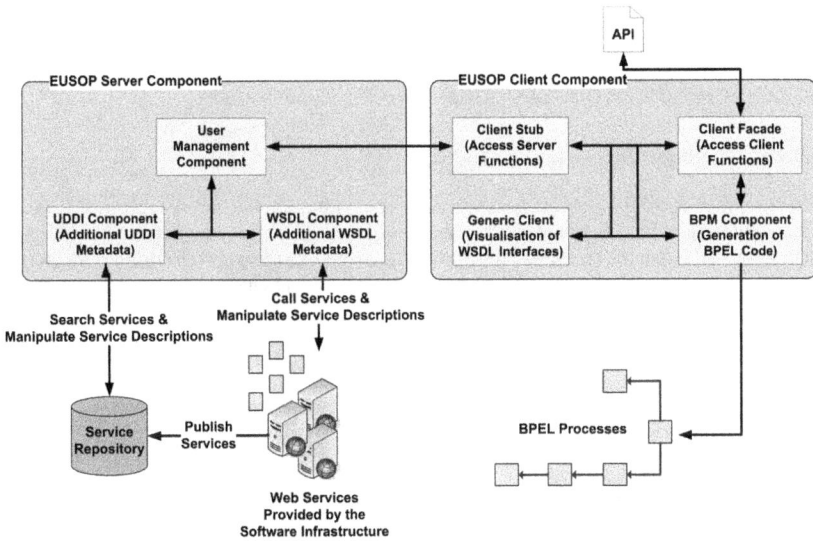

Figure 29: EUSOP's Architecture

EUSOP's two main components are the *client* and the *server component*. The user *management component* is part of the server component and provides a basic user and role concept. The *UDDI component* communicates with the UDDI repository. It simplifies the API calls of jUDDI and provides the functionality to store additional metadata as key-value pairs for any service or service provider in the repository.

The *WSDL component* provides the functionality to store additional metadata in the WSDL file of a service. Since this metadata is stored within the documentation elements of the WSDL files, the modification conforms to the WSDL specification. However, the original WSDL files cannot be modified directly because the service providers host them. Therefore,

---

[36] http://eusop.sourceforge.net/

[37] GNU General Public License, see http://www.gnu.org/licenses/gpl.html

the WSDL component describes the modifications to these files as XSLT transformations. Applying these transformations on the original WSDL files creates the modified WSDL files. The *client facade* is a part of the client component and accumulates all functions of EUSOP as an API, making them accessible by external applications. The *client stub* provides access to the functions of the server component. The so-called *generic client* generates specific 'clients', i.e. stub classes, for accessing the specific Web services. These stub classes are for instance used by the *BPM component* for the generation of workflow models. The BPM component is based on a generic component and container model which allows the generation of different composition descriptions. However, currently it is only possible to generate BPEL code.

5.5.3. SiSO: A Graphical Workflow Modelling Tool

SiSO (Simple Service Orchestration) is a graphical workflow modelling tool built on top of EUSOP. Frank Paczynski has developed large parts of SiSO and provides a thorough description of an earlier version of the system (Paczynski, 2008). Below, I provide an overview of the design of SiSO's graphical user interface as well as its architecture.

5.5.3.1. Graphical User Interface

The design of SiSO's graphical user interface takes into account the specific needs of end users, requiring only little technical knowledge. Figure 30 is a screenshot of the user interface, which is divided into three main activity areas. It enables users to search for services (*search area*), to model workflows (*modelling area*), and to read and change the description of services (*information area*).

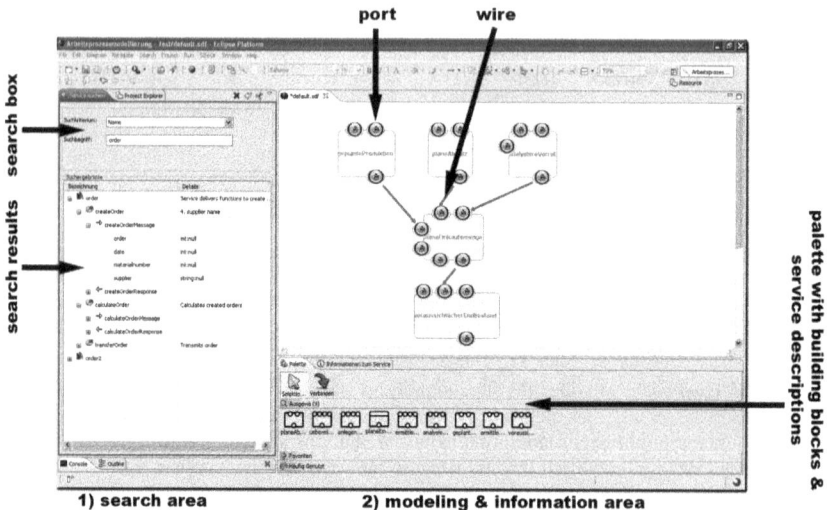

Figure 30: SiSO's Graphical User Interface

The *search area* is located on the left side of the user interface. It has a search box that gives users the option to select the search criterion (e.g. name of service, keyword). A successful search results in a list of services. Users can get additional information about service functions by pressing the small 'plus' buttons on the left side of the result list. Expanding a service entry shows its functions as well as a description of these functions. Functions can be expanded to display their parameters and parameter can be described to make them understandable.

The *modelling area* is located in the centre of the user interface and enables users to wire service functions to create a workflow. The service functions are shaped as boxes. Different icons are used for the visualisation of the input- and output ports depending on the data type of the port. A simple syntax check has been implemented to prevent users from connecting output port with output port or input port with input port or to connect ports with different data types. Composition tools like FreEvolve, ECHOES, OVAL, and Yahoo Pipes have inspired the design of the modelling area in terms of functionality and graphical representation. The implementation of the box & wire metaphor is relatively simple since it only allows the modelling of sequential workflows. This limits the modelling power of SiSO in comparison with business process and workflow modelling tools that have been designed for professionals. On the other hand, this limitation decreases the cognitive demands for using SiSO.

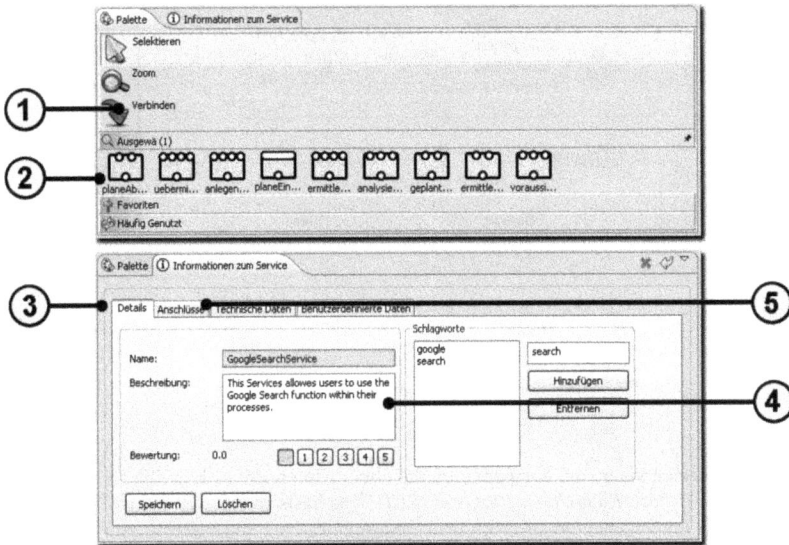

Figure 31: SiSO's Information Area

Figure 31 shows SiSO's *information area* which is located below the modelling area. The information area provides additional support functions for the two aforementioned areas. It provides a toolbox which offers tools (#1) for selecting and connecting the services collected (#2) in the modelling area. In addition, it provides explanations and information about a selected service and its ports (#3) to supplement the information displayed in the search area. The information consists mainly of different non-technical descriptions such as descriptions of the service (#4), its functions, and keywords. There are also technical descriptions such as parameter names and data types (available when opening tab #5). It is important to emphasize that the system allows users to change these descriptions in a 'wiki-like manner'[38].

5.5.3.2. Architecture

SiSO was built on top of EUSOP as illustrated in Figure 32. It should be noted that SiSO has been released on Sourceforge[39] under GPL in spring 2009.

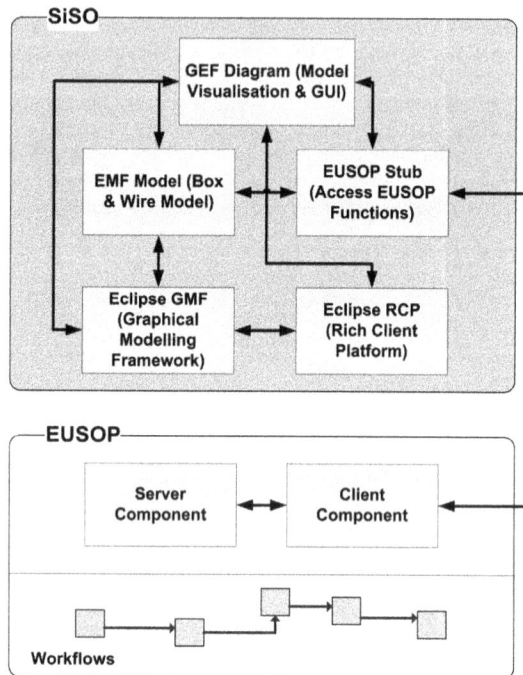

Figure 32: SiSO's Architecture

SiSO is connected via a stub component to the client component of EUSOP. Its implementation uses the *Eclipse Rich Client Platform (RCP)*[40] as basis. Eclipse RCP provides a framework for the implementation of rich client Java applications and offers a powerful plug-in mechanism. One of these plug-ins is the *Eclipse Graphical Modelling Framework (GMF)*, which includes the *Eclipse Modelling Framework (EMF)*. EMF provides basic functionalities for the implementation of the composition model, which is based on a box & wire metaphor.

---

[38] 'Wiki-like manner' refers to the easy interaction concept of creating and changing information in wiki systems.

[39] http://siseor.sourceforge.net/

[40] http://wiki.eclipse.org/index.php/Rich_Client_Platform

The composition model is visualised within SiSO's modelling area by using another Eclipse plug-in called *Graphical Editing Framework (GEF)*. GEF is a supplementation of EMF which can be used for the automatic generation of a graphical representation of the EMF model. GEF and RCP were also used for the implementation of SiSO's graphical user interface.

5.6. Discussion

The main design objective of the business process modelling environment was to keep the technical skill levels required as low as possible to enable end- and super users to model business processes and workflows. This was achieved in two ways. First, the design of the environment was guided by the previously identified EUD design principles (see section 2.1.7). SiSO provides users with non-technical information about Web services. This information makes it easier for users to understand and select appropriate services for the composition of workflows. In addition, the modelling area of SiSO uses the accepted and easily understandable 'tailoring by composition' mechanism. Second, PaSeMod has a paper-based user interface which was developed to support creative collaborative processes in early stages of the business process modelling process.

In the following, I discuss how each requirement has been realised in the business process modelling environment.

Requirement 1: The system must use a programming language, i.e. an adaptation mechanism, based on a box & wire metaphor, which is closely connected to users' mental model.

SiSO and PaSeMod make use of a 'tailoring by composition' mechanism based on the box & wire metaphor. The metaphor has proven to be closely connected to users' mental model (see section 5.3). However, the composition mechanisms of SiSO and PaSeMod are limited since they support only sequences as basic control flow pattern (cf. van der Aalst et al., 2003a). This comparatively simple implementation was considered to be adequate in this context since the problems identified in the application domain were also rather simple (cf. chapter 4).

Requirement 2: The system must provide an easy search function for Web services to overcome the limitation of UDDI's keyword search.

SiSO's search function allows users to distinguish between several search criteria: service names, tags, and community-generated service descriptions. However, it is not possible to use all criteria at the same time. Furthermore, the system offers no functionality to search for related services, which is considered to be an important issue (Jeong et al., 2009).

Requirement 3: The system must provide an improved information structure in the WSDL files and the UDDI for the description of Web services.

EUSOP provides functionalities for including additional usage-related metadata in the WSDL and UDDI data structures. The existing data is extended by a limited set of metadata. Services, service functions and parameters can be annotated with descriptions and services can be tagged. In addition, it is possible to rate services by using a five-point scale. Jeong et al. (2009) postulated design principles for Web-based documentation systems, which could also be applied to APIs, such as WSDL interfaces. They propose the integration of 'how-to-use' information for the documentation, clear names for services, and the provision of code examples.

Requirement 4: The system must support the collaboration of users, e.g. by providing mechanisms for sharing artefacts and documentation.

SiSO supports the collaborative creation of the documentation (see requirement #3) in a 'wiki-like manner'. The created artefacts, i.e. BPEL workflows, could be published in the UDDI directory, making them accessible for all users. Even if BPEL workflows are technically compatible with the UDDI standard, this functionality has so far not been implemented (see section 5.1).

Requirement 5: The system must have an architecture that supports the (re-)design of workflows during use time.

EUSOP is implemented on top of a SOA supporting the re-design of workflows during use time.

Requirement 6: The technical skill requirements for using the system should be as low as possible.

The design of SiSO and PaSeMod make use of the TAILOR design principles (see section 2.1.7) which aim at the design of easy to use EUD tools. SiSO hides the technical complexity of the Web services technology from users and PaSeMod provides a 'natural' pen-and-paper-based interaction concept.

Requirement 7: The system's user interface should be designed by using end-user-oriented concepts (e.g. point and click, hyper linking).

SiSO uses well-known interface concepts like a familiar layout of the interface, point and click, and tree-structures. Users know these concepts well because they are also used in enterprise systems (e.g. ERP systems and office tools).

Requirement 8: The system should reduce the transformation gap between the business process model and the workflow model as much as possible.

Support functions for the transformation of the business process models (created with PaSeMod) into workflow models (usable in SiSO) have so far not been implemented. Model transformations from any notation into BPEL or the other way round are considered to be challenging and have already been the subject of a substantial amount of research (MaWeidlich2008).

Requirement 9: The system should use a minimalistic design for the elements of the modelling notation, similar to those used in the PD workshop. In particular, the elements should be easy to understand and to distinguish.

SiSO and PaSeMod use a set of modelling elements which are similar to those that have been used in the conducted PD workshop. In the case of PaSeMod, the elements are easy to sketch and to recognise (Green and Petre, 1996). The elements used in SiSO, are also easy to distinguish.

Requirement 10: The system should clearly separate the process view, the search view, and the description of activities.

SiSO's user interface is divided into three distinct areas: the search area, the modelling, and the information area.

Requirement 11: The system should use a technology to overcome the restrictions of the screen.

PaSeMod uses the Anoto pen and paper technology to overcome this issue. As users can use any number of sheets of paper for creating business process sketches, there is virtually no restriction in size for these models.

Requirement 12: The sketches created should be transformed automatically into a digital model, which can then be processed by a computer.

PaSeMod transfers the business process sketches into a digital representation which can be transformed into several output formats. However, as stated in requirement #8, the transformation of PaSeMod's business process model into SiSO's workflow model has so far not been implemented.

Requirement 13: The system should facilitate the learning of tailoring mechanisms by supporting tailoring on different levels of complexity.

PaSeMod and SiSO have different levels of complexity, allowing users to choose how they want to participate in the business process development process. Either they participate by sketching business process models with PaSeMod in the first step, which has the lowest complexity, or they participate by creating workflow models with SiSO in the second step, which has a higher complexity.

Requirement 14: The system should be fault tolerant, allowing users to correct inputs and business process and workflow models.

SiSO and PaSeMod provide functions that allow the deletion and (re-)wiring of elements.

Requirement 15: The system should make it difficult for users to commit syntactic errors.

SiSO offers a basic validation mechanism that permits users to wire syntactically different elements. However, the system does not provide advanced debugging, testing and verification mechanisms, such as those described in section 2.1.3.

Requirement 16: The system must support informal annotations.

PaSeMod allows users to create informal annotations which are also preserved in the digital model.

Requirement 17: The system must have a semi-formal modelling notation to encourage creativity in early design phases.

PaSeMod's modelling notation is semi-formal, allowing users to create business process models that consist of formal and informal elements. Informal elements (see requirement #16) could be used for instance for the creation of new modelling elements which have not been implemented (e.g. gates). However, the use of secondary notations like colours is not supported in the paper-based model since the pens used all have the same colour.

Chapter 6

"But as personal computers become widespread, and most new domestic appliances incorporate microprocessors, many people are engaging in programming-like activities in domestic or non-professional contexts. Such users often have less motivation and more obstacles to programming, meaning that they may be unlikely even to take the first steps."

Blackwell, 2002, p.2

6.   Evaluation and Redesign

In this chapter, I discuss the evaluation of PaSeMod and SiSO. EUSOP was evaluated only implicitly as it is a substantial part of SiSO. A detailed description of PaSeMod's evaluation can be found in (Borggräfe, 2008).

In section 6.1, I discuss the method for my evaluation. My main evaluation criteria are the *usability* and *usefulness* of SiSO and PaSeMod in the application domain.

In section 6.2, I present the results of my evaluation. As will emerge, PaSeMod and SiSO support the process development process. PaSeMod is useful in the creative phase of the development process. It provides easy access for end users, who have limited experience with business process modelling. SiSO proved to be a suitable tool for the automation of processes but requires super users to have an understanding of the basic concepts of process and workflow modelling.

In section 6.3, I propose a redesign of SiSO in order to address shortcomings identified by my evaluation of the original system. Most important was the redesign of SiSO's search function aiming to improve its search algorithm and its search interface. I then evaluate the redesigned search function in terms of its usability.

6.1.   Evaluation Method and Setting

PaSeMod and SiSO are innovative systems and cannot easily be implemented in the SMEs without further technical and organisational adjustments. Therefore, I could not at this stage evaluate the systems in users' actual work contexts. Instead, I evaluated the systems in a laboratory setting, using exploratory methods to obtain feedback from users of the application domain.

My literature review identified some specific case-based prototyping approaches (e.g. Blomberg et al., 1996; Eriksson and Dittrich, 2007) which served as basis for my evaluation design. The strength of case-based prototyping approaches is their close alignment with the application domain and their involvement of users in the design process.

According to Walsham (1993), exploratory case studies can be used to explain, describe, illustrate and explore certain topics of interest. My main evaluation criteria were the perceived *usability* and the perceived *usefulness* of the tools as both are indicators for technology acceptance (Davis, 1989). However, these are not the only factors relevant to technology acceptance. Therefore, my evaluation also takes into account some additional factors (e.g. job-fit, relative advantage, complexity) of the United Theory of Acceptance and Use of Technology (UTAUT)[41] (Venkatesh and Davis, 2000; Venkatesh et al., 2003).

I aim to provide answers to these evaluation questions:

- How did participants approach their tasks?
- How effective were participants in performing their tasks?
- What problems did participants struggle with?
- How could the tools be used to solve problems in participants' work contexts?

---

[41] UTAUT was designed based on eight specific models (e.g. the theory of planned behaviour and technology acceptance model) of the determinants of intention and usage of information technology.

In the case of SiSO, the evaluation involved six participants who were employed by three different SMEs (participants no. 5, 6, 8, 9, 18, 20 in Table 8). All three SMEs had participated in the empirical pre-study (see chapter 4) and two of the employees (participants no. 8, 9 in Table 8) had also participated in the participatory design workshop (see section 5.3). The Participants selected came from different departments, with job descriptions such as purchasing manager, IT manager, product manager, controller, accounting manager, and production manager. In the case of PaSeMod, the evaluation was carried out with two of the six participants (participants no. 8, 9 in Table 8) from the SiSO study: a purchasing manager and an IT manager, both of whom had participated in the participatory design workshop.

The evaluation took place in a computer laboratory at my university. It used a realistic setting that was constructed informed by the empirical pre-study.

For the evaluation of PaSeMod it was important to create a 'natural' use-situation, i.e. a collaborative setting. The process chosen, shown in Figure 33, was part of the scenario identified in the empirical pre-study (see section 4.2) and was well-known to both participants.

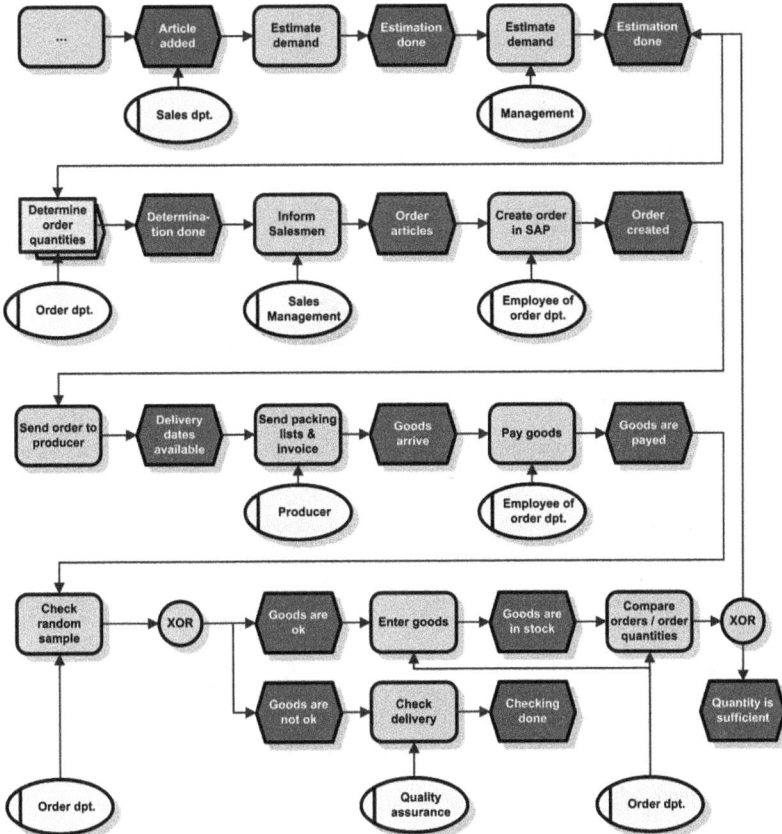

Figure 33: Purchasing Process, used for PaSeMod's Evaluation

In the case of SiSO, I simulated a service-oriented ERP system. I deployed eight self-created Web services, each with up to three functions, to an application server and registered them within SiSO. The services provided the necessary functionality for the scenario. All services were annotated with additional non-functional metadata, i.e. descriptions of services, functions and ports. It was a challenging task to create a scenario that was suitable for all participants. I created a generalisation of the process 'determine order quantities' (see Figure 34). The process is a sub-process of the purchasing process shown in Figure 33 and has been used before in the participatory design workshop (see section 5.3). Therefore, I consider it to be a representative scenario.

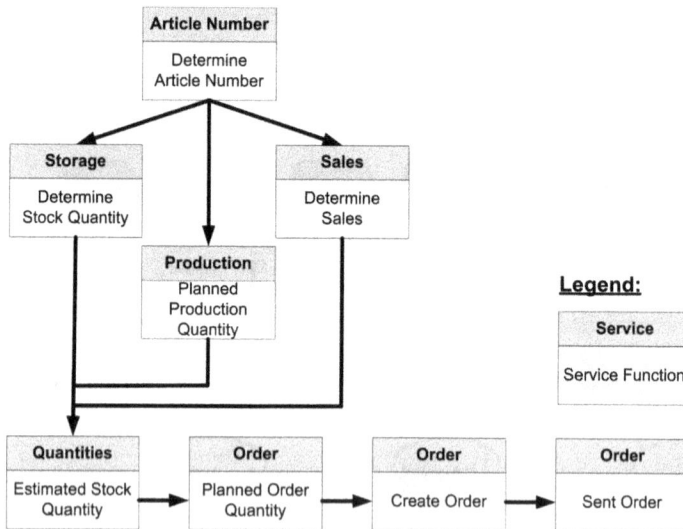

Figure 34: The 'Determine Order Quantities' Process, used for SiSO's Evaluation

A usability testing system consisting of a screen recorder and a video camera was used for the evaluation. The screen recorder was used to record the systems' user interfaces. The video camera was placed behind the participants to record their actions in front of the computer (when using SiSO) or the 'workspace' (when using PaSeMod) as well as participants' spoken utterances. The video streams of the screen recorder and the camera were sent to a computer. It ran a special usability testing software which recorded both video streams synchronously and allowed annotations. The computer was placed in a corner of the room to be more or less invisible to the participants.

For SiSO, separate evaluation sessions were arranged for each participant. For PaSeMod, the two participants worked together in a single evaluation session. Before we started, we sought consent from participants to video recording and note taking during the sessions. Then we gave participants an explanation of the purpose of the evaluation as well as an introduction to the system and its functionalities. Afterwards, we talked participants through the scenario to ensure they completely understood it.

We asked participants to verbalise their thoughts during the evaluation sessions. It was recorded on videotape by using the *think aloud* method (Ericsson and A.Simon, 1993; Robson,

2002). I observed the participants and asked exploratory and open-ended questions to encourage responses regardless of whether they were consistent with or differed from my expectations. I explicitly asked participants what information they found incomprehensible and what they liked and disliked. A second researcher participated as an observer and made notes about critical use-situations. In the case of PaSeMod, a third researcher assisted as second moderator and technical 'consultant'. In the case of SiSO, participants had to solve the following two tasks:

1. Model the workflow, illustrated in Figure 34, and

2. Annotate any service.

In the case of PaSeMod they had as well two tasks:

1. Model a part of the business process illustrated in Figure 33, and

2. Model another part of the business process by using Post-its®.

After accomplishing both tasks, my colleague(s) and I conducted short semi-structured interviews with each participant. We used an interview guideline (see appendix A 1.5) and addressed the usefulness of the systems beyond technical and graphical design.

I analysed the transcripts of the interviews and videos in light of the evaluation questions. The analysis was divided into five steps (Reichling et al., 2007; Schmidt, 2003):

1. I structured the transcripts according to the questions of the interview guideline. Often, statements taken from the transcripts shed light on participants' reactions during the session, as recorded by the video camera.

2. Based on the transcripts, I constructed ex-post categories for the analysis. This categorisation included the identification of critical use situations, overall design issues, the knowledge required to use the system, organisational aspects of its implementation in the application domain and recommendations for improvements.

3. I used these analytical categories to create a coding guideline. It helped me to cluster the data in terms of meaningful units to focus on specific problems. I made critical data anonymous and generalised the data into meaningful patterns.

4. I constructed nodes of correlating units which provided a quantitative overview of the material.

5. I created hypotheses which had been derived from the previous steps.

6.2. Results

The results section is split into two sub-sections. The sub-section on SiSO provides a detailed analysis of the results, while the sub-section on PaSeMod focuses only on the most important findings. A full discussion of PaSeMod's evaluation can be found in (Borggräfe, 2008).

6.2.1. PaSeMod

This section is structured according to the evaluation questions, which focus on the *procedure, success, usability* and *usefulness* of PaSeMod. I analyse the use strategies employed by participants and identify problems with the design of the system, including the underlying interaction concept.

As will emerge, feedback from participants on PaSeMod was generally positive, but helped to identify remaining problems which could usefully be addressed going forward.

6.2.1.1. Procedure and Success

Participants started to 'play' with the system to get familiar with it. They explored the basic functionality, such as process elements and pen modes, which is necessary to model a business process with the system. Afterwards they started with the first task, the modelling of the purchasing process shown in Figure 33. While the participants were working on the task, they sometimes asked the moderators how they could use specific functions like changing the semantics of sketched elements or saving the process. Having finished task one, the concept of modelling by using Post-its® was introduced to them. They were asked to use them to perform the second task. Using the Post-its® worked quite well, but they struggled with connecting them to the process paper and moving and removing them.

In general, participants had no big problems with solving their tasks. Their feedback on the procedure offered by PaSeMod was generally quite positive. However, they noted that it took some time to get familiar with the handling of the system:

- *"[...] It was only a handling problem and once you figure out how to do it, it is easy to use ."*[42]

- *"You have to get familiar with the pen, which takes some time; then it is easy."*

6.2.1.2. Usability

This section covers issues related to the overall design of PaSeMod which unnecessarily complicate its use. These usability-related issues either relate to the modelling or the interaction concept. The next paragraphs discuss each of these categories in detail.

Modelling concept: This focuses particularly on the abstraction of processes and activity descriptions as well as the design of the process notation and the combination of formal and informal aspects. The comprehensibility of the modelling concept was crucial for the usability of the system.

The syntax and semantic of the process notation were quickly understood by the participants. Only the mapping of colours and elements had to be looked up on the action cards. The power of the process notation was considered to be too low. He noted: *"[...] it would be interesting to have the option of creating such things [elements]."*

Participants did not combine and integrate the formal and informal process elements as much as they could have done. They tried to keep the digital business process model as 'clean' as possible, trying to avoid using informal elements. However, this lead to more strokes on the sheet of paper than necessary, making the paper model unclear and leading to a divergence between the digital and the paper model.

Interaction and feedback concept: The idea of having different pen modes was accepted and understood by the participants. However, one participant misunderstood the meaning of the annotation mode. He sometimes switched to this mode to annotate a formal element even if

---

[42] I have translated participants' comments from German to English.

the system offered easier ways to do this, for instance by creating a 'comment' element. Also, participants did not always realise which pen mode was active:

- *"I was aware [that there are different modes]. However, I initially did not realise that it is possible to see them in the upper right corner of the window [of PaSeMod's GUI]."*

- *"At first, I didn't look [at the user interface] to check which mode is active. Therefore, I had some problems at the beginning."*

Participants found the concept of selecting functions and pen modes by means of activity cards very intuitive. They appreciated the option to change the syntax of the elements, in part because the system sometimes recognised activities as comments. Participants also were positive about the idea of connecting Post-its® to the process paper. They generally found the feedback from PaSeMod helpful when trying to connect a Post-it® to the process paper: *"There it [the system] provides some instruction, some kind of online-help."*

Participants had some problems with moving Post-its® on the process paper. They said the logic of moving a Post-it® was not intuitive. First, Post-its® had to be 'deleted' with a pen stroke, while the pen was in the deletion mode. Afterwards, the Post-it® could be reconnected to the process paper. They asked for a special mode for moving Post-its®. In addition, they were irritated at times by the feedback provided by the system: *"When you deleted a connection, you got the instruction to connect it [the Post-it®] again. This was irritating at first. [...] It would have been good to get more specific instruction."*

The audio feedback was created e.g. when changing the pen mode. Participants found it helpful as it allowed them to take their eyes of the screen at times. However, they noted that this kind of feedback would be distracting in meetings: *"During a meeting it would be not that good; being alone you can avoid to look up [on the screen]."* One participant suggested making the audio feedback optional.

6.2.1.3. Usefulness

This section discusses the participants' view of the system's likely usefulness in their work context. In general, participants had a positive attitude of the system. They said:

- *"I like it [the system]. [...] It reduces the work."*

- *"Quite funny. [...] I enjoyed playing with it."*

Especially the second statement is interesting, as it shows that the system could motivate users to use it. Regarding the systems' usefulness in their work context, users had contradictory opinions:

- *"I could really make use of it."*

- *"I would use the computer anyway for the development [of business process models]".*

The first participant said she is used to sketching things (e.g. tables, models) on paper which are later transferred into digital representations within the computer: *"If I already had a precise and structured process in mind, I would use the PC right away. [...] I would use it [PaSeMod] in the creative phase [...] and for brainstorming."* Consequently, PaSeMod supported her work practice. This perception of the system matches perfectly with the two-step business process development process (see section 5.4) and with the distinct aims of PaSeMod and SiSO. The second participant had a different practice and said that he did not need to sketch things (e.g. models, processes) on a sheet of paper: *"I would like to create it [the busi-*

ness process model] electronically because it [PaSeMod] would not be used in a context where you don't have a computer. He did not see any advantages for himself in creating business process models on sheets of paper.

Another aspect was PaSeMod's focus of supporting collaborative modelling situations. One participant described meeting situations in which they create sketches on flipcharts. These sketches are then photographed with a digital camera and attached to the meeting protocol. This process could be optimised with PaSeMod as the digital representation of the paper sketch is created directly. This participant also considered the system to be useful in discussions about the optimisation of business processes. The other participant said the system could help to save time, but he did not think it would be useful for the discussion of business process models. He named the inflexibility of paper-based models as reason: *"If you develop [something] together, it must be possible to move things [activities] easily."*

6.2.1.4. Discussion

The evaluation provided answers to the evaluation questions. Participants were successful in executing the given tasks. However, they remarked that it took some time to get familiar with the system as it had a different interaction concept than other applications they were used to.

Participants asked to be given the option to extend the set of available modelling elements. This extension should increase the power of the modelling notation. In addition, they pointed out the problem of divergent models. This problem arose when elements were 'deleted' because they remained visible in the paper but not in the digital model. Using Post-its® minimised this problem. The only things that remained in the paper were the short 'connection strokes' between the Post-its® and the paper but not the 'deleted' elements. However, participants found it very cumbersome to delete and rearrange Post-its®. They therefore asked to be given a specific function for moving Post-its®.

Participants had conflicting views of the usefulness of PaSeMod. One participant thought that the system should be used in the first phase of the business process modelling process to support the brainstorming and creation of process sketches. This was how I had in fact intended the system to be used. The other participant considered the system to be inappropriate for supporting his work, because he already thought in well-specified business process models which could be created directly in a workflow tool like SiSO. Using PaSeMod was the same for him as modelling a business process on a sheet of paper and scanning it afterwards.

In conclusion, the evaluation showed that PaSeMod could be useful in participants' work context if used in the first phase of the business process modelling process. One of the participants considered PaSeMod to be inappropriate for his work context, because he did need to create sketches to approach his modelling tasks. However, this was because he was looking for a more advanced system which supports him in creating very formalised business process models. This suggests it is important to properly introduce the tool and clarify what modelling tasks it should be used for.

The evaluation also showed that PaSeMod is useful in the creative phase of the business process development process. It provides easy access for end users, who have limited experience with business process modelling as it is based on an intuitive interaction concept with a semi-formal modelling notation.

6.2.2. SiSO

The evaluation of SiSO focused on *procedure*, *success*, *usability*, and *usefulness*. These aspects cover:

• Overall design issues

• The description of usage strategies

• The exploration of the knowledge required by end users to model workflows

• A discussion of organisational preconditions for the deployment of the system in the application domain

6.2.2.1. Procedure and Success

In this section, I describe participants' strategies for using the system to perform the tasks assigned to them. I discuss what skills were required for that purpose and how often super users successfully completed the tasks. I discuss each participant's experience separately to do justice to the different strategies chosen.

Participant 1: Participant number one approached the first task (modelling the workflow in Figure 34) by searching for services. She then read the descriptions of the services she had found in the result list of the search area. This helped her to understand some but not all of these services. She used the information area later on, but that did not help her to better understand the services. Before trying to model the workflow in SiSO, she sketched on paper how she would do so in Excel to get a better grasp of the problem. She then turned to SiSO. Unfortunately, she merely created some connections between different functions and did not manage to model the whole workflow. Her problems with the task can be related to two issues. First, she struggled to understand the services available in SiSO. Second, she had a wrong perception of the system. She tried to use it like Excel, i.e. she tried to create formulas that use services instead of table cells, and did not try to create a workflow that arranges services in a structural order.

She successfully completed the second task (annotate any service). She suggested making available more domain specific information in SiSO.

Participant 2: Participant number two also approached task one by searching for services. He used the information area to locate detailed information about services and their functions. Having found suitable service functions for the workflow, he added the functions to the modelling area and annotated one port with the 'notepad' tool, being provided by Eclipse GMF. After finishing to model the workflow, he documented a service for other 'ordinary' users to make it more accessible: *"In this way, I will create a description for the user, ensuring he will understand what happens here."*[43]

He considered the system to be useful for the selection of services to be used for modelling workflows.

Participant 3: Participant number three was puzzled in the beginning and did not know how to start. She looked for concrete data like stock quantities which she considered to be 'imaginable': *" Where have the results of this 'determine stock quantities' function gone? It must be possible to see the current stock somewhere."*

---

[43] I have translated all comments of the participants from German to English.

As she did not find such data, she searched for other services and tried to understand them by reading the documentation in the search result list. However, the hierarchy of the list, consisting of services, service functions, and input- and output ports, remained unclear to her. Despite these problems, she managed to connect several functions on the modelling area, but without properly understanding the setup of the system. In the interview she just repeated the introduction of the system that was given to her by the moderator: *"[The system] probably makes it easier because it is possible to pre-define different processes, which can be – as the boss [the moderator] said – executed on the push of a button. Therefore, I don't have to perform every work step each time, but instead I have a schema which is processed automatically."*

She said that she lacked experience with purchasing which left her struggling to understand the details of the workflow.

In a weak attempt to perform the second task, she created a tag for a service.

Participant 4: Participant number four already had some experiences with business process modelling and used the systems as intended. He started to search for services, used the descriptions in the information area to understand them, collected the necessary service functions in the palette and started to model the workflow. However, he found it difficult to distinguish the different ports on the modelling area due to inadequate signposting: *"[Ports must be more clearly distinguishable]; if I click here, it says number, which is probably the type, but the name of the input [port] is missing."*

He retrieved this 'missing' information by combining the descriptions in the result list with the descriptions in the information area. He experienced no other difficulties while completing the first task. He noted that he would usually have started by sketching the process on paper before attempting to model the workflow: *"[...] If I started to model a particular process, I would maybe start by writing down how I imagined the steps that I knew and then [...] I would sketch a model. In the second step I would search the web services for the different steps.*

This suggests that PaSeMod simplified his strategy for performing the tasks in question. In fact, participant number four said explicitly that the system was useful for the visualisation of business processes and their automation in form of workflows.

Participant 5: Participant number five also had some experience with modelling business processes. He started to search for services using a particular datum, i.e. a real material number instead of an abstract data type. He initially struggled to understand business process models used in this context for the creation of workflows that allow the automation of tasks. After he worked a while with the system and asked some questions he managed to achieve the required understanding. He read the documentation in the result list to understand the functions of the different services. Like participant 4, he found it difficult to distinguish the different ports in the modelling area.

During the second task, participant 5 struggled with the documentation in the information area, which was not very clearly set out. Nevertheless, he managed to change the description of a service. He considered the system to be useful for creating business processes to be used for calculations.

Participant 6: Participant number six started right away to search for services. He used the documentation in the result list to understand the different services and their functions and browsed only quickly through the documentation in the information area. Like other participants, he had some problems during the modelling of the workflow because it was difficult to distinguish the different input- and output ports on the modelling area.

He was able to complete the second task without any problems. He considered the system to be useful for the automation of different business processes. He suggested connecting SiSO with other systems like SAP so that SiSO can access data and services from these systems.

6.2.2.2. Usability

The usability-related issues were grouped into six categories, the *user interface, affordances, logic, testing, understanding,* and *features*.

Interface: Most participants said that the application had a good design and was clearly set out. However, they noted that it took them some time to familiarise themselves with SiSO: *„I think it [the user interface] is clearly arranged. If you know how to use it, [...] it is actually easy. I would say it is not hard to understand it."*

One participant disliked the design of the modelling area because he found it too small for large workflows. The modelling area is limited in height and, like everyone else, he modelled top down: *"If I have large workflows with ten to fifteen different services, it is necessary to scroll."*

One participant thought the representation of workflows as boxes & wires in the modelling area was pretty standard: *"I assume that boxes & wires are always used in some form for the representation of processes. I think there are not many variants."*

Affordances: Some participants found the system self-explanatory: *"There is nothing that scares me (about the system), where I need to acquire school certificates or the like; it is basically self-explanatory."*

One participant considered the system to be an easy instrument for modelling, but had some problems with adding functions to the modelling area and understanding the structure of the information area. Another participant thought that she needed some time to 'play' with the system before using it. A third participant considered the system to be good except for some specific use problems. He criticised the unclear visualisation of the ports in the modelling area. A fourth participant struggled to understand how to work with the system and asked for an extensive introduction of the system. Others considered an introduction to be unnecessary, because they could learn how to use the system by themselves.

All participants said they expected to be able to drag functions from the result list in the search area or from the palette to the modelling area: *"I would appreciate it if I could use drag & drop [to move functions to the modelling area]."*

This suggests that drag & drop functionalities should be added to SiSO.

Users expected to have a wildcard operator in SiSO's search function for calling up all services registered in the system. Such a function has not been implemented because I assumed that the system would have too many services (>1000) in a real world setting for it to be useful to list all of them. Another problem related to the search function was the search algorithm itself. It used the simple keyword search of the UDDI repository and only returned results if users typed in at least part of the service name they were looking for.

A minor problem in this category was related to the context menus. Right-clicking on the properties of a service, service function or port did not refresh the description in the information area.

Logic: Participants found it cumbersome to add all service functions to the palette prior to using them. They said that this step was unnecessary: *"It would be nice if I didn't have to do the intermediate step and could drag it [functions] directly from here [search result list] over there [modelling area]. The intermediate step might have advantages, but I would like to drag it directly."*

Another logic-related problem was the lack of data representations, such as manually entered input data. Participants expected to have the option to enter real data at specific input ports of the functions added to the modelling area: *"[...] but where are they [input data]. I don't understand that"*.

Participants expected to have filter functions for selecting specific sub-sets of the data provided by services: *"But I would need some possibility to tell him [the system] which articles [i.e. data] I'm interested in; theoretically, article a, b, c; but there must be a possibility to enter that."*

Testing: Participants expected to have functions for testing particular service functions and the modelled workflow with real data because they wanted to see how they 'worked' to get a better understanding:

- *"Well, now I would like to execute them [the functions] to see what they are doing. [...] Therefore, I probably have to connect and activate them."*
- *"So, now I would like to test it to see how it works."*

One participant said that he likes to test his workflow, but admitted that it is sometimes hard to 'see' what really happens in a workflow. Furthermore he suggested implementing functions such as syntax checks which prevent the creation of 'wrong' workflows.

Understanding: Participants had problems with the visualisation of ports of a service function on the modelling area. Ports were designed as 'circles' having different icons, but it was hard to tell which port could be connected to which other port: *"Now I again have the problem of seeing what can be connected with what; I can't see that here."*

Others said they could not distinguish the ports at all:

- *"It was comprehensive, like I said. The temporary names of the services, in particular these fields [services and ports in the modelling area] were a little irritating."*
- *"[...] You could not see what was really there as those numbers [the icons of the ports] were always '123'."*
- *"[...] It [visualization of the ports] was pretty confusing;"*

Therefore, participants asked for a clear and significant descriptions of the ports: *"As I said, these symbols should not always be '123', but should rather contain the article or colour, making them meaningful; four symbols with a '123' do not say anything."*

The most severe problem was the absence of appropriate descriptions of port names outside the information area. The modelling area only indicated the data types of the ports, but not the port names: *"Where can I see which one is this one [relation of a function on the modelling to the entries in the result list]?"*

Providing extended service descriptions was one objective of SiSO's information area. Nevertheless, participants struggled with technical terms and criticised the descriptions available which did not tell what data was needed by a function or how the data could be processed by a function:

- *"This [descriptions in the information area] was rather technical. After I found a service, there were different variants [i.e. functions provided by the service] and I could not decide [between them]. The first variant [i.e. function] calculated the amount and the second variant read it."*

- *"There is not much information [description of services in the information area] which would be of interest to me".*

One participant compared the technical nature of the descriptions in SiSO's information area with the descriptions in the SAP Business Warehouse which were not understandable to her: *"There [in the Business Warehouse] were also only technical terms, like H-456, which are not comprehensible for 'normal' users."*

She suggested extending the available information with more domain specific information, created by the users: *"The descriptions could be complemented by personal things like: 'Warning, if you select this, you have to activate it as well'."*

Another participant was puzzled by the technical term *message*[44]. He wondered: *"This 'generate table message'; is it a message which is sent to the users?"*

Regarding the structure of the information area, participants struggled to understand how to use the information area. Some of them preferred the structure of the result list of the search area.

Some participants mentioned that the modelling was difficult without having a runtime perspective with real data since they had to imagine how the system would process data. Another issue was related to the visualisation of the result list of the search area. One participant said that the arrows used for the input- and output ports were difficult to distinguish. A third issue was the tagging of services. One participant did not consider this functionality to be useful, while another considered it to be very useful.

Features: Participants also had some ideas for new features for the system. They suggested the implementation of a "generic formula" service which could be used to enter mathematical formulae to perform calculations within a workflow: *"I would like to have a function that allows you to enter a formula; [...] this number multiplied by this number minus this number."*

Other participants wished to have a printable version of the created models to use them for instance in meetings:

- *"[The models...] are often printed and discussed in meetings; therefore it would be nice to have such a function."*

- *"[I would like to print it] to archive it or to give it to colleagues [...] as not all colleagues might have the program [to open the file]."*

One participant suggested enlarging the modelling area because he found it too small for his workflow models. Another participant suggested allowing service names to be edited as they were sometimes not adequate: *"If I created this service, I would have named it differently. I would have called it 'sales'."*

Participants also proposed to improve the mapping between port descriptions in the result list of the search function and the ports in the modelling area: *"I would do it like this: if I click here [function or port on the modelling area], the corresponding row with the number should be highlighted blue [in the result list]."*

---

[44] Messages are used in the Web service technology to encapsulate the input- and output ports of a service.

6.2.2.3. Usefulness

In this section, I discuss participants' assessment of the system's usefulness in their work context. The assessment covers both the conditions for the successful implementation of the system and its job performance once implemented.

Job performance: Most participants believed that the system could be useful in their work context. One said the system enabled her to define workflows only once, allowing automatic execution later on. This automation could increase her efficiency: *"The effort would have to be made only once. I would have to build it [the workflow] once and then I would have less work, as I would just have to 'refresh' it."*

Another participant thought the system would be useful for his product calculations, for which he needs prices of raw materials delivered by various suppliers. He said the system could increase his efficiency as he could use the system to obtain prices directly from the suppliers: *"Well, in my area I could imagine using it [the system]. When I do my calculations, I often need raw material prices from suppliers; therefore it would make sense [...] to get them directly from the supplier and not from the purchasing department."*

One participant said he could use the system for his work in the IT department for the aggregation of data, e.g. for consolidating production data and employee data to measure their performance. Another participant said there was only a small application area for the system in his work context (product management). However, he compared the system to another modelling tool which he used to automate a simple process and concluded that SiSO is probably easier than his current tool: *"[In the other tool...] you have to have technical knowledge to be able to use the different things; it is really a developer tool which is inappropriate for end users."*

Both participants mentioned that the system could be useful in all departments where processes recur like in the production.

However, two participants were unable to assess the usefulness of the system in their real work context on the basis of the evaluation sessions: *"[Using the system in the work context] could be possible; that fits; [...] but I have only had minimal exposure to the system. It would be interesting for me to see how they [the workflows] really look on the screen. Right now I have only seen the formula-perspective. It would have been interesting to see the real visualisation [the run-time perspective of the system]."*

Deployment preconditions: Participants identified a range of preconditions for the deployment of the system in their organisations. One condition related to the security of the system. One participant was sceptical about the confidentiality of data coming from external systems because he does not receive a written reference as confirmation. Another precondition was the independence of participants enabling them to use the tool without the help of consultants: *"Well, if the modelling could be done by everyone [...], I would not need a consultant who creates a process for me every time."*

Another issue was the integration of SiSO with other systems of the software infrastructure, such as SAP and Excel. One participant expected to have an export function for creating Excel sheets. Furthermore, he wanted to have the option to use Excel sheets as data sources and some basic Excel functions within SiSO: *„I basically need some Excel functions like pivot tables and filters in here."*

The proper documentation of services was also identified as a pre-condition for the successful implementation of SiSO. One participant said that this documentation should be written completely by developers and not by users. He also thought that 'ordinary users', unlike super users, were not very interested in service details: *"I could describe where the data comes from [...] although this should not be interesting for the user; he just wants to know: 'I enter some data at the top; I get a return at the bottom'."*

One participant also mentioned that 'ordinary users' should not be allowed to use the system since they do not have the knowledge to use it.

6.2.2.4. Discussion

The presentation of the evaluation results provided answers to my evaluation questions listed in section 6.1. It included a detailed description of the way participants approached the tasks assigned to them. Four out of six participants successfully completed these tasks. Looking at the issues they struggled with, I conclude that users must have at least a basic understanding of the underlying concepts of business processes and workflows in order to use SiSO effectively. That does not mean that they have to become experts in workflow modelling, Rather, it means that they should know what process and workflow descriptions look like, which elements are used and which pros and cons formal descriptions have. It could be argued that users need support (either training or help within the system) in order to develop a 'designer mindset' (Fischer and Scharff, 2000).

The evaluation also explored usability issues. In general, participants did not perceive the system to be too difficult. They thought it took only little time to get started. However, well-known functions, like drag & drop were missing. The search function caused some difficulties because it was implemented as a basic keyword search, making it difficult to obtain suitable results. Participants also suggested adding functions for filtering data because they wanted to select specific data ranges as the inputs of service functions.

Another major issue was the design of the information area. Its structure and the technical terms used confused the participants and made it difficult for some of them to understand the descriptions of services, service functions, and ports. In the modelling area, participants struggled to distinguish different ports by their symbols or colours. The unclear marking made it difficult for them to determine which port could be connected to which other port."

In addition, participants asked for testing functions (Dittrich et al., 2006) for services and workflows. This request was foreseeable, but was not the focus of this work (see section 5.1). Testing functionalities could be realised for example by the implementation of validity checks (Won, 2004), exploration environments (Wulf, 2000; Wulf, 2001) or question-based debugging systems like Whyline (Myers et al., 2004). Participants also suggested the implementation of a print function for printing the workflow models as well as a generic formula service for performing calculations within workflows.

Participants offered different views on the usefulness of SiSO in their work contexts. They named two different application fields for using SiSO. One of them was the visualisation and automation of business processes. The second was the creation of calculations using data from different systems and sources. However, participants identified several preconditions for the successful deployment of SiSO in their organisations. The system would have to provide access controls, ensure the confidentiality of data and be compatible with the existing software infrastructure including applications like SAP and Excel.

In conclusion, the evaluation showed that SiSO is a suitable tool for the automation of business processes but requires super users to have an understanding of the basic concepts of business process and workflow modelling.

6.3. Redesign of SiSO

The results of SiSO's evaluation helped to identify of requirements for its redesign. Considering the scope of my research (see section 5.1), the redesign focused on requirements related to SiSO's modelling, information and search area. Figure 35 shows the old user interface, while Figure 36 shows the redesigned interface.

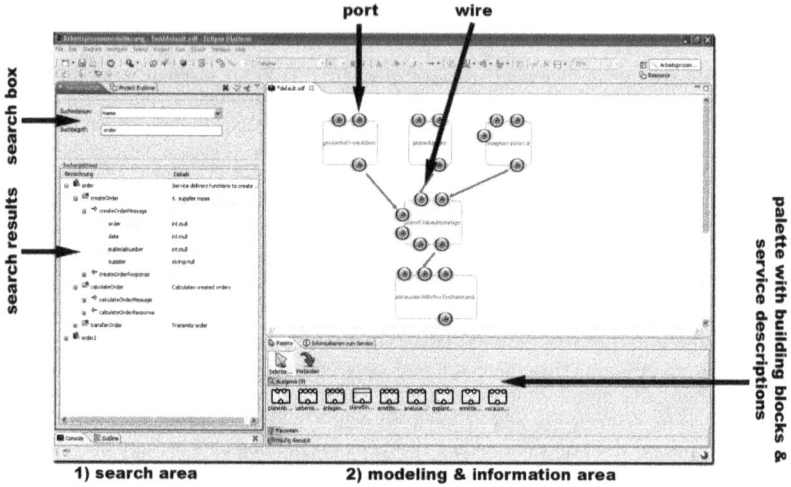

Figure 35: The Old User Interface of SiSO

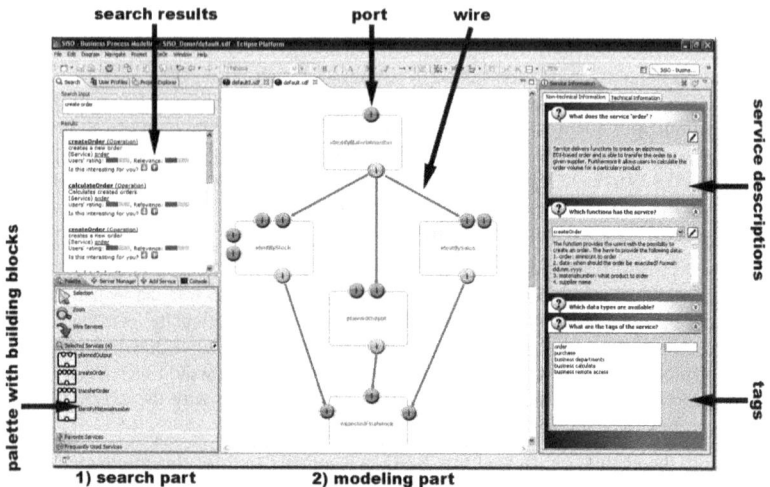

Figure 36: The Redesigned User Interface of SiSO (according to Dörner et al., 2009)

The evaluation indicated that the modelling area was too small in size and used poor port visualisations. Hence, I redesigned the modelling area in order to provide more space for vertically arranged workflows. I also improved the visualisation of the ports. They now have clearly distinguishable icons. Moreover, the input ports have been coloured yellow and output ports blue. The modelling area now provides additional information about the ports, i.e. port names and data types, if users point the cursor at them. I also created a highlighting function that shows the ports which can be connected to an output port that was selected by the user.

The information area had an inappropriate structure. It used technical terms and was usually hidden since it was designed as a tab sharing its space with the palette (see Figure 35). I therefore moved the information area to the right side of the user interface. In addition, I structured the information in this area more clearly, providing answers to the four questions:

1. What does the service 'x' do?

2. Which functions does the service have?

3. Which data types are available?

4. What are the tags of the service?

Table 15 summarises the differences between SiSO's old and the redesigned user interface. The next section describes the redesign of the search function, which required much more effort.

	Old Interface	Redesigned Interface
Search Area	Keyword-based search system; result list is visualised as tree	Interface and algorithm follow the design of Web search engines; search algorithm includes additional non-functional metadata and provides personalisation functions
Modelling Area	Horizontally optimised	Vertically optimised; clearly distinguishable and differently coloured icons
Information Area	Technically oriented structure, separating services, ports, and data types; 'hidden' behind the 'palette tab'	Structured more clearly, providing answers to four questions; moved to the right side of the user interface to be always visible

Table 15: Differences between SiSO's Old and Redesigned User Interface

6.3.1. Redesign of SiSO's Search System

Thorsten Theelen re-implemented the search system having the aim of providing an easy-to-use search function to overcome the limitations of UDDI's keyword search (Theelen, 2009). The two major improvements were its graphical user interface and the search algorithm. The user interface follows the design of popular Web search engines. Hence, users are likely to be familiar with it.

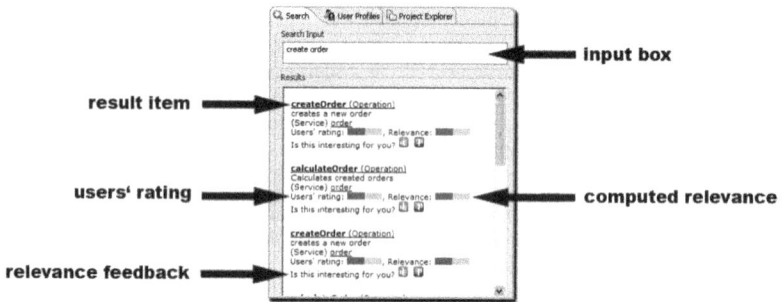

Figure 37: SiSO's Redesigned Search Interface

Figure 37 shows the search interface. It has an input box for entering search terms in plain text. Users neither have to learn a specific syntax nor do they have to specify if they search for a service name, tag or anything else. The presentation of the search results follows the design of Web search engines. Result items have a headline containing the service or function name. In the case of functions, users can click on the headline to add the item to the palette. The next lines below the headline contain a preview of the service's documentation. A further line contains two ratings of the item. The bar on the right displays the computed relevance of the item in relation to the keywords entered. The bar on the left displays users' rating, i.e. their assessment of the usefulness of the item. The last line allows users to vote. They can click either on the green 'thumb icon' if they consider the item to be relevant or on the red one if they do not. The votes are saved in relation to the keyword entered since the relevance of the results depends on it.

The redesign of the search algorithm is more significant than the redesign of the search interface. The limitation of SiSO's search system was the basic keyword search, which made it difficult for end users to find services that were suitable for solving a particular problem. Due to the different backgrounds of users and service providers, it is not easy to identify common keywords that have the same connotations in both contexts. Furthermore, service documentations may be incorrect and incomplete and are usually rather short. This makes it particularly difficult to obtain appropriate results for a set of keywords. The search algorithm addresses these issues as follows:

- It increases the number of results by computing semantically similar services and service functions. Service functions are particularly interesting because they provide the necessary functionalities for creating workflows. Services only bundle certain functions, just like classes in programming languages.

- It processes user-generated content, i.e. metadata like descriptions and tags. This metadata represents a domain specific documentation that is closely related to users' mental model.

- It displays the relevance of the computed search results by using two different indicators, i.e. users' rating and computed relevance.

- It allows users to rate search results. These ratings are used to create personalised search results. In the long term this might produce more precise results than any algorithm as it moves the relevance decision into users' hands.

- The personalisation of results is further improved by using user profiles for clustering sub-groups.

Figure 38 presents the design of the new search algorithm, showing the search process and the data used for computing the results in each step.

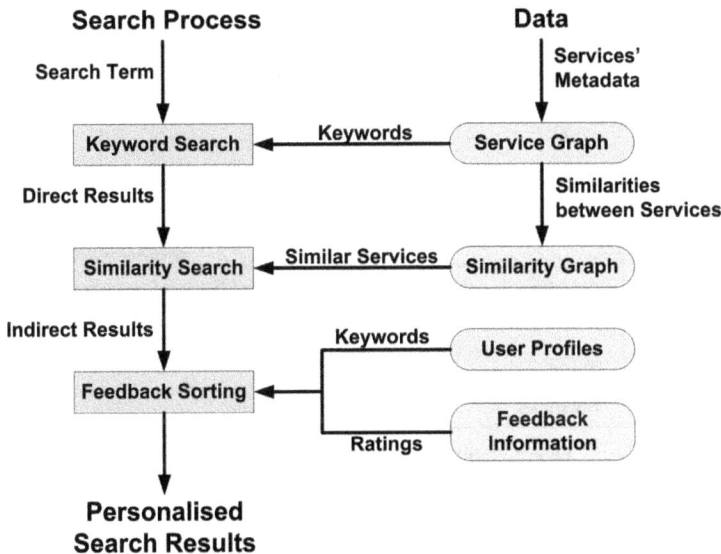

Search Process   **Data**

Search Term   Services'
                                             Metadata

Keyword Search ◄── Keywords ── Service Graph

Direct Results   Similarities
                                             between Services

Similarity Search ◄── Similar Services ── Similarity Graph

Indirect Results
                     Keywords   User Profiles

Feedback Sorting ◄──

                                             Feedback
                     Ratings   Information

**Personalised
Search Results**

Figure 38: SiSO's Redesigned Search Algorithm (according to Theelen, 2009)

In the first step the algorithm generates a service graph that is based on the services' metadata, consisting of the extended WSDL and UDDI descriptions provided by EUSOP. The service graph is used as basis for a keyword-based search that matches the search term with the metadata of all services to return 'direct results'. The service graph is also used to generate the so-called similarity graph, which describes the semantic relations between services and service functions. The similarity graph is used to add 'indirect results', i.e. similar services and service functions, to the search results already generated. In the last step the search algorithm sorts the all results in line with user profiles and feedback information, i.e. users' ratings and keywords from user profiles. The algorithm returns a list of personalised search results for the search term entered.

The redesign of the search function had implications for SiSO's architecture. Figure 39 shows the redesigned version of SiSO's architecture. The blue boxes on the right represent the new components, i.e. the *search interface* and the *search logic*.

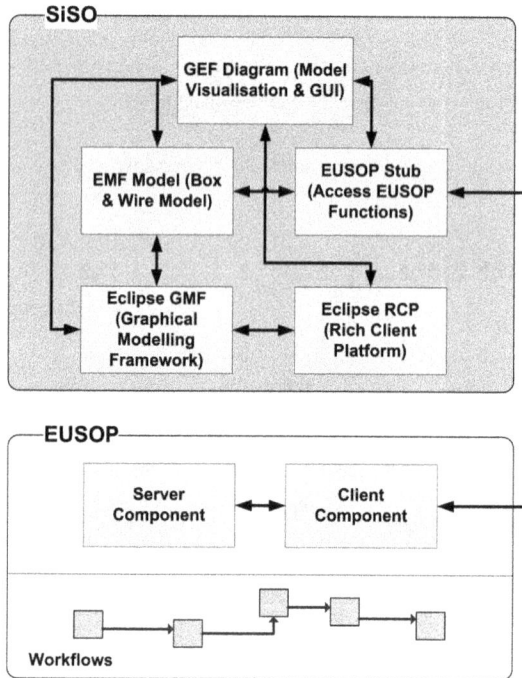

Figure 39: SiSO's Architecture after its Redesign

6.3.2. Evaluation of SiSO's Search System

We[45] evaluated SiSO's redesigned search system in a separate study, without considering any other aspects. Below, I discuss the main results of the evaluation. A more detailed discussion can be found in (Theelen, 2009).

6.3.2.1. Evaluation Goal, Method and Setting

The evaluation of the system's usability explored which concepts worked well and which did not. The search system was compared to a search engine for Web services called Seekda[46], which is freely available on the Web. The evaluation was based on a method for evaluating Web search engines (Su, 2003a; Su, 2003b). We gave participants the task of searching Web services with both systems. During this task, participants had to evaluate both systems using a questionnaire (see appendix A 2.2), which focused on the quality of the search results as well as on the performance and usability of both systems. After finishing the task, participants had to complete a second questionnaire (see appendix A 2.3), which involved a comparison of the

---

[45] In the following I use the pronoun *we* since the evaluation was done together with Thorsten Theelen.

[46] See http://www.seekda.com/

two systems. The questionnaire responses were used to determine which system delivered the best results and was most efficient.

Both questionnaires used a scale from 1 to 7 in combination with a free text field for each question. We had to make minor changes to the questionnaires proposed by Su (2003) to adapt them to our context. Participants had some problems with the questions as they were written in English. As a result, they sometimes provided answers that did not match the questions. The questionnaires were analysed by using qualitative rather than quantitative methods as the number of participants was too small to generate statistically significant results. Structuring the answers along ex-post generated categories of answers (Pandit, 1996) addressed the problem of the mismatch between questions and answers.

Eight students were selected as participants for the evaluation. All of them had a background in information systems, but not necessarily in Web services. Each participant received a free lunch as compensation for his efforts. The evaluation was done in two sessions as the number of available computers was limited. Each session took between one and two hours. The sessions took place in a computer laboratory at our university.

Seekda is a kind of Web service repository offering extensive information about the registered Web services as well as some advanced search functions. To have similar service repositories, we registered the same services in SiSO that were available in Seekda and were related to our scenario. The information about these Web services was also copied from Seekda to SiSO. In addition, we registered some other services in SiSO. They were not directly related to the scenario. They increased the number of services available and provided some false positives. Altogether, we registered approximately 50 Web services, containing approximately 450 functions, in SiSO.

At the beginning of the sessions, users received the questionnaires and were allowed to ask questions to make sure they understood the questions. Afterwards, the scenario was introduced. Participants were supposed to search for a Web service that delivered a weather forecast for the next days for any city. They were asked to search for the Web service described in each of the systems and to complete the three questionnaires. To reduce learning effects that could result from using both systems sequentially, one half of the participants started with SiSO while the other half started with Seekda. Participants were supposed to use three to five different *search strategies* to find an appropriate Web service. A search strategy involved a combination of different search terms. In case of Seekda, it could also involve the usage of the advanced search function. Participants had to select the most successful search strategy, which then formed the basis for answering the questions of the first questionnaire. Finally, participants had to complete the second questionnaire which compared both systems.

6.3.2.2. Results

In this section I present the main results of the evaluation. The section is separated into issues related to the search algorithm and to the user interface.

Some participants criticised the precision of SiSO's search algorithm since it delivered too many irrelevant results. They wrote that the system probably 'misunderstood' their search terms. This encouraged a trial and error approach finding suitable services. It should be noted that the same issue arose in Seekda.

The sorting of search results in SiSO was sometimes inappropriate. Participants asked for customisation options for sorting the results according to different criteria. In addition, some participants suggested the implementation of an advanced search function that should enable them to search for specific criteria.

The implementation of SiSO's search system uses a logical OR function for connecting the entered keywords. This will usually result in a greater number of search results if participants enter additional keywords. However, this was not what participants expected. They expected that the system would return fewer results if they entered more keywords.

SiSO's search system returned services and service functions as results. This was considered to be a major improvement compared to Seekda, which only returned services. However, participants were normally unable to distinguish services and functions in the result list. This may be due to either the improper visualisation of the two different elements or some participants' limited knowledge about Web services.

Participants were happy with the overall performance of SiSO's search system since it displayed the results quickly. They were also content with the usability of the system. However, participants criticised some aspects of the user interface. Some of them asked for a button for starting the search. In the current implementation, this could only be achieved by pressing the 'enter' key on the keyboard. Others suggested adding a counter to determine the number of items in the result list. SiSO could also be improved by connecting the different services on the basis of similarity between the tags entered, as it is realised in Seekda. In Seekda, they could click on a tag to find all services related to this tag.

6.3.3. Discussion

The evaluation of SiSO's redesigned search system had several limitations:

- Only a small number of students participated in the evaluation.
- The evaluation sessions took place in a laboratory setting using a fictive scenario.
- The system was only compared with one other system.
- The evaluation did not cover technical issues like response times and the precision of the algorithm (e.g. number of false positives and false negatives).

Despite these limitations, the evaluation results indicated that SiSO's redesigned search system is somewhat better than Seekda. The better performance and usability as well as the inclusion of service functions in the result list were particularly important.

However, the redesign of SiSO not only aimed to re-implement the search system, but also to improve the modelling and information area. In relation to the requirements set out in section 5.2, the following improvements have been achieved:

Requirement 2: The system must provide an easy search function for Web services to overcome the limitation of UDDI's keyword search.

SiSO's search function is now more advanced as it includes service names, function names, tags and community-generated non-functional metadata, and provides personalisation mechanisms for improving the quality of search results. In addition, it does not only return services but also service functions. These improvements fulfil the sub-requirement of presenting related services as search results.

Requirement 3: The system must provide an improved information structure in the WSDL files and the UDDI for the description of Web services.

The presentation of this information turned out to be incomprehensible in the first evaluation. After the redesign of the information area, the information is now structured along four questions. However, so far, we have not achieved the integration of 'how-to-use' information in the documentation guide, customisable names for services, and the provision of code examples.

Requirement 9: The system should use a minimalistic design for the elements of the modelling notation, similar to those used in the PD workshop. In particular, the elements should be easy to understand and to distinguish.

The icons and colours used for the visualisation of ports on SiSO's modelling area were not clearly distinguishable. They have been redesigned by using new icons and colours for the visualisation of input- and output ports.

Requirement 15: The system should make it difficult for users to commit syntactic errors.

Users did not understand which output ports could be connected with which input ports. The redesign of the modelling area addresses this issue by providing a highlighting function. It indicates which output port could be connected with which input ports. However, SiSO still fails to provide advanced debugging, testing and verification mechanisms, such as the ones discussed in section 2.1.3.

Chapter 7

"The next logical step in the evolution of the Business Web will be eBay-like marketplaces for business services. Individual developers and entrepreneurs, whether they are located in Shanghai, Bangalore, or Silicon Valley, will be able to write applications, plug their innovations into Web platforms like Salesforce.com, and leverage the marketing and distribution strength of these Web platforms to sell globally, without the heavy investment that is required today to commercialize software. "

Friedman, 2006, p. 89

7. Summary and Future Work

This chapter discusses the overall achievements of my research. In section 7.1, I highlight its contributions to theory and practice. I also identify open questions in section 7.2, which could be addressed by future research. In section 7.3 I summarise my work. Section 7.4 concludes.

7.1. Contribution

The objective of my research was to answer the question how service-oriented architectures could be used to support the tailorability of software infrastructures by end users. This question was addressed by developing and evaluating a business process modelling environment which uses 'tailoring by composition' as tailoring mechanism. The environment provides technology support for a user-centred business process modelling approach which consists of two steps: the creation of a business process model and the transformation of this model into a workflow. I briefly summarize the contributions of my research:

- I enabled end users to tailor heterogeneous software infrastructures by themselves.

- I developed two innovative modelling mechanisms: a paper-based mechanism for business processes and a screen-based mechanism for workflows.

- I extended the EUD discourse, which focuses on component-based technologies, by the introduction of service-oriented architectures as the next generation of adaptable technologies.

- I improved the metadata structures of SOAs by enabling users to create, store, and retrieve usage-related information. This can increase the comprehensibility of Web services by end users.

- I developed an advanced search system for Web services which uses the previously described improved metadata structures. The system returns similar services and service functions and provides personalisation mechanisms.

In the following I provide a detailed description of the contributions.

General contribution: My work's focus on software infrastructures instead of standalone systems blurs the boundaries of different systems and allows users to focus on problems rather than systems since they no longer need to distinguish between different systems. The business process modelling environment enables end users to adapt their software infrastructures by themselves. It helps them to overcome problems related to the limited functionality of these infrastructures and reduces end users' dependency on externals, such as consultants and software vendors.

I developed two different modelling mechanisms, a paper-based mechanism in PaSeMod and a screen-based mechanism in SiSO, to allow different user groups with varying skill levels to participate in the modelling process. Paper-based mechanisms have the potential to facilitate the use of composition tools. Their informal character, e.g. the virtually unrestricted options to create annotations can encourage end users' creativity. Thus, these achievements provide answers to the following research sub-questions: *'How can process sketches be created and transferred to a computer?'* and *'How can the professional skill levels required for using BPM tools be reduced?'*

Besides these general contributions, there are also several specific contributions in the fields of computer-supported cooperative work, end-user development, and service-oriented architectures.

Contribution to research on CSCW: My research focuses on a collaborative innovation in workplace infrastructures. It addresses the imprecise description of work practices by using formal constructs, i.e. business processes and workflows. Reviewing research in this field, Brahe and Schmidt concluded that *"[...] we are far from a situation where ordinary workers are able to define and compose their own local computational workflows."* (Brahe and Schmidt, 2007, p. 257) My work addresses this issue. It provides an example of how end users could describe their sequential work practices themselves by using formal constructs (business processes and workflows) to (semi-)automate them. The (partial) automation achieved can save time spent on repetitive tasks reduce delays between process and workflow changes, and improves the decision support provided as information becomes available more quickly. This ultimately also enhances organisations' efficiency and speeds up reaction times to environmental changes.

Contribution to research on EUD: Considering the research on EUD, tailoring of heterogeneous software infrastructures still poses a challenge for research (Eriksson and Dittrich, 2007; Pipek and Kahler, 2006). My research introduces new software engineering technologies, i.e. service-oriented architectures, in the EUD discourse. It transfers the 'tailoring by composition' mechanism to SOAs enabling designers to construct flexible EUD tools based on these architectures. One example is the workflow modelling tool SiSO, which allows super users to adapt software by orchestrating Web services into workflows. This contributes to the realisation of the vision of Klann et al. (2006), who argued that service composition might in future become an activity of end users. My contribution to research on EUD answers the research sub-question: *'How can tailoring by composition be realized in service-oriented systems?'*

Contribution to research on SOA: SOAs are a reliable base for the implementation of systems on top of heterogeneous infrastructures since they allow the integration of the different technologies by using common interfaces, described in XML. However, using SOAs is still difficult for end users. Two of the most important issues in this context are the limitations of Web service descriptions to functional metadata, i.e. the documentation in WSDL files and the UDDI repository (Beaton et al., 2008; Hoyer et al., 2008), and the limitation of UDDI's search mechanism to keywords (Turner et al., 2003).

In terms of the first issue my work shows how the comprehensibility of services could be increased. EUSOP is a platform which enhances the metadata structures of SOAs by providing extended facilities to store usage-related metadata. The integration of this metadata has been achieved by extending the WSDL files and the UDDI repository. This contributes to research on SOAs and provides an answer to the following research sub-question: *'How can non-functional descriptions be integrated in WSDL and UDDI?'*

The second issue is addressed by my implementation of an advanced search system for Web services. It includes service names, function names, tags, and usage-related metadata and identifies similarities between services and service functions. In addition, it provides personalisation mechanisms to improve the quality of search results even further. This extension of the system overcomes the limitations of UDDI's keyword-based search. Unlike semantic Web service approaches, the developed concepts aim to support users when searching and selecting Web services instead of automating these tasks. This contributes to research on SOAs and provides an answer to the following research sub-question: *'How can effective UDDI search functions, usable by end users, be realized?'*

7.2.   Open Questions and Scope for further Research

This section identifies important open questions which could be addressed by future research. The first issue is related to the pre-study. Additional studies would be useful to cross-check the results of the study even further.

The evaluation of SiSO and PaSeMod was carried out in a laboratory setting since it would not have been possible to implement both systems in the SMEs at this time. Therefore, it is necessary to perform long-term studies within SMEs to properly evaluate the community-related functionalities of SiSO, such as the feedback concept of its search system and the usage-related Web service documentation. However, before long-term evaluation studies can be carried out, the following organisational and technical obstacles to deploying the system in the application domain need to be overcome.

At a technical level, organisations have to expose all their systems' functionalities as services while further improving the business process modelling environment until it is ready to be deployed in a real world context. Critical improvements are related to the service granularity as current Web services are usually optimised based on technical requirements to facilitate reuse. It is also important to organise process models hierarchically so that business processes can be used as parts of higher-level processes.

The composition mechanisms of PaSeMod and SiSO, based on the box & wire metaphor, used a limited set of modelling elements, which did not support advanced control flow patterns. This could be improved in the future making it possible to model more complex business processes and workflows.

The evaluation of PaSeMod showed that inconsistencies between the paper model and the digital model can cause problems in a practical setting. Further research could improve the alignment between the paper model and the digital model.

The evaluation of SiSO suggested that users have to have appropriate access controls and testing functionalities. Implementing such mechanisms is important, as the workflows created have to be syntactically and semantically valid. Research on End-User Software Engineering (EUSE) offers a variety of mechanisms for validation and quality assurance (Burnett et al., 2004) which could be helpful in this context.

In addition, PaSeMod and SiSO should be connected with each other, supporting the modelling process end-to-end. To achieve this, it is necessary to implement a converter for transforming PaSeMod's XML model into SiSO's EMF model. One of the most challenging programming issues is the implementation of a runtime perspective, i.e. several user interfaces, which enables users to interact with the created workflows. Ideally, users should be put in a position to create these interfaces themselves, without support from professionals. The WSGUI approach may help to achieve this because it provides concepts for the automatic generation of user interfaces for Web services (Spillner, 2006).

At an organisational level, successful end-user development requires several actions: education, motivation and tools to master the complexity of software development (Bandini and Simone, 2006). The evaluation of SiSO showed that users needed at least an understanding of the basic concepts underlying business process and workflow modelling to be able to use the system successfully. The development of education concepts should be subject to future research, given that *"EUD cannot turn the intrinsically complex process of design into a simple one by employing clever interfaces, no matter how intuitive they claim to be."* (Repenning and Ioannidou, 2006)

The creation of workflow models within SiSO has no direct visible effects on the software infrastructure leading to the loss of direct manipulation (Blackwell, 2002). Users must take an intermediate step first. They have to deploy the created workflows to a workflow engine and shift from the 'design perspective' to the 'use perspective' before they can see any effect. Education could help users to deal with this loss of direct manipulation. Even then, it would probably take some time to become familiar with workflow modelling. Improved support of collaborative processes, i.e. the delegation of adaptation tasks, communication about adaptation problems and a culture of sharing the created processes could speed up the successful implementation of the system in SMEs.

Studying the adaptation of software infrastructures showed their reflexive characteristics as they can be used in their own (re-)design. This calls for more specific studies on the nature of this kind of infrastructures which may lead to a different understanding of the term infrastructure (Pipek and Wulf, 2009).

7.3. Summary

The tailorability of software infrastructures by end users is an important research topic. Modern, non-tayloristic work environments require organisations to have flexible business and work processes (Gurram et al., 2008; Wulf and Rohde, 1995). Quickly and effectively adapting to external change helps firms to address customers' needs and stay ahead of the competition (Carr, 2004). Organisations' software infrastructures have to reflect this need for flexibility.

One 'adaptation mechanism' of particular interest is the modelling of business processes. Business process modelling strengthens the link between strategy and execution which were historically not perfectly aligned (Silver, 2009; Stevens et al., 2006). It could also reduce the coordination effort of cooperative activities (cf. Schmidt, 1997). Technically, business processes are usually implemented as workflows, connecting different services, or more precisely service functions, to provide an acceptable level of functionality. SOAs have become the most popular implementation concept for workflows over the last years (Brahe, 2007).

In my research I explored the adaptation of software infrastructures by modelling business processes and developed a business process modelling environment, enabling super users of small and medium enterprises to model business processes and workflows.

Current EUD tools and CSCW applications, like Oval, ECHOES, MILANO, and FreEvolve, are mainly component-based and not usable in a service-oriented environment (cf. Agostini and Michelis, 2000; Malone et al., 1995; Mørch and Mehandjiev, 2000; Stiemerling, 2000; Wulf et al., 2008). Research on BPM offers a broad spectrum of professional business process and workflow modelling tools which are usually modules of ERP systems. Workflow management systems were widely adopted by firms several years ago (Leymann and Roller, 2000) when it became easier to integrate legacy systems.

Even so, *"[...] we are far from a situation where ordinary workers are able to define and compose their own local computational workflows."* (Brahe and Schmidt, 2007, p. 257). Therefore, there remains scope for research that aims to facilitate the use of business process modelling in a practical work context. A critical issue was the reduction of the required skills, which could for instance be achieved by using innovative user interfaces. The implementation of PaSeMod contributes to this research by using a paper-based user interface. As such interfaces utilise *pen and paper* as interaction concept, they encourage users' creativity and lower the usage barriers (cf. Nakagawa et al., 1993).

132 Summary and Future Work

The tailoring of heterogeneous software infrastructures posed a major challenge for research on tailorable systems (Eriksson and Dittrich, 2007; Pipek and Kahler, 2006). This challenge was met by the business process modelling environment, which allows such tailoring. It uses 'tailoring by composition' as tailoring mechanism. The transfer of this mechanism to service-oriented systems posed another challenge (Wulf et al., 2008) which has been addressed successfully by my work.

SOAs were designed as adaptive, i.e. automatically adapting systems, but not as adaptable systems, changeable by end users. The focus of SOAs on machine-to-machine interaction means they are very difficult to use by end users (Schroth and Janner, 2007). Two of the most severe issues in this context were the limitation of service descriptions to functional metadata and the limitation of UDDI's search mechanism to keywords.

Service descriptions are sometimes incomplete, incorrect or even inadequate and the service providers may only include a few non-functional parameters (e.g. different quality of service values) in the service descriptions (Abramowicz et al., 2006) which could lead to usability problems (Beaton et al., 2008). The issue of imprecise service descriptions was addressed in SiSO by utilising a Web 2.0 approach which enables end users to contribute usage-related information to the service descriptions.

UDDI's search mechanism sometimes fails to return any results, as there is no relation between the description concepts used by service providers and those used by clients (Aguilera et al., 2007; Kawamura et al., 2005). In other cases UDDI returns a number of services, making the selection of appropriate services time-consuming (Liu et al., 2007). SiSO has an advanced search system which addresses these issues. It makes use of the aforementioned advanced service descriptions, returns related services and service functions, and limits the number of search results through personalisation options.

My review of research in the field was accompanied by an empirical pre-study with employees from several SMEs which explored the domain and identified existing problems. The study aimed at the identification of any relevant practical problems related to the usage of software in SMEs. It was designed as case study based on a pluralist approach, combining both qualitative and quantitative research methods. The major problems were a lack of process support, the limited functionality of the firms' systems, and imprecise service descriptions. Those issues make it necessary to tailor software systems to overcome the existing problems. Furthermore, the empirical studies were used for the identification of the requirements for system design.

Having identified practical problems and gaps in research, the business process modelling environment was designed and implemented. It supports a two-step modelling process of end- and super users:

1. *Analysis phase*: Initial sketching of a business process model on a sheet of paper (supported by PaSeMod)

2. *Specification phase*: Transformation of the business process model into a workflow model (supported by SiSO and EUSOP)

Its design followed several EUD design guidelines which aimed at improving its usability for end users. It consists of three EUD tools: PaSeMod, SiSO, and EUSOP.

PaSeMod enables end users to sketch business process models on sheets of paper by using an electronic pen. The system uses a semi-formal modelling notation consisting of formal elements, i.e. activities, comments, and wires, and any informal elements which can be sketched on a sheet of paper. The created business process sketches are transferred into an electronic representation and can then be processed by a computer. If desired, the digital models can be transformed in a second step into a workflow model by using a workflow tool like SiSO.

SiSO enables super users to transform the previously created business process models into workflow models. It is based on EUSOP and provides several functions to support the transformation. SiSO offers advanced search functions for Web services and has an improved modelling component, which facilitates the modelling of workflows and provides additional information about service functions and ports. Furthermore, it enables users to document services with additional (usage-related) metadata.

EUSOP is a platform that enhances the metadata structures of SOAs by providing extended facilities to store usage-related metadata. It provides mechanisms for storing metadata in WSDL files and the UDDI repository. In addition, it abstracts from the technical layers of the Web service technology and supports the development of workflow modelling environments.

The evaluation of the business process modelling environment showed that PaSeMod has low entry barriers for end users. By contrast, SiSO requires super users to have sufficient knowledge about the underlying concepts of business process and workflow modelling, i.e. how process descriptions look like, which elements are used in a workflow and which pros and cons business process descriptions have.

The evaluation also explored usability issues. The main issues of SiSO related to the search function, the information area, and the modelling area. The issues have been addressed in the redesign phase of the system, but have so far not been evaluated completely. In the case of PaSeMod, participants demanded to have the option of extending the set of formal modelling elements to increase the power of the process notation. In addition, they pointed out the problem of divergent models, which could result from the 'deletion', i.e. crossing out, of elements in the paper model.

The last evaluation issue concerned the usefulness of the tool in the participants' work contexts. They named the visualisation and automation of processes as well as the creation of calculations as two major application areas for SiSO. PaSeMod was considered to be a support tool for the first phase of the business process modelling process.

Having achieved the postulated goal of implementing a business process modelling environment for end users, my work has several contributions to the body of research. The contributions are achieved by providing technology support for a user-centred business process modelling approach. The enhancement of the documentation within WSDL files and UDDI increases the understanding of services for end users as well as professional programmers. The environment also introduced an advanced search mechanism for Web services, which includes usage-related metadata and provides a personalisation mechanism.

In addition, I introduced 'tailoring by composition' as an adaptation mechanism for SOA. So far, 'tailoring by composition' has only been regarded as a useful tailoring approach for component-based systems (Teege, 2000). My research changed this view by applying it to workflow composition, based on SOAs. This changes the 'nature' of 'tailoring by composition', as it is no longer only used as a structural composition mechanism, but as a composition mechanism that takes the execution order of services into account (Alda et al., 2007).

7.4. Conclusion

Wulf et al. raised the question of how to connect tailoring activities with processes of organisational development and change (Won et al., 2006; Wulf and Jarke, 2004). This research is relevant to this question. It introduces the modelling of business processes, including their technical representations as workflows as a new form of 'tailoring by composition', uniting the business and IT perspective. The framework of Integrated Organisation and Technology Development (Rohde, 2007; Wulf, 2001; Wulf and Rohde, 1995) describes this unified view of understanding organisational and technological realities as an interrelated work system. The unification of business and IT moves the 'problem world' (here an organisation, represented as set of business processes) closer to the 'programming world' (here a workflow implementation of a business process), facilitating problem solving as the need for 'translations' from one world to the other is reduced significantly (cf. Green and Petre, 1996; Pane and Myers, 2006).

The strong correlation of problem and programming world might help to realise Szyperski's vision of component markets, in form of service markets (Szyperski, 2002). Going forward, we may see eBay-like marketplaces for business services (Friedman, 2006) where super users can select services and integrate them into their business processes, leveraging their strength without depending on others.

Appendix

A 1 Interview Guidelines

A 1.1 Interview Guideline, Pre-Study, Session I, Medium SME

Einleitung:

Hinweis auf die geplante Länge des Interviews: ca. 90 min.

Hinweis auf die Vertraulichkeit der Interviewinhalte: Interviewinhalte werden in keinem Fall außerhalb der in EUDISMES forschenden Organisationen SAP, Buhl Data und der Universität Siegen zugänglich gemacht, und dort nur den am Projekt direkt beteiligten Mitarbeitern. Darüber hinaus werden Interviewdaten lediglich in anonymisierter und akkumulierter Form publik gemacht. Die persönlichen Daten der Interviewten werden getrennt von den Interviewinhalten gespeichert.

Hinweis auf die Aufzeichnung des Interviews durch Mitschrift und Audioaufzeichnung; einholen des Einverständnisses über die Audioaufzeichnung des Interviews. Wird diese verwehrt, wird die Audioaufzeichnung sofort gestoppt.

Gegebenenfalls darauf hinweisen, dass die Erhebung und Verwendung der empirischen Daten mit dem Betriebs-/Personalrat abgesprochen wurde.

Persönliche Daten Interviewte/r:

Daten werden später von den Interviewdaten getrennt gespeichert.

Name:

Alter:

Dauer der Betriebszugehörigkeit:

Stellung im Unternehmen:

Kurzbeschreibung der eigenen Erfahrung in den Bereichen IT und Unternehmensplanung:

A Basisdaten

1. Unternehmensalter

2. Branche, typische Aufträge/Produkte

3. Auslastung

4. Anzahl der Angestellten

5. Umsatz

B Technik

1. Welche Anwendungen werden in Ihren Betrieb eingesetzt?

    a. IT-Architektur allgemein

    b. SAP-Module/Bürosoftware

    c. Weitere Software für Projektmanagement, Planung (Workflow-/Task-management, Monitoring/Reporting), Sonstiges (z.B. CAD/CAM, branchenspezifische Software)

2. Welche Systeme oder Netzwerke benutzen Sie in Ihrem Betrieb? Ist weitere Hardware in die Infrastruktur eingebunden (Maschinen, Produktionsstrassen, Scanner, Drucker, etc.)? Spielen mobile Geräte eine Rolle?

3. Benutzen Sie internetbasierte Kommunikations- und/oder Kooperationstechnologien?

C Techniknutzung

1. Wer benutzt die beschriebenen Technologien wie (Abdeckung Unternehmen/Abteilungen)? Welche Rollen gibt es dafür im Unternehmen? Wie kommunizieren diese Rollenträger miteinander?

2. Arbeiten Sie auch mit externen Leuten zusammen (IT-Unternehmensberater/Entwickler)? Wie sieht die Zusammenarbeit aus?

3. Wie sieht die Spezialisierung/Aufteilung der Fachabteilungen aus?

4. Gibt es technische Schnittstellenprobleme zwischen den Systemen und wie sieht der Umgang damit aus?

D Orga: Unternehmensplanung/ - management

1. Wie läuft die Projekt-/Bereichsplanung ab?

2. Wie funktioniert die Kapazitäts-/Ressourcenplanung?

3. Wie verläuft die Finanzplanung? Was wird wie von wem vorgegeben?

4. Wie werden Verantwortlichkeiten aufgeteilt? Gibt es eine festgelegte Hierarchie?

5. Vergeben Sie Teile eines Projektes an externe Partner (Outsourcing)?

6. Wie funktioniert das Auftragsmanagement?

E Orga: Arbeitsteilung und Kooperation im Technikmanagement

1. Wie sehen die Struktur und die Arbeitsteilung im Technikmanagement aus?

2. Welche Abteilungen in ihrem Unternehmen sind dafür zuständig? Wie läuft die Betreuung der Nutzer in den Fachabteilungen?

3. Wer übernimmt die Technikplanung: Requirements Analysis, Beschaffung, Anpassung, Schulung?

4. Haben sie eine eigene Softwareentwicklung? Für/in welchen Abteilungen? Für welche Aufgaben und wie sehen die zugehörigen Prozesse aus?

5. Wie sehen interne Projekte zur Weiterentwicklung der Infrastruktur aus (Dauer, Teilnehmer, Endbenutzereinbeziehung)?

6. Haben Sie Netzwerke zur Unterstützung bei Problemen?

   a. Ansprechpartner bei technischen Fragen?

   b. Ansprechpartner bei Konfigurationsproblemen?

   c. Übernehmen externe Partner einige Aufgaben des Technikmanagements (Outsourcing)?

   d. Welche anderen, unternehmensexterne Wissensquellen nutzen Sie?

F Spezialfragen Task Management (Optional):

1. Prozessszenarien: Welche Geschäftsprozesse oder Arbeitsabläufe sind von Interesse und warum?

   a) Standardisierung/Auditing existierender Prozesse

   b) Optimierung existierender Prozesse durch Integration oder Design

   c) Sichtbarmachung verborgener Prozesse, die zwar existieren aber verborgen sind und formal nicht unterstützt sind

   d) Erstellung neuer Prozesse

   e) Firmenübergreifende Prozesse

   f) Systemübergreifende Prozesse

2. Prozessstrukturen: Beschreiben Sie einige Kernprozesse, die

   a) in einem gewissen Ausmaß eine feste Struktur besitzen und

   b) im Arbeitsalltag wiederholt vorkommen

   c) ein höheres Maß an Abstimmungsbedarf zwischen Mitarbeitern besitzen

   d) bei denen Mitarbeiter ihren Beitrag effizienter leisten können, wenn sie

      i) ähnliche Fälle in einem Archiv einsehen können

      ii) Einblick und Verständnis in den Gesamtprozess jenseits ihres persönlichen Beitrags erlangen

   e) von derzeitigen Workflow Systemen nicht unterstützt werden?

(Beispiel: Anfertigung eines Kooperationsvertrags...)

3. Mitarbeiter-Interaktion in Bezug auf miteinander kooperierende Mitarbeiter, die sich abstimmen müssen: Welche Kommunikationsform werden genutzt oder würden Idealerweise genutzt werden?

   a) Workflow Systeme

   b) Email

   c) Telefon

   d) Besuch im Nebenzimmer

   e) browserbasierte von unterwegs/Home Office

4. Vertiefung: Welche Mitarbeiter (mit Offenheit und etwas Vision) können wir als Key- oder End-User zu ihren Problemen, Wünschen und Visionen im Umgang mit Workflow- oder Kollaborationssystemen interviewen?

G Spezialfragen Analytik/Reporting (optional)

1. Wie wichtig ist es für Ihr Unternehmen, ad-hoc Berichte und Analysen erstellen zu können?

2. Wie viele Mitarbeiter haben hierfür Bedarf / sind in der Lage sie zu erstallen?

3. Wie groß ist der potentielle Anwenderkreis?

4. Wie wichtig ist hierbei Interoperabilität zwischen verschiedenen Systemen?

5. Wie wichtig ist hierbei eine Integration mit Microsoft Excel?

6. Was sind die aktuellen Problemstellen im Bereich Analytik/Reporting

H Allgemein

1. Wie würden Sie Ihre wichtigsten vorhandenen Probleme bei der Verwaltung ihrer Infrastruktur beschreiben? Ist etwas bisher noch nicht zur Sprache gekommen?

2. Wo besteht ein möglicher Verbesserungsbedarf?

3. Endbenutzer für Befragungen/Evaluation

A 1.2 Interview Guideline, Pre-Study, Session I, Small SME

Einleitung:

Hinweis auf die geplante Länge des Interviews: ca. 90 min.

Hinweis auf die Vertraulichkeit der Interviewinhalte: Interviewinhalte werden in keinem Fall außerhalb der in EUDISMES forschenden Organisationen SAP, Buhl Data und der Universität Siegen zugänglich gemacht, und dort nur den am Projekt direkt beteiligten Mitarbeitern. Darüber hinaus werden Interviewdaten lediglich in anonymisierter und akkumulierter Form publik gemacht. Die persönlichen Daten der Interviewten werden getrennt von den Interviewinhalten gespeichert.

Hinweis auf die Aufzeichnung des Interviews durch Mitschrift und Audioaufzeichnung; einholen des Einverständnisses über die Audioaufzeichnung des Interviews. Wird diese verwehrt, wird die Audioaufzeichnung sofort gestoppt.

Gegebenenfalls darauf hinweisen, dass die Erhebung und Verwendung der empirischen Daten mit dem Betriebs-/Personalrat abgesprochen wurde.

Persönliche Daten Interviewte/r:

Daten werden später von den Interviewdaten getrennt gespeichert.

Name:

Alter:

Dauer der Betriebszugehörigkeit:

Stellung im Unternehmen:

Kurzbeschreibung der eigenen Erfahrung in den Bereichen IT und Unternehmensplanung:

A Basisdaten

1. Unternehmensalter
2. Branche, typische Aufträge
3. Auslastung
4. Anzahl der Angestellten
5. Umsatz

B Technik

1. Welche Anwendungen werden in Ihren Betrieb eingesetzt?

    a. Betriebssysteme

    b. Bürosoftware

    c. Buchhaltung/Planung

    d. Sonstiges (CAD/CAM)

2. Welche Hardware (Scanner, Drucker etc.) oder Netzwerke benutzen Sie in Ihrem Betrieb?

3. Nutzen Sie Internetanwendungen (Email, Web)?

    a. Wenn ja, wer und von wo hat man Zugangsmöglichkeiten?

C Techniknutzung

1. Wie läuft in Ihren Betrieb die Buchhaltung ab?

    a. Gibt es ein Zusammenspiel zwischen der Buchhaltung und sonstigen Anwendungen?

2. Arbeiten Sie auch mit externen Leuten zusammen (Steuerberater)? Wie sieht die Zusammenarbeit aus?

3. Gibt es in Ihrem Betrieb auch eine Spezialisierung einzelner Mitarbeiter auf bestimmte Bereiche?

D Orga: Unternehmensplanung/ - management

1. Wie läuft die Projektplanung ab?

2. Wie funktioniert die Kapazitätsplanung?

3. Wie verläuft die Finanzplanung?

4. Wie werden Verantwortlichkeiten aufgeteilt? Gibt es eine festgelegte Hierarchie?

5. Vergeben Sie Teile eines Projektes an externe Partner (Outsourcing)?

6. Wie funktioniert das Auftragsmanagement?

E Orga: Arbeitsteilung und Kooperation im Technikmanagement

1. Wie sehen die Struktur und die Arbeitsteilung im Technikmanagement aus?

2. Haben Sie Netzwerke zur Unterstützung bei Problemen?

    a. Ansprechpartner bei technischen Fragen?

    b. Ansprechpartner bei Konfigurationsproblemen?

    c. Übernehmen externe Partner einige Aufgaben des Technikmanagements (Outsourcing)?

F Allgemein

1. Wie würden Sie Ihre vorhandenen Probleme beschreiben?

2. Wo besteht ein möglicher Verbesserungsbedarf?

3. Endbenutzer für Befragungen/Evaluation

A 1.3 Interview Guideline, Pre-Study, Session II

I. Einführung

- EUDISMES Projekt kurz erklären: Forschungsprojekt (Uni, KMUs)
- Kurzvorstellung der eigenen Person
- Zweck dieses Interviews kurz erörtern (Infrastruktur und Anpassungsprozesse verstehen)
- Anmerkung bzgl. Aufnahme und Datenschutz

II. Interview

1. Allgemeiner Teil:

1.1. Welche Rolle spielen Sie in dem Unternehmen; was sind Ihre Aufgabenbereiche?

    1.1.1. Sind Sie für diese Aufgabenbereiche alleine verantwortlich?

    1.1.2. Welche Software unterstützt Sie in den einzelnen Bereichen?

1.2. Skizzieren Sie bitte kurz eine typische (möglichst komplexe) Aufgabe aus ihrem Verantwortungsbereich.

1.3. Was für ein PC-Nutzertyp sind Sie? (erfahren, mäßig erfahren, unerfahren)

1.4. Welche Software nutzen Sie gerne und warum? (Bei welchen Arbeitsprozessen wird diese Software eingesetzt?)

    1.4.1. Wenn keine Software gerne genutzt wird, dann insb. auch nach dem Warum fragen.

1.5. Welche Software ist Ihrer Meinung nach am einfachsten zu bedienen?

    1.5.1. Wie zufrieden sind Sie mit dieser Software?

    1.5.2. Was macht die Software so einfach und intuitiv bedienbar?

    1.5.3. Vermissen Sie Funktionalitäten, die Ihnen diese Software nicht bietet?

1.6. Wie erlernen Sie am Liebsten eine neue Software? (Z. B. Kurse, learning by doing, Handbücher)

1.7. Wie erlernen Sie tatsächlich eine neue Software?

1.8. Wer entscheidet im Unternehmen, welche Software Sie nutzen (Sie, Leitung, IT, etc.)

1.9. Empfinden sie die IT-Unterstützung Ihrer Arbeit als Bereicherung/Erleichterung?

1.10. Wie ist Ihre IT-Landschaft aufgebaut? (Eigener Arbeitsplatz, Gesamtkonzept)

    1.10.1. Nachfrage bzgl. Internet-Zugang (analog, ISDN, DSL,…)

    1.10.2. Ist hier eine Veränderung in den nächsten Wochen/ Monaten/ Jahren geplant?

1.11. Wie würden Sie Ihre Software-Umgebung hinsichtlich des Funktionsumfangs einschätzen?

    1.11.1. Sie bietet mir alle notwendigen Funktionen

    1.11.2. Sie bietet zu viele (und versteckte) Funktionen

    1.11.3. Sie bietet zu wenige Funktionen

1.12. Sind die Funktionen immer dann erreichbar, wenn Sie diese brauchen?

1.13. Glauben Sie, dass Sie mit dem vollen Funktionsumfang der Software-Systeme vertraut sind?

2. **Problembewältigung (Wenn nicht bereits beantwortet)**

2.1. Inwiefern treffen die von Ihrer Software bereitgestellten Funktionalitäten Ihre individuellen Bedürfnisse? (zufrieden, unzufrieden, Wunsch nach Anpassungen, etc.)

2.2. Was machen Sie, wenn sich bei der Software-Nutzung Probleme ergeben?

    2.2.1. Greifen Sie auf die IT-Abteilung zurück? Wenn ja, wie oft und bei welchen Problemen?

    2.2.2. Welche anderen Formen der Unterstützung nutzen Sie? (Hotline, Handbuch, integrierte Hilfe, EDV-Abteilung oder Kollegen fragen, etc.)

3. **Fragen zum Verständnis von Anpassbarkeit**

3.1. Ist Ihnen bekannt, dass Sie Software selbst anpassen können? (Kurze Erklärung, was Modifikationen sind; z. B. Excel Makro, Word-Vorlage, Skripte)

3.2. Sehen Sie Bedürfnisse/Notwendigkeiten Ihre Software-Umgebung besser an Ihre individuellen Arbeitsprozesse anzupassen? Wie gehen sie bislang damit um?

3.3. Informieren Sie sich über die Anpassungsmöglichkeiten ihrer Software? Welche Informationsquellen nutzen Sie?

3.4. Haben Sie an Ihrer Software bereits einmal Anpassungen durchgeführt (Oder Anpassungen z.B. durch die IT veranlasst?)

3.5. Ja-Zweig: Nutzer hat eine Software bereits selbst angepasst

    3.5.1. Welche Vorteile bringt die Anpassbarkeit von Software Ihnen in Ihrem Arbeitsalltag? (Z. B. Produktivitätssteigerung) Beschreiben Sie ein konkretes Beispiel eines solchen Vorteils.

    3.5.2. Wie häufig haben Sie schon Anpassungen durchgeführt?

    3.5.3. Was bietet Ihre Software für Möglichkeiten/Hilfsmittel zur Anpassung?

    3.5.4. Wie oft war diese Anpassung erfolgreich?

    3.5.5. Wie lange brauchen Sie in etwas, um Ihre Software anzupassen?

    3.5.6. Führten die Anpassungen wirklich zu einer Arbeitserleichterung?

    3.5.7. Wie häufig kommt es vor, dass sie Anpassungen an der Software vornehmen möchten, aber nicht die Möglichkeit dazu haben?

    3.5.8. War die Anpassung auch für andere Beteiligte hilfreich oder nur für Sie alleine?

    3.5.9. Wollen Sie Anpassungen lieber in Eigenregie vornehmen oder durch eine autorisierte Fachperson durchführen lassen?

    3.5.10. Wie viel Aufwand würden Sie in Anpassungen investieren?

3.6. Nein-Zweig: Nutzer hat eine Software noch nicht selbst angepasst

    3.6.1. Was waren Hindernisgründe für eine Anpassung?

    3.6.2. Wie stellen Sie sich die Anpassung einer Software vor?

    3.6.3. Wären grundsätzlich bereit, Zeit in eine Anpassung zu investieren?

4. Anpassungskultur

    4.1. Werden Maßnahmen zur Anpassung von Kollegen oder der Geschäftsleitung eher ungern gesehen oder sogar unterstützt?

    4.2. Gibt es Anreize/Möglichkeiten, die Anpassungen an Andere weiterzugeben?

    4.3. Bei welcher Gelegenheit haben Sie zuletzt mit ihren Kollegen über Ihre Werkzeugnutzung gesprochen?

    4.4. Bei welcher Gelegenheit haben Sie zuletzt mit jemandem aus der IT Ihre Werkzeugnutzung gesprochen?

    4.5. Aus welchen Gründen denken sie über die Nutzung und Verbesserung Ihrer Anwendung nach?

    4.6. Haben Sie Ihre Nutzungspraxis einmal geändert, weil die Software ihre alte Praxis nicht gut unterstützt hat?

        4.6.1. Wie haben Sie diese Änderung nach einigen Tagen bewertet?

        4.6.2. Wie bewerten Sie diese heute?

    4.7. Bitte beschreiben Sie, wie Sie die Software ändern würden, damit diese besser zu Ihrer Arbeitspraxis zu passt? Wie viel Zeit würden Sie selber aufwenden, um die Software zu verbessern? *(Doppelte Fragenstellung (Verständnis-Block) beabsichtigt!)*

A 1.4 Expert Interview Guideline, Pre-Study Danske Bank

I. Introduction (Estimated time: 5-10 min.)

*   Organization Issues:
    o   The estimated length of the expert interview should be about 45 minutes to an hour.
    o   We would like to record the call to be able to hear important or missed details again. The record will be used anonymised. Is this ok for you?

*   Background and aim of the expert interview:
    o   The main focus of my thesis is to develop an interaction concept for a modelling environment that enables end users to participate in the development of business processes. The focus of my work is on processes in service-oriented architectures. Thus I want to create an end-user oriented interaction concept for the orchestration of web-services.
    o   To figure out how such an interaction concept has to be designed I want to understand how modelling/orchestration takes place in real practice, how and to what extend users from the departments are involved in the modelling of business processes and which relevance collaborative aspects have.

II. Expert Interview

1. Short information about personal data and organizational knowledge (5 min.)

*   What is your Job in the organization? / Where are you located within the organization?
*   In which department do you work and how many people work there?
*   What tasks do you typically have to process?
*   How long do you work for the company?

2. Understanding und type of processes (10 min.)

*   What is a process in your eyes? How would you define it?
    o   Do user interactions play a role in these processes?
    o   Is this process understanding shared in the whole organization?
*   What kind of processes do you model within the organization? (Automatic/user-centred)?
    o   How complex are those processes?
    o   How critical are they?
    o   Do you have any private processes?
*   Which problems are solved by the processes?
*   How many processes do you have in your organization?

3. Process Development (20-30 min.)

- Process Evolution (5 min.)
  Can you try to estimate how often processes and single services have to be changed?
- How often you create new processes?
- How long does it take to develop a typical process?
- How often are single services used in different processes?
- Process modelling (10-15 min.)

  o Is there some kind of model, which should be followed during the process?

  o Which persons are involved in the modelling process and which competencies do these persons have?

    - What contribute the departments?

    - What contributes the IT?

    - How much influence/power should the departments have in the development of processes?

    - How important is collaboration between the departments in the IT in the modeling process?

  o How do you capture requirements to model the process?

    - Which media and visual representations do you use when you talk with the users from the departments about the processes?

    - Do you also use whiteboards, paper, etc.?

    - In which spatial context does the modelling take place?

    - Is there a special formalism (e.g. modelling language xyz)?

    - Do you capture formal and/or informal aspects? How?

    - What is the result of the analysis? A process model?

  o Which tools and techniques are used to model?

    - What are the reasons for those tools?

    - (Do you use BPEL or BPMN?)

  o How detailed (how many aspects are included – exception handling, message flows, etc.) are the processes that you model?

  o What are typical problems during the modelling process?

  o To what extend do you think have users the ability to model processes?

- Process development (10 min.)

  o How does the transformation from requirements to process models work?

  o Does the process modelling have iterations?

  o What do you do, if the process is specified imprecise?

  o Is it possible to reuse parts of the processes in other processes?

  o Are processes/services are shared within the company?

o Which processes could be adapted by end users (from a business point of view)?

o Is there a kind of beta-testing?

- Feedback fort the design idea

o How would you imagine the modelling of processes on digital paper? (First give a short impression of our solution idea of paper-based modelling)

4. Technical details (10 min.)

- How good are services/interfaces documented?

o What is missing?

o Is there any user documentation?

- How do you know, which services exist? How does the "search process" work?

o Is there a central repository?

- Do you use internal and/or external services?

o Services are sliced according to which criteria?

- Think about a function that could recommend services? Would it be useful and why?

5. Reconcilement (5 min.)

- What are main differences between processes in your previous environment and your post-SOA environment?

148   Appendix

A 1.5 Interview Guideline, Evaluation, SiSO and PaSeMod

1. Was bietet das System? Was kann man mit dem System machen?

2. Wie ist generell Ihr "erster" Eindruck von diesem System? (Hat das System die Erwartungen erfüllt, die Sie im Vorfeld an ein solches System stellen?)

3. Wie war der Umgang mit dem System?

   a. War der Umgang mit dem System mit (vielen) Problemen behaftet?

   b. Konnten Sie die Aufgaben, die Sie mit dem System gelöst haben, ohne Umschweife lösen? Gab es vielleicht Probleme mit der Navigation?

   c. Präsentiert das System die Informationen klar und verständlich?

   d. Haben Sie das Gefühl, dass Sie Unterstützung benötigen, wenn Sie das System verwenden?

   e. Sind die Hinweise und Antworten durch das System hilfreich? Wie gut haben Ihnen insbesondere die Rückmeldungen des Systems genützt?

   f. Waren für Sie die Informationen und Interaktionselemente (wie Knöpfe, Menüs, etc.) verständlich?

   g. Konnten Sie ohne großen Aufwand Fehler korrigieren oder rückgängig machen?

4. Sehen Sie einen grundsätzlichen Bedarf nach einem solchen System (bei Ihnen selbst, bei Kollegen, in Ihrer Firma)?

5. Wie müsste ein solches System gestaltet sein/verbessert werden, damit Sie das System in Ihrem Arbeitsalltag nutzen (bzw. was wären die Voraussetzungen/Bedingungen)?

   a. Wie wichtig ist es, das ein solches System (im Arbeitsalltag) übersichtlich gestaltet und klar gegliedert ist?

6. (Wie) müssten die Prozesse oder Ihre Arbeitsaufgaben im Unternehmen verändert werden, damit ein solches System für Sie hilfreich und nutzbar wäre?

7. Meinen Sie, dass das System gut mit den anderen Systemen/Programmen zusammenarbeitet, die Sie sonst an Ihrem Arbeitsplatz nutzen?

8. Glauben Sie, dass die Bedürfnisse der Benutzer in diesem System berücksichtigt worden sind?

9. Gibt es etwas, dass Sie sich wünschen würden, was dieses System bis jetzt noch nicht bietet?

A 2 Questionnaires

A 2.1 Questionnaire, Pre-Study, Online Survey

Einleitung:

Sehr geehrte Teilnehmerin, sehr geehrter Teilnehmer,
auf den folgenden Seiten führt der Lehrstuhl „Wirtschaftsinformatik und Neue Medien" der Universität Siegen eine Online-Befragung zum Thema „Modellierung und Anpassung von Geschäftsprozessen" durch.

Die Befragung dient der Erprobung eines von unserem Lehrstuhl entwickelten Systems, das die Modellierung von Geschäftsprozessen ermöglicht. Diese Umfrage soll zum einen Aufschluss darüber geben, in welchen Bereichen dieses System eingesetzt werden kann und zum anderen in welchen Fällen ein konkreter Nutzen dadurch erzielt werden könnte.

Die Teilnahme erfolgt anonym, es werden daher keine personenspezifischen Daten erfasst. Die Ergebnisse der Studie dienen ausschließlich der wissenschaftlichen Forschung. Die Studie endet am dd.mm.yyyy.

Die Bearbeitungszeit des Fragebogens dauert in etwa 15 Minuten.

Vielen Dank für Ihre Teilnahme!

Fragen

1. Haben Sie schon einmal Erfahrungen mit der Beschreibung oder Modellierung von Geschäftsprozessen gesammelt?, Pflichtfeld

   1.1. Wenn Ja: Wie sahen Ihre Erfahrungen/Beschäftigungen mit Geschäftsprozessen genau aus? (Ich habe Prozessbeschreibungen gelesen, Ich habe Prozessbeschreibungen (mit) angefertigt, Ich habe Geschäftsprozesse optimiert, Ich habe Geschäftsprozesse in Software abgebildet, Andere, nämlich: [Freitext])

   1.2. Wie schwer ist es in der Regel, Geschäftsprozessbeschreibungen zu verstehen oder sie anzufertigen? (4 Punkte Bewertung: leicht, mittel, schwer, zu schwer)

   1.3. Wie waren diese Geschäftsprozesse beschrieben? (In einem Textdokument, In einer Tabelle, In einer Prozesssprache (z.B. Aris, BPMN))

      1.3.1. Wenn Prozesssprache: Welche Prozesssprache wurde verwendet? (Freitext), Pflichtfeld

      1.3.2. Wurde der Geschäftsprozess mit Hilfe einer Software beschrieben? (ja, nein, keine Angabe), Pflichtfeld

         1.3.2.1. Wenn ja: Welche Software wurde verwendet? (Freitext), Pflichtfeld

2. Haben Sie schon mal etwas am Computer programmiert (zum Beispiel mit Java, Visual Basic, C++, C#)? (ja, nein, keine Angabe), Pflichtfeld

3. Mit welchen dieser Programme arbeiten Sie regelmäßig in Ihrem Unternehmen (häufiger als 1 Mal im Monat)? (SAP, MS Navision, MS Excel 2000/2003/2007, MS Word 2000/2003/2007, MS Outlook 2000/2003/2007, Andere... [Freitext]), Pflichtfeld

4. Wie gut kennen Sie sich mit diesen Programmen aus? (gleiche Programme wie zuvor; 4 Punkte Bewertung von sehr gut – schlecht. + keine Angabe)

5. Geben Sie Kollegen Tipps bei der Nutzung von Programmen oder helfen Sie Ihren Kollegen, wenn diese Probleme mit einem der Programme haben, mit denen Sie sich gut auskennen? (Ja, nein)

    5.1. Wenn ja: Bei welchen Problemen/Programmen helfen Sie? (Freitext), Pflichtfeld

    5.2. Wie oft helfen Sie in etwa? (täglich, mehrmals wöchentlich, einmal wöchentlich, mindestens einmal monatlich, seltener), Pflichtfeld

    5.3. Ist diese Hilfe ein Teil Ihrer Arbeitsaufgaben, oder mehr eine Nettigkeit gegenüber den Kollegen? (Eher Teil meiner Pflichtaufgaben, eher eine Nettigkeit gegenüber den Kollegen), Pflichtfeld

6. Sind Sie SAP Key User in ihrem Unternehmen (Ja, Nein, keine Angabe)?, Pflichtfeld

7. Wie wichtig sind Geschäftprozessbeschreibungen in Ihrem Arbeitsalltag? (4 Punkte Bewertung + Keine Angabe), Pflichtfeld

8. Sind Sie an Geschäftsprozessbeschreibungen und -entwicklungen beteiligt? (ja, nein, keine Angabe), Pflichtfeld

    8.1. Wenn nein: Wer ist dafür zuständig? (Sie brauchen nur die entsprechende Position anzugeben.) (Freitext, keine Angabe), Pflichtfeld

    8.2. Wie wichtig ist es nach Ihrer Einschätzung, dass die Geschäftsprozesse formal beschrieben sind? (4 Punkte Bewertung + Keine Angabe), Pflichtfeld

    8.3. Wie werden diese Beschreibungen gegebenenfalls erstellt?

9. Kennen Sie Geschäftsprozesse aus Ihrem Unternehmen, an denen auch andere Abteilungen als Ihre eigene beteiligt sind? (Ja, nein)

10. Kennen Sie Geschäftsprozesse aus Ihrem Unternehmen, an denen auch andere Unternehmen mit beteiligt sind? (Ja, nein)

11. Werden Geschäftsprozesse in Ihrem Unternehmen mit Hilfe von Software abgebildet (z.B. in SAP)? (Ja, Nein, weiß nicht), Pflichtfeld

    11.1. Wenn ja: Wie sieht diese Abbildung genau aus? (Freitext), Pflichtfeld

    11.2. Mit welcher Software erfolgt die Abbildung?

12. Wie wichtig ist es in Ihren Augen, dass Sie Geschäftsprozesse in Software abbilden können? (4 Punkte Bewertung)

13. Würden Sie gerne selbst Einfluss auf die Abbildung von Geschäftsprozessen nehmen? (Ja, Nein), Pflichtfeld

    13.1. Wenn ja: In welcher Form würden Sie gerne Einfluss auf die Abbildung von Geschäftsprozessen nehmen? (Ich würde gerne bei der Beschreibung von Geschäftsprozessen mitwirken, Ich würde die Geschäftsprozesse gerne gemeinsam mit Beratern in die Software einpflegen, Ich würde die Geschäftsprozesse gerne mit Kollegen in die Software einpflegen, Ich würde die Geschäftsprozesse gerne selbst in die Software einpflegen), Multiple Choice, Pflichtfeld

    13.2. Würde die durch Sie beeinflusste Abbildung der Geschäftsprozesse in Software, in Ihren Augen zu einer Arbeitsoptimierung führen? (Ja, nein, Keine Angabe), Pflichtfeld

14. Kommt es im Allgemeinen gelegentlich vor, dass Sie Funktionen in Ihrer Software vermissen, oder manche Arbeiten nur sehr umständlich gelöst werden können? (ja, nein), Pflichtfeld

    14.1. Wenn ja: Wie häufig vermissen Sie Funktionen oder können Probleme nur umständlich lösen? (täglich, mehrmals wöchentlich, einmal wöchentlich, mindestens einmal monatlich, seltener)

    14.2. Welche der folgenden Beschreibungen treffen Ihre Probleme am besten? (Die Probleme hängen scheinbar mit der Darstellung am Bildschirm zusammen, Die Probleme scheinen nur zu existieren, weil mein Anwendungsfall sehr speziell ist, Die Probleme existieren scheinbar, weil der Softwarehersteller schlechte Arbeit geleistet hat, die Probleme scheinen zu entstehen, weil verschiedene Programme nicht gut miteinander zusammenarbeiten, andere ... [Freitext])

    14.3. Wie lösen Sie auftretende Probleme/Schwierigkeiten? (Ich finde meist selbst eine Lösung, Ich frage eine(n) Kollegen/Kollegin, Ich hole mir Hilfe von Außerhalb (z.B. von einem Berater), Ich finde eine Lösung im Internet, gar nicht), andere... Freitext

    14.4. Könnte Ihnen eine Anpassung von Software an Ihre speziellen Arbeitsaufgaben dabei helfen, einen Teil Ihrer Probleme zu lösen? (Ja, weil... / Nein, denn), Pflichtfeld

    14.5. Wäre es für Sie hilfreich, wenn Sie eine solche Software-Anpassung an Ihre Arbeitsaufgaben mit einfachen Mitteln selbst vornehmen könnten? (Ja, weil / Nein, denn)

15. Ihr Geschlecht (m, w, keine Angabe), Pflichtfeld

16. Ihr Alter (< 20, 20 - 30, 31 - 40, 41 - 50, > 50, keine Angabe), Pflichtfeld

17. Wie groß ist das Unternehmen in dem Sie arbeiten? (<10, <50, <250, <1000, < 10000)

18. Wie lange arbeiten Sie in Ihrem Unternehmen? (<1, 1-5, >5), Pflichtfeld

19. In welcher Abteilung arbeiten Sie? (Freitext), Pflichtfeld

20. Welche Ausbildung haben Sie? (Freitext, keine Angabe), Pflichtfeld

A 2.2 Questionnaire, Evaluation, SiSO's Redesigned Search System

1.   Participant number:

2.   Name of search engine:

3.   Starting time (When you are connected to the search engine, e.g., 3:45 p.m.): _____

4.   Search strategies: Please start searching on your topic. You must use at least three different strategies and record them as you go along. Choose the best strategy for your search by evaluating the relevancy of search results from each strategy. Check the box of the strategy that produces the best results.

Search strategy # 1 _____ ☐

Search strategy # 2 _____ ☐

Search strategy # 3 _____ ☐

Search strategy # 4 _____ ☐

Search strategy # 5 _____ ☐

5.   How many of the first 20 results of the best strategy are... relevant ____ partially relevant ____ not relevant ____

6.   Finishing time (When above tasks are completed): _____

7.   Evaluation of features of the search engine: Please give a satisfaction rating for each of the following system features and interaction and indicate your reasons for the particular rating:

Response time How satisfied are you with the time taken by the engine from the submission of a search command till the display of search results in response to your query?

Extremely unsatisfactory O 1 O 2 O 3 O 4 O 5 O 6 O 7 Extremely satisfactory
Reasons:_____

Search interface How satisfied are you with the search forms and commands provided by the engine?

Extremely unsatisfactory O 1 O 2 O 3 O 4 O 5 O 6 O 7 Extremely satisfactory
Reasons:_____

Online documentation How satisfied are you with online search help and instructions (e.g., database description, search tips, help, or FAQs)?

Extremely unsatisfactory O 1 O 2 O 3 O 4 O 5 O 6 O 7 Extremely satisfactory
Reasons:_____

Output display: How satisfied are you with the format and components of search output (e.g., abstract, URL, number of hits, relevance score, and hyperlinks, etc.)?

Extremely unsatisfactory O 1 O 2 O 3 O 4 O 5 O 6 O 7 Extremely satisfactory
Reasons:_____

Interaction How satisfied are you with the information exchange between you and the search engine in general or in particular related to some specific aspect of the search process?

Extremely unsatisfactory O 1 O 2 O 3 O 4 O 5 O 6 O 7 Extremely satisfactory
Reasons:_____

A 2.3 Post-Session Questionnaire, Evaluation, SiSO's Redesigned Search System

1.   Searcher's judgment concerning precision ratio. Please indicate your degree of satisfaction with the proportion of relevant services using a 7-point scale, 1 representing extremely unsatisfactory, and 7, extremely satisfactory.

SiSeOr-Searchsystem:
Extremely unsatisfactory O 1 O 2 O 3 O 4 O 5 O 6 O 7 Extremely satisfactory
Reasons:_____

seekda.com:
Extremely unsatisfactory O 1 O 2 O 3 O 4 O 5 O 6 O 7 Extremely satisfactory
Reasons:_____

2.   Time saving. Does using the engine to find services save you time?

SiSeOr-Searchsystem:
No time saving at all O 1 O 2 O 3 O 4 O 5 O 6 O 7 Saving me a lot of time

seekda.com:
No time saving at all O 1 O 2 O 3 O 4 O 5 O 6 O 7 Saving me a lot of time

3.   Searcher's judgment concerning value of search results as a whole. Taking the set of search results with summaries and other information, when available, as a whole, its value or usefulness in meeting your need or resolving your problem is:

SiSeOr-Searchsystem:
Extremely unsatisfactory O 1 O 2 O 3 O 4 O 5 O 6 O 7 Extremely satisfactory
Reasons:_____

seekda.com:
Extremely unsatisfactory O 1 O 2 O 3 O 4 O 5 O 6 O 7 Extremely satisfactory
Reasons:_____

4.   Overall performance (SUCCESS). Considering your experience in using the engine to retrieve information for your information problem, how would you rate the overall success of the engine in providing help for your information need or problem?

SiSeOr-Searchsystem:
Extremely unsatisfactory O 1 O 2 O 3 O 4 O 5 O 6 O 7 Extremely satisfactory
Reasons:_____

seekda.com:
Extremely unsatisfactory O 1 O 2 O 3 O 4 O 5 O 6 O 7 Extremely satisfactory
Reasons:_____

Thank you for your participation in this research project.

References

Abramowicz, W., Kaczmarek, M., Kowalkiewicz, M., and Zyskowski, D. "Architecture for Service Profiling," Proceedings of the IEEE Services Computing Workshops, IEEE Computer Society Press, (Chicago, IL, 2006), pp. 121 - 130.

Adamopoulos, D.X. "Enhancing Web Services in the Framework of Service-Oriented Architectures," Proceedings of the PDCAT '06, IEEE Computer Society Press, (Taipei, Taiwan, 2006), pp. 260 - 265.

Agostini, A., and Michelis, G.d. "A Light Workflow Management System Using Simple Process Models", Computer Supported Cooperative Work (9:3-4) 2000, pp. 335 - 363.

Agostini, A., Michelis, G.d., and Grasso, M.A. "Rethinking CSCWSystems: the Architecture of MILANO," Proceedings of the ECSCW '97, Kluwer Academic Publishers, (Lancaster, UK, 1997), pp. 33 - 48.

Aguilera, U., Abaitua, J., Diaz, J., Bujan, D., and Lopez de Ipina, D. "A Semantic Matching Algorithm for Discovery in UDDI," International Conference on Semantic Computing (ICSC 2007), IEEE Computer Society Press, (Irvine, CA, 2007), pp. 751 - 758.

Alda, S., Kuck, J., and Cremers, A.B. "Tailorability of personalized BPEL-based Workflow Compositions," IEEE Congress on Services, IEEE Computer Society Press, (Salt Lake City, UT, 2007), pp. 245 - 252.

Alvarez, F., Vaquero, A., Sáenz, F., and Buenaga, M.d. "Bringing Forward Semantic Relations: Issues and Proposals," International Conference on Intelligent Systems Design and Applications (ISDA '07), IEEE Computer Society Press, (Rio de Janeiro, Brazil, 2007), pp. 511-519.

Andersen, R., and Mørch, A. "Mutal Development," Proceedings of the Second International Symposium on End User Development, Springer, Berlin, LCNS, (Siegen, Germany, 2009), pp. 31 - 49.

Anderson, C. The Long Tail: Why the Future of Business Is Selling Less of More Hyperion Books, New York City, NY, 2006.

Åsand, H.-R.H., and Mørch, A.I. "Super Users and Local Developers: The Organization of End-User Development in an Accounting Company", Journal of Organizational and End User Computing (18:4) 2006, pp. 1 - 21.

Bandini, S., and Simone, C. "EUD as Integration of Components Off-the-Shelf," in: End User Development, H. Lieberman, F. Paternò and V. Wulf (eds.), Springer, Dordrecht, The Netherlands, 2006, pp. 358 - 380.

Bartonitz, M. "Wachsen die BPM- und Workflow-Lager zusammen," BPM-Netzwerk.de, http://www.bpm-netzwerk.de/articles/66, last access: 15.06.2009.

Baskerville, R.L. "Investigating Information Systems with Action Research", Communications of AIS, Article19 (2) 1999.

Baskerville, R.L., and Wood-Harper, A.T. "A Critical Perspective on Action Research as a Method for Information Systems Research", Journal of Information Technology (11) 1996, pp. 235 - 246.

Beaton, J., Jeong, S.Y., Xie, Y., Stylos, J., and Myers, B.A. "Usability challenges for enterprise service-oriented architecture APIs," IEEE Symposium on Visual Languages and Human-Centric Computing, VL/HCC 2008, IEEE Computer Society Press, (Herrsching am Ammersee, Germany, 2008), pp. 193 - 196.

Beringer, J. "Reducing Expertise Tension", Commun. ACM (47:9) 2004, pp. 39 - 40

Berners-Lee, T., Hendler, J., and Lassila, O. "The Semantic Web", Scientific American Magazine (Mai 2001) 2001, pp. 29 - 37.

Bernstein, M., Robinson-Mosher, A., Yeh, R., and Klemmer, S. "Diamond's Edge: From Notebook to Table and Back Again," Conference supplement to Ubicomp 2006 (Poster), ACM, (Irvine, CA, 2006).

Bianchini, D., Antonellis, V.D., Pernici, B., and Plebani, P. "Ontology-based methodology for e-service discovery", *Information Systems* (31:4) 2006, pp. 361 - 380.

Black, A. "Visible planning on paper and on screen: The impact of working medium on decision-making by novice graphic designers", *Behaviour & Information Technology* (9:4) 1990, pp. 283 - 296.

Blackwell, A.F. "First Steps in Programming: A Rationale for Attention Investment Models," Proceedings of the Symposium on Human Centric Computing Languages and Environments (HCC'02), IEEE Computer Society Press, (Washington, D.C., 2002), pp. 2 - 10.

Blomberg, J., Giacomi, J., Mosher, A., and Swenton-Wall, P. "Ethnographic field methods and their relation to design," in: *Participatory design: Principles and practices*, D. Schuler and A. Namioka (eds.), Lawrence Erlbaum Associates, Hillsdale, NJ, 1993.

Blomberg, J., Suchman, L., and Trigg, R.H. "Reflections on a Work-Oriented Design Project", *Human-Computer Interaction* (11:3) 1996, pp. 237 - 265.

Bødker, K., Kensing, F., and Simonsen, J. *Participatory IT design : designing for business and workplace realities* MIT Press, Cambridge, MA, 2004.

Bødker, S. "Creating conditions for participation: conflicts and resources in systems development", *Human-Computer Interaction* (11:3) 1996, pp. 215 - 236.

Boehm, B., Abts, C., Brown, A., Chulani, S., Clark, B., Horowitz, E., Madachy, R., Reifer, J., and Steece, B. *Software Cost Estimation with COCOMO II* Prentice Hall PTR, Upper Saddle River, NJ, 2000.

Borggräfe, B. "Papiergestützte Service-Modellierung für Endbenutzer," Diploma thesis, Fachbereich 5 – Wirtschaftswissenschaften, Wirtschaftsinformatik und Wirtschaftsrecht, Universität Siegen, Siegen, Germany, 2008.

Borggräfe, B., Dörner, C., Heß, J., and Pipek, V. "Drawing services: towards a paper-based interface for end-user service orchestration," Proceedings of the 4th international workshop on End-user software engineering, ACM, (Leipzig, Germany, 2008), pp. 66 - 70.

Bowen, P.L., Heales, J., and Vongphakdi, M.T. "Reliability factors in business software: volatility, requirements and end-users", *Information Systems Journal* (12:3) 2002, pp. 185 - 213.

Brahe, S. "BPM on top of SOA: Experiences from the Financial Industry," BPM 2007, Springer, Heidelberg, (Milano, Italy, 2007), pp. 96 - 111.

Brahe, S., and Schmidt, K. "The story of a working workflow management system," Proceedings of the CSCW '07, ACM, (Sanibel Island, FL, 2007), pp. 249 - 258.

Brancheau, J.C., and Brown, C.V. "The Management of End-User Computing: Status and Directions", *ACM Computing Surveys* (25:4) 1993, pp. 437 - 482.

Brooks, F.P.J. "No silver bullet: essence and accidents of software engineering", *IEEE Computer* (20:4) 1987, pp. 10 - 19.

Burnett, M. "What Is End-User Software Engineering and Why Does It Matter?," Second International Symposium on End-User Development, Springer, Berlin, LCNS, (Siegen, Germany, 2009), pp. 15 - 28.

Burnett, M., Cook, C., and Rothermel, G. "End-user software engineering", *Commun. ACM* (47:9) 2004, pp. 53 - 58.

Burstein, M., Bussler, C., Finin, T., Huhns, M.N., Paolucci, M., Sheth, A.P., Williams, S., and Zaremba, M. "A semantic Web services architecture", *IEEE Internet Computing* (9:5) 2005, pp. 72 - 81.

Carr, N.G. *Does IT Matter? Information Technology and the Corrosion of Competitive Advantage* Harvard Business School Press, Boston, MA, 2004.

Cervantes, H., and Hall, R.S. "Technical Concepts of Service Orientation," in: *Service-oriented Software System Engineering*, Z. Stojanović and A. Dahanayake (eds.), Idea Group Publishing, Hershey, PA, 2005, pp. 1 - 26.

Chang, C.W.E. "Atomserv Architecture: Towards Internet-scaled Service Publish, Subscription, and Discovery," International Conference on e-Business Engineering (ICEBE), IEEE Computer Society Press, (Shanghai, China, 2006), pp. 571 - 578.

Chen, Q., Grundy, J., and Hosking, J. "An e-whiteboard application to support early design-stage sketching of UML diagrams," Proceedings of the Symposium on Human Centric Computing Languages and Environments (HCC'03), IEEE Computer Society Press, (Auckland, New Zealand, 2003), pp. 219 - 226.

Chung, J.-Y., Lin, K.-J., and Mathieu, R.G. "Web services computing: advancing software interoperability", *IEEE Computer* (36:10) 2003, pp. 35 - 37.

Costabile, M.F., Fogli, D., Mussio, P., and Piccinno, A. "End-User Development: The Software Shaping Workshop Approach," in: *End User Development*, H. Lieberman, F. Paternò and V. Wulf (eds.), Springer, Dordrecht, The Netherlands, 2006, pp. 195 - 217.

Crabtree, A. "Design in the absence of practice: breaching experiments," Proceedings of the DIS '04, ACM, (Cambridge, MA, 2004), pp. 59 - 68.

Cypher, A. *Watch What I Do: Programming by Demonstration* MIT Press, Cambridge, MA, 1993.

Damm, C.H., Hansen, K.M., and Thomsen, M. "Tool support for cooperative object-oriented design: gesture based modelling on an electronic whiteboard," Proceedings of the CHI '00, ACM, (The Hague, The Netherlands, 2000), pp. 518 - 525.

David, J.S., Dunn, C.L., McCarthy, W.E., and Poston, R.S. "The Research Pyramid: A Framework for Accounting Information Systems Research", *Journal of Information Technology* (13:1) 1999, pp. 7-30.

Davis, F.D. "Perceived usefulness, perceived ease of use, and user acceptance of information technology", *MIS Quarterly* (13:3) 1989, pp. 319 - 340.

Davison, R.M., Ou, C.X.J., Li, M.Y., Martinsons, M.G., and Bjorksten, J. "The Multimethodological Investigation of Knowledge Sharing Practices in Eastwei," Proceedings of the ICIS '08, Paper 166, (Paris, France, 2008).

Deboeser, A. "Webservices steigern Effizienz," Computer Zeitung, September 8th 2008, p. 19.

Dittrich, Y., Lindeberg, O., and Lundberg, L. "End User Development as Adaptive Maintenance " in: *End-User Development* H. Lieberman, F. Paternò and V. Wulf (eds.), Springer, Dordrecht, The Netherlands, 2006, pp. 308 - 326.

Divitini, M., and Simone, C. "Supporting Different Dimensions of Adaptability in Workflow Modeling", *Computer Supported Cooperative Work* (9:3-4) 2000, pp. 365 - 397.

Donaldson, A., and Williamson, A. "Pen-based Input of UML Activity Diagrams for Business Process Modelling," Proceedings of the HCI 2005 Workshop on Improving and Assessing Pen-based Input Techniques, (Edinburgh, UK, 2005), pp. 31 - 38.

Dörner, C., Draxler, S., Pipek, V., and Wulf, V. "End Users at the Bazaar: Designing Next-Generation Enterprise-Resource-Planning Systems", *IEEE Software* (26:5) 2009, pp. 45 - 51.

Dörner, C., Heß, J., and Pipek, V. "Improving Information Systems by End User Development: A Case Study," Proceedings of the ECIS '07, University of St. Gallen, (St. Gallen, Switzerland, 2007), pp. 783 - 794.

Dörner, C., and Rohde, M. "Software-Anpassungspraxis von Kleinen und Mittelständischen Unternehmen", *HMD - Praxis der Wirtschaftsinformatik*, Heft 269, 2009, p. 87 - 95.

Dourish, P. "Implications for Design," Proceedings of the CHI '06, ACM, (Montréal, Québec, Canada, 2006), pp. 541 - 550.

Ehn, P., and Kyng, M. "The Collective Resource Approach to Systems Design," in: *Computers and Democracy - a Scandinavian Challenge,* G. Bjerknes, P. Ehn and M. Kyng (eds.), Avebury, Aldershot, UK, 1987, pp. 17 - 57.

Eisele, M., Kolb, R., Kraus, E., and Ehrenstein, C.v. "SAP NetWeaver: Slicing the fridge ", *Informatik Spektrum* (30:6) 2007, pp. 407 - 412.

Ennals, R., Brewer, E., Garofalakis, M., Shadle, M., and Gandhi, P. "Intel Mash Maker: join the web", *SIGMOD Rec.* (36:4) 2007, pp. 27 - 33.

Ericsson, K.A., and A.Simon, H. *Protocol analysis : verbal reports as data,* (2 ed.) MIT Press, Cambridge, MA, 1993.

Eriksson, J., and Dittrich, Y. "Combining Tailoring and Evolutionary Software Development for Rapidly Changing Business Systems", *Journal of Organizational and End User Computing* (19:2) 2007, pp. 47 - 64.

Esteves, J., and Pastor, J. "Enterprise Resource Planning Systems Research: An Annotated Bibliography", *Communications of AIS* (7:8) 2001, pp. 2 - 54.

Faustmann, G. "Configuration for Adaptation – A Human-centered Approach to Flexible Workflow Enactment", *Computer Supported Cooperative Work* (9:3-4) 2000, pp. 413 - 434.

Feurer, S. "Enterprise Architecture – IT meets Business," SAP Deutschland AG & Co. KG, https://www.sdn.sap.com/irj/scn/go/portal/prtroot/docs/library/uuid/403fd993-56d9-2910-eaa4-9c5bcd1b82d, last access: 15.06.2009.

Fischer, G. "Seeding, Evolutionary Growth and Reseeding: Constructing, Capturing and Evolving Knowledge in Domain-Oriented Design Environments", *Automated Software Engineering* (5:4) 1998, pp. 447 - 464.

Fischer, G. "End-User Development and Meta-Design: Foundations for Cultures of Participation," Proceedings of the Second International Symposium on End User Development, Springer, Berlin, LCNS, (Siegen, Germany, 2009), pp. 3 - 14.

Fischer, G., and Giaccardi, E. "Meta-Design: A Framework for the Future of EUD," in: *End User Development,* H. Lieberman, F. Paternò and V. Wulf (eds.), Springer, Dordrecht, The Netherlands, 2006, pp. 427 - 457.

Fischer, G., Giaccardi, E., Ye, Y., Sutcliffe, A.G., and Mehandjiev, N. "Meta-design: a manifesto for end-user development", *Commun. ACM* (47:9) 2004a, pp. 33 - 37.

Fischer, G., and Girgensohn, A. "End-User Modifiability in Design Environments," Proceedings of CHI '90, (Seattle, WA, 1990), pp. 183 - 191.

Fischer, G., Grudin, J., McCall, R., Ostwald, J., Redmiles, D., Reeves, B., and Shipman, F. "Seeding, Evolutionary Growth and Reseeding: The Incremental Development of Collaborative Design Environments," in: *Coordination Theory and Collaboration Technology,* G. Olson, T. Malone and J. Smith (eds.), Lawrence Erlbaum Associates, Mahwah, NJ, 2001, pp. 447 - 472.

Fischer, G., McCall, R., Ostwald, J., Reeves, B., and Shipman, F. "Seeding, evolutionary growth and reseeding: supporting the incremental development of design environments," Proceedings of the CHI '94, ACM, 1994), pp. 292 - 298.

Fischer, G., and Scharff, E. "Meta-design: design for designers," Proceedings of the DIS '00, ACM, (New York City, NY, 2000), pp. 396 - 405.

Fischer, G., Scharff, E., and Ye, Y. "Fostering Social Creativity by Increasing Social Capital," in: *Social Capital and Information Technology* M. Huysman and V. Wulf (eds.), MIT Press, Cambridge, MA, 2002, pp. 355 - 399.

Fischer, G., Scharff, E., and Ye, Y. "Fostering Social Creativity by Increasing Social Capital," in: *Social Capital and Information Technology*, M. Huysman and V. Wulf (eds.), MIT Press, Cambridge, MA, 2004b, pp. 355 - 399.

Fischer, L. *Workflow Handbook 2001* Future Strategies, Lighthouse Point, FL, 2000.

Floyd J. Fowler, J. *Survey Research Methods*, (3 ed.) Sage Publications, Thousand Oaks, CA, 2002.

Friedman, T.L. *The World Is Flat: A Brief History of the Twenty-First Century*, (2 ed.) Farrar, Straus and Giroux, New York City, NY, 2006.

Gallivan, M.J., and Keil, M. "The user–developer communication process: a critical case study", *Information Systems Journal* (13:1) 2003, pp. 37 - 68.

Gantt, M., and Nardi, B.A. "Gardeners and gurus: patterns of cooperation among CAD users," Proceedings of the CHI '92, ACM, (Monterey, CA, 1992), pp. 107 - 117.

Germonprez, M., Hovorka, D., and Collopy, F. "A Theory of Tailorable Technology Design", *JAIS* (8:6) 2007, pp. 351 - 367.

Gold, N., Mohan, A., Knight, C., and Munro, M. "Understanding service-oriented software", *IEEE Software* (21:2) 2004, pp. 71 - 77.

Golombek, B. "Implementierung und Evaluation der Konzepte 'Explorative Ausführbarkeit' und 'Direkte Aktivierbarkeit' für anpassbare Groupware," Master thesis, Mathematisch-Naturwissenschaftliche Fakultät, Universität Bonn, Bonn, Germany, 2000.

Green, T.R.G., and Petre, M. "Usability analysis of visual programming environments: a "cognitive dimensions" framework", *Journal of Visual Languages and Computing* (7:2) 1996, pp. 131-174.

Gurram, R., Mo, B., and Gueldemeister, R. "A Web Based Mashup Platform for Enterprise 2.0," in: *WISE 2008, LCNS 5176* S. Hartmann (ed.), Springer, Berlin, Germany, 2008, pp. 144 - 151.

Harper, R., Hughes, J.A., and Shapiro, D.Z. "Working in harmony: An examination of computer technology in air traffic control," Proceedings of the ECSCW' 89, Computer Sciences House, (Gatwick, London, UK, 1989), pp. 73 - 86.

Harrison, W. "The Dangers of End-User Programming", *IEEE Computer* (21:4) 2004, pp. 5 -7.

Heath, C., and Luff, P. "Collaboration and Control: Crisis Management and Multimedia Technology in London Underground Control Rooms", *Computer Supported Cooperative Work* (1:1) 1992, pp. 69 - 94.

Henderson, A., and Kyng, M. "There's no place like home: continuing design in use," in: *Design at Work: Cooperative Design of Computer Systems* J. Greenbaum and M. Kyng (eds.), Lawrence Erlbaum Associates, Boston, MA, 1991, pp. 219 - 240.

Henn, C. "Der Graben zwischen IT und Fachabteilung schließt sich," Computer Zeitung, October 27th 2007, p. 16.

Hevner, A.R., March, S.T., Park, J., and Ram, S. "Design Science in Information Systems Research", *MIS Quarterly* (28:1) 2004, pp. 75 - 105.

Hofmann, M., Ley, B., and Dörner, C. "Endbenuztergerechte Anpassung von serviceorientierten Softwaresystemen," Proceedings of the MKWI 2008, TU Munich, (Munich, Germany, 2008).

Hoyer, V., Stanoesvka-Slabeva, K., Janner, T., and Schroth, C. "Enterprise Mashups: Design Principles towards the Long Tail of User Needs," IEEE International Conference on Services Computing, IEEE Computer Society Press, (Honolulu, HI, 2008), pp. 601 - 602.

Hughes, J., King, V., Rodden, T., and Andersen, H. "Moving Out from the Control Room: Ethnography in System Design," Proceedings of the CSCW '94, ACM, (Chapel Hill, NC, 1994), pp. 429 - 439.

Hughes, J.A., Randall, D., and Shapiro, D. "Faltering from ethnography to design," Proceedings of the CSCW '92, ACM, (Toronto, Ontario, Canada, 1992), pp. 115 - 122.

Hummes, J., and Merialdo, B. "Design of Extensible Component-Based Groupware", *Computer Supported Cooperative Work* (9:1) 2000, pp. 53 - 74.

Iacucci, G., Pipek, V., Jacucci, G., and Kuutti, K. "Continuing Design in Use of Tangible Computing Environments," The Good, the Bad and the Irrelevant - The User and the Future of Information and Communication Technogy (COST 269 conference), (Helsinki, Finnland, 2003), pp. 209 - 216.

Jeong, S.Y., Xie, Y., Beaton, J., Myers, B.A., Stylos, J., Ehret, R., Karstens, J., Efeoglu, A., and Busse, D.K. "Improving Documentation for eSOA APIs through User Studies," Second International Symposium on End-User Development, Springer, Berlin, LCNS, (Siegen, Germany, 2009), pp. 86 - 105.

Kahler, H. "From Taylorism to Tailorability: Supporting Organisations with Tailorable Software and Object Orientation," Proceedings of the HCI '95, Elsevier, (Tokyo, Japan, 1995), pp. 995 - 1000.

Kahler, H. "Supporting Collaborative Tailoring, Department of Communication, Journalism and Computer Science, Roskilde University, Roskilde, Denmark, 2001.

Kaplan, B., and Maxwell, J.A. "Qualitative Research Methods for Evaluating Computer Information Systems," in: *Evaluating Health Care Information Systems: Methods and Applications,* J.G. Anderson, C.E. Aydin and S.J. Jay (eds.), Sage Publications, Thousand Oaks, CA, 1994, pp. 45 - 68.

Kawalek, P., and Leonard, J. "Evolutionary software development to support organizational and business process change: a case study account", *Journal of Information Technology* (11:3) 1996, pp. 185 - 198.

Kawamura, T., Hasegawa, T., Ohsuga, A., Paolucci, M., and Sycara, K. "Web services lookup: a matchmaker experiment", *IT Professional* (7:2) 2005, pp. 36 - 41.

Kieser, A., and Ebers, M. *Organisationstheorien*, (6 ed.) Kohlhammer, Stuttgart, Germany, 2006.

Klann, M., Paternò, F., and Wulf, V. "Future Perspectives in End-User Development," in: *End User Development,* H. Lieberman, F. Paternò and V. Wulf (eds.), Springer, Berlin, Germany, 2006, pp. 481 - 492.

Krafzig, D., Banke, K., and Slama, D. *Enterprise SOA : service-oriented architecture best practices* Prentice Hall PTR, Indianapolis, IN, 2005.

Kumar, K., and Hillegersberg, J.v. "ERP Experiences and Evolution", *Commun. ACM* (43:4) 2000, pp. 23 - 26.

Kvale, S. *Interviews: an introduction to qualitative research interviewing* Sage Publications, Thousand Oaks, CA, 1996.

Kyng, M. "Scandinavian design: users in product development," Proceedings of the CHI '94, ACM, (Boston, MA, 1994), pp. 3 - 9.

Landay, J.A., and Myers, B.A. "Interactive sketching for the early stages of user interface design," Proceedings of the CHI '95, ACM, (Denver, CO, 1995), pp. 43 - 50.

Landay, J.A., and Myers, B.A. "Sketching Interfaces: Toward More Human Interface Design", *IEEE Computer* (34:3) 2001, pp. 56 - 64.

Leadbeater, C., and Miller, P. *The Pro-Am Revolution: How Enthusiasts are Changing Our Society and Economy* Demos, London, UK, 2004.

Legner, C., and Wende, K. "The Challenges of Inter-organizational Business Process Design - a Research Agenda," Proceedings of the ECIS '07, University of St. Gallen, (St. Gallen, Switzerland, 2007), pp. 1643 - 1654.

Leymann, F., and Roller, D. *Production Workflow: Concepts and Techniques* Prentice Hall PTR, London, UK, 2000.

Liao, C., Guimbretièr, F., and Hinckley, K. "Papiercraft: a command system for interactive paper," Proceedings of the 18th Symposium on User interface software and technology, ACM, (Seattle, WA, 2005), pp. 241 - 244.

Lieberman, H. *Your Wish Is My Command: Programming by Example* Morgan Kaufmann, San Fransisco, CA, 2001.

Lieberman, H., Paternò, F., and Wulf, V. *End User Development* Springer, Dordrecht, The Netherlands, 2006.

Lin, J., Wong, J., Nichols, J., Cypher, A., and Lau, T.A. "End-user programming of mashups with vegemite," Proceedings of the 13th international conference on Intelligent user interfaces, ACM, (Sanibel Island, FL, 2009), pp. 97 - 106.

Linn, C. "Semantic Reliability in Distributed Systems: Ontology Issues and System Engineering," IEEE/WIC International Conference on Web Intelligence (WI '03), IEEE Computer Society Press, (Halifax, Canada, 2003), pp. 292 - 300.

Little, G., Lau, T.A., Cypher, A., Lin, J., Haber, E.M., and Kandogan, E. "Koala: capture, share, automate, personalize business processes on the web," Proceedings of the CHI '07, ACM, 2007), pp. 943 - 946.

Liu, X., Huang, G., and Mei, H. "Towards End User Service Composition," Computer Software and Applications Conference, COMPSAC 2007, (Beijing, China, 2007), pp. 676 - 678.

Liu, Y., Zhuang, M., Wang, Q., and Wang, H. "A novel approach for service capabilities representation based on statistical study on WSDL," Third International Conference on Internet and Web Applications and Services (ICIW '08), IEEE Computer Society Press, (Athens, Greece, 2008), pp. 97 - 102.

Ma, K.J. "Web Services: What's Real and What's Not?" *IT Professional* (7:2) 2005, pp. 14 - 21.

Mackay, W.E. "Patterns of sharing customizable software," Proceedings of the CSCW '90, ACM, (Los Angeles, CA, 1990), pp. 209 - 221.

MacLean, A., Carter, K., Lövstrand, L., and Moran, T. "User-tailorable systems: pressing issues with buttons," Proceedings of the CHI '90, ACM, (Seattle, WA, 1990), pp. 175 - 182.

Malone, T.W., Lai, K.-Y., and Fry, C. "Experiments with Oval: a radically tailorable tool for cooperative work", *ACM Transactions on Information Systems* (13:2) 1995, pp. 177 - 205.

March, S.T., and Smith, G.F. "Design and Natural Science Research on Information Technology", *Decision Support Systems* (15:4) 1995, pp. 251 - 266.

Markus, M.L., Petrie, D., and Axline, S. "Bucking the Trends: What the Future May Hold for ERP Packages", *Information Systems Frontiers* (2:2) 2000, pp. 181 - 193.

McKean, E. *The new Oxford American dictionary* Oxford University Press, Oxford, UK, 2005.

Medina-Mora, R., Winograd, T., Flores, R., and Flores, F. "The action workflow approach to workflow management technology," Proceedings of the CSCW '92, ACM, (Toronto, Ontario, Canada, 1992), pp. 281 - 288.

Mehandjiev, N. "User Enhanceability for Information Systems through Visual Programming," PhD thesis, University of Hull, Hull, UK, 1997.

Mehandjiev, N., and Bottaci, L. "User-enhanceability for organizational information systems through visual programming," CAiSE '96, Springer, Berlin, LCNS, (Heraklion, Crete, Greece, 1996), pp. 432 - 456.

Melão, N., and Pidd, M. "A conceptual framework for understanding business processes and business process modelling", *Information Systems Journal* (10:2) 2000, pp. 105 - 129.

Merton, R.K., and Kendall, P.L. "The focused interview", *American Journal of Sociology* (51) 1946, pp. 541 - 557.

Miles, M.B., and Huberman, A.M. *Qualitative data analysis: An expanted sourcebook*, (2 ed.) Sage Publications, Thousand Oaks, CA, 1994.

Mingers, J. "Combining IS Research Methods: Towards a Pluralist Methodology", *Information Systems Research* (12:3) 2001, pp. 240 - 259.

Mintert, S. "Implementierung von Webservices - REST vs. SOAP?" *Wirtschaftsinformatik* (47:1) 2005, pp. 63 - 65.

Mocan, A., Moran, M., Cimpian, E., and Zaremba, M. "Filling the Gap - Extending Service Oriented Architectures with Semantics," International Conference on e-Business Engineering (ICEBE), IEEE Computer Society Press, (Shanghai, China, 2006), pp. 594 - 601.

Mørch, A., and Mehandjiev, N.D. "Tailoring as Collaboration: The Mediating Role of Multiple Representations and Application Units", *Computer Supported Cooperative Work* (9:1) 2000, pp. 75-100.

Mørch, A.I. "Three Levels of End-user Tailoring: Customization, Integration and Extension," in: *Computers and Design in Context,* M. Kyng and L. Mathiassen (eds.), MIT Press, Cambridge, MA, 1997, pp. 51 - 76.

Muller, M.J. "PICTIVE - an exploration in participatory design," Proceedings of the CHI '91, ACM, (New Orleans, LA, 1991), pp. 225 - 231.

Muller, M.J. "Retrospective on a year of participatory design using the PICTIVE technique," Proceedings of the CHI '92, ACM, (Monterey, CA, 1992), pp. 455 - 462.

Muller, M.J. "Participatory Design: The third space in HCI," in: *The Human-computer Interaction Handbook: Fundamentals, Evolving Technologies, and Emerging Applications,* J.A. Jacko and A. Sears (eds.), Lawrence Erlbaum Associates, Mahwah, NJ, 2003, pp. 1052 - 1065.

Myers, B.A., Pane, J.F., and Ko, A. "Natural programming languages and environments", *Commun. ACM* (47:9) 2004, pp. 47 - 52.

Myers, M.D. "Qualitative Research in Information Systems", *MIS Quarterly* (21:2) 1997, pp. 241 - 242.

Myers, M.D. "Investigating Information Systems with Ethnographic Research", *Communications of AIS, Article 23* (2) 1999, pp. 1 - 20.

Myers, M.D. *Qualitative Research in Business & Management* Sage Publications, London, UK, 2009.

Nakagawa, M., Kato, N., Machii, K., and Souya, T. "Principles of pen interface design for creative work," Proceedings of the Second International Conference on Document Analysis and Recognition, IEEE Computer Society Press, (Tsukuba Science City, Japan, 1993), pp. 718 - 721.

Nardi, B.A. *A small matter of programming: perspectives on end user computing* MIT Press, Cambridge, MA, 1993.

Nardi, B.A., and Miller, J.R. "Twinkling lights and nested loops: distributed problem solving and spreadsheet development", *International Journal of Man-Machine Studies* (34:2) 1991, pp. 161 - 184.

Niehaves, B. "On Episemological Diversity in Design Science: New Vistas for a Design-Oriented IS Research?," Proceedings of the ICIS '07, Paper 133, (Montréal, Québec, Canada, 2007).

Nielsen, J. *Usability Engineering* Academic Press Ltd., London, UK, 1993.

Oberquelle, H. "Situationsbedingte und benutzerorientierte Anpaßbarkeit von Groupware," in: *Menschengerechte Groupware - Software-ergonomische Gestaltung und partizipative Umsetzung,* A. Hartmann, T. Hermann, M. Rohde and V. Wulf (eds.), Teubner, Stuttgart, Germany, 1994, pp. 31 - 50.

Orlikowski, W., and Baroudi, J. "Studying information technology in organizations: Research approaches and assumptions", *Information Systems Research* (2:1) 1991, pp. 1 - 28.

Orlikowski, W.J. "The Duality of Technology: Rethinking the Concept of Technology in Organizations", *Organization Science* (3:3) 1992, pp. 398 - 427.

Oviatt, S. "Human-centered design meets cognitive load theory: designing interfaces that help people think," Proceedings of the 14th International conference on Multimedia, ACM, (Santa Barbara, CA, 2006), pp. 871-880.

Paczynski, F. "Vereinfachte Modifikation serviceorientierter Software durch Abstraktion und Transformation am Beispiel von Web Services," Diploma thesis, Fachbereich 5 – Wirtschaftswissenschaften, Wirtschaftsinformatik und Wirtschaftsrecht, Universität Siegen, Siegen, Germany, 2008.

Paetau, M. "Configurative technology: adaptation to social systems dynamism," in: *Adaptive User Support: Ergonomic Design of Manually and Automatically Adaptable Software,* R. Oppermann (ed.), Lawrence Erlbaum Associates, Hillsdale, NJ, 1994, pp. 194 - 234.

Palvia, P., En Mao, P., Salam, A.F., and Soliman, K.S. "Management Information Systems Research: Whats There in a Methodology?" *Communications of AIS* (11) 2003, pp. 289 - 308.

Palvia, P., Leary, D., En, M., Midha, V., Pinjani, P., and Salam, A. "Research Methodologies in MIS: an Update", *Communications of AIS* (14) 2004, pp. 526 - 542.

Pandit, N.R. "The Creation of Theory: A Recent Application of the Grounded Theory Model", *The Qualitative Report* (2:4) 1996.

Pane, J.F., and Myers, B.A. "More Natural Programming Languages and Environments," in: *End User Development,* H. Lieberman, F. Paternò and V. Wulf (eds.), Springer, Berlin, Germany, 2006, pp. 39 - 58.

Panko, R.R. "What we know about spreadsheet errors", *Journal of End User Computing* (10:2) 1998, pp. 15 - 21.

Paolucci, M., Kawamura, T., Payne, T.R., and Sycara, K. "Semantic Matching of Web Services Capabilities," First International Semantic Web Conference, Springer, Berlin, LCNS, (Sardinia, Italy, 2002), pp. 333 - 347.

Papert, S.A. *Mindstorms: Children, Computers and Powerful Ideas* Basic Books, New York City, NY, 1980.

Pasley, J. "How BPEL and SOA are Changing Web Services Development", *IEEE Internet Computing* (9:3) 2005, pp. 60 - 67.

Peltz, C. "Web services orchestration and choreography", *IEEE Computer* (36:10) 2003, pp. 46 - 52.

Pfeiffer, S., Ritter, T., and Treske, E. *Work Based Usability Produktionsmitarbeiter gestalten ERP-Systeme 'von unten' - Eine Handreichung* ISF aktuell, Munich, Germany, 2008.

Pipek, V. "From Tailoring to Appropriation Support: Negotiating Groupware Usage," PhD thesis, Department of Information Processing Science, University of Oulu, Oulu, Finland, 2005.

Pipek, V., and Kahler, H. "Supporting Collaborative Tailoring," in: *End User Development,* H. Lieberman, F. Paternò and V. Wulf (eds.), Springer, Dordrecht, The Netherlands, 2006, pp. 327 - 355.

Pipek, V., Rosson, M.B., Ruyter, B.d., and Wulf, V. *Proceedings of the Second International Symposium on End User Development* Springer, Berlin, Germany, 2009.

Pipek, V., and Syrjänen, A.L. "'Infrastructuring' as Capturing In-Situ Design," 7th Mediterranean Conference on Information Systems, AIS, (Venice, Italy, 2006).

Pipek, V., and Wulf, V. "Infrastructuring: Towards an Integrated Perspective on the Design and Use of Information Technology ", *JAIS* (10:5) 2009, pp. 447 - 473.

Powell, A., and Moore, J.E. "The Focus of Research in End User Computing: Where Have We Come Since the 1980s?" *Journal of End User Computing* (14:1) 2002, pp. 3 - 22.

Randall, D., Harper, R., and Rouncefield, M. *Fieldwork for design: Theory and Practice* Springer, New York City, NY, 2007.

Rapoport, R.N. "Three Dilemmas in Action Research", *Human Relations* (23:6) 1970, pp. 499 - 513.

Reichling, T., Veith, M., and Wulf, V. "Expert Recommender: Designing for a Network Organization", *Computer Supported Cooperative Work: The Journal of Collaborative Computing (JCSCW)* (16:4) 2007, pp. 431 - 465.

Repenning, A., and Ioannidou, A. "What makes End-User development Tick? 13 Design Guidelines," in: *End User Development* H. Lieberman, F. Paternò and V. Wulf (eds.), Springer, Dordrecht, The Netherlands, 2006, pp. 59 - 98.

Rettig, C. "The Trouble with Enterprise Software", *MIT Sloan Management Review* (49:1) 2007, pp. 21 - 27.

Rittel, H., and Webber, M.M. "Planning Problems are Wicked Problems," in: *Developments in Design Methodology,* N. Cross (ed.), John Wiley and Sons, Chichester, UK, 1984, pp. 135 - 144.

Robson, C. *Real world Research: a resource for social scientists and practitioner-researchers* (2 ed.) Blackwell Publishers, Oxford, UK, 2002.

Rohde, M. "Integrated organization and technology development (OTD) and the impact of socio-cultural concepts: a CSCW perspective," PhD thesis, Department of Computer Science, Roskilde University, Roskilde, Denmark, 2007.

Rohde, M., Stevens, G., Brödner, P., and Wulf, V. "Towards a paradigmatic shift in IS: designing for social practice," Proceedings of the 4th International Conference on Design Science Research in Information Systems and Technology, ACM, (Philadelphia, PA, 2009), pp. 1 - 11.

Scaffidi, C., Shaw, M., and Myers, B. "Estimating the Numbers of End Users and End User Programmers," Proceedings of the VL/HCC'05, (Dallas, TX, 2005), pp. 207 - 214.

Schmidt, C. "Analyse von Leitfadeninterviews," in: *Qualitative Forschung: Ein Handbuch,* U. Flick, E.v. Kardorff and I. Steinke (eds.), Rowohlt Taschenbuch Verlag, Hamburg, 2003, pp. 447 - 456.

Schmidt, K. "Riding a tiger, or computer supported cooperative work," Proceedings of the ECSCW '91, Kluwer Academic Publishers, (Amsterdam, The Netherlands, 1991), pp. 1 - 16.

Schmidt, K. "Of Maps and Scripts - The Status of Formal Constructs in Cooperative Work," Proceedings of the GROUP '97, ACM, (Phoenix, AZ, 1997), pp. 138 - 147.

Schroth, C., and Janner, T. "Web 2.0 and SOA: Converging Concepts Enabling the Internet of Services", *IT Professional* (9:3) 2007, pp. 36 - 41.

Sellen, A.J., and Harper, R.H.R. *The myth of the paperless office* MIT Press, Cambridge, MA, 2002.

Shi, X. "Sharing service semantics using SOAP-based and REST Web services", *IT Professional* (8:2) 2006, pp. 18 - 24.

Silver, B. "SAP NetWeaver BPM White Paper," Report Number, Bruce Silver Associates, Aptos, CA, pp. 1 - 18.

Simon, H. *The Sciences of the Artificial*, (3 ed.) MIT Press, Cambridge, MA, 1996.

Sirin, E., Parsia, B., and Hendler, J. "Filtering and Selecting Semantic Web Services with Interactive Composition Techniques", *IEEE Intelligent Systems* (19:4) 2004, pp. 42 - 49.

Song, H., Guimbretière, F., Hu, C., and Lipson, H. "ModelCraft: capturing freehand annotations and edits on physical 3D models," Proceedings of the 19th Symposium on User interface software and technology, ACM, (Montreux, Switzerland, 2006), pp. 13 - 22.

Spahn, M., Dörner, C., and Wulf, V. "End User Development of Information Artefacts: A Design Challenge for Enterprise Systems," Proceedings of the ECIS '08, National University of Ireland, Galway, (Galway, Ireland, 2008a), pp. 303 - 314.

Spahn, M., Dörner, C., and Wulf, V. "End User Development: Approaches Towards a Flexible Software Design," Proceedings of the ECIS '08, National University of Ireland, Galway, (Galway, Ireland, 2008b), pp. 482 - 493.

Spierling, D. "Die SOA ist die Perestroika der Softwareindustrie," Computer Zeitung, June 2nd 2008, p. 11.

Spillner, J. "Entwicklung eines Editors zum Entwurf von Benutzerschnittstellen für Web Services auf Basis der abstrakten UI-Beschreibungssprache WSGUI," Diploma thesis, Technische Universität Dresden, Dresden, Germany, 2006.

Sprott, D. "Enterprise resource planning: componentizing the enterprise application packages", *Commun. ACM* (43:4) 2000, pp. 63 - 69.

Stal, M. "Using architectural patterns and blueprints for service-oriented architecture", *IEEE Software* (23:2) 2006, pp. 54 - 61.

Stevens, G., Quaisser, G., and Klann, M. "Breakin It Up: An industrial case study of component-based tailorable software design," in: *End User Development*, H. Lieberman, F. Paternò and V. Wulf (eds.), Springer, Dordrecht, The Netherlands, 2006, pp. 269 - 294.

Stiemerling, O. "Component-Based Tailorability," PhD thesis, Mathematisch-Naturwissenschaftliche Fakultät, Universität Bonn, Bonn, Germany, 2000.

Stiemerling, O., Kahler, H., and Wulf, V. "How to make software softer — designing tailorable applications," Proceedings of the DIS '97, ACM, (Amsterdam, The Netherlands, 1997), pp. 365 - 376.

Strauss, A., and Corbin, J. *Basics of Qualitative Research: Techniques and procedures for developing grounded theory*, (2 ed.) Sage Publications, Thousand Oaks, CA, 1998.

Su, L.T. "A comprehensive and systematic model of user evaluation of web search engines: I. theory and background", *J. Am. Soc. Inf. Sci. Technol.* (54:13) 2003a, pp. 1175 - 1192.

Su, L.T. "A comprehensive and systematic model of user evaluation of web search engines: II. an evaluation by undergraduates", *J. Am. Soc. Inf. Sci. Technol.* (54:13) 2003b, pp. 1193 - 1223.

Subrahmonia, J., and Zimmerman, T. "Pen Computing: Challenges and Applications," 15th International Conference on Pattern Recognition (ICPR'00), IEEE Computer Society Press, (Barcelona, Spain, 2003), p. 2060.

Suchman, L. "Systematics of office work: Office studies for knowledge-based systems," Proceedings of the Office Automation Conference '82, ACM, (San Francisco, CA, 1982), pp. 409 - 412.

Suchman, L. *Plans and Situated Actions: The Problem of Human-Machine Communication* Cambridge University Press, Cambridge, UK, 1987.

Susman, G., and Evered, R. "An Assessment of The Scientific Merits of Action Research", *Administrative Science Quarterly* (23:4) 1978, pp. 582 - 603.

Sutcliffe, A., and Mahandjiev, N. "End-User Development", *Commun. ACM* (47:9) 2004, pp. 31 - 32.

Szyperski, C. *Component Software: Beyond Object Oriented Programming*, (2 ed.) Addison-Wesley, New York City, NY, 2002.

Tapscott, D., and Williams, A.D. *Wikinomics: How Mass Collaboration Changes Everything* Penguin Group, New York City, NY, 2006.

Taylor-Cummings, A. "Bridging the user-IS gap: a study of major information systems projects", *Journal of Information Technology* (13:1) 1998, pp. 29 - 54.

Teege, G. "Users as Composers: Parts and Features as a Basis for Tailorability in CSCW Systems", *Computer Supported Cooperative Work* (9:1) 2000, pp. 101 - 122.

Theelen, T. "Entwicklung eines Suchsystems für Webservices," Diploma thesis, Fachbereich 5 – Wirtschaftswissenschaften, Wirtschaftsinformatik und Wirtschaftsrecht, Universität Siegen, Siegen, Germany, 2009.

Tian, F., Xu, L., Wang, H., Zhang, X., Liu, Y., Setlur, V., and Dai, G. "Tilt menu: using the 3D orientation information of pen devices to extend the selection capability of pen-based user interfaces," Proceedings of the CHI '08, ACM, (Florence, Italy, 2008), pp. 1371 - 1380.

Turner, M., Budgen, D., and Brereton, P. "Turning Software into a Service", *IEEE Computer* (36:10) 2003, pp. 38 - 44.

Ulrich, W. *Critical Heuristics of Social Planning* John Wiley and Sons, Chichester, UK, 1994.

van der Aalst, W.M.P., Hofstede, A.H.M.t., Kiepuszewski, B., and Barros, A.P. "Workflow Patterns", *Distributed and Parallel Databases* (14:1) 2003a, pp. 5 - 51.

van der Aalst, W.M.P., ter Hofstede, A.H.M., and Weske, M. "Business Process Management: A Survey," Proceedings of the 1st International Conference on Business Process Management, Springer, Berlin, LCNS, (Eindhoven, The Netherlands, 2003b), pp. 1 - 12.

Venkatesh, V., and Davis, F.D. "A theoretical extension of the technology acceptance model: Four longitudinal field studies", *Management Science* (46:2) 2000, pp. 186 - 204.

Venkatesh, V., Morris, M.G., Davis, G.B., and Davis, F.D. "User Acceptance of Information Technology: Toward a Unified View", *MIS Quarterly* (27:3) 2003, pp. 425 - 478.

Verheecke, B., Vanderperren, W., and Jonckers, V. "Unraveiliny crossoutting concerns in Web services middleware", *IEEE Software* (23:1) 2006, pp. 42 - 50.

Vinoski, S. "Old measures for new services", *IEEE Internet Computing* (9:6) 2005, pp. 72 - 74.

Volkoff, O., Strong, D., and Elmes, M. "Between a Rock and a Hard Place: Boundary Spanners in an ERP Implementation," Proceedings of the 8th Americas Conference on Information Systems (AMCIS '02), AIS, (Dallas, TX, Paper 135, 2002), pp. 958 - 962.

Vollmer, K. "The Forrester Wave™: Integration-Centric Business Process Management Suites, Q4 2008," Forrester, http://www.tibco.com/resources/solutions/bpm/forrester_wave_ic_bpms_q42008.pdf, last access: 23.06.2009.

Volmering, T. "Gemeinsame Umgebung für Fachabteilung und IT-Manager," Computer Zeitung, March 16th 2009, p. 17.

von Hippel, E. *Democratizing Innovation* MIT Press, Cambridge, MA, 2005.

Walsham, G. *Interpreting Information Systems in Organizations* John Wiley and Sons, Chichester, UK, 1993.

Wellner, P. "Interacting with paper on the DigitalDesk", *Commun. ACM* (36:7) 1993, pp. 87 - 96.

Wilde, T., and Hess, T. "Forschungsmethoden der Wirtschaftsinformatik - Eine empirische Untersuchung", *Wirtschaftsinformatik* (49:4) 2007, pp. 280 - 287

Winograd, T. "From Programming Environments to Environments for Designing", *Commun. ACM* (38:6) 1995, pp. 65 - 74.

Won, M. "Interaktive Integritätsprüfung für komponentenbasierte Architekturen," PhD thesis, Mathematisch-Naturwissenschaftliche Fakultät, Universität Bonn, Bonn, Germany, 2004.

Won, M., Stiemerling, O., and Wulf, V. "Component-based Approaches to Tailorable Systems," in: *End User Development*, H. Lieberman, F. Paternò and V. Wulf (eds.), Springer, Dordrecht, The Netherlands, 2006, pp. 127-153.

Wong, J., and Hong, J.I. "Making mashups with marmite: towards end-user programming for the web," Proceedings of the CHI '07, ACM, (San Jose, CA, 2007), pp. 1435 - 1444.

Wu, C., and Chang, E. "AtomServ Architecture: Towards Internet-scaled Service Publish, Subscription, and Discovery," Proceedings of the IEEE International Conference on e-Business Engineering, IEEE Computer Society Press, 2006), pp. 571 - 578.

Wulf, V. "Anpaßbarkeit im Prozeß evolutionärer Systementwicklung", *GMD-Spiegel* (24:3) 1994, pp. 41 - 46.

Wulf, V. "Let's see your search-tool! - Collaborative use of tailored artifacts in groupware," Proceedings of GROUP '99, ACM, (Phoenix, AZ, 1999), pp. 50 - 59.

Wulf, V. "Exploration Environments: Supportung Users to Learn Groupware Functions", *Interacting with Computers* (13:2) 2000, pp. 265 - 299.

Wulf, V. "Zur anpaßbaren Gestaltung von Groupware: Anforderungen, Konzepte, Implementierungen und Evaluationen," Habilitation, Fachbereich Informatik, Universität Hamburg, Hamburg, 2001.

Wulf, V. "Theorien sozialer Praktiken zur Fundierung der Wirtschaftsinformatik: Eine forschungsprogrammatische Perspektive," in: *Wissenschaftstheorie und Gestaltungsorientierte Wirtschaftsinformatik*, J. Becker, H. Krcmar and B. Niehaves (eds.), Springer/Physika, (in print), 2009.

Wulf, V., and Golombek, B. "Direct Activation: A Concept to Encourage Tailoring Activities", *Behaviour & Information Technology* (20:4) 2001, pp. 249 - 263.

Wulf, V., and Jarke, M. "The economics of end-user development", *Commun. ACM* (47:9) 2004, pp. 41 - 42.

Wulf, V., Pipek, V., and Won, M. "Component-based tailorability: Enabling highly flexible software applications", *International Journal of Human-Computer Studies* (66:1) 2008, pp. 1 - 22.

Wulf, V., and Rohde, M. "Towards an integrated organization and technology development," Proceedings of the DIS '95, ACM, (Ann Arbor, MI 1995), pp. 55 - 64.

Wulf, V., Stiemerling, O., and Pfeifer, A. "Tailoring Groupware for Different Scopes of Validity", *Behaviour & Information Technology* (18:3) 1999, pp. 199 - 212

Ye, Y., and Fischer, G. "Designing for Participation in Socio-Technical Software Systems," Proceedings of 4th International Conference on Universal Access in Human-Computer Interaction, Part I, Springer, Heidelberg, (Beijing, China, 2007), pp. 312 - 321.

Yeh, R.B., Brandt, J., Klemmer, S.R., Boli, J., Su, E., and Paepcke, A. "Interactive Gigapixel Prints: Large Paper Interfaces for Visual Context, Mobility, and Collaboration," Technical Report, Computer Science Department, Stanford University, Stanford, CA, 2006.

Yeung, L., Plimmer, B., Lobb, B., and Elliffe, D. "Levels of formality in diagram presentation," Proceedings of the 19th Australasian conference on Computer-Human Interaction, ACM, (Adelaide, Australia, 2007), pp. 311 - 317.

Yin, R.K. *Case Study Research: Design and Methods*, (4 ed.) Sage Publications, Thousand Oaks, CA, 2008.

Zhou, C., Chia, L.-T., and Lee, B.-S. "Semantics in service discovery and QoS measurement", *IT Professional* (7:2) 2005, pp. 29 - 34.

www.ingramcontent.com/pod-product-compliance
Lightning Source LLC
Chambersburg PA
CBHW070722220326

41598CB00024BA/3257

PROSTATE CANCER IS CURABLE

by

SANTIAGO VILAS, Ph.D.

YAGO EDITORIAL, LLC

TABLE OF CONTENTS

Foreword

From this first line that you are reading to when you have finished this page, at least one more man has been diagnosed with prostate cancer in the United States alone. Another man will have died of this disease by the time you complete this Chapter. In 2006, about 234,460 men will be diagnosed with prostate cancer (1.02% more than in 2005, 6.03% more than in 2003) and 27,350 would die. **Prostate Cancer is Number 1 among all cancers** (33%, the highest incidence of new cases); Number 2 is female breast cancer, 31%.

Prostate misbehavior can dramatically change men and their partners forever. It can make a man's life miserable —and kill him, too. The risk of a man being diagnosed with prostate cancer is **one in six**, but certain circumstances increase that risk exponentially. For example: if the man is **obese**, he has an additional 30% risk, if he has a **family history** of prostate cancer (one diagnosed close relative: father, brother) his risk is twice as high, if he has two relatives his risk is five times higher, and with three relatives the likelihood of his developing prostate cancer is 97%. And if he is **black,** he still has a 40% to 50% higher risk and twice the probabilities of dying of this disease. Black population has the highest incidence and mortality of cancer rates in the U.S., 70% higher than white population. Lifetime probability of a man developing prostate cancer is 46%.

No single cause has been identified yet. **No single means to prevent it** has been discovered either. However, we now know that **prostate cancer is curable**. The difference between dying of prostate cancer and having a good probability of being cured rests on **early diagnosis**, when the cancer is still localized within the gland. Most men are unaware of that difference, and a large percentage of those who know do believe they will not develop prostatic troubles. Many do not even know, until diagnosed, that they have a gland named **prostate**, and the TV media once confused it with the word "prostitute" —as do some word processors to replace the word "prostatitis".

This book, ***PROSTATE CANCER is CURABLE*** (second version of its predecessor ***On the way to Fighting Prostate Cancer)***, has been **patient-designed as an informative and educational vehicle**. Its objectives: to induce the ***patient-to-be*** (a) to assume a more active **responsibility for monitoring his health**, (b) to develop, by anticipation before he becomes a ***patient***, an **attitude of confrontation with the illness** and **of positive cure**, and (c) to gather enough data to be able to make educated decisions that are most favorable to him **as an individual**. Such data would be almost impossible for him to compile in the short period of time between his finding out that he has prostate cancer and the decisions demanded of him to *do something about it –right away!*

Whether this is your first excursion into the intricacies of **prostate [mis]behavior** or another search for information, this book should be of help. It addresses a multiplicity of issues with provocative stimuli and arguments seldom found in other studies. A patient's ability to make wise decisions depends on a combination of complex factors, among them: prevention, identification of symptoms, age, physical condition, philosophy of living, ancestry awareness, diversity of treatments, the patient's and his partner's preference for the quality-of-life consequences, however predictable or unpredictable they may be. This book also **"dissects" for discussion most of the contemporary direct influences on the patient**, e.g., attitude, statistics, drugs, physicians, HMOs, treatments, his rights and responsibilities. It includes a historical perspective of discoveries and advancements as well as current circumstances, thus unveiling the peaks and valleys of the unique prostate landscape. That is, **it looks at the prostate from introspective, provocative angles seldom explored; one may say that this book is *different*.**

The data gathered for this book and digested into summaries are the result of a five-year study from a variety of sources:

- Books written by physicians, by patients or by a collaboration of both, and personal correspondence with some of those authors,
- Medical news and articles published in newspapers, magazines and medical journals as well as speeches delivered at conventions, symposia and public meetings in several countries,
- Research in School of Medicine Libraries,

3

- Personal meetings, correspondence and telephone and Internet conversations with prominent urologists and oncologists in the USA, Mexico, Spain, Denmark, and Japan,
- Personal conversations with over 100 prostate cancer patients and their partners from the USA, Great Britain, Canada, New Zealand, Poland, Spain, and China,
- Incalculable number of pages posted by hundreds of doctors, patients, organizations and pharmaceutical companies from all over the world on that formidable communication wonder known as the Internet,
- Direct contacts with, and studies and pamphlets released by international organizations promoting cancer prevention, care and treatment,
- The experience of having the door virtually slammed in my face at the Department of Urology of one of the prime hospitals in Spain while asking for statistics –the head urologist on duty insisted, *"We have to protect ourselves!"*
- My own personal insights.

The book delineates a man's journey commencing with simple and necessary informative and anatomic introductions to his healthy prostate, going through loving it, and ending with various strategies on how to kill it. Background narratives, separation of data, touches of humor, interviews, and insertion of photos and birth and death dates and places of world-renowned scientists are included for two purposes. First, to help to defuse the myth and fear traditionally linked to cancer of the prostate (or any cancer, for that matter). It comforts a patient to be able to associate and visualize (*humanize*) his intimate *prostatic circumstance* with the graphic presentation, age and geographic root of those who have made possible for him to find cure. Second, this book pays a tribute of gratitude and admiration to those eminent giants of Science and specifically Medicine who throughout the years have discovered or furthered advancements to diagnose and to cure prostate cancer. They have saved the lives of millions of men all over the world. This book is the first such compiled graphic tribute known to this Author. Likewise, the **Chronology of Events** section (also the first known to this Author) and the historic data appearing in all chapters are inserted to impress upon the patient that **he is not alone** and that **he is not the first man** to be concerned about his prostate. Undoubtedly, some sections and comments may also apply to men affected by other cancers, and even to women too, but this book is mainly concerned with a man's prostate.

Technically,

- Although themes are compartmentalized in independent chapters sometimes data and names need to overlap,
- Statistics, some still unpublished by their authors at the time of this writing, are used frequently as a practical illustration of the issues and for the patient's awareness, rather than for strict clinical comparison,
- The *Chronology of Events* and the content of the book are by no means definitive since it would be impossible and beyond the purpose of this book to include the whole history and data spectrum of each of the issues discussed,
- The English leans toward its international style avoiding odd contractions (don't, he's, what's, it's, etc.) and it uses the masculine form to cover both genders,
- Words for race descriptions are *white* when referring to Caucasian and *black* when referring to African-American,
- There are no footnotes; needed explanations are given within the text,
- The following symbols have the indicated meaning: $<$ *less than*, $\leq$ *equal to or less than*, $>$ *more than*, $\geq$ *equal to or more than*, $=$ *equal to* or *resulting in*, $\pm$ *plus or minus* (a variance in whatever direction), and $\sim$ *about, more or less, approximately.*

Irrespective of any personal interpretation a reader may make (for which this Author and the publisher assume no responsibility), (a) no photo or graphic or name herein inserted implies the personal endorsement of this book, and (b) nothing herein is offered as, or is, or can, or should be construed in content or form as medical advice or medical judgment. A patient has the right and the responsibility for obtaining as much information as possible to monitor his health. Only a medical doctor has the jurisdiction and the responsibility for giving medical and medication advice.

Santiago Vilas, Ph.D.
Baton Rouge, Louisiana (USA)
August 2006

The famous *"Mannekin Piss Fountain"* **(Brussels, Belgium), with the** *"Little Boy Piss"* **statue displaying the European Union flag during a festivity**.
(*Photo courtesy of* The Office of Tourism, Belgium)

The *Mannekin Piss Fountain* and its *Little Boy Piss* statue, located in central Brussels, Belgium, have been part of the landscape, the history and the hearts of Belgians since 1388. Citizens of Brussels say they have adopted the *Little Boy Piss* as a somewhat irreverent symbol of their city.

The present statue, the second, was made in 1619 by Jerome Duquesnoy to replace the original, by an unknown artist, which had been destroyed. Ever since, the *Little Boy* has been continuously pissing water from the pedestal into the stone basin. The statue represents a cute 5-year-old boy with curly hair, ½ meter (~20 inches) tall. Hundreds of thousands of tourists photograph it every year. In *La Maison du Roi* (*King's House*), the building facing the basin, the statue is honored with a Museum displaying over 300 costumes donated by entities from all over the world, the first one sent by King Louis XV of France in 1747 —although no one knows why.

This Author believes that the *Little Boy*, with his stream of piss *uninterrupted for 384 years*, merits being **The Urological Symbol of the Ideal Healthy Male.**

6

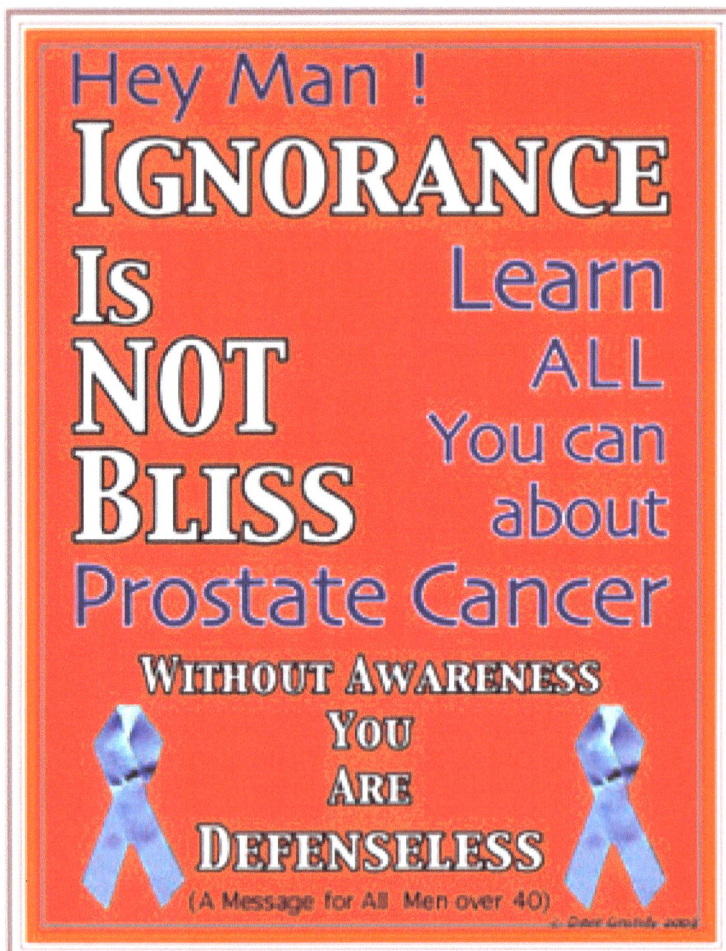

Prostate Cancer Awareness Poster
(*Courtesy of* Dave Grundy, Canada)

CHRONOLOGY OF SELECTED EVENTS

RELEVANT TO PROSTATE *mis*BEHAVIOR

L et us accept from no man the emotional cry **"W***hy me?***"** as if he were **the first** or **the only one** affected by or dealing with prostate misbehavior. It should comfort him and all of us to remember that, since the beginning of History, thousands of scientists and experts in multiple fields worked and many devoted their entire lives to paving the road for us, men of the 21st century, to have the best medical care mankind has ever enjoyed for treating prostate diseases. The following summary is **the shortest list** the Author could compile; it constitutes a tribute to those scientists who for centuries, in one way or another, worked or are working **for** us.

* * *

Greek physician **Hippocrates** (circa 460-377 B.C.) transforms traditional Religion, Superstition and even Philosophy into scientific thinking and observation – curative Medicine; leaves the legacy of his **Hippocratic Code of Ethics** or **Oath** that will inspire worldwide medical conduct until 1973 when the U.S. Supreme Court rejects it as a *guide to medical ethics and practice*. **Father of Medicine.**

Greek physician **Herophilus** (335-280 B.C.) uses the term **prostate** when referring to the position of a gland in front of the bladder (Greek *pro*=before; *histania*=to set). However, the word **prostate** is coined by French surgeon **Dr. Ambrose Pare** (1509-1590), pioneer of **prostate studies**, when describing the gland's role as *the guardian of the bladder*.

8

Radical prostatectomy: The word **prostatectomy** derives from Greek *pro=* before; *histania=*to stand, to set; *ek=*out; and *tommein=*to cut; that is, *to cut out what stands before [the bladder]*. **Radical**=surgical removal of the whole prostate and seminal vesicles.

1500 B.C. **Cancer** (Latin *cancer=*crab) is first mentioned in the Ebers papyrus written about 1500 B.C.; the Greeks used *gangrene* and the Romans *lupus* ("because it consumed like a wolf"). **Antyllus** recommends in 300 A.D. that cancers should be disregarded because *"they were inoperable"*.

1257   (circa) **Roger Bacon** (1214-1294) outlines the principles of a **microscope** and a **reflecting telescope**.

1817   American surgeon **Dr. George Langstaff** (1780-1846) first in describing the **Carcinoma of the Prostate.**

1825   British actuary **Benjamin Gompertz** (1779-1865) publishes his book *Law of Mortality* formulating his **Exponential Growth Theory** (**Kinetics**), applied still today to determine the constant geometric progression of the division of cells.

1842   May 25: **Dr. Christian Andreas Doppler** (Salzburg, Austria 1803-Venice, Italy 1853), who had studied Mathematics, Mechanical and Astronomy, presents his paper *On the coloured light of the double stars and certain other stars of the heavens*, thus, creating the so-called **Doppler principle**, based on ultrasonography and setting up the structure of advancements into colored Radiography.

1846   American **Dr. Oliver Wendell Holmes** (1804-1894) discovers **Anesthesia**.

1854   Although the Greeks created the first "tax-supported public physicians service", the first Compulsory Health Insurance Law is proclaimed by Prussia in 1854, followed by Germany in 1883, then it spreads over Europe as **Social Insurance** or **Social Medicine**, government plan still prevalent today in most countries except the U.S.

1865   Czech Augustine monk **Johan Gregor Mendel** (1822-1884) discovers, while studying plants and experimenting in plant hybridization, that *traits are determined by discrete 'factors'* (later known as **Genes**, which in humans are inherited unchanged from the parents). He transforms agricultural breeding into a science and, as a result, discovers the **fundamental laws of inheritance**. His revealing article *Experiments on hybridization of plants,* covering his 1856-1863 research, is published in the modest *Transactions of the Society of National History* magazine of Brünn, Austria. **Father of Genetics.**

1867   German surgeon **Dr. Theodor C. Billroth** (1829-1894), of the University of Vienna, Austria, performs the first **Radical Perineal Prostatectomy for Cancer**, by resection.

9

1869   Swiss scientist **Dr. J. Friedrich Miescher** (1844-1895) first to isolate **DNA** and to suggest a **genetic code**.

1889   **Dr. Edwin Klebs** (Vienna, Austria 1834 - relocated to the U.S. where he died in 1913) noted an abnormality of chromosomes in cancer cells, hence pioneering the **genetic heritage**.

1891   American **Dr. George E. Goodfellow** (1855-1910), physician of the South Pacific Railroad, Tucson, Arizona, writes, "*I made a pure perineal prostatectomy, the first, so far known to me*". It is unknown why he waited several years to make the announcement; that is why Dr. Hugh Hampton Young (see entry 1897) is recognized as performing the first **Prostatectomy**. (Bilingual, Dr. Goodfellow is one of the negotiators for Spain's surrender of Cuba, Puerto Rico and Filipinas to the United States, July 1898).

1895   American urologist **Dr. Eugene Fuller** (1858-1930) performs the first **supra pubic prostatic adenomectomy**.

1895   November 8: Holland-born German **Dr. Wilhelm Konrad Röntgen** (1845-1923), professor at the University of Würzburg, accidentally discovers a milestone in Science: the **Röntgen Rays**, later called by him "**X-Rays**" (**X** = *unknown* because he did not know what they exactly were). Experimenting how electricity could be conducted in a dilute gas, he surprisingly noticed a strange fluorescent glow irradiating from the darkened lab when he activated a type of vacuum known as "the Crooke's tube". The impressions of the glow penetrated wood, cardboard and even his wife's hands and caused an instant revolution in the scientific world. First to take a radiography; **First Radiographer**. Used promptly in the U.S. (Dartmouth, MA 1896). Wins the first Nobel Prize in Physics, 1901. Profoundly an altruist (rejects a German title of nobility, does not patent his X-Rays "*to allow the world to benefit*", donates his Nobel Prize money to his university) dies virtually bankrupted.

1896   February 24: French **Dr. Henri Becquerel** (1852-1908) announces in Paris the discovery of **Uranium**. French **Dr. Pierre Curie** (1859-1906) and his wife and former disciple of Becquerel **Dr. María Sklodowska Curie** (Poland 1867-France 1934) discover **Polonium** and **Radium** in 1898 and find out that both materials emitted rays of much higher intensity and speed than Becquerel's uranium. Madame Curie starts calling the phenomenon **Radioactivity**. The three share the Nobel Prize 1903. Madame Curie, the first woman ever to receive it, wins a second Nobel Prize, Chemistry 1911. Ironically, Pierre's health deteriorated due to carrying in his pockets pieces of uranium to show to his scientist friends. He dies tragically, run over by a horse-drawn carriage near Paris, April 16, 1906; María dies in 1934 of leukemia caused by radiation. The Curies, archetypes of the ideal scientist, are also responsible for many other discoveries, from **Symmetry** in Physics that precipitates great advances in Medicine, to **Quartz** that transforms forever the way watches are made. When the French Government wrote notifying him of an official decoration, Dr. Pierre Curie responded, "*he had enough honors, but what he needed was a new laboratory to pursue his experiments*".

1897   American **Dr. Hugh Hampton Young** (September 18, 1870-August 23, 1945), director of the Urology Department at Johns Hopkins University in Baltimore, Maryland, one of the giants of the History of Urology, introduces the actual technique for **Suprapubic Prostatic Adenomectomy**. He also introduces in 1902 a technique for **perineal prostatic adenomectomy**, which he further improves in 1903, and performs on April 7, 1904 the first **Radical Prostatectomy** removing the gland and adjacent tissue. **Father of American Urology.**

1902   September 5: Dies in Berlin due to a fall from a streetcar the eminent German scientist **Dr. Rudolph Carl Virchow**, born in Prussia October 13, 1821. By age 25 had already discovered numerous diseases, including **Leukemia**. Changes traditional theory of disease by discovering that the causes are internal (*"Diseased cells come from already diseased cells"*, thus furthering **Genetics**). Published 2,124 works. **Father of Modern Pathology**.

1903   **Alexander Graham Bell** (Edinburgh, Scotland, March 3, 1847-Nova Scotia, U.S., August 2, 1922), inventor of the telephone, writes, *"There is no reason why a tiny fragment of radium sealed in a fine glass tube should not be inserted into the very heart of the cancer, thus acting directly upon de disease material"*, a phrase construed by some radiation historians as pioneering the concept of **Brachytherapy**.

1905   Use of **Radiology** begins at the Swedish School of Medicine, mainly thanks to the pioneering anatomist **Dr. Gosta Forsell** (March 2, 1876-1950) for his studies on the stomach and duodenum. (Modern Radiology starts in the U.S. shortly after World War II at Stanford University, California)

1906   American **Dr. A. L. Gray** (1873-1932) introduces **Radiotherapy** to treat the **Carcinoma** of the bladder. Soon the technique is also used for **Cancer of the Prostate**.

1909   **Dr. Joaquín Albarrán y Domínguez** (1860 - 1912), Cuban of Spanish descent, defines the **Median Perineal Prostatectomy**.

1911   French **Dr. Octave Pasteau** first in inserting radioactive material (radium) into the prostate by using a catheter through the urethra, thus actually pioneering **Brachytherapy**.

1913   Ten physicians and five community leaders create in New York the Society for the Control of Cancer, reorganized in 1945 as the **American Cancer Society**, a non-profit organization dedicated to *eliminating cancer as a major health problem*. It is now headquartered in Atlanta, Georgia, and represented in 3,400 communities by over two million Americans. Its foundation marks a milestone in the world history of public health.

1917   American **Dr. Benjamin Stockwell Barringer** (1878- ?), of Memorial Sloan-Kettering Cancer Center Hospital of New York, performs the first **Interstitial Brachytherapy** by inserting radium needles transperinneally into

11

the prostate guided by a finger inserted in the rectum. He also shows in 1938 that prostate cancer causes elevation of acid phosphatase (PAP).

1920   Cubist painter, writer and poet **Josef Capek** (Czechoslovakia 1887-1945) coins the word **Robot** during a casual conversation with his brother **Karel Capek** (1890-1938) when suggesting him to use it to identify the "artificial workers" Karel was using in his forthcoming play "*R.U.R.*", which he publishes later, in 1920. **Robotics** revolutionizes surgery techniques in 2000.

1929   **Dr. Michael Shadid** starts in the U.S. the first **Pre-Paid Health Care Plan**, designed for a rural Farmers Cooperative in Elk City, Oklahoma; precursor of the **HMOs**. The initiative expands and by 1933, 5,000 workers are enrolled in Los Angeles by Dr. Sidney Garfield; Henry J. Kaiser contracts Dr. Shadid to provide healthcare to his company's employees, makes the plan public and by 1959 the Kaiser Plan has a half million persons enrolled. Another precursor of the HMOs, **Blue Cross**, is also founded in 1929 at the University of Baylor, Texas.

1931   March 2. **Dr. Gosta Forsell** (1876-1950) of Sweden coins the term **Brachytherapy** when he improves Dr. Pasteau's technique (see entry 1911) to use radium for treatment of carcinoma of the cervix. Immediately adopted in England, Germany and Switzerland.

1933   Foundation in Geneva, Switzerland, of the *Union Internationale Contre Cancer* (International Union Against Cancer), a non-governmental, non-profit, independent association of 290 organizations in 84 countries devoted to all aspects of the worldwide fight against cancer; it will later contribute to the development of the **TNM Cancer Staging** method (see entry 1992).

1934   June: American urologist **Dr. Frederick E. B. Foley** (1891-1966), of the University of Minneapolis, Minnesota, announces his invention of the rubber balloon **Catheter** (Greek=*let down*) that will become the "gold standard" for continuous urinary drainage held by its own configuration. Although rudimentary catheter devices, from onion stalks to soaked and dried woven and to metals, had been used throughout centuries, this new definitive invention becomes so popular that still today we refer to a catheter as simply a "**Foley**".

1935   August 14: U.S. President Roosevelt signs a landmark in American History: the **Social Security Act**.

1941   Canadian-born, American relocated **Dr. Charles Benton Huggins** (1901-1997), of the University of Chicago, after removing the testicles of dogs with prostate cancer discovers **Hormones** (hormonal therapy) that will revolutionize treatment of prostate cancer and other diseases. First urologist to be awarded the Nobel Prize (1966).

1942   Austrian neurologist-psychiatrist **Dr. Karl T. Dussik** (1908-1947) **first in using ultrasound for medical diagnosing**, furthering the *Doppler color/ power principle* discovered 100 years before (see entry 1842); introduces **Hyperphonography** to detect tumors.

12

1944   American **Dr. Oswald Theodore Avery** (Nova Scotia, Canada, 1877-relocated to the U.S., dies in Nashville, TN, 1955) publishes in the *Journal of Experimental Medicine* his research discovering that a gene is made of **deoxyribonucleic acid (DNA)** that serves as genetic material, that DNA is a genetic molecule, and that DNA is packaged in a chromosome. One of the founders of **Immunochemistry**, was proposed several years for but never received the Nobel Prize. Forerunner of the ultimate discovery and characterization of DNA (see entry 1953).

1947   British **Dr. Terrence Millin** (January 9, 1903-July 3, 1980) performs the first **Retropubic Prostatic Adenomectomy** caused by urinary obstruction, by complete removal of the gland.

1948   After 18 years of "trials", **Dr. Arnold A. Kegel** (February 24, 1894-1976), professor of Gynecology at the University of Southern California School of Medicine, describes in his article "*Non-surgical Treatment of Genital Relaxation*" an innovative method of controlling incontinence in women following childbirth or menopause and designs the instrument *Perineometer*. Known since as **Kegel Exercises**, the method is practiced all over the world to help also men suffering of incontinence due to prostatic diseases and post-surgery.

1950-1951   American urologist **Dr. Willet F. Whitmore, Jr.** (Long Island, New York, December 13, 1917-May 8, 1995), of Memorial Sloan-Kettering Cancer Center Hospital of New York, and **Dr. Hugh J. Jewett** (September 26, 1903-May 6, 1990), of Johns Hopkins University, Baltimore, Maryland, design **The ABCD Whitmore-Jewett Cancer Staging Method** to define expansion of the cancer of the prostate. Used all over the world for many years until the announcement of the more detailed and technically advanced method known as **International TNM** (T=Tumor, N=Nod, M=Metastasis), first designed in 1972, revised several times.

1951   At the start of Nuclear Medicine, American **Dr. Rubin H. Flocks** (May 7, 1906-May 17, 1975), chief of Urology at the University of Iowa, performs the first actual **Brachytherapy** by using radioactive colloidal gold (Au 198) to treat carcinoma of the prostate. With his colleague **Dr. David A. Culp**, publishes in 1960 the textbook *Radiation Therapy of early Prostate Cancer*.

1953   February: American **Dr. James Dewey Watson** (Chicago April 6, 1928-   ) while studying in England joins British **Dr. Francis Harry Crick** (Northampton June 8, 1916-San Diego, California, July 29, 2004) and together publish in the journal *Nature* (April 25, 1953) an article entitled "*The Double Helix*" announcing the discovery of the actual structure of the **molecule** that stores the genetic **Code of Life**, the deoxybonucleic acid or **DNA** (the most important discovery in the History of Biology). Their second article explains the structure's genetic implications. Will revolutionize many fields including Medicine. Dr. Watson was 24 at the time. Both share with **Dr. Maurice Hugh Frederick Wilkins** (New Zealand 1916-   ) the Nobel Prize 1962. The other co-discoverer, British **Dr. Rosalind Elsie Franklin** (London 1920-1958), who precipitated the actual landmark, dies of cancer at 37, five years

13

before the announcement. Wilkins and Franklin were professors at King's College.

1955   British **Dr. John Julian Wid** (England 1914 - relocated to the U.S.   ) and American **Dr. John Reid** (1926-   ) invent the **Transrectal Scanning Transducer**, followed next year by the **Rectal Scanner**.

1956   **Dr. Malcolm A. Bagshaw** (Adrian, Michigan June 24, 1925-   ), director of the Radiology Department at Stanford University, California, initiates **External Beam Irradiation** for prostatic cancer, demonstrates in 1962 that high dose of radioactive gold celluloid radiation can be effective treatment for early-detected prostate cancer. **Father of American Radiotherapy**.

1958   American statisticians **E. L. Kaplan** and **P. Meier** describe in the *Journal of American Statistical Association* their study *"Nonparametric Estimation from Incomplete Observations"* that becomes the **Survival Statistics Method** utilized since by most medical scientists all over the world.

1962   Scientists at Stanford University, San Francisco, California, led by **Dr. Malcolm A. Bagshaw** (see entry 1956) build the first **Linear Electron Accelerator** for medical use, the **Electron-Gamma-Shower** or **EGS** available since in most hospitals for **cancer radiation treatment**.

1965   July 30: U.S. President Lyndon B. Johnson signs the first healthcare insurance law, **Medicare**, under the Social Security Act of 1935, after decades of great controversy and opposition from medical, pharmaceutical, and hospital associations.

1967   Japanese **Dr. Hiroki Watanabe** (Chiba, Japan January 20, 1935-   ), Professor, Department of Urology of the Kyoto Prefectural University of Medicine in Kyoto, performs the first worldwide clinical application of **Sonography**.

1969   The diagnosing technique **Biopsy by compound Sonography** is developed in Sweden and causes great advances in Medicine (not utilized in the U.S. until 1987).

1970   American immunologist **Dr. Richard J. Ablin** (May 15, 1940 -   ), of State University of New York at Buffalo, New York, announces in the *Journal of Reproduction and Fertility* and in the *Journal of Immunology* his discovery of **"Identification of the tissue-specific antigens of the normal and pathologic prostate"**, thus establishing the foundation for the so-called **PSA test**.

1971   U.S. President Richard Nixon announces the development of the **Health Maintenance Organizations (HMO)** that Congress passes two years later, in 1973.

1971   December 23: U.S. President Richard Nixon signs the Proclamation of the **National Cancer Act**.

1972   British electrical engineer **Godfrey Newbold Hounsfield** (August 28, 1919-
August 12, 2004), of EMI Laboratories, invents the **Computed Tomography
(CT) Scan** imaging machine (from Greek **tomos**=*slice* or *section*, and
graphia=*describing*), also known as **Computed Axial Tomography (CAT)
Scan**. Independently, physicist **Allan McCleod Cormack** (South Africa February 23, 1924-Relocated to the US, Massachusetts, May 7, 1998) worked
also on the same advancement. Both shared the 1979 Nobel Prize for Medicine and Science. Using X-Rays technology and complex computer science,
it creates a 3-dimensional cross sectional slice of the body and each image
provides detailed anatomy of that location or slice, later recomposed into a
whole picture. Can show in a matter of seconds extremely high detail of body
structures such as bones, soft tissue, brain, organs, and blood vessels. Revolutionizes diagnostic Medicine.

1972   American urologist **Dr. Willet F. Whitmore, Jr.** (see entry 1950-1951),
teaming with **Dr. Basil S. Hilaris** (September 3, 1928-   ), then also of
Memorial Sloan-Kettering Hospital of New York, perform the **First Prostate
Implant** using **Iodine-125 seeds**; brachytherapy by open surgery.

1976   **Dr. J. Michael Bishop** (York, Pennsylvania, February 22, 1936-   ) and
Dr. Harold E. Vermus (1940-   ), professors at the University of San Francisco, California, discover **Oncogenes in Normal DNA**, demonstrating that a
normal gene already in a cell has the potential of becoming an oncogene
(cancerous). Share Nobel Prize 1989.

1977   American Pathologist **Dr. Donald F. Gleason** (Minneapolis, October 5,
1921-_____), of the Veterans Administration Hospitals, devises the **Gleason
Grading System** to identify and classify the progressive transformation of
the prostatic cells from normal or well-differentiated to cancerous and poorly-
differentiated. Prostate cancer pathologic diagnostics are since based worldwide on the Gleason Cancer Grading System.

1978   American **Dr. Patrick Craig Walsh** (Akron, Ohio, February 13, 1938 -   ),
Director of the Brady Urological Institute of Johns Hopkins University, in
Baltimore, Maryland, describes a revolutionary technique **to control bleeding from the Dorsal Vein Complex** that for the first time allows the surgeon,
literally, to "see" what he is doing while performing a radical prostatectomy.

1979   **Dr. T. Ming Chu** (Taiwan April 18, 1938–Relocated to and educated in the
U.S.   ), Chair of Diagnostic Immunology Research at Roswell Park Cancer
Institute in Buffalo, New York, announces the completion by his researching
team of a nine-year program: the "identification and purification of the **prostate-specific antigen**" that will lead them to make the first **PSA test** (1980), a
landmark in Urology. They also discover the **FreePSA test** (1998). With the
digital rectal examination (DRE), PSA becomes worldwide the most important test for prostate diseases. Approved by the FDA in 1986 to monitor and
in 1994 to diagnose prostate cancer.

1982   April 26: American **Dr. Patrick Craig Walsh**, one of the giants of Urology
(see entry 1978) sets a Medicine milestone and redefines surgical techniques

by "re-discovering" the male anatomy. Demonstrates that continence and sexual nerves do not run *through* the prostate but rather *outside* of the prostate capsule, and that they can be saved during surgery. As a consequence, defines what he calls **Anatomical Approach to Radical Prostatectomy** (or **Nerve-Sparing**) and drastically changes surgical techniques. Such nerves are since known as **The Walsh Nerves**. Proves for the first time that **a man can live without his prostate and still preserve his urinary and sexual normal functions**.

1982   Danish urologist **Dr. Hans Henrik Holm** (Copenhagen, September 1931-_____) of the Herlev Hospital in Copenhagen, performs the first worldwide non-surgical **Perineal Brachytherapy implanting radioactive Iodine-125 seeds by using transrectal ultrasound guide**.

1984   Upon completion of a monumental clinical research, American **Dr. William J. Catalona** (Cleveland, Ohio November 14, 1942 -   ), then Director of Washington Urological Medical Center in St. Louis, Missouri, Illinois, decisively impresses upon the Food and Drug Administration (FDA) the approval of the **Prostate Specific Antigen test (PSA)** for diagnostic purposes. Along with the **FreePSA** approved later in 1998 and the Digital Rectal Examination (DRE), it will become universally *the gold standard diagnostic tool* to explore prostate diseases, especially cancer. (See entry 1979)

1985   November 6: Urologist **Dr. Haakon Ragde** (Oslo, Norway July 26, 1927- Relocated to and educated in the U.S.   ), then director of the Pacific Northwest Cancer Foundation in Seattle, Washington, teaming with American oncologist **Dr. John Charles Blasko** (St. Louis, Missouri 1943-   ), then Medical Director of the Northwest Tumor Institute of the Northwest Hospital, in Seattle, Washington, improve Dr. Holm's techniques (see entry 1982) and perform in the United States the first **Non-Surgical Transrectal Ultrasound-Guided Brachytherapy** to cure prostate cancer by **implanting Palladium-103 radioisotope seeds** in the gland after external beam radiation, hence confirming that **a man can live with a "dead" prostate inside the body and preserve his urinary and sexual functions**.

1987   Urologist **Dr. Haakon Ragde** (see entry 1985) performs the first world-wide **Transrectal Ultrasound-Guided Biopsy** to explore cancer of the prostate, which revolutionizes diagnostic techniques by avoiding open surgery. Becomes the *gold standard* of prostate biopsy procedure.

1989   **Dr. Frank A. Critz** (1945-   ), Director of Radiotherapy Clinics of Georgia, Decatur, modifies the non-surgical transrectal ultrasound-guided Brachytherapy by **implanting Iodine-125 radioisotopes seeds followed by external beam radiation**. His technique and Drs. Ragden-Blasko's will challenge the cancer treatment procedure known until 1985 as the *gold standard*: radical prostatectomy.

1989   British **Tim Berners-Lee** (London 1955-   ) creates the **World Wide Web (www)**, an Internet global project for a hypertext that enables the whole world to work jointly on the Web, thus revolutionizing the world of commu-

16

nications and facilitating the instantaneous exchange of information. The Web becomes the most common source of information for millions of prostate patients worldwide.

1993-1997   May 17, 1997: Scientists at the Brady Urological Department of Johns Hopkins University in Baltimore, Maryland, led by **Dr. Alan W. Partin** (May 16, 1961-   ) and **Dr. Patrick C. Walsh** (see entries 1978, 1982) announce a revision of the set of tables or nomograms created in 1993 by introducing more sophisticated formulas based on PSA level, Gleason score, and Staging to track prostate cancer prognosis. The formulas are later coined "**The Partin Tables**" by **Dr. Stephen B. Strum** (Jamaica, NY September 17, 1942), Prostate Oncology Specialist and co-founder of the Prostate Cancer Research Institute, California.

1997   The U.S. Congress amends the Social Security Act approving the **Prostate Cancer Screening tests DRE and PSA** for early detection of the disease.

1998   March 10: U.S. Food and Drug Administration (FDA) approves the first **FreePSA** diagnostic test after the convincing screening of over 35,000 men conducted by **Dr. William J. Catalona** (see entry 1984). This new test, in conjunction with the Total PSA and the Digital Rectal Examination (DRE), will further revolutionize diagnosis of prostate illnesses by being able to detect 95% of cancers several years before they become symptomatic.

2000   **Statistical milestone in prostate cancer awareness**, greatly due to the use of the PSA test: the cases of diagnosed prostate cancer in the United States alone jumps from 9,000 the year 1900 to 200,000 in 2000, thus facilitating early treatment and saving thousands of lives.

2000   May: First **Laparoscopic Robotic Nerve-Sparing Prostatectomy** in the world performed in May in Frankfurt, Germany. First performed in the U.S. in November, in Richmond, Virginia. **Intuitive Surgical, Inc.** of California builds the system, named "**da Vinci**", which revolutionizes surgery.

2001   June: The FDA approves Intuitive Surgical's technique **Laparoscopic Robotic Prostatectomy**.

2001   The U.S. Congress approves a Resolution designating September as the **National Prostate Cancer Awareness Month.**

17

During the intricate, lengthy research and screening of prostate-related data for this *Chronology of Events,* the first of its kind known to the Author, particular care was devoted to accuracy. Conflicting records or lack of within some target entities in the U.S., and the limited information available from sources in other countries were not always verifiable in spite of my efforts. Although data are assumed now correct, the Author welcomes reference to any discrepancy or completion in a datum. He sincerely appreciates the help of those who wrote him upon the release of the first version of this book.

SANTIAGO VILAS, Ph.D.

Prostate Cancer Awareness Poster
(*Courtesy of* Dave Grundy, Canada)

Chapter 1

Preparedness, Readiness

A man is **not alone** when fighting a prostate illness. And the fight is not new and not a characteristic of modern life or environment. Prostate illness is not and should not be a *stigma* either, whether personal or social. It is not contagious. In addition, it is **curable –if caught early!**

Yet, in spite of the thousands of scientists who for centuries paved the way for us to diagnose and cure prostate illnesses, and in spite of the 234,460 Americans who in 2006 are finding out that they have prostate cancer, each man feels **truly alone** when facing that discovery. **No one else can take his place in sickness or in death**.

To be prepared if that event arrives and due to the high probability that it may, prudence advises us to prepare ourselves for an attitude conducive to fighting prostate anomalies –**successfully**. In the U.S., as per current predictions, one man in six, and one in three if black or having family history of the disease, will develop prostate cancer, that is, between 56 and 92 million Americans. The "Law of

Mother Nature" is axiomatic: *all of us will die*. However, Mother Nature does not prevent our learning how to fight, how to prolong out life, and how to preserve the best quality of life possible –**to have quality of life** defined as "**able to continue performing tasks that cause enjoyment**".

A man must educate himself while he still is a **patient-to-be**, before he becomes a **patient**. We shall review in this Chapter a few of the main factors that influence and may help a man to develop an attitude of readiness and preparedness –and thus, to make more educate treatment decisions when the time comes.

Personal Attitude

The **anguish** the average man feels when abruptly diagnosed with prostate cancer is mainly **due to the unknown** –to his lack of knowledge of what to expect when, what to do, and how his life will change. Implicitly, not knowing anything about the matter reveals his neglect of trying to learn. It is surprising that a mature adult (who naturally may have urinated about seven times a day or 2,555 times a year during, say, 40 years, that is, after 102,200 repetitions) may never have wondered about **the intricacies that make his plumbing system work** –and whether or not he knows anything about his prostate. By comparison, the same men, by age 40, surely know considerably more about how their automobile systems work. Hence, the cry of *being devastated, depressed ("**Why me?**")* by the news of prostatic illnesses is **intrinsically senseless although it may be emotionally understandable**.

Many prostate cancer patients surveyed by this Author confessed years of neglecting to go to the urologist even after experiencing symptoms. It is interesting that in two thirds of the instances **their wives were the ones urging** for their appointments and the ones ending up making them and the ones leading the conversation with the doctor –men made the initial appointment only 30% of the times.

Men's indifference is even more notable when compared to women's attitude toward breast cancer, a similar medical event (statistics of new incidences of prostate cancer, 234,460 new cases in 2006, are comparable of those statistics for breast cancer, 212,920 in the same year). Let us review the discrepancies in funding cancer research: in 1998, $87 million were spent on prostate cancer research but $250 million on breast cancer research; three years later, in 2001, $250 million were spent on prostate cancer research and $475 million

20

on breast cancer research. **Perhaps the time has come for some men to listen to and to learn from women**.

The value of motivation for awareness was eloquently demonstrated as far back as 1936 when the Women's Clubs Committee to Recruit Volunteers made the famous proposal to the American Cancer Society: **to be allowed to form an "all-women legion of volunteers"** for all types of cancers. By the end of 1938, that is, in only two years, women had increased all over the U.S. the number of people active in cancer awareness, education and control from 15,000 to 150,000.

Another result of awareness activity: the U.S. Postal Service released on July 29, 1998 a 415-million awareness/fund-raising **Breast Cancer Stamp Series** and as of June 15, 2001, it had sold 305 million stamps that generated $21 million for research. The following year, on May 28, 1999, the U.S. Postal Service released also a 78.1-million awareness/fund-raising **Prostate Cancer Stamp Series**; on September 30, 2001, after having sold 53.8 million, the Postal Service removed from the market the remaining inventory of 24.3 million stamps (however, more Breast Cancer Stamp Series were subsequently released in 2002 and 2005).

Furthermore, women were instrumental in having approved by Congress legislation requesting physicians and HMOs to provide a doctor's second opinion after a patient be diagnosed with breast or prostate cancer.

And women's aggressiveness to protect their [e.g., breast] health has been and still is as consistent as men's passiveness regarding their [e.g., prostate] health, as demonstrated once again in 2006. In April-May, the U.S. Senate was debating bill S. 1955, "*Health Insurance Marketplace Modernization and Affordability Act of 2006*", which, if approved, would pre-empt laws in 49 states requiring health insurance providers to cover cancer screenings (all cancers) and equipment and supplies for other diseases (e.g., diabetes). Hundreds of newspapers and magazines published full-page campaign ads illustrated with large pictures of brassieres and phrases protesting, "*Don't*

21

*let the U.S. Senate have women exposed", "Mammograms save lives",
"Tell the Senate to protect coverage for mammograms"*, etc. Only one
small line in the whole page indicated, *"Coverage of other lifesaving
cancer screenings is also at risk".* Interestingly, this campaign was not
led or supported exclusively by "just a group of women" but rather by
the American Cancer Society. (Bill S. 1955 was defeated)

A man's responsible attitude for personal readiness and preparedness starts with, among other issues:

---

* **Learning when to start being tested.**
* **Learning what to expect from and how to relate to
his physician.**
* **Preparing an itemized record of his *Medical and
Clinical History* and updating it by faithfully recording
the results of every test and analysis –available from
his doctors. (A sample spreadsheet is inserted in this
Chapter; some data and tolerance baselines should be
adjusted with the doctor's input. The man's clinical
history will help both the patient and the physician and
save valuable time for exploring other issues during
the visit to the doctor).**
* **Executing a *Durable Power of Attorney* (giving
someone else authority to make decisions in case of
surgery or emergency), and a *Living Will* (notifying
physicians and hospitals of his wishes regarding life-
sustaining procedures and devices). Most hospitals are
now requiring these two documents prior to surgery.
In some states, the legal language must have specific
provisions. Drafts adjusted to each state law are
downloadable free from several websites.**

The Physician-Patient Relationship

The **Physician-Patient relationship is not a marriage**. One
cannot survive without the other. The dynamics of this relationship
experienced drastic changes in the past few decades. External pres-
sures have affected their respective unilateral autonomy.

The "**central position**" of the patient has remained substantially unchanged until recently. The patient seeks the help of the physician when known or unknown anomalies breach his physical or
mental security mechanisms; he receives treatment or medication to

restore health and chemical balance. Then, he pays directly from his own pocket or indirectly through the HMO he supports (either the entire amount or a **co-payment** with or without a deductible, or by means of taxes). In countries other than the U.S., he pays through his government in support of a healthcare system known as "Socialized Medicine". We shall see that circumstances in recent years **are forcing patients to revise their historic passive attitude**.

Physicians themselves already have been subjected to multiple influences that essentially have altered the classic dynamics of the doctor-patient relationship and of medical practice in general. For example: sophisticated but highly costly new technological equipment (over one million dollars for a machine, unaffordable to most physicians individually), proliferation of private healthcare-controlling insurers or HMOs other than Medicare, demand for adoption of business-efficiency methods to increase a physician's productivity (="mass production"), pressure from the drug industry regarding prescription of new products, and the necessity to adopt unique defensive or survival mechanisms in a litigious society such as the U.S. due to the high cost of malpractice insurance –the penalty upon all for the mistakes of some. Additionally, an ongoing debate is attempting to define whether the bulk of future care of prostate cancer patients may switch from the traditional urologist-surgeon specialist to the modern prostate-oncologist specialist.

This **new medical era** is not only requiring more diverse training of new physicians, but also has caused practitioners to re-evaluate their own approach to medical practice –thus, affecting the patient. For example, patients traditionally liked to keep the same doctors, a trend distorted by HMOs when imposing their own medical staff. In the midst of conflicting stimuli, some physicians relocated to accept jobs elsewhere, others have abandoned practice to pursue vocations as researchers either signing up with pharmaceutical companies and research institutions or alternating practice with research. Others have discovered the economic advantages of medical partnerships. Some have stopped their practice and gone back to school, as faculty or to pursue studies toward an MBA (Master of Business Administration) to learn how to lead hospitals or HMOs. A few for a brief while suggested being called **artist** instead of **practicing physician** or **scientist**, perhaps to resurrect the early Greek assumption of *the art of the physician*, reflected in the *Hippocratic Oath*.

MEDICAL & CLINICAL RECORDS

Name_____ DOB_____ Race_____
Place of birth_____Country_____
Family history: Prostate Cancer #:_____ Breast Cancer #:_____

Results of Test/Analysis	Normal Tolerance	←Date Performed– mm/dd/yy→		
Height				
Weight				
Current Medications	---			
Allergies	---			
Blood Pressure:				
Diastolic	< 80			
Systolic	< 120			
Cholesterol: Total	120-199			
HDL – "Good"	40-75			
LDL – "Bad"	63-29			
Colonoscopy	Unremarkable			
Sigmoidscopy	Unremarkable			
Stool (blood in)	Negative			
DRE (digital rectal)	Undetectable			
EKG	Unremarkable			
Glucose	70-115			
Physical Exam	Unremarkable			
Prostate Biopsy	Negative			
Prostate size/volume	≤ 30 cc			
Pulse				
PSA: Total (*)	≤ 2.5 ng/ml			
Free	≥ 0.25 ng/ml			
Velocity	< 0.75 ng/ml			
Radiology: Bone Scan	Unremarkable			
Chest X-Rays	Unremarkable			
CT Scans	Unremarkable			
MRI	Unremarkable			
ProstaScint	Unremarkable			
Surgery Performed				
Testosterone	200-1600-or0 <20 ng/dl			
Triglycerides	63-202			
Urinalysis				
OTHER:				
(*) Adjust for Age				

To complicate matters, the *U.S. Prescription Drug and Medicare Improvement Act of 2003* impacts the medical facilities owned or operated by physicians, thus implicitly denying patients the possibility of saving money by going to a doctor-owned facility. Furthermore, the Medicare Act affected the income of many specialists by reducing reimbursement for drugs (injections) personally administered to their patients. The **spread** (the difference between the price physicians used to pay for the drugs and the reimbursement from Medicare) ranged from 12% to 77%, according to the American Society of Clinical Oncology.

Never until recently have physicians been subjected to **public accountability**. In this new medical era, the patient must face the challenge, among others, of learning a new strategy: **how to select, retain, and interact with his physician**. It is now essential for the patient-to-be to become aware of the circumstances characterizing this new relationship and to discover **in time** the limitations of his doctor's autonomy in order to program his own healthcare. **As a doctor has prepared himself to deal with the patient, a man must now prepare himself before the time arrives for him to become a prostate patient.**

Moreover, it has probably seldom occurred to him that he should know:

- **How to determine the physician's autonomy, substantially reduced by HMOs.**
- **When and how to request which tests and why.**
- **How to understand the significance of the test results.**
- **How to proceed to exercise his legal right to ask for a second opinion from another physician (urologist>oncologist or oncologist>urologist) within or outside his HMO staff.**
- **If he has the right and how to ask for a different treatment center offering his needed protocol, and which one or who will be responsible for providing follow-up care after the treatment.**
- **How to request and evaluate adequate statistics to understand his own individual situation.**
- **What questions to ask and how to ask –a number of questions will be suggested throughout this book. Many patients are afraid to ask, while many doctors maintain a de-**

fensive position that "they cannot answer un-asked questions" –a situation easily resolved when the patient takes
with him to the visit a written list of questions and concerns
about his health.

• How accessible is the chosen doctor.

• How to impress upon his physician and upon his
HMO that he, the patient, must be given sufficient information to make a treatment decision, and that he has the right
to receive a copy of all of his tests and analyses; and,

Notwithstanding the above, it would be unrealistic to expect
that **today's physician** is going to teach a prostate patient **all the
facts of illness and death** within the ≤15 minutes allocated for an
appointment. The new medical era has made the patient responsible
for learning by himself as much as possible. For example, one cancer
entity expresses the advice to and the responsibilities of patients as
follows: "*A man should discuss elevated PSA test results with his doctor.*" A more logical way would be: "*It is the **doctor's responsibility**
to discuss with the patient the results of any test administered.*" The
man, as a rule, has no clue of the meaning of the tests (and precisely
to help him acquire some knowledge is one of the main motivations
for this book).

Of the over 100 prostate cancer patients this Author surveyed
personally, most said that they would have liked to have received
more data from their primary-care physicians and urologists (in both,
quantity and quality), and some resented the telephone call from the
clinic's clerk instead of from the urologist to inform that the biopsy
was positive –cancer. Over 33% changed their specialists for that reason; more than half complained about difficulties with their HMOs in
obtaining tests or desired treatments, even in obtaining a copy of their
own tests and analyses. Most protested that, once diagnosed, they had
to make treatment decisions by themselves **after doing their own
research** ("*a lot of research*"). Their main source of data was the
fabulous Internet, which can flash in 0.08 seconds over 27 million hits
on the word Prostate –using only one search engine.

This shift **from the consultation room to the Internet** to give
and to find answers is exemplified by the result of a survey revealing
that 8,953 (63.7%) of the 14,046 urologists in the U.S. were accessible via e-mail and that 888 of them had their own website. Ironically,
another survey of doctors, sponsored by the California Health Care

Foundation, has shown that **top-rated medical websites gave accurate information only 45% of the time.**

Regardless of who his physician is,
(a) At the slightest symptom of prostatic anomalies a man should see a medical doctor.
(b) Only a medical doctor has the knowledge and training to diagnose, evaluate and give advice, prescriptions and answers.
(c) A patient should never attempt "to cure by himself" or use unapproved commercialized alternative compounds without prior consultation with his doctor.
(d) A patient should keep an accurate record of all medical experiences and test results.
(e) A patient should never wait for the prostate symptom to go away by itself –it will nest and grow...and often kill.

Social Attitude

For generations, **"cancer"** has been a somehow **taboo word** in the so-called "private society culture" in the U.S., as well as **"dying"**, **"sex"**, or **"castration"** –some English dictionaries define more explicitly a dog's spay than a man's castration, and one defines it as just **"to unman"**.

In the U.S., not until the mid-1950s some physicians started using the word cancer when talking to their own patients. There was a time when to be told, *"You have cancer"* was a diagnosis akin to a death sentence, confessed a doctor. The psychiatrist **Dr. Elizabeth Kübler-Ross** (Zurich, Switzerland, 1926-Scottsdale, Arizona, 2004) revolutionized the traditional physician-patient verbal communication with her book *On Death and Dying* (1969), in which she openly defined and explained (and urged doctors to share when their patients) the progressive series of five steps a person experiences when facing dying *–denial, anger, bargaining, depression and, finally, acceptance.*

Fortunately, with few exceptions, the characterization of prostate cancer as *social stigma* has disappeared. Doctors are less reserved and **today's patient is more willing to discuss the issue** with family and friends. Celebrities in the world of politics, military, movie acting, sports, and business prominence have publicized their prostate cancer cases in the media, thus embedding the words, the concept and

27

the inevitable reality of prostate cancer into everyday conversation – without embarrassment.

Various organizations have adopted cancer awareness ribbons, e.g., pink for breast cancer, red for AIDS. Prostate cancer survivor Rick Ward, of San Antonio, Texas, created in 1997 a metal blue ribbon and a gold nut pin to promote awareness. In November 1999, the CaP Cure Organization started the use of a cloth blue ribbon as a symbol for prostate cancer (ribbon=*First Place*, blue=*Blue for Boys*). In 2001, the U.S. Congress designated September as the National Prostate Cancer Awareness Month.

In recent years, the so-called **Prostate Cancer Support Groups** have increasingly adopted the target of **education and attitude-development** to replace the old **compassionate support**.

The prostate cancer *awareness* has spread to social gatherings. When visiting friends at home for social encounters, one can easily recognize the host who is or has been a prostate cancer patient. Upon the greetings at the door, he will immediately inform the male guests of **the precise location of each bathroom in the house**. Further, a non-patient may be surprised when overhearing how some patients introduce themselves to a peer group. The following dialog, with a hand shaking, is an example:

—*Hi, I am PSA 14, Gleason 8 (4+4).*
—*Nice meeting you, PSA 14. I am PSA 2.5, and Gleason 8 also.*
—*Just a moment! Did you say that you are "PSA 2.5" and have cancer? What happened to you?*
(And so on)

Statistics

This book uses abundant statistical data throughout, in numerous fields, as informative illustrations to the text and for the patient's reference and awareness –not for clinical comparison. **Statistics are part of our life. Statistics help us to know ourselves better.** For example, it is statistically very important to find out how many times average men get up during the night to urinate, how frequently their voiding hesitates. When we demand answers to our concerns on

"How normal am I?", the reply is full of statistics. But statistics have different value and meaning depending upon the perspective from which we look at them, the original purpose and the objective of the research and how it was conducted, how the data were analyzed, etc.

By their own nature, statistics are supposed to be, in and by themselves, intrinsically accurate and truthful when answering one-dimensional questions: how many patients visited a clinic last year and their age, race, etc. However, it is not so simple to establish the quality of medical information when we want to compare statistics from various sources. For example, if a patient wants to compare statistics from different institutions, clinics, or doctors (which were caused by various purposes) in order to evaluate by himself the accuracy or the cure rate of a treatment he may be contemplating. Such comparison may be useless and, worse, misleading unless 100% of the variables are 100% identical in all compared surveys –a very rare, if ever true, occurrence. **The variables and the components to be matched and the total input are seemingly endless**: number of patients studied, for how long, patients taken from the pre- or the post-PSA era, PSA levels and circumstances under which tests were made, age, pre-existing physical condition and history, cancer scores, staging, psychological factors, processes used for follow-ups at 3, 5, 10 or more years, and a galaxy of others. (Most of those issues are discussed in later chapters.)

Further confounding the search for answers through statistics, the director of quality control of one of the largest brachytherapy clinics in the U.S. confided to this Author that, of the thousands of patients treated for over 15 years, his staff had **never found two prostates 100% identical** –like snowflakes or fingerprints. Even doctors frequently argue among themselves and fuel strong controversies due to different test qualifications, criteria, and interpretation of their own statistics. In essence, a study of one clinic reporting, for instance, an 80% treatment disease-free results might in fact be worse than another reporting, say, 65%, because of the different standards or definitions of "disease-free", or the criteria used, or the objective of the study.

A humorous anecdote: American writer Mark Twain (1835-1910) popularized in the U.S. the famous quote from his contemporaneous, England Prime Minister and novelist Benjamin Disraeli (1804-1881): *"There are three kinds of lies: Lies, Damned Lies, and Statistics"*.

The main value of a statistical study, by itself, rests upon **the proven integrity of the doctor or entity that originated it**, the established criteria and the purpose for which it was designed. To the newly diagnosed prostate patient, the most meaningful value rests ultimately on the **individualization** of those statistics. It is crucial. The patient wants to know from the urologist and oncologist the trend of national cure rates **as a barometer to evaluate a treatment**, but particularly he wants to be informed of:

- How frequently and how many times has **his** specialist performed such treatment. Eminent specialists urge that a surgeon should have 150 supervised radical prostatectomy operations or 100 supervised brachytherapy procedures **before working** *in solo*. Although many doctors argue that such high requirements are **unrealistic**, studies have shown that patients are "three-times as likely to die" or to have more severe side effects when treatment is performed by a "low-volume" surgeon.

- His specialist's **own cure statistics** (in numbers and percentages), including how many patients achieved a PSA of ≤0.2 ng/ml and when and for how long after treatment.

- How many of his patients recovered continence and potency and when, and how many of them just died.

- What is the prognosis for cure and for preserving the quality of life to which the patient wants to adhere based on his **personal, individual cancer circumstances** and not on those of any other patient and treated by any other doctor – not even by such doctor's clinic or university or hospital. The patient likes to hear **how others did** but he is fundamentally concerned with *"What is in those statistics for me?"*, *"What is that doctor, personally, capable of doing for me?"* The patient is going to be treated by a doctor, not by an entity or a building. And finally,

- The advisability to contact some of the patients the specialist has previously treated. A patient told this Author that he was diagnosed with prostate cancer and that his urologist advised him to have a radical prostatectomy right away. The doctor outlined his potential cure using statistics that showed a very high chance of preserving life, continence, and potency after surgery. **The data sounded like the records** achieved by the surgeon recognized as the #1 in the world. Early the following morning, the patient decided to go back to the clinic to ask his urologist for confirmation of the data as being *his own* surgical statistics. The answer, *"I do not have time for that paper work, I am a surgeon, not an accountant".* A great urologist suggested, *"The patient should ask his urologist for the name and telephone of 10 patients the doctor has operated on".* Another renowned surgeon shared his own policy with this Author: He asks each of his treated patients, *"Would you be willing to telephone and talk to my future patients about your experience?"*

The Health Maintenance Organization (HMO)

The healthcare insurers concept (Preferred-Provider Organization, Pre-Paid Health Care Plan, Health Maintenance Organization, etc., summarized here under the general term **HMO**) has revolutionized the medical practice in the United States and, in general, the way patients have or do not have access to the medical care of their choice.

The concept was originally intended to make it possible for a company, association or group to provide its workers or members and their families healthcare that by themselves, they, individually, would not be able to afford. The physician **Dr. Michael Shadid** in 1929 started the first **Prepaid Health Care Plan** for the Rural Farmers Cooperative in Elk City, Oklahoma. The innovation expanded rapidly. **Henry J. Kaiser**, president of the Grand Coulee Dam, is credited for the definite expansion of the new idea. He made the Plans public and by 1959 the **Kaiser Permanent Health Plan** had a half million employees enrolled. In 1942, the Government helped greatly by making **health insurance premiums tax deductible –for the employers**.

The proliferation of healthcare insurers has drastically changed, more than anything else, today's perception and practice of Medicine. Both doctor and patient have learned the dichotomy: cheaper access to healthcare versus the power to override a doctor's recommendation for tests and treatments, and the limitation of patients' choices.

In 1965, President Johnson signed the **Medicare Law** to provide medical insurance to people age ≥65, and in 1971 President

31

Nixon announced the development of the **Health Maintenance Organizations (HMOs)**, passed by Congress in 1973.

HMOs are here to stay. When researching to select his new HMO, it is important for our man to ascertain that the terms of the contract provide:

> • **For his current and contemplated healthcare needs. When considering a new job, many men carefully scrutinize the services for pregnancy and infant care, but neglect to research those applicable to prostate screening and prostate cancer treatment.**
> • **For flexibility, allowing him to choose doctors and facilities –in many instances the patient cannot.**
> • **Doctor's autonomy to decide on tests and treatments, or else, what process should be followed and by whom for approval when special treatments become necessary (such as for prostate cancer). Otherwise, the patient may find out too late that the treatment of his choice is not covered or, worse, that his HMO, based on an internal technicality, may refuse paying the bill for services *already rendered*.**

Notable is the language used in the *Patient Rights & Responsibilities* brochures displayed in the examination rooms of some HMOs. One says, *"You have the right to receive understandable information regarding your medical condition, treatment and prognosis..."*, **but**, *"You are responsible for attempting to understand the options and treatment process of your care"*. In still another location, more significantly, *"You have the right to inspect and/or obtain a copy of information [we] maintain about you"*, **but followed by**, *"We may deny your request to inspect or obtain a copy of your information"*.

Affordability of Medicines

Drug manufacturers have not been immune to the radical mutations experienced by the medical care field in the last decades. The business trajectory of a small and modest one-product apothecary has been mentioned to exemplify the dimension and power gained by drug companies. Founded in 1888 in Chicago by the physician **Dr. Wallace C. Abbott**, his company's global conglomerate in 2004 had

70,000 employees, a capitalization of $60 billion and gross sales of $17.6 billion.

Indeed, patients have benefited from such formidable financial strength. It has enabled research and development of drugs to eradicate or mitigate numerous diseases and discomforts. Further, drug companies have contributed to the education of patients and have been active in charitable assistance. A few years ago, several major drug manufacturers implemented generous programs to provide drugs free of charge to needy prostate cancer patients.

On the other hand, aggressive promotional methods have both made a presence in the medical profession and contributed to the ever-high cost of medicines. The Food and Drug Administration caused a significant economic booster to the drug companies when it lifted in 1997 the **strict ban on advertising prescription medications directly to patients**. Marketing then shifted from a target of thousands of doctors visited in their offices to an audience of millions of persons, whether or not already patients. One result of the lift has been the investment of millions of dollars to inundate TV and magazines with ads written in medical jargon and printed in tiny compressed font size, some of them hardly readable particularly by the patients for whom the product is precisely made. The ads have the repeated kick, "*Ask your physician*".

The "side effects" of this new public image of the gigantic empire include, first, the tremendous pressure by patients on doctors asking for prescriptions of new or brand-name drugs they saw advertised; and second, an understandable emphasis on developing blockbuster products (e.g., for cholesterol, depression) and less to other conditions (e.g., prostate cancer). What directly and adversely affects the patient is the **high cost of the drugs for prostatic anomalies**. These patients appear to have gained an [*unsolicited*] "wealthy status": $1,800 for a shot repeated every three months, $400 for a one-month supply of 30 pills within a treatment to last several years, etc. Many patients have learned to urge their doctors to spend an extra moment **researching for less expensive drugs** –a generic brand or another "old" drug with a different name but the same therapeutic effects, and many of them (>50%) manufactured by the same company that makes the brand-name drug. As declared by the Food and Drug Administration, **generic drugs, for approval, must have the same stability, purity, quality and strength as the brand-name drugs**, and therefore, both have the same benefits and risks.

33

Ironically, one year after the FDA lifted the ban on advertising directly to patients, the International Federation of the Drug Industry of Europe and the United Kingdom adopted an *Ethics Code* (*"The European Code of Good Practice for the Promotion of Medicines"*) with strict rules to control pharmaceutical advertising. Among them: (a) advertising of medicines **must be directed exclusively to professionals of Medicine**, (b) the value of **any gift to a physician** cannot exceed 19 € (euros) = ~$25, and (c) manufacturers violating this *Code* (created and enforced by the pharmaceutical manufacturers themselves) will be fined a minimum of 6,000 € = ~$7,020, a maximum of 350,000 € = ~$409,500.

Chapter 2

When the Prostate behaves

The man's prostate is like the center of a masterpiece of engineering design. As the "central station" of the urinary/sexual/reproductive system, it controls the speed, strength and frequency of urination, it has jurisdiction over ejaculation, and it therefore decisively influences also the very essence of the male's being (*masculinity, manhood*) and of his intimacy with a partner –not to mention his life.

It would be fascinating to be able to watch internally, *in vivo*, **like children observing an electric train for the first time**, the motion of fluids and secretions in their own liquefied nature running up and down and around defying gravity in one- or two-way conduits before exiting the body. From the kidneys to/through the penis, fluids cross tunnels and valves that open and close automatically, as light-signal posts by the side of the railroad tracks, contingent upon physiological needs, pleasure desire, mental instructions and physical condition of the individual. It is a unique combination of skillful design, high technology, and plumbing mastery. Amazingly, this extremely complex and delicate piece of "soft machinery" may endure perfect functioning for 40, 50, 60 or more years –when in good behavior.

(We enjoy, of course, other similarly marvelous systems in our body, but we are concerned here with our prostate.)

As a substitute for that "natural observation tower", and thanks to some Internet graphics gurus and interactive human atlas, it is possible and impressive to watch on a computer monitor animated CD programs of the prostatic landscape in full operation and color.

Masculinity

The concept of *masculinity*, with its superlative popular or colloquial expression *machismo*, has played throughout History a fundamental role in defining men's character. In current times, this concept has changed to influence, for better or for worse, most men's approach to their prostate upon being diagnosed with cancer.

Macho, from Latin *mas* and Italian *maschio*, was introduced into Spanish culture centuries ago and subsequently passed into other cultures and spread as well all over Spanish America. One of the definitions of **machismo** in the *Diccionario de la Real Academia Española* is, *The attitude of preponderance of a man with respect to women.* The English **Webster Dictionary** says that machismo is, A *strong, exaggerated, sense of masculine pride,* and that **macho** is, A*ggressively virile.* Conceptually, the so-called macho is a complex male, vain, loud, eager to prove his manhood utilizing as vehicle the conquering of women, and he must have an audience to show-off. In some Spanish American countries, it is still an ingredient of the popular folklore. In the U.S., the concept has been for decades the inspiration of and the theme for countless movies (the first sound movie, Barrymore's *Don Juan* in 1926, the "Old West" style, *Don Giovanni Unmasked*, etc.), of songs (*Macho Man*), and even of children's toys. All media frequently use the word macho, and many choose this word to define "all Mexicans". Interestingly, it even expanded to women: *"She walks like a macho".*

The monk **Fray Gabriel Téllez** (1584-1648), one of the giants of the *Edad de Oro* (*Golden Age*) of Spain's Literature (mid-XVI century to 1681), better known by his penname **Tirso de Molina,** created the immortal character of the conqueror *Don Juan* in his masterpiece play *El Burlador de Sevilla* (1630). The play covers a variety of themes to which people were sensitive at the time, from religion and philosophy to the mixture of history and legends and myths. It caused tremendous impact and the theme inspired writers and composers in many countries, among them the French Molière (1665) and Baudelaire (1861), and Austrian Mozart's *Don Giovanni* (1787). However, it was **José Zorrilla** (1817-1893), the *National Poet* of Spain, who perfected the universal archetype of masculinity and of the macho in his immortal play in verse **Don Juan Tenorio**, premiered in Madrid in 1844 but with the action situated in Sevilla in the year of 1545. In the opening Act, the main character, Don Juan, reports on a bet over his macho rival Don Luis and claims to have conquered seventy-two women in one year, "*from a royal princess to a fisherman's daughter*". To affirm credibility, he kept a record of each conquest, attested by witnesses.

Historically, the essential implication has been that **the stereotyped male** is more of a man in relationship to his true (or faked) potency to conquer women –that is, to the power of his testicles.

Masculinity and the Prostate

But we now know that the legend initiated by Molina and perfected by Zorrilla is not quite accurate.

First, masculinity, as we will see in a later chapter, is particularly with age greatly influenced by a tiny gland surrounded by muscles and veins and tissues known as the **prostate (something that neither Molina nor Zorrilla had any clue about)**. When that gland fails, the concept and the feeling of masculinity, as applied to self-awareness and self-identity, are in serious jeopardy. Based on the principle that *everything is as strong as its weakest part*, what makes a male "feel like a man" are not just his testicles, but rather **the healthy function of his prostate**. During our younger years, the prostate seems to us men so unimportant that we hardly remember it even after a course in Anatomy (and some books do not even mention it). As a norm, seldom if ever are we as children taught at home to watch out for that tiny gland.

Second, today's male, when he becomes a prostate cancer patient, is very concerned about the impact that **his physical [in]ability to perform sexually** may have on his appreciation of his own masculinity (thus, of his own identity) as well as on his partner's.

And the psychological reaction to the news of having prostate cancer, a sensitive issue to all men, becomes even **more crucial when intersecting the traditional social stigma of both "cancer" and "homosexuality"**. The concerns of a gay patient about his sexuality relative to his prostate cancer diagnosis extend to **how to communicate with and which reaction to expect from his partner**, the impact on his life style and social environment and, to worsen his anxiety, the uncertainty of finding medical specialists who understand the

37

gay patient's emotional and psychological trauma in addition to his prostate condition.

The differences between the man of the legend and the man of our times are essential to fully understand many men's reactions when their prostate misbehaves, as well as to understand the attitude of their wives or partners.

When the Prostate behaves

When it behaves, the **prostate** has the approximate shape of a walnut and measures about 1½ inch long. The exterior is not as hard as a walnut but not as fragile as a little egg either. The texture is uniform, fine, elastic, muscular, composed of tissues. It is positioned in

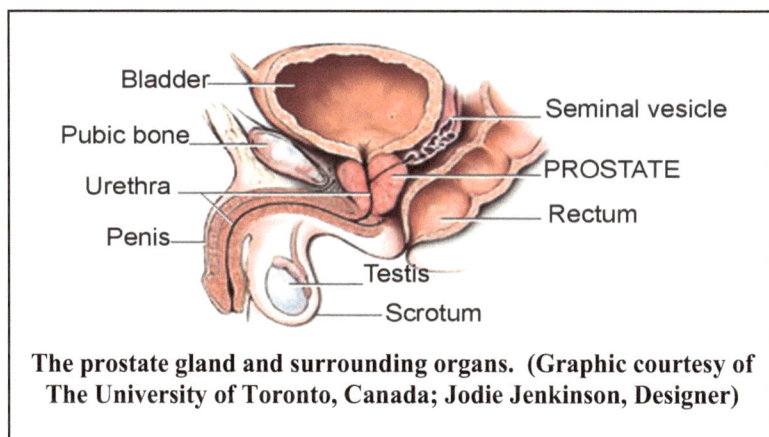

The prostate gland and surrounding organs. (Graphic courtesy of The University of Toronto, Canada; Jodie Jenkinson, Designer)

the **pelvis** between the bladder (above) and the **rectum** (below and behind), in vertical configuration. Sticking out, though at an angle, are the **seminal vesicles,** like two vigilant TV antennas or rabbit ears. The nerves and muscles that control **sexual erection** and **continence** of urine run at both sides. The **ureters**, 2 one-way muscular tubes one foot long by ½ inch wide, carry the **urine** from each of the two **kidneys** (average size 4" x 2" x 1") to the bladder. The **bladder** expands to hold about one pint of liquid and contracts to expel the urine through the **urethra** (8 inches long), which the prostate wraps around like a donut as it crosses through the center of the gland to carry the urine through the penis for voiding.

Making this system more complex, the prostate is one of the glands that produces most of the **semen**, the milky fluid transporting the **sperm** (made by the testicles or testes and stored for maturing in the epididymis) out through the urethra and the penis when the male ejaculates at sexual orgasm.

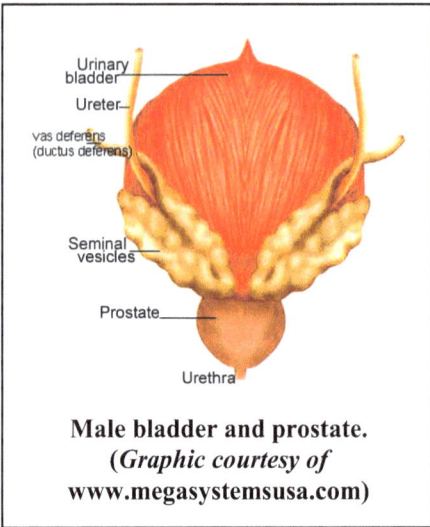

Male bladder and prostate.
(*Graphic courtesy of*
www.megasystemsusa.com)

The **epididymis** is a small single coiled tube, about 20 feet long if un-coiled, of very small diameter; it lies along the top and the side of each testis; the sperm cells are temporarily stored here after leaving the testes and until instructed to exit by **ejaculation**. The **vas deferens** (plural, **vasa defer-entia**) is each of the two tubes (45.72 cm or 18" long x a tiny 3 mm or 0.11811" in diameter) running as an extension of the epididymis zone on each side of the pros-tate; they transport sperm up from the testes to the base of the prostate and then through the ejaculatory duct, the ure-thra and finally out through the penis.

A **muscular valve** lo-cated in the neck of the blad-der directs the traffic, like the switchman in the imaginary electric train route mentioned above. At orgasm, this valve shuts down and forces the sperm fluid to exit through the urethra and the penis in-stead of back into the blad-der. (The **[mal]function of this valve** after surgery and radiation will become par-ticularly important at ejacula-tion, as it will be discussed in

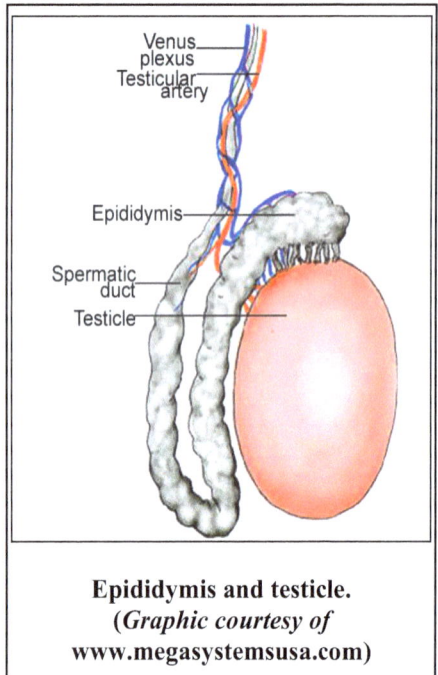

Epididymis and testicle.
(*Graphic courtesy of*
www.megasystemsusa.com)

Chapter 6) The prostate however, has no bearing on the **orgasm**, which is triggered by the brain in response to certain stimuli.

The average **sperm cells** daily production or count is about 100 million little swimmers per milliliter (ml) of seminal fluid, and **seminal fluid** is produced at an average of 2 ml per day. The two **seminal vesicles**, each 2 inches long, are pouch-like glands situated above the prostate and they ensure the consistency of the semen.

The two **testicles** or **testes**, each about 2 inches long by 1 inch wide (±4 x 5.5 cm), the size of a plum and the shape of an egg, are the factory for sperm, the main source of **the male reproductive cells** (spermatozoa and sperm) and of male **hormones.**

Testosterone is the male hormone responsible for fertility and that at a certain age starts also influencing *masculinizing* characteristics, such as post-pubertal **body hair** and **deepening of the voice**.

The testes are housed in the bag called **scrotum** and they produce ±85% to 95% of the testosterone; the **adrenal glands**, on top of the kidneys, make the other ±5% to 15%. The scrotum provides the ideal temperature for the production of sperm cells in the testicles.

The **testosterone**, also called **androgen**, comes from the testes, circulates in the blood at the discretion of the hypothalamus and regulates the prostate. The amount produced is believed to be one of the determining factors in **the growth of cancer of the prostate**, much as kerosene fuels a fire or much as fertilizer enhances the growth of plants.

This intense traffic of fluids ends up exiting through the **penis**, which is composed of nerves, muscles, blood vessels, and erectile and connective tissue sheathed in skin. The penis serves two purposes: **voiding of urine** and **ejaculation**. The dynamics of its arteries and veins cause an erection when the arteries continue their function of pumping blood into the penis but the veins close down the engorged or the circulation of the blood so that the penis can remain "inflated" during sexual arousal.

The penis may start developing as early as 9 years and it reaches its adult size at ±17 years of age. Some experts maintain that its size (as well as its color and shape) is related to hereditary factors; it ranges from the shortest 1½ inches (3.8 centimeters) to the longest 6½ inches (16½ centimeters), the average being 4½ to 5 inches (11½ to 12.7 centimeters). A flaccid penis fully stretched measures as much as the same penis erect.

The **volume/size** and the **weight** of the prostate increase progressively from about 4cc (cc = cubic centimeter) or 4 grams at age 15, to 20cc and a weight of 20 grams at age 20. At age 50, tissues begin to show certain changes, **enlargement**, in 75% of the males. The size of adult healthy prostate averages 15cc to 30cc.

Such multiplicity of parts, so tiny, so independent and yet functioning in interwoven coordination with each other, are located in an area so small that, for centuries, surgeons could not find some of those parts, immersed as they were in a pool of blood, or else, they could not determine the exact location of most until the year 1978, as we will discuss in Chapter 6 - *"Radical Prostatectomy"*.

The prostate is divided into three parts or **lobes**: right, left, and middle, or into five **zones**: anterior, peripheral, central, pre-prostatic, and transition. The transition zone surrounds the urethra, which runs through it at a 35° angle. **Excessive growth of the gland** will consequently choke it, obstruct the urine flow and cause illness.

THE MALE URINARY AND SEXUAL SYSTEM
(*Items in* **bold** *correlate the drawing with the caption*)

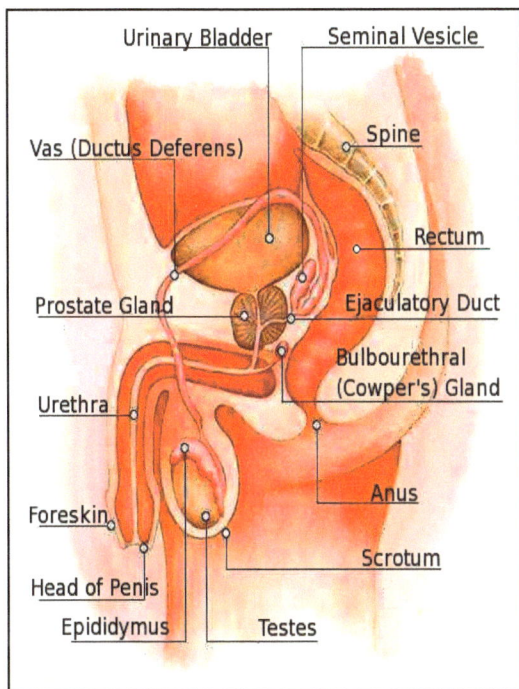

The **bladder** is emptied by way of the **urethra**, a tube passing through the **prostate gland**. The main function of the prostate is to supply fluid for sperm that has been collected in the **seminal vesicles**. Ejaculation occurs when the seminal vesicles and the prostate empty at orgasm.

The seminal vesicles are supplied by the **vas deferens** from the **epididymis**, a tightly coiled tube next to the **testicles** or **testes** that provides for the storage, transmission, and maturation of sperm.

Before ejaculation, the **Cowper's glands** secrete an alkaline fluid that neutralizes any urine that may be left in the urethra. The fluid also has a lubricating quality. Because these glands are often spared in a prostatectomy or are damaged by radiation, they may continue to function even though there is no ejaculate through the penis (it is called a "dry-ejaculate").

The drawing also shows how the location of the prostate favors an easy digital rectal examination (DRE), rectal ultrasound, and rectal biopsy.

(Adapted from "*You and Your Prostate*", produced by the Australia Department of Veterans Affairs - © and *Courtesy of* The Commonwealth of Australia)

Chapter 3

When the Prostate misbehaves

In spite of the prostatic anatomic environment being such an amazing "masterpiece of design", the controlling gland itself is an astonishing irony. **First**, perhaps for being one more human part, the prostate is not as perfect as it appeared at first sight. **It is fickle, it may fail** –it may be a matter of time or circumstances. **Second**, and worse, it is intrinsically **dispensable, disposable –although not replaceable.** We did not know it until 1982, confirmed in 1985. The eminent urologist **Dr. Patrick Craig Walsh** (Akron, Ohio February 13, 1938-   ) in 1982 rediscovered its anatomy and reasserted that, after its *removal*, men can live and continue performing two important functions: to urinate in the toilet and to have sex, both at will. And in 1985 another urologist, **Dr. Haakon Ragde** (July 26, 1927-_____), teaming with oncologist **Dr. John Charles Blasko** (1943-_____), accomplished substantially the same results but by virtually *killing* the prostate and leaving it *inside* resting in peace. In essence, after so many centuries, scientists were able to reconfigure and re-evaluate our prostatic anatomy.

Noting the significance of those events, we might like (if feasible) to simply overhaul the entire system by eliminating some pieces and rerouting others to allow more room for the surgeon to reach hidden parts and for the radiation oncologist to avoid damage to tissues surrounding the gland. However, it is beyond doubt that new generations **shall be born with the same original configuration**. Consequently, we must learn **how to love and care for the prostate** while it behaves and **how to fight it and kill it or dispose of it** if necessary when it does not.

When it starts misbehaving, the prostate may develop three main pathologies or diseases:

1. **Infection, inflammation (Prostatitis)**
2. **Benign Prostatic Hyperplasia (BPH)**, abnormal increase of the number of cells, **enlargement** of the gland
3. **Cancer**.

(The first two are benign and produce symptoms while the third, the worst, cancer, is usually asymptomatic –in its beginnings.)

1. Infection, Inflammation

It may be caused by **Bacterial Infection**. Some of the symptoms are fever and chills, muscular pain, pain in lower back, irritation and obstruction of the urinary tract, burning sensation, ejaculatory pain, and warmth and tenderness felt by the urologist's rectal palpation examination. The actual cause is unknown. Some theories suggest that a man may develop it due to bladder infection or caused by a catheter or other instrument inserted into/through his urethra. Doctors usually request a urinalysis and perform a digital rectal examination (DRE). During this exam, they massage the prostate to force some fluid out of the gland to send it to the laboratory for analysis.

Non-bacterial Prostatitis, also of unknown cause, is characterized by similar symptoms as those described above and will urge the urologist to prescribe drugs (mainly relaxants, since antibiotics will not help in the absence of bacteria) and to further explore with tests as those performed for BPH. Studies show that prostatitis is not sexually transmitted.

2. Benign Prostatic Hyperplasia (BPH)

44

It is an enlargement of the gland and generally not related to the process of malignancy. It is considered not cancerous. However, it can coexist with cancer and therefore, share the same symptoms. Additionally, one of the causes of the enlargement is the production of the hormone metabolite dihydrotestosterone (**DHT**), judged by many experts to be greatly responsible for benign prostate enlargement and possibly for prostate cancer. Studies link it also to high fat diets and family history.

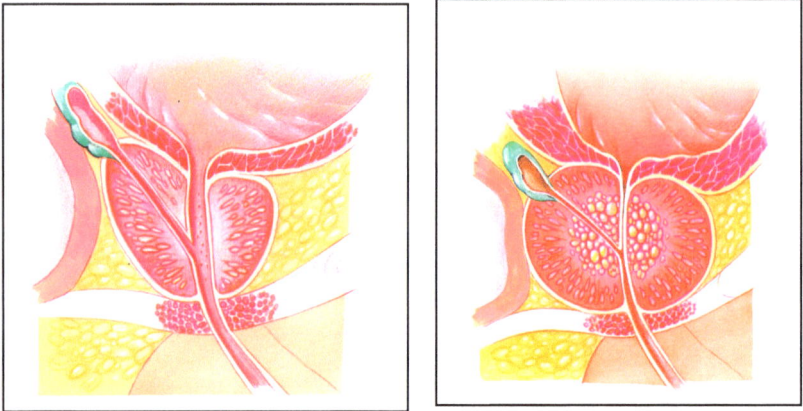

Left: Normal prostate. Right: Prostate showing Benign Prostatic Hyperplasia (BPH); the enlargement presses against the urethra and the bladder, consequently narrowing the flow of urine.
(*Graphics courtesy of* Merck Research Laboratories of Merck & Co.)

Puberty (14 to 18 years) is considered the period of "maturation" of the prostate, which grows until the third decade. After the 30s and until age 45-50, it has a so-called "stationary size"; afterwards, it may suffer enlargement (BPH) or progressive atrophy. In the U.S., 25% of white **men experience prostate enlargement starting at about age 40, 50% at age 50**. For black men these numbers are 25% at age 35 and 50% at age 45 –**always 5 years earlier for blacks**. For every decade increase in age, the percentage of all men with probability of prostate enlargement also increases by ten: at age 60, 60% have prostate enlargement; at 70, 70%; at 80, 80%; at 90, 90%, and when/if we reach 100…*Bingo!* all of us are "expected" to somehow have an enlarged prostate. BPH is the most common cause of urinary symptoms in men age ≥70.

Due to its strategic location in the man's anatomy, the prostate, when enlarged, will cause formidable chaos to the otherwise functional harmony of the gland and neighboring organs. Most critical: strangulation of the urethra and obstruction of the flow of urine from the bladder to/through the penis.

- **Incomplete emptying:** Sensation of not emptying the bladder completely after urinating is finished.
- **Frequency:** Measured by the number of times one has to urinate again less than two hours after having urinated; or >8 times in a 24-hour period.
- **Intermittency:** Stopping and starting again several times during urination.
- **Urgency:** Difficulty in postponing urination upon first feeling the need without warning.
- **Weak-stream:** Weak urinary stream, low flow.
- **Straining and Hesitancy:** Necessity of pushing or straining to begin urination, waiting for a long time for the flow to begin.
- **Dribbling:** After completing urination, leakage of urine in the underpants, an occurrence mainly in men age >70.
- **Disuria:** Burning sensation when urinating; caused by urethritis or possibly because the urine may have already formed calculus in the vesicles.
- **Nocturia:** Disrupted sleep; getting up frequently (more than two times) at night to urinate before it is time to get up in the morning.

Hematuria (*hemat*=blood, *uria*=urine) or presence of blood in the urine is considered not necessarily a symptom of prostatic illness. If the urine is abnormally colored pink, red or brown the man should see his urologist immediately because there is a possibility of other grave anomalies in the urinary tract —such as kidneys, ureters, bladder, prostatic urethra and the rest of the urethra.

Interestingly, the feeling of some of the above symptoms may be abruptly *amplified* by cold temperature, the sound of running water, a long trip or…**when using an electric shaver or toothbrush**, which suddenly produce the urge to stop the task and go immediately to urinate.

Several organizations and urological groups have developed various questionnaires to help doctors (and patients by "self-testing") in an initial evaluation of the urinary function. Following is a sample –the higher the score ranging from 0 to 35, the greater the warning of urinary anomalies.

SELF-TEST OF URINATING PATTERNS (Circle the number that applies to you)						
Generally, during the last 4 weeks or so I felt...	Never	< 1x in 5	< ½ time	~ ½ time	> ½ time	Always
After finishing, a sensation of not having emptied the bladder completely:	0	1	2	3	4	5
An urge to urinate again in less than 2 hours:	0	1	2	3	4	5
A sensation of stopping and starting again several times while urinating:	0	1	2	3	4	5
Difficulty in waiting or post-poning:	0	1	2	3	4	5
Weak urinary stream:	0	1	2	3	4	5
A need to push or strain in order to begin:	0	1	2	3	4	5
Getting up frequently at night to urinate (how many times?):	0	1	2	3	4	5

TOTAL SCORE...................: _____

SCORE: ≤7=Mild BPH; 8-11=Moderate BPH; 20-35=Severe, **see your urologist as soon as possible.**

Cancer

Because it is generally asymptomatic in the beginning, probably the cancer is already advanced when symptoms are felt, as discussed later.

Diagnosing Methods

Following are the most common diagnosing tests that the patient may go through (and this is the right time for the man to update the *Medical and Clinical Records* spreadsheet inserted in Chapter 1).

DIGITAL RECTAL EXAMINATION (DRE)

This is the first and most common test. It is universally performed to explore and diagnose pathologies of the prostate. It is done in the doctor's examination room. The patient takes his pants down and leans forward on the table; the doctor inserts a gloved, lubricated finger into the patient's rectum to reach and feel the prostate and to identify possible lumps, irregularity or asymmetry in form, scars, etc. that could suggest a prostatic disease.

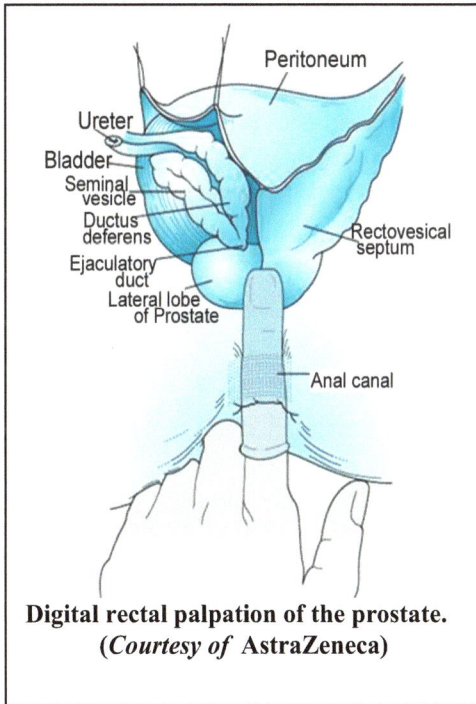

Digital rectal palpation of the prostate.
(*Courtesy of* AstraZeneca)

Dr. Willet F. Whitmore, Jr. (Long Island, New York, December 12, 1917-May 8, 1995), Memorial Sloan-Kettering Hospital, New York, **popularized in 1956 in the U.S. the use of the DRE** to explore by tact abnormalities in the prostate gland suspicious of cancer; and **Dr. Hugh J. Jewett** (1903-1990), of Johns Hopkins University, Baltimore, Maryland, was in 1975 **the first to classify the spread of local tumor based on the DRE**.

This is a simple test and lasts a few moments under no anesthesia. Even currently, it is erroneously assumed that the expertise of the doctor and the size of his finger are solely responsible for making it uncomfortable. The discomfort is caused when the finger tries to reach the back of the gland or has to massage it, a brief unpleasant process augmented when the man has BPH or a large prostate. Men who are overweight complain more vehemently.

Nevertheless, most men dislike it. This test is particularly significant in some cultures, and American men are not an exception. Many consider the DRE test **unbecoming to their masculinity** and the urologist must convince a patient to allow him to perform this exam. A great urologist in Mexico confided to this Author that, when he tells a patient that he *is not* going to perform the DRE at that time, the patient responds as if *he is already cured* of whatever problem for which he went to see him. In Latin American countries, the attitude of "fear" of the DRE varies from nation to nation, being the strongest in Mexico –where the feeling of machismo is also the strongest. Such attitude remains attached to Latin American immigrants when they first come to the U.S.

The DRE is the most important initial test performed for prostate abnormalities diagnosis. By itself however, it is not enough. When performing routine physical examinations, and based on the result of the DRE and the age of the patient, urologists complement the DRE with another test, the PSA.

PROSTATE-SPECIFIC ANTIGEN (PSA)

Prostate-Specific Antigen (abbreviated **PSA**) is a type of enzyme produced primarily in the man's prostatic gland and concentrated in its tissue. Its chemical reaction, the protein, carries the semen (the fluid that propels the sperm at sexual orgasm) and helps to keep it in its liquid form.

PSA is made by healthy as well as by prostatic cancerous cells. **A healthy prostate keeps or locks in the gland the major portion of PSA**, and therefore, levels in the blood are very low, "undetectable". However, when the prostate begins to misbehave, a higher amount of PSA "leaks" from the gland into the blood stream. Consequently, the PSA level has become a crucial marker: generally, the higher its amount in the blood, the more cause for alarm that something abnormal is going on inside the gland. When the doctor during the DRE detects abnormalities in, for example, volume or symmetry of the gland, or bumps, or soft/hard spots, he recommends a *PSA blood test*.

The PSA test has had a varied and complex history, encompassing events from its discovery to current controversies on random screening.

It all began with two articles published in 1970 in the *Journal of Reproduction and Fertility* and in the *Journal of Immunology* by one of the pioneers of immunology of the prostate, **Dr. Richard J. Ablin** (May 15, 1940-   ), then with the University of New York at Buffalo and now Director of Scientific Investigation of Innapharma, Inc., New Jersey. *"While looking for tumor-specific antigens to distinguish between benign versus malignant disease of the prostate"*, Dr. Ablin explained to this Author in January of 2003, *"we discovered the tissue-specific antigens of the normal and pathologic prostate, the basis for the Prostate-Specific Antigen test (PSA test), developed by others later, and the prostatic acid phosphatase (PAP)"*.

Photo courtesy of
Dr. Richard J. Ablin

A few years later, **Dr. T. Ming Chu** (Taiwan April 18, 1938- relocated to and educated in the U.S._____), then Chair of Diagnostic Immunology Research at Roswell Park Cancer Institute, Buffalo, New York, now Emeritus, grouped and directed a team of remarkable scientists to embark on a research program supported by the State of New York and the National Cancer Institute. His goal was, as he explained to this Author, *"to identify, purify and characterize prostate tumor-specific or associated antigens and to develop a blood test for early detection of prostate cancer."* He announced in 1979 the extraordinary success of the first phase of the program and confirmed the pursuit of developing PSA tests.

As a result, the first test **to diagnose prostate cancer** was complete in 1980, and the second in 1981 **to monitor post-treatment**. The Food and Drug Administration **approved in 1986 the first PSA test** for monitoring prostate cancer treatment and recurrence, in 1994 for diagnosis, and in 1998 the fPSA (FreePSA) and the cPSA (ComplexedPSA).

Physicians welcomed the new test. It enabled them to detect tumors sometimes between 5 and 7 years **before they became palpable**. Moreover, eminent specialists worked diligently to experiment the tests and to suggest improvements.

Photo courtesy of
Dr. T. Ming Chu

The scientists that precipitated the universal generalization of the PSA test were in the team directed by **Dr. William J. Catalona** (Cleveland, Ohio, November 14, 1942-   ), then Chief of Urologic Surgery at Washington University Medical Center, St. Louis, Missouri, and since 2003 Professor of Urology at Northwestern University School of Medicine, Chicago, Illinois. Dr. Catalona structured two extensive investigative trials to prove the value of the test as a screening tool. In his landmark article published in 1991 in the *New England Journal of Medicine,* he reported the results of the first successful large series (screening of 1,653 asymptomatic men over 50 years of age). In 1993, to satisfy the FDA requirements for approval, he completed another study involving 10,251 asymptomatic men over age 50 in seven urologic centers of excellence at universities all over the U.S. And he was also the leader of a complex screening campaign with an enrollment of 35,000 men.

These screenings showed that, in conjunction with a digital rectal examination, the PSA test was the most effective way to detect possible prostate cancer. Furthermore, 90% of prostate cancers detected through PSA screening are considered "clinically significant" cancers but still in organ-confined early stages, that is, with strong probability of being cured.

Col. Judd W. Moul, M.D. (February 8, 1957-   ), former Director of the Prostatic Disease Center and Professor of Surgery, Uniformed Services University, Walter Reed Army Medical Center in Rockville, Maryland, now Chief of the Urology Department at Duke University, Durham, NC, directed several milestone researches. In a ten-year study of 2,042 men, he noticed that the prostate cancer survival rate increased from 81.7% (18.30% death) in 1988-91 to 98.3% (only 1.70% death) in 1995-1998 thanks to screening, and that prostate cancer metastases decreased dramatically from 14.1% in 1988 to only 3.3% in 1998.

Photo courtesy of
Dr. William J. Catalona

At the same time, Dr. Moul confirmed that **black population registered up to 50% higher** incidence of prostate cancer than white did, and a similarly unbalanced mortality rate (24.7 per 100,000 population among whites, 55.1 per 100,000 among blacks). As possible causes, hormonal, nutritional, genetic, behavioral, socioeconomic status, and literacy have been mentioned. In 2002, the American Council on Science and Health confirmed that **black men have 69% higher risk of developing prostate cancer than white men**.

The PSA test undoubtedly is the most significant advancement in the management of men's diagnosis as well as in post-treatment evaluation of cancer of the prostate. Some urologists flag caution on how to interpret the results. The reason: PSA is **prostate-specific** (specifically made in/by the prostate) but it is **not cancer-specific** (it does not specifically and necessarily constitute evidence of the presence or absence of cancer), an argument of great importance for the patient's own interpretation of his PSA levels. **This test has become an indispensable tool**. The U.S. Congress in 2000 passed an Act whereas all Medicare and Medicaid patients can receive an annual PSA test as part of their benefits.

Nevertheless, neither the DRE alone nor the PSA alone is sufficient basis to make diagnosis and treatment decisions –urologists insist in that **both** should be administered. In 1992, the American Cancer Society recommended both the DRE and the PSA tests as part of the annual physical examination.

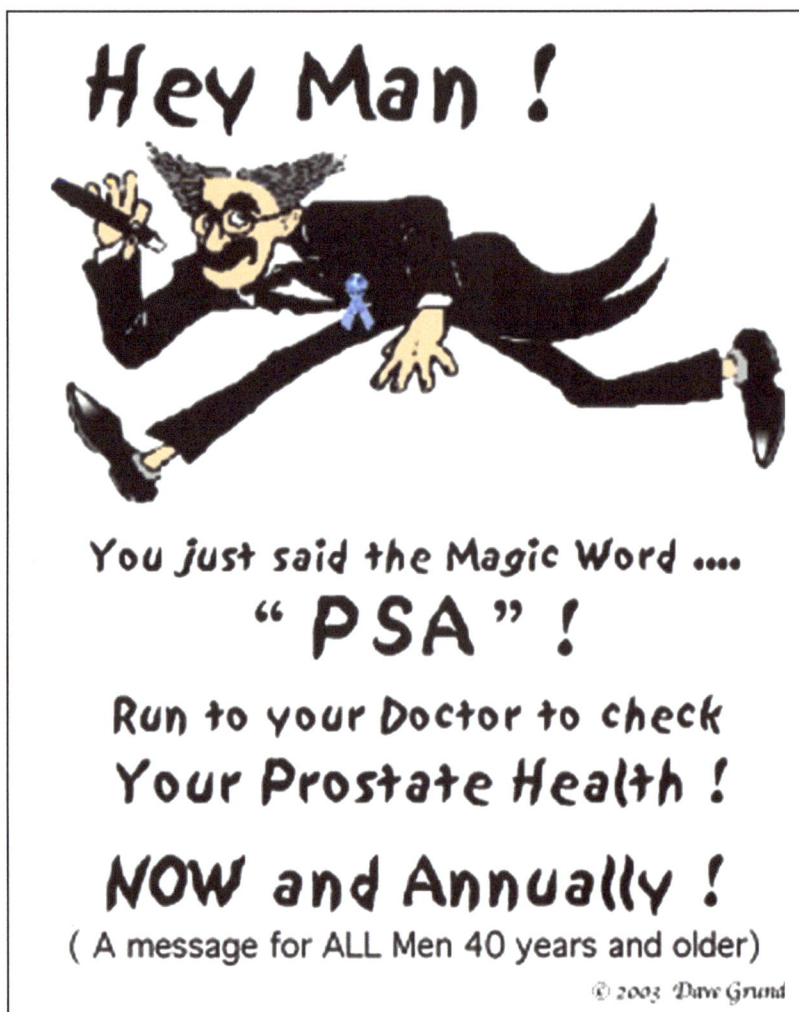

Prostate Cancer Awareness Poster
(*Courtesy of* **Dave Grundy, Canada**)

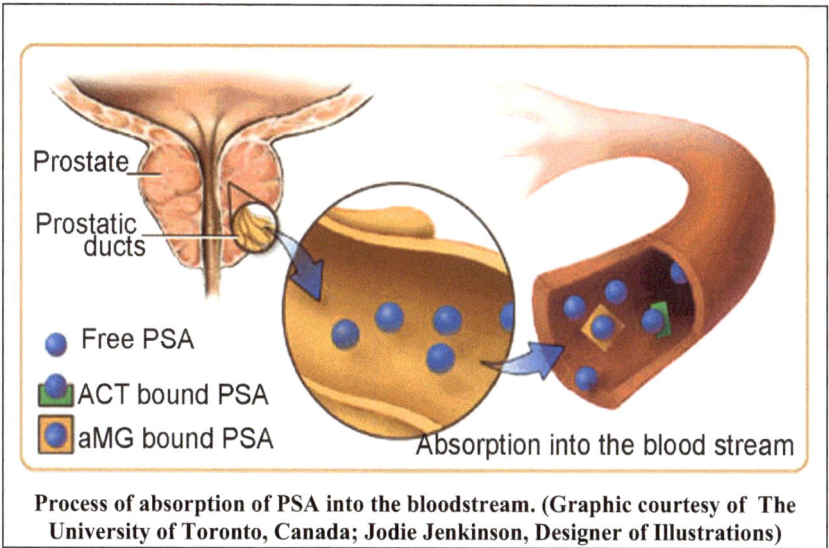

Process of absorption of PSA into the bloodstream. (Graphic courtesy of The University of Toronto, Canada; Jodie Jenkinson, Designer of Illustrations)

Scientists vigorously pursued research to improve the PSA tests, as shown in the following summary, and the details are or will be of great concern to all men age 30 and older.

TotalPSA or tPSA (generally, just PSA)

It is the first and the basis of **the PSA family of tests**. It measures the total amount of PSA leaking from the prostate into the blood stream. The measurement is expressed in **nanograms per milliliter of serum**, abbreviated **ng/ml** (to express test sensitivity accuracy, many laboratories and doctors write measurements as, for example, 0.03 ng/ml, but the same number is also found in general literature written, for simplicity, as 3.0 ng/ml., that is, x 100).

The American Cancer Society had suggested the use of ≤4.0 ng/ml as the **baseline between healthy and abnormal prostate**. However, researchers discovered through another test, the biopsy, and during radical prostatectomy surgery that more than 22% of men registering a PSA of ≥2.6 to ≤4.0 ng/ml turned out to have cancer already, and that 81% of those had a pathologically "organ-confined" cancer –curable, because of early detection. Consequently, in 1995, Dr. William J. Catalona proposed lowering the baseline from ≤4.0 ng/ml to ≤2.5 ng/ml. Studies suggest that the new threshold allows detecting more cases of cancer and that a man registering a PSA of ≥2.5 ng/ml at any age should be explored for possible prostate cancer.

Recent studies recommend to lower the baseline even more, to ≤2.0 ng/ml, and advise men with >2.0 to have FreePSA and PSA-Density tests as well.

A healthy prostate generally leaks ≤1.0 ng/ml of PSA into the blood. Levels between 2.5 to 4.0 ng/ml are considered borderline, levels of 4.0 to 10 ng/ml should be cause for alarm and suggest further testing and a biopsy, and levels of >10.0 ng/ml indicate the probability of cancer.

GROUPS/LEVELS OF PSA	
0.0 – 2.5 ng/ml	2.6 – 4.0 ng/ml
4.1 – 10.0 ng/ml	10.1 – 20.0 ng/ml
20.1+ ng/ml	

Some renowned specialists suggest that the PSA levels in the chart above frequently correlate with cancer that has already penetrated outside the capsule (risk of metastasis). For example:

PSA GROUP	CAPSULE PENETRATION PROBABILITY
0.0 – 4.0 ng/ml	25%
4.1 – 10.0 ng/ml	50%
10.1 – 20.0 ng/ml	75%
≥ 20.1 ng/ml	~100%

In Austria, a group of researchers completed in 2006 a study on 3,446 men that underwent PSA screening and then had a biopsy. Alarmingly, prostate cancer was detected in 21% of men with a PSA of 2.0 to 3.9 ng/ml, and 30% in the group 4.0 to 10.0 ng/ml.

Several factors may alter PSA test results. Research shows that they may be substantially (though temporarily) increased or decreased by certain conditions unrelated to malignancy. Awareness of those conditions may assist both patient and doctor to consider rescheduling the PSA test. For example,

- **Ongoing prostatic infection:** The physician may prescribe antibiotics and wait about six weeks before giving the test.
- **Digital Rectal Examination:** Experts recommend taking the blood before the exam or 2+ weeks after. The gland is known to release larger amounts of PSA after its manipulation or massage.
- **Sexual ejaculation:** Tends to elevate PSA level. Doctors advise abstaining from sexual activity for 2 to 3 days before the test.
- **Bicycle or Horseback riding:** Same as for Digital Rectal Examination.
- **After a prostatic Biopsy:** This procedure may affect the PSA level for at least six weeks.
- **Cytoscopy:** Can elevate PSA level for at least two weeks.
- **Medications:** Some may temporarily reduce the PSA level by as much as 50%.
-

FreePSA (fPSA)

Two major types of PSA exist *in vivo*: **Total** or **Complexed** (=bounded to proteins and that accounts for ~90%) and **Free, Floating** or **Uncomplexed** (=unbounded to proteins and that accounts for ~10%). Significantly, the higher the TotalPSA in the blood above of certain baseline (>2.5 ng/ml) the more risk that cancer is already growing, and the lower the percent of FreePSA in the blood below of certain baseline (<25%) the more risk that cancer is already developing. Researchers discovered that **the predictive numbers move in opposite directions**. Renowned prostate oncologists strongly urge having the FreePSA test **before** and **not after** designing a diagnostic.

The formula is: FreePSA divided by TotalPSA x 100 (and expressed in percent). For example, if the FreePSA is ≥25% the probability of cancer is only ~8%. But if it is <10%, the probability of cancer increases to 70%. Furthermore, experts relate FreePSA% level to the probability of cancer extra-capsular invasion. Investigators have arrived at several prediction tables; the following relationships are samples of the probability of cancer depending on TotalPSA and the FreePSA%.

CORRELATION BETWEEN *PSA* & *% FreePSA* AND *CANCER PROBABILITY*			
STANDARD PSA	PROBABILITY OF CANCER	% FREE PSA	PROBABILITY OF CANCER
0 - 2 ng/ml	1%	0.0 - <10%	70%
2 – 4 ng/ml	15%	10% to <11%	58%
4 – 10 ng/ml	25%	11% to <15%	46%
> 10 ng/ml	>50%	15% to <20%	20%
		20% to 24%	23%
		≥ 25%	8%

PSA-Velocity (PSAV)

Velocity shows the change at which the PSA level increases within a certain period, therefore, improving the ability to diagnose cancer and to evaluate its prognosis. Some experts sustain that "**no single value of PSA is as important as the PSA Velocity**" and that it can detect the cancer five years or more before it is diagnosed. It is done at about three months apart over an 18-month period and **always by the same assay laboratory**. A [PSA] velocity increase of ≥25% per year suggests high probability of cancer even if the TotalPSA is not very elevated.

Patients monitoring their own prostate health may wish to download **PSAV automatic calculators** available in several Internet websites, for example, http://www.prostate-cancer.org.

PSA-Density (PSA-D)

Density is PSA reading per volume-unit of gland: PSA divided by the gland volume. The precise volume or size of the prostate can be measured by the test **Transrectal Ultrasound of the Prostate (TRUS or TRUSP)** or by the endorectal **Magnetic Resonance Imaging (MRI)**. Cancerous cells release into the bloodstream more PSA per volume unit than the benign cells or BPH. The formula is: Prostate Volume x 0.066 = the amount of serum PSA attributable to benign prostate cells due to gland enlargement. By subtracting this amount from the TotalPSA, we find out the **"excess" PSA** that may be assumed due to tumor activity. For example, if the patient has a PSA of 6.0 and a gland of 30cc, the formula would be: 30 x 0.066 = 2.0 ng/ml; and 6.0 –2.0 ng/ml = 4.0 ng/ml, which is the PSA unaccounted for and possibly related to prostate cancer. The level of PSA in the blood is normally 15% of the weight or volume of the gland, and a reading above that figure differentiates between BPH and risk of prostate cancer. The higher the number, the higher the chance of cancer. This test is considered very useful to also explore the aggressiveness of localized cancer.

PSA-Double Time (PSA-DT)

PSA *Double* or *Doubling Time* is the time in which the PSA level doubles its value. Like the PSAVelocity, this is done at least three months apart over an 18-month or longer period and using always the same assay laboratory. Research revealed that **prostate cancer shows a slow PSA lineal phase followed by a quick growth**, and that the PSA level continues toward a phase of **exponential increment several years before it is diagnosed**. Most cancerous tumors have an average PSA-DT of four years, that is, **the number of cancerous cells may double in four years**. However, many double in shorter periods. Renowned specialists insist in that a doubling time faster than 1.5 to 2 years suggests the presence of cancer and may prove life threatening. This constitutes another factor against theories arguing that prostate cancer is a constant, and therefore, very slow-growing malignancy –and another proof that men should start being tested at an early age and then every 6-12 months.

SUMMARY OF THE *PSA TESTS*		
	NORMAL TEST TOLERANCE	RESULTS THAT WARN OF CANCER
TotalPSA	≤ 2.5 ng/ml	≥ 4.0 ng/ml.
FreePSA%	≥ 0.25%	≤ 0.25%
PSA Velocity	≤ 0.25%	≥ 0.25%
PSA Density	≤ 0.15ng/ml	≥ 0.15 ng/ml
PSA Doubling	0	1.5 to 2 years

PSA Ultrasensitive Test → "Third Generation"

When first released in the late 1980s, the immunoassays for PSA ("First Generation") possessed analytical sensitivities of 0.3 ng/ml to 0.6 ng/ml, average 0.4 ng/ml. In many countries other than the U.S., and even by few urologists in the U.S., the 0.4 ng/ml baseline is still used, meaning that a PSA reading between zero and 0.39 ng/ml is considered in those countries and by those urologists "normal" or with "no detectable cancer". In the 1990s, a "Second Generation" of PSA assays was developed with an analytical sensitivity of

0.1 ng/ml to 0.2 ng/ml, providing a more valuable tool to identify the risk of cancer already developing even in men registering <0.4 ng/ml.

In 1997, a "Third Generation" **Ultrasensitive PSA** assay was released to the market with a detection limit as low as 0.003 ng/ml, an analytical sensitivity of 0.003 ng/ml and a functional sensitivity of 0.01 ng/ml. The original first two generations of PSA tests were designed for **screening and diagnosing purposes**, while the third generation test has been designed *exclusively* **for the management/evaluation of patients following surgery –but not for screening**.

PSA Age-Specific

This is not a PSA test but rather a set of guidelines. A number of specialists stressed the need for adjusting the PSA results according to the age of the man because PSA levels may increase with age (*Age-Specific Reference Ranges* or *ASRRs*). However, many other doctors strongly sustain that the baseline should remain the same for all ages at ≤2.5 ng/ml.

Nadir PSA

This is not a PSA test either but rather an essential definition of post-treatment measurement of cure (discussed in Chapter 6-"*Radical Prostatectomy*").

OTHER DIAGNOSING TESTS

The First Urine Test: uPM3

Bostwick Laboratories of Virginia released in 2005 **the first urine-based genetic test for prostate cancer**, the uPM3. It is based on the so-called PCA3, a specific gene identified exclusively in prostate cancer tissue –the only human tissue known to produce PCA3. It is estimated to predict cancer with an overall 81% accuracy. The sample urine is collected immediately after a digital rectal examination performed by a physician, who massaged the gland to cause cells to shed into the urine. The urine that tests positive for PCM3 suggests that the patient has a high likelihood of already developing cancer in the prostate. This advancement, some experts affirm, may revolutionize the way we test the probabilities of a man having prostate cancer.

Urine Analysis or Urinalysis

This test is used to exclude or to identify possible infections. The urine sample is analyzed in few minutes at the doctor's office or sent to a laboratory.

Cystoscopy

A procedure used **to visually inspect the bladder and the urethra**. The urologist inserts a cystoscope or telescope through the penis to view the urethra, the bladder, and the prostate in order to evaluate possible pathology. It is a long flexible fiberoptic instrument slightly narrower than the urethra and with a powerful light at its tip. The procedure lasts 5-10 minutes and seldom causes great discomfort.

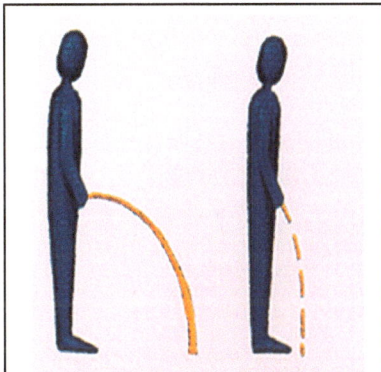

Left: Urination curve of a man with a healthy prostate. **Right:** Curve showing symptoms of prostate abnormalities. (From the Spanish poster "*Próstata*". © 2006 by and Courtesy of 3B Scientific, Hamburg-Germany, www.3bscientific.com)

Uroflowmetry

This test is taken both for diagnostic investigation and as a follow-up to measure the success of treatment for obstructed urination. Customarily, it is done in many clinics after brachytherapy procedure.

The man urinates in a machine called *uroflowmeter* that records the volume, strength and duration of the voiding or flow. An attached computer/printer automatically registers the results and prints out the numeric and graphic curves for evaluation by the doctor and awareness by the patient.

UROFLOWMETRY: FOUR SAMPLE PRINTOUTS

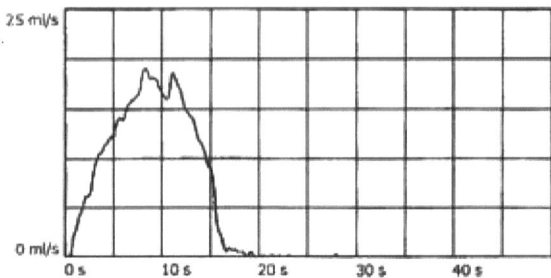

1: Urine flow curve of a man with a normal prostate.

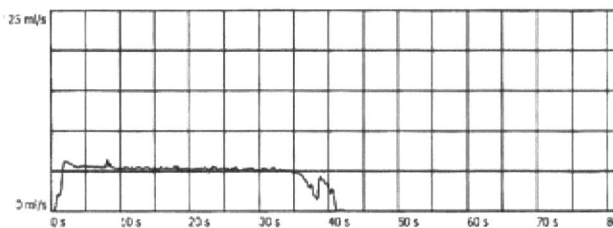

2: Urine flow curve of a man with Bladder Outlet Obstruction or BOO, due to Benign Prostatic Hyperplasia (BPH).

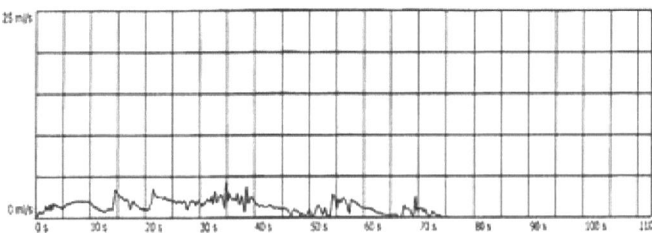

3: Urine flow curve of a man with urethral stricture.

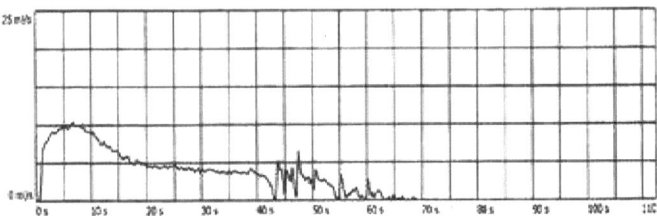

4: Improved urine flow curve after treatment (urothroctomy).

(© 2006 by and *Courtesy of* Medtronic, Inc)

61

BIOPSY

Urologists generally require the **third fundamental test, the Biopsy**, when the results of the DRE and the PSA red flag something wrong in the gland and to verify the cause of elevated PSA levels. It consists of extracting a few samples of the prostatic tissue, which are then submitted to a pathologist for examination under a microscope.

Urologists performed surgical biopsies for decades. They used to make an incision in the lower abdomen or perennially between the scrotum and the anus to reach the gland and extract several samples. It was surgery, sometimes causing abundant loss of blood and devastating side effects. The procedure was frequently postponed until the urologist opened the patient for surgical removal of the prostate; tissues were then analyzed by a waiting pathologist to determine if cancer had already spread beyond the gland.

Photo courtesy of
Dr. Hiroki Watanabe

In 1987, **Dr. Haakon Ragde** (July 26, 1927-   ), then Director of the Pacific Northwest Cancer Foundation in Seattle, Washington, and now Director of the Ragde Prostate Cancer Foundation, revolutionized prostate diagnosing techniques when he performed the first worldwide **Trans-Rectal Ultrasound-Guided (TRUS) Biopsy** by removing non-surgically the prostatic samples through the rectum. Urological ultrasound technology was already advanced in Japan by **Dr. Hiroki Watanabe** (Chiba, Japan, January 20, 1935-   ), then with the Department of Urology, Kyoto Prefectural University of Medicine in Kyoto, and now at the Meiji University of Oriental Medicine in Funaigun, Kyoto, who performed **the first worldwide clinical application of Sonography** in 1967. Ultrasonic techniques were also advanced in Denmark in the early 1980s by the great urologist **Dr. Hans Henrik Holm** (September 1931-   ), then Head of the Urology Department of the Herlev Hospital in Copenhagen, now Emeritus. One of the world pioneers of Sonography that had been very successful in applying ultrasound to various medical procedures, Dr. Holm also developed the first ultrasound scanner for bladder tumor staging (1974), the first transpirennial ultrasound-guided prostatic biopsy (1981), and the first prostate transrectal ultrasound-guided seed implantation (1983).

Photo courtesy of
Dr. Hans Henrik Holm

Dr. Ragde traveled to Denmark in 1986 to pursue research under Dr. Holm. Upon his return to the U.S., he improved the ultrasound techniques and devised a probe and a gun to reach the prostate through the rectum while the ultrasound produced sound waves that composed an image on the monitor. **This has been the biopsy technique utilized since.**

The biopsy is performed generally without anesthesia in the doctor's clinic and lasts 20-30 minutes. The patient self-administers an enema prior to the session and takes an antibiotic before and after the test. On the examination table, the patient lies on one side. After a complete digital rectal exam (DRE), a lubricated transrectal ultrasound-guided probe (TRUS) a little thicker than a finger is inserted into the rectum while the urologist evaluates the appearance and exact size of the gland on a monitor connected to a computer. Multidimensional views of the prostate appear at each slight movement of the probe. Next, the urologist introduces through the same TRUS instrument a long, spring-loaded, hollowed 18-gauge needle that crosses through the rectum wall to go with great accuracy to the areas of the prostate suspected of housing cancerous cells. The doctor "pulls" the trigger, which sounds like a spring-shot, and the needle instantaneously grasps a tiny piece or cylinder of tissue. The process is repeated to obtain ~18 samples, one at a time. The samples are especially preserved, packaged and sent to the pathology lab.

For a few hours after the biopsy, the man will feel soreness around his rectum. He can expect to have blood in the stool and urine for several days, and in the semen for up to a month.

Most men dislike the prostate biopsy, although it is more uncomfortable than painful.

There is no evidence that the needle, when retracted or at any time, may leak or spread cancerous cells from the prostate into other areas.

The urologist discusses with the patient the outcome of the test when the pathology lab reports the results in about a week. The results of the biopsy will be either **Negative, Suspicious**, or **Positive**.

Negative and Suspicious Biopsy

The biopsy result may be **Negative**, meaning no cancer was detected. However, sometimes the pathologist's result comes out negative, and yet, microscopic cancerous cells are already quietly "crawling" inside the prostate. The latter is known as "**a false negative biopsy**". Specialists believe that either the cancer in those cells was not yet detectable or else, the urologist did not extract sufficient samples or extracted them from zones other than the one[s] where the cancer is nesting. When the result is **Suspicious**, many specialists advise patients to have a second opinion on the same tissue samples from another pathology laboratory and even a second biopsy done by the same or by another urologist.

Statistically, **a first biopsy detects about 85% of cancers** and reveals that only 25% to 35% of elevated PSA levels are truly caused by cancer –a formidable diagnosing device. A second biopsy may miss only 10% of cancers.

Although the urologist and the pathologist are not infallible, the biopsy is considered the most accurate means to judge that there is not cancer or prove that there is. **It is an indispensable aid to making diagnosis and treatment decisions.** Millions of prostate biopsies are performed annually worldwide.

On the other hand, statistics show that 33% of men whose specimens were rated by the pathologist as Gleason scores of 2 to 6 turned out to have Gleason 7 to 10 in radical prostatectomy specimen. Oncologists specialized in brachytherapy have observed similar underrating. Pathologists explain that, **when in doubt between grades, the lower grade may be assigned**.

Reacting to criticisms by urologists and oncologists of those pathologists who fail to find cancerous cells when later, at radical prostatectomy, it becomes evident that cancer was already in the prostate, **Dr. Anthony V. D'Amico** (June 9, 1961-   ), Professor of Radiation Oncology at the Brigham and Women's Hospital of Harvard Medical School, Boston, Massachusetts, explains the first-biopsy errors as follows:

> "The reason why people with rising PSA and multiple biopsies have still negative results is the sampling error. Let me just tell you the math on this because it is very interesting. A biopsy core with an 18-gauge needle is 1 x 1 millimeter in cross section. The back of the prostate, the peripheral zone in a man whose prostate is not enlarged, is 3 x 3 centimeters = 30 x 30 millimeters. That is, a 900 millimeter squared surface, of which you take out one millimeter squared every time you do a biopsy. Therefore, if you take out 6, you have sampled 6 out of 900 in terms of a cross sectional area. If you take out 50, that is 50 out of 900. Are you going to do 900 biopsies to sample the whole prostate? The sample technique is very poor for prostate. It is not like breast cancer where a mammogram shows you right where it is and you put the needle right to it and you know the area. In prostate, it is a guessing game and that is why the biopsy is done in a random fashion. It is a random sampling."
>
> ***(Courtesy of*** **Dr. Anthony V. D'Amico)**

A **Negative Biopsy** will indicate one of three conditions:

(a) The most welcomed: there is **nothing wrong** in the man's prostate –at least, not right now. Or,

(b) The man has a **Benign (non-cancerous) Prostatic Hyperplasia (BPH)**. Or,

(c) The man has **Prostatic Intra-epithelial Neoplasia (PIN)**. In this finding, the pathologist has judged that some cells in the samples **are *not cancerous* but that they are *not non-cancerous* either**. That is, they are **atypical**, not looking good or bad, strange, unclassifiable –yet. They are believed to be **suspicious, *pre-cancerous***. The pathologist will label them **PIN1** (meaning, **mild**), **PIN2 (moderate) and PIN3 (severe)** according to their atypical growth stage. As shown by subsequent biopsies 3, 6 or 12 months later, cancer is in gestation in PIN2 and PIN3 (*higher grade* PIN

In the **(b)** case above, the BPH, the urologist will advise the best treatment for the patient tailored to his individual circumstance: **Do Nothing** (no need for treatment, at least right now), **Medication**, or **Surgery**. Regarding surgery,

65

* For many years, the most common surgical protocol used to be the **Trans-Urethral Resection or Excision of** [part of] **the Prostate** (**TURP**), a procedure popularly known as *roto-rooter*. Under anesthesia, a resectoscope with a light was inserted through the penis and the urethra to the bladder that allowed the urologist to observe the enlargement. He might cut/scrape and resect the excessive growth in small pieces. Modern technology facilitates other minimally invasive techniques as an alternative to TURP. Less invasive, for example, are:

* The **Trans-Urethral Needle Ablation (TUNA)**. It consists of the delivery through needles of low-level radiofrequency energy directly into the hyperplasic prostate to heat the tissue enough to produce significant coagulative necrosis or death of the cells. And,

* The **Trans-Urethral Microwave Thermotherapy (TUMT)**. It induces coagulation necrosis within the prostate tissue by using microwave frequencies.

Positive Biopsy

When **the biopsy is Positive**, whether at the first or subsequent attempts, the diagnosis is unquestionable: **Cancer**. This is the beginning of an entirely new phase in the life of the patient and his family, as well as of a new chapter in our book.

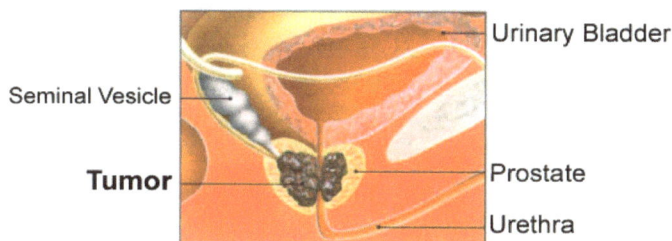

(*Graphic courtesy of* **AstraZeneca**)

Pathology Report
Daniel Freeman Marina Hospital

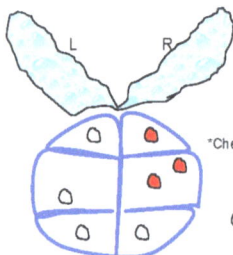

Patient Name (Last, first):	Smith, John
Date of biopsies	July 10, 2001
Number of cores obtained *	7

*Check here if each core placed in separate container ☐

◯ Pr   = No Prostate Cancer   🔴 = Prostate Cancer

SPECIMEN DETAILS

Site	Length (mm)	PC (Yes/ No)	PC	Gleason score
1 left base	10	N	-	-
2 left mid	7	N	-	-
3 left apex	5	N	-	-
4 right base	5	Y	5 (100)	3,3
5 right mid	8	Y	4 (50)	3,4
6 right mid	7	Y	7 (100)	3,3
7 right apex	12	N	-	-
Totals	57 mm	3/7	16 (250) =total % % (of specimen)	-

Description:

_____

_____

Sample of a Biopsy Pathology Report. (*Courtesy of* **The Prostate Cancer Research Institute, Los Angeles, California**)

By now, we have completed the first major part of this book. ***Prostate Cancer is Curable*** has covered from "scratch" to "positive biopsy". That is, we began with the assumption that the man, still a **patient-to-be**, knew nothing about his prostate and prostate cancer and we led him to knowing now that he has become a **patient** diagnosed with the disease.

"TO KNOW OR NOT TO KNOW", that is the question

Most practitioners and cancer institutions favor testing and screening for prostate cancer, beginning at age 40 for white men and at 30-35 for black men and for any men with known family history of prostate cancer or breast cancer. We have found so far abundant statistics showing the wisdom, indeed the necessity, of early testing for early discovery of malignancy, and therefore, allowing for having considerably higher chance of cure. However, some doctors and HMOs in the U.S. and movements generated in few other countries medically operating under governmental Socialized Medicine, have raised opposition to screening **unless and until the man experiences symptoms** –that is, until it is **all too often too late for cure**. Here are some of their main arguments against screening, followed by a discussion of patients' reactions:

- **Should a man know whether he has prostate cancer, and how much information should he have?**
- **Are most men prepared for knowing?**
- **Should he be tested, screened to find out whether he has cancer?**
- **Is the effort of finding a man's cancer worth the cost of screening (to an HMO or a government)?**
- **How old or how mature must a man be to make educate decisions about his own health?**
- **Cost of screening.**
- **Likelihood of unnecessary procedures.**
- **Patient's anxiety when considering treatment, or possibility of distressing side effects.**
- **Screening may disclose diseases of the prostate, but not specifically cancer.**
- **It has not been documented that treatment of prostate cancer increases the life span of the patient.**
- ***Watchful Waiting*** **is adequate when there are no symptoms.**

Cost

Never more than today would patients welcome any campaign aimed at *truly* reducing their cost of healthcare. But reality has repeatedly demonstrated that when the medical profession and/or hospitals or HMOs and/or drug manufacturers and/or the Government announce **a cost-cutting campaign**, the result is **an increase in the cost to the patient.** The increase may take the form of higher premium or higher co-payment or higher deductible, fewer days allowed for hospitalization or the patient's full payment of the first several days in the hospital, restrictions on tests, etc. And such increases due to the provider's "cost-cuts" are generally not just a couple of dollars but actually 50%, 70%, 100% and more over the previous cost to the patient, or new charges never applied before, such as those disguised as "materials used" when, say, extracting blood for an analysis.

Unquestionably, as history demonstrates, **treatment for a cancer detected early is much more likely to be shorter and more effective** –therefore, **less costly**– than treatment for a cancer detected later, when it is more invasive.

The great scientist **Dr. T. Ming Chu**, part as we have seen of the PSA test discoveries, contradicted those arguments on the cost of testing by telling this Author:

> "Let us analyze costs versus prostate cancer detected and life potentially saved. There are 27 million men age 50 years or older, and approximately 40% or 10 million men will have histological (autopsy confirmed) prostate cancer. Based upon actual screening experience, the number of cancers detected by PSA screening would be 1.84 million cases. Therefore, the cost per one cancer detected would be ($11.89 billion divided by 1.84 million cancers) $6,500, or the cost per one man's life potentially saved will be ($6,500 x 3.3) $21,000."
>
> **(*Courtesy of* Dr. T. Ming Chu)**

Notwithstanding all of the above, it is indeed a waste when a patient requests or is asked to have tests (biopsy or otherwise, for prostate cancer, cholesterol, etc.) unless his attitude is to act upon the results –whatever they may be.

69

Anxiety

Any medical test and procedure is cause for apprehension. Uncertainty, that is, **the unknown, causes anxiety**. Psychology postulates that the goal of **anxiety therapy** is precisely *to help the patient gain control*. Our typical man of today can make decisions but only when and if he has the necessary knowledge acquired by tests that have given him awareness of his health –or lack of. PSA screening does inspire a feeling of calm and wellbeing in men whose PSA tests are repeatedly "normal". However, without being tested and without the doctor's educational explanation, a patient may indeed develop what humorously may be called "**PSAitis**" –real anxiety generated by ignorance of his PSA levels and of the significance of the testing.

And the Patient?

Perhaps the most relevant issue has not been dealt with in the years-long screening controversy among specialists, HMOs and governments: *Where is the patient?* This Author has been unable to find comparable studies showing what patients think, feel or want regarding being tested or screened. It is somewhat like the attitude in "traditional old fashioned" homes where everybody argued and made decisions about younger members without concern for their voice, not to mention for their vote. The difference is that, in our case and in our times, the patient is the center upon whom the whole healthcare is built and the one who pays for all of the components of his healthcare environment. Interestingly, all over the world (and especially in the U.S.) men for many years have enrolled for screening projects voluntarily and by the hundreds of thousands, but some entities and doctors still **must be further convinced** in order to administer testing. Statistics show that PSA testing has caused a substantial decrease of incidence of metastatic disease at the time of diagnosis by 75%, and a decreased death rate of 25%.

A few doctors and entities have gone as far as suggesting that **men should be required to sign a** *Consent Agreement* document before undertaking a PSA test, a request that, even if "unintentionally", carries an implication of discouragement, resulting in fear and anxiety. Patients might think that **it would be equally fair that those doctors should be required to sign another** *Acceptance of Responsibility* document when they omit or refuse to test a man's prostate as part of a physical examination. Moreover, the latter may be a forthcoming legal issue upon which to reflect: knowing that a man's family history of prostate cancer constitutes a decisive factor in develop-

70

ing the disease at a much earlier age, a doctor's or insurer's refusal or omission (or even lack of advice) of prompt, early and regular testing may open to them an unwanted loophole of legal vulnerability.

Following is a summary of comments by the over 100 prostate cancer patients from seven countries that this Author surveyed:

---

* **Over 90% expected, and wanted, more information from their urologists and oncologists. Additionally, two patients, who were medical doctors in general practice and in cardiology, respectively, said that their medical practice had changed dramatically since they were diagnosed because now for the first time they interpret healthcare from the patient's viewpoint.**
* **70% received from their doctors no specific information on the intricacies and significance of the various tests, PSA included, and consequently they had no clue on how to interpret the results.**
* **100% were in favor of screening, of testing. If they were starting all over, they said they would be much stronger (a) in pressing their doctors for tests at an earlier age, including biopsy, and (b) in fighting their HMOs to approve tests and procedures.**
* **Two patients were deeply appreciative of their urologists: in spite of a PSA level of only 2.5 ng/ml, the doctors, suspicious, ran a biopsy and the results were Gleason scores 7 and 8 –advanced cancer.**
* **Only a few doctors encouraged patients to seek a second opinion.**
* **Most doctors recommended exclusively the treatment on which they had specialized –for example, radical prostatectomy, radiation. And when recommending a treatment, the majority used cure statistics published by eminent surgeons, or else, national statistics –not their own.**

The importance of "to know or not to know" by means of screening and testing was already summarized years ago by the American Cancer Society and several professional medical associations that released the following recommendation to doctors:

71

> **Men who ask their clinician to make the testing decision on their behalf should be tested. A policy of not discussing testing or [of] discouraging testing in men who request early prostate cancer detection tests *is inappropriate*.**

It is an **eloquent irony** that, countries where screening and precautionary testing are not prevalent reflect a higher mortality and metastasis rates due to prostate cancer –thus, refuting some of the anti-screening arguments listed above. For example, prostate cancer mortality in the U.S. is 19% of all men diagnosed with this disease. In Canada (one of the countries fighting screening) it is 25%, in New Zealand 30%, in Australia 35%, in Germany (where the PSA test is not even covered by the social healthcare system) 44%, in France 49%, and in the United Kingdom 57%. By using another statistical method, the prostate cancer Age-Adjusted Rates formula as applied to deaths per 100,000 population, the three countries with the highest prostate cancer death rates in the world are precisely the ones that have raised the most opposition to screening: Switzerland with 22.4 deaths per 100,000 population, Norway 22.0, and Sweden 20.9.

Notwithstanding the country (if otherwise advanced), it is hard to comprehend how in our times a man's neglect may reach the tragic end that he himself described in this letter:

> **"I am one of those men who awake one day with a diagnosis of prostate cancer, advanced and highly aggressive: PSA 45, Gleason 9, 80%-90% tumor, T3b, right seminal vesicle invaded, prostate size 60 grams. It is strange but it is so. I cannot change the facts. I knew nothing. I was advised prostatectomy but it was not enough, followed by radiation therapy and it was not enough either, then drugs…and nothing is sufficient. Please, what else can I do? What I do now is warn people to take care of themselves and be active in patients' associations helping others with what I know."**
>
> (Summary of the anguished *"Help!"* message written by a patient, 56 years young when diagnosed in January 2003, e-mailed to the U.S. from his home on The Netherlands-France border in 2006.)

72

The renowned Prostate Oncology Specialist Dr. Stephen B. Strum recently wrote to a patient,

> **"Your being diagnosed with a PSA of 20 ng/ml is a reflection of your own self-neglect or that of your doctors or perhaps both. (…) The approach we use toward a possession such as a valuable car is the same approach we should take toward something as priceless as our [prostate] health."**

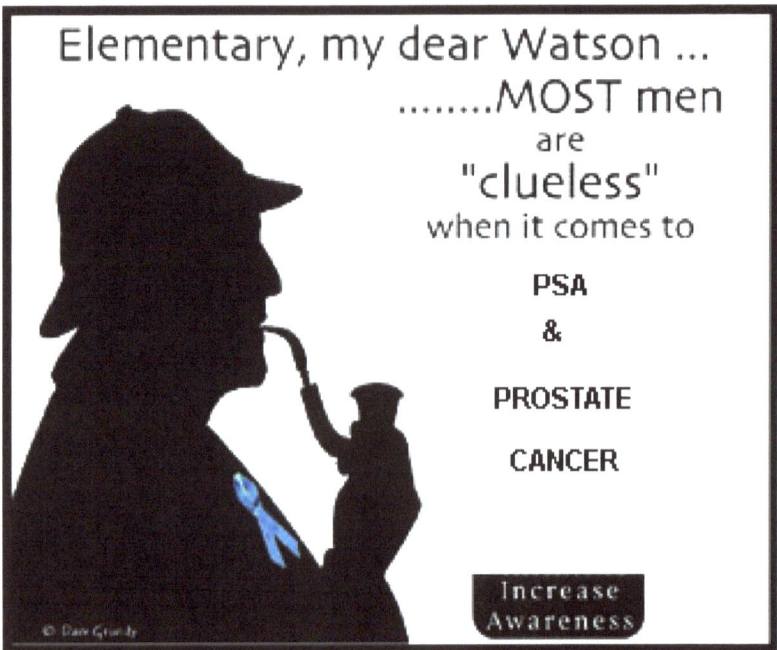

Prostate Cancer Awareness Poster
(*Courtesy of* Dave Grundy, Canada)

Chapter 4

Gotcha!

If the biopsy is positive…

…Our man has **Prostatic Adenocarcinoma = Cancer**. Feared, expected, albeit unwelcome. **It is Number 1 in incidents among all cancers.** Yet, if the man has been preparing for the event, he may wish to *celebrate* the news of the discovery if at an early stage –when it is curable.

There are **many types of cancers** and they are named after the part of the body where they originate: prostate cancer, lung, breast, testicles, etc. Each requires its own treatment specifically tailored to both the cancer tumor characteristics and the patient. Furthermore, when three men have prostate cancer, each is a different cancer because **it is fundamentally individual.** There are two main groups of cancerous tumors: **Carcinoma** and **Sarcoma**. Carcinoma starts in the epithelial tissue (skin or lining of inner organs), sarcoma starts in connective tissue (bones, cartilage). **The tumor of the prostate is a carcinoma** in 95% of the cases.

Irrespective of when it is discovered and of the severity of the disease, **the diagnosis of prostate cancer dramatically changes the life of the man**. His struggle will extend also to his wife or partner and to their families –they all are impacted by the man's ambivalent target of **wanting to find answers** and **wanting to survive.** It stirs up in his sensitivity a whole spectrum of issues –somehow unresolved by many men. Upon the diagnostic event, a sector of men accept it blindly, they suspect being a *victim* ("*Why me?*"), others will research and fight the disease and will not be affected by inner struggles, while still others find their values stirred up by uncertainties on unresolved questions on Life and Death –but are determined to fight anyway. Essentially, those with a fighting attitude become *heroes* of their own life and merit respect and admiration.

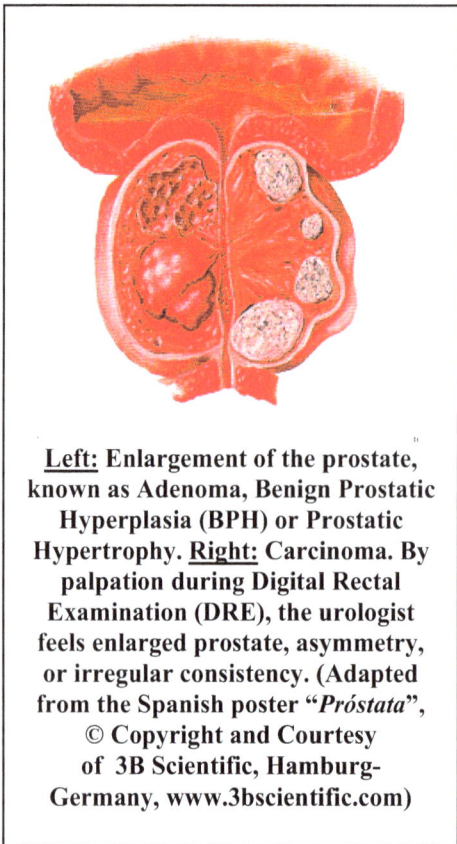

Left: Enlargement of the prostate, known as Adenoma, Benign Prostatic Hyperplasia (BPH) or Prostatic Hypertrophy. Right: Carcinoma. By palpation during Digital Rectal Examination (DRE), the urologist feels enlarged prostate, asymmetry, or irregular consistency. (Adapted from the Spanish poster "*Próstata*", © Copyright and Courtesy of 3B Scientific, Hamburg-Germany, www.3bscientific.com)

"*How did I get cancer?*"

The desire to identify the cause or causes that originate prostate cancer is as old as cancer itself. The search has been increasingly aggressive since the 1950s when revolutionary advances in science and technology precipitated unprecedented access into the intricacies of how the human body functions. Specialists in all professional fields, industries ranging from farming to manufacturing, spiritual advocates, and of course, the average patient, all joined efforts attempting to unveil the **mystery**. A number of suggestions have been proposed: family history, viruses, venereal diseases, sexual activity or lack of, occupation, smoking, environment, surgical procedures such as vasectomy, masturbation, what we eat or do not eat, age, obesity, hormones, lack or excess of vitamins and minerals...

We do know that **prostate cancer is not contagious**. It is not transmitted like HIV, flu, or bacterial infection. It is not transmitted either by physical contact (kiss, saliva, sexual intercourse). **It targets men of all origin and of all socio-economic status**, business executives, high-rank clergy, rich and poor, royalty, prominent politicians, even medical doctors themselves. Indeed, throughout history, prostate illness has impacted world affairs and the life of leaders and their countries. For example, Carlos I of Spain (1500-1558), the most powerful Emperor ever, abdicated in 1556 due to his prostate anomalies, among others; and François Mitterrand (1916-1996), the longest ruling President of France, strictly kept secret his prostate cancer diagnostic until 1996 when he was already dying of the advanced disease.

Although one single cause has not been identified, two factors are known to contribute to the growth of prostate cancer. One is **age**, beginning normally at 40 depending on the individual and his family history –and **the age factor is irreversible**. Another is the **biochemistry** of the man, including his hormones (testosterone, androgen) and **his genetics and immune system**. Scientists all over the world are discovering increasing evidence that **Genetics** and specifically **certain genes** have decisive influence.

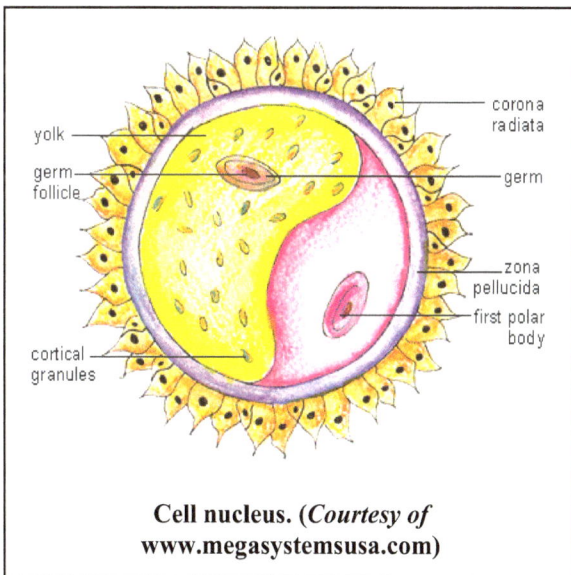

Cell nucleus. (*Courtesy of* www.megasystemsusa.com)

Trillions of microscopic cells compose our human body. They provide its organic structure, and they manufacture the essential ingredients to sustain life. They are programmed to reproduce and to die in an orderly cycle.

Groups of cells (either similar or

76

working together) perform all of the specific functions of the organism (e.g., how we smile, how we perceive the humor in things) and elaborate or produce certain "raw materials" (molecules or proteins) that compose tissue and organs, enzymes, and antibodies. Consistent with their own laws, **each new cell is ideally an exact copy of the parent cell**; and each of the 100 trillion cells in the human body contains a copy of almost the entire human genome.

Instructions to comply with the **"law of the cells"** originate in the double-helix molecule known as **deoxy-ribo-nucleic acid** or **DNA**, a central database. **The organism's complete set of DNA is the Genome**.

In spite of the enormous number of kinds of cells, researchers have discovered in the DNA only four building blocks molecules: **A**denine, **C**ytosine, **G**uanine, and **T**hymine, known by their initial letters. Scientists' interpretation of the *law* of DNA indicates that the four groups cannot mess around: only a molecule A can pair with molecule T, only C with G. **The "mating" A-T, C-G is controlled by the structure of the four coding molecules themselves.** Each pair fits together very much the same way as a lock and key fit together in order to function.

This sequence of pairing molecules is the heart of the genetic code. Graphically, it is represented by a spiral

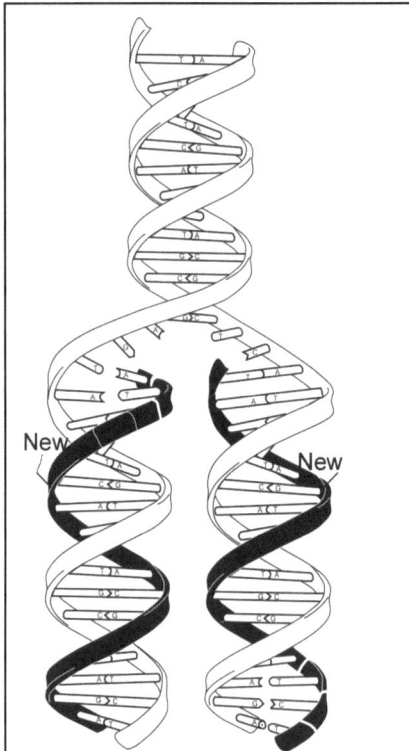

DNA replication: The base pair of single-strands of DNA in the original Double Helix, like the steps of a ladder (top), splits into two new single-strands. In this division or replication of a cell the genetic material is passed on to both daughter-cells, which should be identical to the parent-cell —unless a "copying error" occurred, causing the "mutation" of the new cell[s] and possibly a disease. (Graphic courtesy of the NHGRI)

staircase, where the two handrails are the deoxyribose-phosphate backbone chains, and each step represents a molecule pair –two pieces that fit together in the middle, and each molecule a half of a stair step. The sequence of molecules conveys information by the order of the sequence of the mating, just as a Morse code message conveys information by the order of the dots and dashes.

Each of the DNA molecules is grouped in chromosomes, and each chromosome contains 30,000 to 35,000 genes. **Humans have 46 chromosomes** divided into two pairs: one pair is inherited from the mother and the other from the father –plus one more from each, which differentiates the sex.

When normal, **cells have a very orderly life** and follow predetermined patterns of similar behavior. However, for reasons still unknown, one or more of those cells may "decide" to rebel and ignore the instructions from the DNA, it hangs around, attempts pairing with a molecule of another letter –misbehaves. It is believed that **cancers begin with a defect in one gene**, in its chemical substance DNA. It is called **mutation**: a change in DNA-spelling. **A copying error or mutation occurs once in every one million divisions**. It then develops and grows without control in number and quality, and this new group of cells is called **Tumor**.

THE PULSE OF OUR CELLS

1. …and there was Nothingness.
2. Two kinds of cells mix, generally during intercourse: **sperm** of a male and **egg** of a female.
3. **A human being**: starts with one cell and grows into 100 trillion **cells** with different forms, locations and missions to make this human being function, and all contain a copy of the entire genome.
4. The **nucleus** of each cell contains 6 feet of DNA packed into 23 pairs of microscopic structures called **chromosomes**, one of each pair from each of the parents, including one pair that determines the sex of the offspring.
5. Each of the DNA molecules contains 30,000 to 35,000 **genes**, which influence our looks, personality, vulnerability to diseases, indeed our whole being.
6. Each gene is composed of a segment of DNA, several thousand base pairs long, copied into a molecule of *ribonucleic*

acid or **RNA**. The RNA transports the instructions to make one specific kind of protein. **Proteins** are building-blocks and workers, laborers that form tendons and hair; they are messengers to the cells.
7. Those proteins, directed by RNA, govern and provide the formation and maintenance of the **functions and structures of the body** of each of us.
8. When one of those genes, or a group of them, does not function according to the established rules (it may be due to internal or external environmental influences on the gene) a deformation or **mutation** occurs and a disease may develop.

When the rebellious cells become more aggressive and the growing volume cannot be restrained to the size of the original site, for example the prostate, the tumor, like a balloon, will "explode" and spill outside. The **cancerous cells will then migrate** to explore and grow in other organs and tissue, particularly the lymphatic system, directly or by sailing through the blood stream. **Such "migration" is called metastasis** and is tragically fatal to those tissue and organs (and eventually to the man's life).

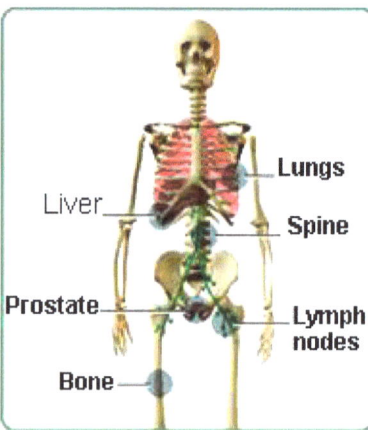

Most common areas to which cancer cells migrate when leaving the prostate —metastasis. At this stage, cancer is generally incurable. (Graphic courtesy of The University of Toronto, Canada; Jodie Jenkinson, Designer of Illustrations)

The rhythm of this complex multiplication is known as **Exponential Growth** or **Gompertzian Growth Theory (*Kinetics*)**, the theory created in 1825 by British actuary **Benjamin Gompertz** (1779-1865) as part of his book *Law of Mortality*. Applied as biomathematics to biological tumor growth, **the division of cells follows a constant geometric progression**. For example, one cell divides to make another identical cell, essentially multiplying itself by 2. Those 2 then multiply into 4, then 4 into 8, then 8 into 16, and so on. The equation for the resulting number of cells produced is 1 multiplied by itself /n/ times, or 2 raised to the /**nth**/ power, or /**2^n/,** where /**n**/ represents the number of doublings that have taken place.

Tissue density is about **1 billion cells per cubic centimeter** (cc), and 1 billion is the approximate result of /2^30/ or only 1 cell that doubled 30 times. And it happens that, **the smallest tumor that is physically detectable** (e.g., by palpation) contains approximately 1 billion cancer cells, weights 1 gram and is the size of a very small grape.

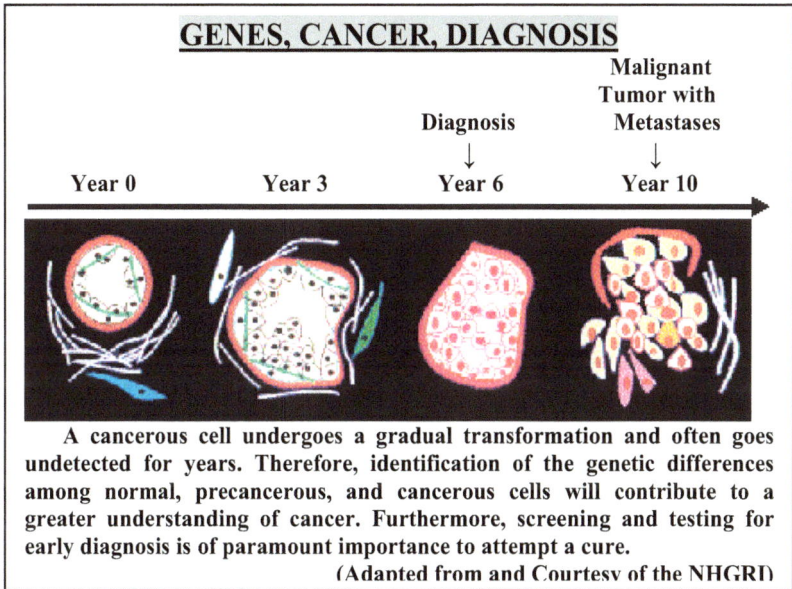

GENES, CANCER, DIAGNOSIS

A cancerous cell undergoes a gradual transformation and often goes undetected for years. Therefore, identification of the genetic differences among normal, precancerous, and cancerous cells will contribute to a greater understanding of cancer. Furthermore, screening and testing for early diagnosis is of paramount importance to attempt a cure.
(Adapted from and Courtesy of the NHGRI)

Interestingly, **cancer clinical symptoms may begin to appear and be detectable by palpation at this point** when cancer exists – hence, the sooner it is detected the better the chances for a successful treatment.

Generally, and for uncertain reasons, prostate cancer tumors do not grow persistently at the same constant speed in an individual, and **the tumor may be detectable or symptomatic within a few months or a few years, or it may start growing slowly and abruptly become very aggressive.**

> Based on this theory of growth measurement and predict-ability, studies estimate that a patient being diagnosed with symptomatic or detectable cancer may have ≤28% chance of long term survival, while if the same patient had been diagnosed 10 months sooner his chance of survival could be 65% and higher.

The **Father of Genetics** is the Czech monk **Gregor Johann Mendel** (1822-1884). Experimenting in plant hybridization, he discovered the fundamental laws of inheritance. Ten years later, Swiss scientist **Dr. J. Friedrich Miescher** (1844-1895) isolated DNA and suggested a **genetic code**.

L-R: Dr. Francis Harry C. Crick, Dr. James D. Watson, and Dr. Maurice H. F. Wilkins. (© The Nobel Foundation. Courtesy of The Nobel Foundation, Sweden)

But the actual genetic revolution began with an article about the discovery of the "**Double Helix**" published April 25, 1953 in the London journal "*Nature*", followed by a second article on the genetic implication of the DNA structure. These articles were authored by British scientist **Dr. Francis H. Crick** (Northampton, June 8, 1916-San Diego, California July 29, 2004) and American scientist **Dr. James D. Watson** (Chicago, Illinois April 6, 1928-   ), who were researching in London together with two professors at King's College: **Dr. Maurice F. Wilkins** (New Zealand 1916-____) and **Dr. Rosalind Elsie Franklin** (London 1920-1958).

Their discovery led to the **unlocking of the mysteries of health and disease** and facilitated the unveiling of fundamental details about ourselves. Watson, Crick and Wilkins shared the 1962 Nobel Prize.

Cancer of the prostate can be detected, identified, graded, scored, staged and cured –but the real single cause, as mentioned above, if there is only one, is still unknown. Scientists affirm that none of the theories, by itself, is conclusive. A group of researchers headed by **Dr. William B. Isaacs** and **Dr. Patrick C. Walsh**, of the

Brady Urological Institute of Johns Hopkins University in Baltimore, Maryland, isolated among others two important defective genes found in Chromosome 1 and Chromosome X. The gene called **Hereditary Prostate Cancer-1 (**or **HPC-1)** was isolated in 1990 and the gene

Hereditary Prostate Cancer-X (or **HPC-X)** in 1995. The events confirmed for the first time the relationship between a man's family history of prostate cancer and his probabilities of developing the disease.

An estimated 250,000 American men carry the defective gene HPC-1 and their susceptibility to developing prostate cancer is very high, though not 100% of them will develop it.

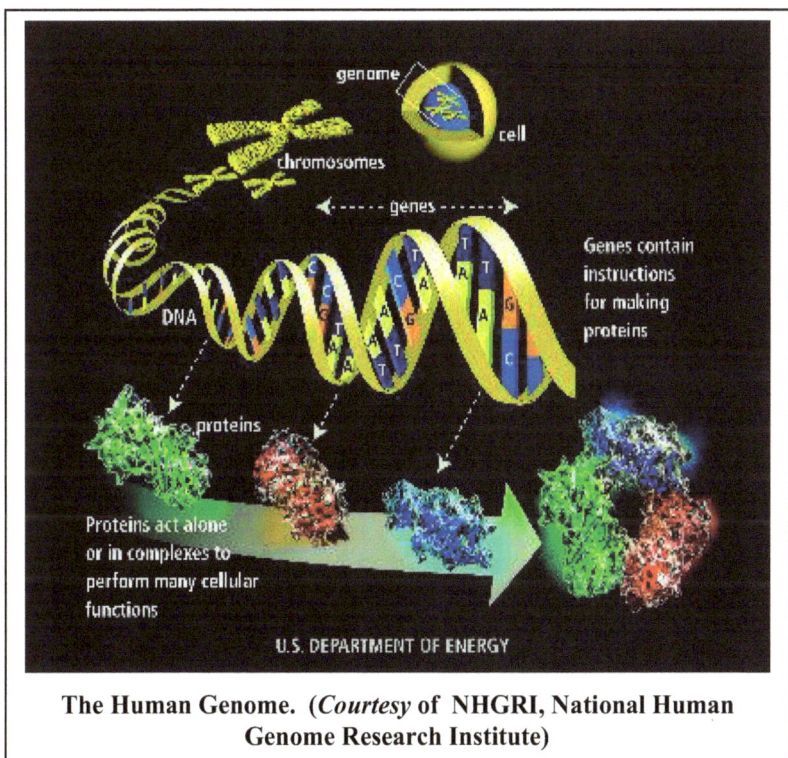

The Human Genome. (*Courtesy* of NHGRI, National Human
Genome Research Institute)**

The discovery had extensive consequences. For instance, in families with a mutated HPC-1:

> **(a)** At least five men in the immediate family or several men in multiple generations have had prostate cancer.
> **(b)** The mean age of the men when diagnosed is <65 years.
> **(c)** There is evidence that the mutated, cancer-inducing genes were transmitted from father to son, although it can be transmitted by either the mother or the father.

Thus, if a daughter inherits the HPC-X mutated gene from either mother or father, **she has a very high risk of developing breast cancer.** If a son inherits the HPC-X mutated gene from his mother, then **he has a very high risk of developing prostate cancer.** Furthermore, **if a man is diagnosed with prostate cancer before age 55, his daughter will have a 50% chance of developing breast cancer.**

On the other hand, if a father was diagnosed with prostate cancer, for example at age 72, his son has the same risk probabilities as any other man, but if the father was diagnosed at age 50, the risk doubles. **For a man with two relatives with a history of prostate cancer, his risk of developing it is 4.9 times greater,** and if with three relatives, then the risk is 10.9 times greater and his chance of developing prostate cancer at age <55 is more likely.

TRANSMISSION OF CHROMOSOMES 1 AND X OR Y

PARENT	CHROMOSOME	TRANSMITTED TO WHOM
Father	Chromosomes 1 and Y	Son
Father	Chromosomes 1 and X	Daughter
Mother	Chromosomes 1 and X	Son, Daughter

(Each chromosome may or may not bear defective genes)

A study of thousands of twins in Europe by a group of scientists concluded in 2000 that as many as **42% of prostate cancer incidences can be caused by or associated with hereditary patterns.**

Other researchers are studying a link between prostate cancer to the gene mutation RNAseL, variant 462Q, suspected of making a man susceptible to viral infection, specifically to the virus XMRV.

In summary, scientists are involved in an enormous task: to characterize which of those 30,000 to 35,000 genes inside one cell sends or receives the message to mutate. They hope then to crack their "**secret code**" in order to alter the instructions and perhaps to trigger a suicide chain-reaction among defective cells –called **apoptosis** or "programmed cell death".

We are in a new scientific era, the **Gene Therapy War**, which will help future prostate cancer patients, and hopefully will eradicate the disease. **The American Cancer Society still hopes to achieve its goal of identifying the cause of cancer by the year 2013.**

A new Artistic Horizon: The inspiration of Genes

Dr. Hunter O'Reilly (San Francisco, California, September 7, 1971-   ), professor of Genetics at the University of Wisconsin-Milwaukee, in 1999 changed the characteristic perspective from which scientists and public in general have looked at genes, DNA, cells, cloning and the like.

120" x 60" oil on canvas representing "The Creation of Organs: Stem Cell Research". (Courtesy of Dr. Hunter O'Reilly)

Based on Genetics, she created a new aesthetic movement, the "**DNArt**", which she teaches as part of her course *Biology through Art*. By using superimposed X-Ray films, CT scan images, digital collage, black drawing, and colored oil on canvas (and many hours on the microscope), Dr. O'Reilly discovered a new appearance of the genetic landscape and *interpreted* the artistic messages "broadcast by its components". Her combination of genetic research and virtual surrealist and cubist art has resulted in aesthetic expressions of unique language. Some of her productions unveil genetic alterations in animals when she uses neon light or ultraviolet rays; others, are photos of viruses that suddenly gain unusual forms and shapes under the microscope; while others are "social visions" of the DNA test that *"may help to identify a murderer but also diseases in a job applicant"*, said the scientist-artist to this Author.

CLASSIFICATION, EVALUATION OF THE CANCER

Ironically, **finding out that one has prostate cancer is not the end but rather the beginning** of an intricate, interesting and challenging new landscape of the journey we are following –no matter how tragic.

Dr. Rudolph Carl Virchow

When the biopsy of the man is positive, the results must be graded, scored, staged, evaluated. He needs to know its speed of growth, the expansion of its growth, its likely behavior, and to compare his with tumors of similar biological characteristics. Historically, pathologists all over the world were accustomed to grading the cancerous cells as seen under the microscope, but always according to their own individual criteria. German **Dr. Rudolph Carl Virchow** (1821-1902) is known as the **Founder of Modern Pathology** and the author of *Cellular Pathology*, the text considered the cornerstone of this medical specialty. Pathology is the study of the nature of diseases, causes and symptoms. Although more than 40 cancer-grading systems had been proposed throughout decades, **there was no uniform method** before 1977 that would allow pathologists to classify and score the progressive transformation of the architecture of the cancerous cells of the prostate.

During his 15 years (1960-1975) as Chief of Laboratory in the U.S. Veterans Administration Cooperative Urologic Research

85

Group Study of Prostate Cancer, the great pathologist **Dr. Donald Floyd Gleason** (Spencer, Iowa, November 20, 1920-   ) compiled the data of and studied more than 4,000 cases of prostate cancer in 20 different VA hospitals. Upon his retirement from the VA in 1975, he moved to Minneapolis, Minnesota, and worked in the Fairview Hospital System for 10 more years. *"I went through a significant personal transformation"*, he humorously told this Author in an interview in January of 2003, and added, smiling, *"Accustomed as I was to dealing with men in the Veterans Administration System, when I retired and joined the "real" world I had to learn all over again because, among other things, I found out that this world was half feminine."*

Courtesy of
Dr. Donald F. Gleason, who autographed his photo to this Author in January of 2003

"Throughout so many years", Dr. Gleason explained, *"I noticed that certain cancer cell patterns were repeated and that those patterns were very closely related to the mortality of the patients"*.

Encouraged by his findings, **Dr. Gleason created a Cancer-Grading Method** to systemize the degree of undifferentiation of the cancerous cells. *"Probably the most important thing I contributed was my drawing of my grading system. Pathologists think in pictures, but a few photomicrographs and a few hundred words did not convey a system. By looking at my drawing of the spectrum of changes, pathologists were able to learn my system without further personal instruction from me."*

Dr. Gleason wrote a study explaining his innovative method and sent it to *"the two foremost pathology journals in the United States"*. And "writer's irony" repeated its history: the study was rejected –*"too long, too many graphs, too many photomicrographs, too many tables, too complex"* were some of the excuses. Discouraged, Dr. Gleason agreed to and was *happy* to give it to a pathologist friend,

Dr. Myron Tannenbaum, who was writing the book *Urologic Pathology: The Prostate* (published in 1977).

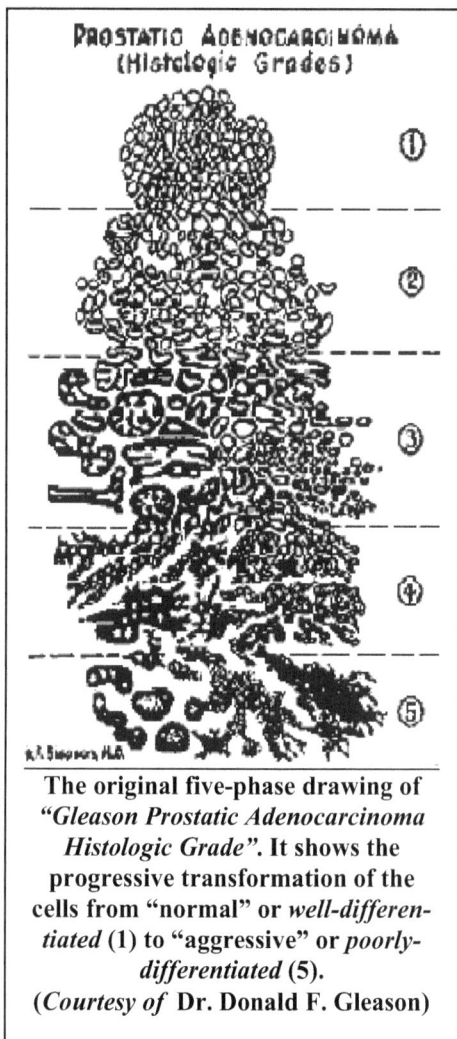

PROSTATIC ADENOCARCINOMA
(Histologic Grades)

① ② ③ ④ ⑤

The original five-phase drawing of *"Gleason Prostatic Adenocarcinoma Histologic Grade"*. It shows the progressive transformation of the cells from "normal" or *well-differentiated* (1) to "aggressive" or *poorly-differentiated* (5).
(*Courtesy of* **Dr. Donald F. Gleason**)

Dr. Gleason's study *"did not cause any impact"*, he said to this Author, *"until ten years later, when in a **Letter to the Editor** six eminent pathologists who read the report in Dr. Tannenbaum's book and used my system recommended that all authors reporting follow-up data or treatment results should use my grading system for uniformity and comparison."*

Since then, the **Gleason Score** appears in all positive biopsy reports and the term is used by millions of doctors and patients all over the world. **It is the single most important prognostic tool for evaluating prostate cancer**.

It is based exclusively on the architectural pattern of the tumor and differentiates between tumors whose structure appears close to normal (**well differentiated cells**, **low-grade cancer**) and tumors whose structure has deteriorated and are very aggressive (**poorly differentiated cells, high-grade cancer**).

Since the cancer of the prostate is multifocal (*heterogeneous,* versus *homogeneous,* centering in several places rather than only one place), an average patient has at least two *foci* or nests of carcinoma,

87

each anatomically different under the microscope. The pathologist assigns a **Gleason grade of 1 to 5** to each phase or deterioration pattern: one grade to the primary or most predominant and aggressive architectural pattern (which must be >50% of the total) and another to the secondary or second most predominant and aggressive (which must be <50%), and then the two grades are added together to make the final **Score**.

THE GLEASON GRADING SYSTEM

Grades 1 and 2.- Resemble normal cells, and reveal low grade, slow growing. Both are "*well differentiated*". **Grade 1** simulates a compact mass and is the closest to the normal cell colonies. **Grade 2** shows some cells attempting to escape or displace towards the edge of the prostate. With these grades, the patient has very high probabilities of being cured.

Grade 3.- Still slow growing, this is the most common grade. In comparison with Grades 1 and 2, Grade 3 shows a larger number of cells attempting to escape and a more evident deterioration of the mass.

Grade 4.- Dangerous, the deterioration is more severe, the overall has lost its cohesive mass. It is "*poorly differentiated*", a cancer which has been nesting for some time.

Grade 5.- Cells are no longer recognizable in comparison with those of Grades 1 & 2 and normal cells. Evidence of advanced cancer, most aggressive. Frequently labeled as "*undifferentiated*" because it has lost its unity characteristics.

(When observing the graphic process of transformation of the architecture of the cancerous cells, an eloquent comparison comes to mind: the 1945 American movie *The Portrait of Dorian Gray*, based on the novel written in 1891 by Oscar Wilde, Dublin 1854-1900).

For example, if the primary or predominant pattern is 3 and the secondary is 4, the score will be 3+4 = **7**; and if both patterns were the same, the score would be 4+4 = **8**. Total scores of 2 to 4 are considered low, 5 to 7 are intermediate, and 8 to 10 are high = advanced cancer deterioration.

The Gleason Score allows experts evaluate also how fast the cancer is growing. For example, the score of 2 to 6 is considered "average growth" and it affects 60% of men; 7 warns that the cancer is growing "fast" and affects 30% to 35% of patients; and scores of 8 to 10, which affect 5% to 10% of men, indicate that the cancer is growing "very fast". Sixty percent of diagnoses register an average score of Gleason 5 to 6.

The system is extremely valuable in identifying the type of cancer, designing treatment, anticipating probabilities of cure, and venturing a prognosis of how long the patient is likely to survive. Studies have summarized the risk of dying of prostate cancer based on Gleason Scores.

RISK OF DYING OF UNTREATED PROSTATE CANCER

GLEASON SCORE	← AGE AT DIAGNOSIS →			
	50-59	60-64	65-69	70-74
2-4	4%	5%	6%	7%
5	6%	8%	10%	11%
6	18%	23%	27%	30%
7	78%	62%	53%	42%
8-10	87%	81%	72%	60%

Dr. William J. Catalona studied the correlation of Gleason Score and progression-free survival rate on 3,459 patients on whom he performed a radical prostatectomy from 1992 to 2005. The following results confirm, once more, the warning that men should start being tested at an early age:

GLEASON SCORE	CORRELATION OF: PROGRESSION-FREE SURVIVAL RATE
< 7	84%
> 7 but < 8	63%
8 – 10	37%

CANCER STAGING

To "stage" the cancer is the process by which specialists determine how far the tumor has progressed.

Based on the digital rectal examination (DRE), the PSA tests and the Gleason Score, urologists and oncologists proceed to the next step to further evaluate the patient's condition and prognosis.

There are **Clinical Staging** and **Pathologic[al] Staging**. In the **Clinical Staging**, based on the digital rectal examination, urologists determine the size and location of the cancerous tumor, and they investigate whether it is localized within the prostate or whether it has already spread. **Pathologic Staging**, more certain, reveals the stage of the disease; the pathologist establishes it when examining under a microscope the actual prostate tissue and the lymph nodes surgically removed at radical prostatectomy.

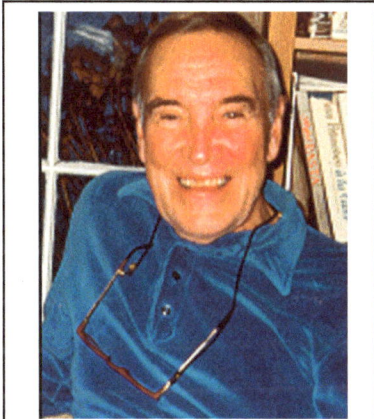

Dr. Willet F. Whitmore, Jr., in Christmas of 1993. (Photo courtesy of his son Dr. Willet F. Whitmore, III and of his daughter Ms. Polly Whitmore)

Although staging systems had been previously devised to evaluate the spread of various diseases, the first method applicable to prostate cancer was **The Whitmore-Jewett "A–B–C-D" Staging System** created in 1950-1951 by **Dr. Willet F. Whitmore, Jr.** (Long Island, NY, December 13, 1917-May 8, 1995), of Sloan-Kettering Hospital, New York, and **Dr. Hugh J. Jewett** (September 26, 1903–May 6, 1990), of Johns Hopkins University, Baltimore, Maryland.

THE WHITMORE-JEWETT
"A-B-C-D" STAGING SYSTEM

A: Early cancer. Tumor is located inside the gland but not yet detectable by DRE. Symptoms: none.

B: The tumor is still within the gland but already lumpy enough to be detectable by DRE. Symptoms: usually none.

C: Cancer is advanced. It is detectable by DRE. Already spread to some areas outside the gland but has not affected other organs. Symptoms: painful and frequent urination, perhaps blood.

D: Cancer has spread (metastasized) even to distant organs, bone, lymph nodes. Symptoms: as above, plus bone, back and joints pain, weight loss, fatigue. Treatment success is questionable. (This D stage was later subdivided into D1 and D2 for further precision.)

Dr. Hugh J. Jewett, who dedicated and autographed this photo to Dr. William J. Catalona.
(*Courtesy of* Dr. Catalona)

The Whitmore-Jewett became universally the most widely used cancer staging system. However, based on more modern technology and research, the Union Internationale Contre le Cancer (UICC) with headquarters in Geneva, Switzerland, which authored the *Classification of Malignant Tumours* system, and the American Joint Committee on Cancer (AJCC), which authored the *Manual for Staging of Cancer* system, in 1972 developed a comprehensive new method suggesting a more accurate prognosis: **The "TNM" Staging**, which stands for **Tumor** (extent of the primary tumor within the prostate), **Node** (whether the cancer has spread to the nearby lymph nodes), and **Metastasis** (absence or spread of the cancer to other organs and tissue).

91

THE "T N M" CANCER STAGING SYSTEM

(T): PRIMARY TUMOR, CLINICAL

Stage Condition

TX	Tumor undetectable
T0	No evidence of primary tumor
T1	Clinically unapparent tumor, neither palpable nor visible by imaging
T1a	Tumor incidental histological finding in ≤5% of tissue resected
T1b	Tumor incidental histological finding in >5% of tissue resected
T1c	Non-palpableTumor identified by needle biopsy (e.g., because of elevated PSA)
T2	Tumor confined within prostate
T2a	Palpable. Tumor involves one lobe
T2b	Tumor involves both lobes
T3	Tumor extends through the prostate capsule
T3a	Extracapsular extension (unilateral or bilateral)
T3b	Tumor invades seminal vesicle(s)
T4	Tumor is fixed or invades adjacent structures other than seminal vesicles: bladder neck, external sphincter, rectum, muscles, and/or pelvic wall

(N): REGIONAL LYMPH NODES

NX	Regional lymph nodes cannot be assessed
N0	No regional lymph node metastasis
N1	Metastasis in a single lymph node ≤2 cm in dimension
N2	Metastasis in a single lymph node ≥2 cm but <5 cm, or in multiple nodes ≤5 cm
N3	Metastasis in a lymph node >5 cm

(M): DISTANT METASTASES

MX	Distant metastasis cannot be assessed
M0	No distant metastasis
M1	Distant metastasis
M1a	Nonregional lymph node(s)
M1b	Bone(s)
M1c	Other site(s)

CORRESPONDENCE BETWEEN
THE "ABCD" AND THE "TNM" SYSTEMS

ABCD	T N M
A	T1,N0,M0
B	T2,N0,M0
C	T3,N0,M0
D1	T4-N0-M0; any T-N1-M0; any T-N2-M0; any T-N3-M0;
D2	any T-anyN-M1

Siminal vesicle

PROSTATE

(Graphics courtesy of AstraZeneca)

THE "PARTIN TABLES"

Before making the incision in the man's abdomen for a radical prostatectomy, surgeons have had great difficulty in predicting what they would find, the specific landscape of the prostatic environment –and whether the cancer actually had spread and how far. In spite of the availability of various calculating formulas, they had to guess.

Photo courtesy of **Dr. Alan W. Partin**

A definitive prediction method was developed by correlating three elements: the serum prostate-specific antigen (PSA) level, the Gleason Score to predict pathologic grade of clinically localized prostate cancer, and the TNM Clinical Stage. The method uses the data acquired from thousands of patients that had undergone radical prostatectomy. Two great urologists, **Dr. Alan W. Partin** (May 16, 1961-   ) and **Dr. Patrick C. Walsh** (February 13, 1938-   ), of the Urological Department at Johns Hopkins University in Baltimore, Maryland, led a group of scientists from several universities to develop in 1993 a set of nomograms ("tables"). The target was to predict simultaneously organ-confined disease, capsular penetration, and seminal vesicle and pelvic lymph node involvement. **The sophisticated computerized formulas permit the doctor and the newly diagnosed patient to evaluate the extent of the cancer and to estimate the survival rate**, therefore, allowing them to make more accurate treatment decisions –with 95% accuracy.

The term "**Partin Tables**" was coined by **Dr. Stephen B. Strum** (Jamaica, NY September 17, 1942-_____), Prostate Oncology Specialist and co-founder and until January 2003 Director of the Prostate Cancer Research Institute in Los Angeles, California.

(See suggestions in page 96 on how to use the Partin Tables)

94

The Partin Tables - Nomogram for prediction (from Clinical Stage) of Final Pathologic Stage

Gleason Score	PSA 0.0-4.0 ng/ml ClinicStage							PSA 4.1-10.0 ng/ml ClinicStage							PSA 10.1-20.0 ng/ml ClinicSta							PSA >20.0 ng/ml Clinical Stage						
	T1a	T1b	T1c	T2a	T2b	T2c	T3a	T1a	T1b	T1c	T2a	T2b	T2c	T3a	T1a	T1b	T1c	T2a	T2b	T2c	T3a	T1a	T1b	T1c	T2a	T2b	T2c	T3a
Organ-confined Disease																												
2 – 4	90	80	89	81	72	77	-	84	70	83	71	61	66	43	76	58	75	60	48	53	-	-	38	58	41	29	-	-
5	82	66	81	68	57	62	40	72	53	71	55	43	49	27	61	40	60	43	32	36	18	-	23	40	26	17	19	8
6	78	61	78	64	52	57	35	67	47	67	51	38	43	23	-	33	55	38	26	31	14	-	17	35	22	13	15	6
7	-	43	63	47	34	38	19	49	29	49	33	22	25	11	33	17	35	22	13	15	6	-	-	18	10	5	6	2
8 – 10	-	31	52	36	24	27	-	35	18	37	23	14	15	6	-	9	23	14	7	8	3	-	3	10	5	3	3	1
Capsular Penetration																												
2 – 4	9	19	10	18	25	21	-	14	27	15	26	35	29	44	20	36	22	35	43	37	-	-	47	34	48	52	-	-
5	17	32	18	30	40	34	51	25	42	27	41	50	43	57	33	50	35	50	57	51	59	-	57	48	60	61	55	54
6	19	35	21	34	43	37	53	27	44	30	44	52	46	57	-	49	38	52	57	50	54	-	51	49	60	57	51	46
7	-	44	31	45	51	45	52	36	48	40	52	54	48	48	38	46	45	55	51	45	40	-	-	46	51	43	37	2
8 – 10	-	43	34	47	48	42	-	34	42	40	49	46	40	34	-	33	40	46	38	33	26	-	24	34	37	28	23	17
Seminal Vesicle Involvement																												
2 – 4	0	1	1	1	2	2	-	1	2	1	2	4	5	10	2	4	2	4	7	8	-	-	9	7	10	14	-	-
5	1	2	1	2	3	3	7	2	3	2	3	5	6	12	3	5	3	5	8	9	15	-	10	9	11	15	19	26
6	1	2	1	2	3	4	7	2	3	2	3	5	6	11	-	4	4	5	7	9	14	-	8	8	10	13	17	21
7	-	6	4	6	10	12	19	6	9	8	10	15	18	26	8	11	12	14	18	22	28	-	-	22	24	27	32	36
8 – 10	-	11	9	12	17	21	-	10	15	15	19	24	28	35	-	15	20	22	25	30	34	-	20	31	33	28	38	40
Lymph Node Involvement																												
2 – 4	0	0	0	0	0	0	-	0	1	0	0	1	1	1	0	2	0	1	1	1	-	-	4	1	1	3	-	-
5	0	1	0	0	1	1	2	1	2	0	1	2	2	3	3	5	1	2	4	4	7	-	10	3	3	7	7	11
6	1	2	1	1	2	2	5	3	5	1	2	4	4	9	-	13	3	4	10	10	18	-	23	7	8	16	17	26
7	-	6	1	2	5	5	9	8	12	3	4	9	9	15	18	24	8	9	17	18	26	-	-	14	14	25	25	32
8 – 10	-	14	4	5	10	10	-	18	23	8	9	16	17	24	-	40	16	17	29	29	37	-	51	24	24	36	35	42

(Graphic adapted from The Partin Tables, 1997 revision, published in *JAMA* 277;1445-51. © Copyright 1997 American Medical Association. *Courtesy of* the American Medical Association.)

To use The Partin Tables: Match at the top the PSA with the T stage, then follow a vertical line until it crosses the horizontal line of Gleason Score in each of the four sections. For example, a man having PSA 10, Stage T2a, and Gleason 7 will show a predictable pathologic stage of 33% probability of organ-confined cancer, 52% of capsular penetration, 10% of seminal vesicle involvement, and 4% of lymph node involvement; whereas another man with PSA 14, Stage T2c and Gleason 8 has a predictable pathologic stage of only 8% probability of organ-confined cancer, but 33% of capsular penetration, 30% pf seminal vesicle involvement, and 29% of lymph node involvement.

OTHER DIAGNOSING/EVALUATING METHODS

After the cancer has been established by a biopsy and after it has been graded, scored and staged, specialists may still want additional tests. The purpose: to evaluate further the quantity, quality and spread of the tumor in order to arrive at the best treatment program for the patient.

Ultrasound, Sonography, precipitated great advances in Medicine. As far back in history as to the era of the Phoenicians, fishermen used rudimentary methods to "hear" the location of fish in the sea. In modern times, the main pioneers of Sonography have been the Swiss physicist **Dr. Daniel Colladen**, who in 1822 used an underwater bell to calculate the speed of sound in the waters of Lake Geneva, and British **Dr. John William Strutt (Lord Rayleigh)** (1842-1919). Rayleigh authored the landmark book *The Theory of Sound*, published in 1877 in England, in which he describes the fundamental physics of **sound vibrations** (waves), **transmission** and **refraction**; he won the Nobel Prize for Physics in 1904.

Ultrasound is sound of higher frequency than humans can hear; its production is based on the *piezo-electric effect* in certain crystals discovered in 1880 by French brothers **Dr. Pierre Curie** (1859-1906) and **Dr. Jacques Curie** (1856-1941). The French physicist **Paul Langevin** developed the **Sound Navigation and Ranging (SONAR)**, used to locate submarines and dangerous obstacles under the sea during World War I. Austrian neurologist-psychiatrist **Dr. Karl T. Dussik** (1908-1947) was the first to use ultrasound for **medical diagnosing** in 1942, and he introduced **hyperphonography** to detect tumors. **Dr. Ian Donald** (Glasgow, 1910-1987) made it possible in 1955 to study pregnancy *"from beginning to end"*, and Glasgow engineer **Dr. Tom Brown** designed the **first contact scanner** in 1956 and the **first automatic scanner** three years later.

Summary of the most commonly performed tests for prostate cancer further evaluation:

Transrectal Ultrasound (TRUS) or
Transrectal Ultrasound of the Prostate Report (TRUSP):
Doctors recommend this test to rule out the possibility of cancer or to evaluate it. Conceptually similar to the examination performed on women to see a fetus inside the womb, it consists of imaging the prostate with the aid of an ultrasound probe inserted into the rectum. The TRUSP is considered a valuable method for determining the volume of the gland in order to decide whether it should be reduced with hormones prior to treatment, the areas of higher concentration of cancer, or the pathologic spread from the capsule onto adjoining areas such as the seminal vesicles.

Computed Tomography (CT) Scan or
Computed Axial Tomography (CAT) Scan:
Based on X-Rays, a section of the scanner rotates around the body while producing images or "slices" of internal organs and tissue. A computer will recompose and convert them into high-resolution 3-dimensional views. Without anesthesia, the man lies down on the scanner bed. X-Rays plates are obtained and then a nurse injects an iodine-based solution intravenously for further imaging contrast of specific areas like the kidneys, pelvis, etc. The CT scan is a valuable aid in both diagnosing metastasized cancer and post-operative follow-up.

Transrectal Ultrasound of the Prostate (TRUSP) Report

Patient Name (last, first)	Smith, Joseph
Date	7/4/01
PSA (ng/ml)	10.0
TRUSP Gland Volume (GV) in cc	40.0
PSA Density (PSA ÷ GV)	0.25
Number of biopsy cores taken *	12
Seminal vesicles normal (Yes vs No)	No
Capsular penetration (Yes vs No)	Yes- left midgland
PSA attributed to benign prostate cells (GV x 0.066)	2.64
Excess PSA (total PSA minus PSA attributed to benign prostate cells)	7.36

* ☒ check box if all pathology specimens placed in separate fixative containers

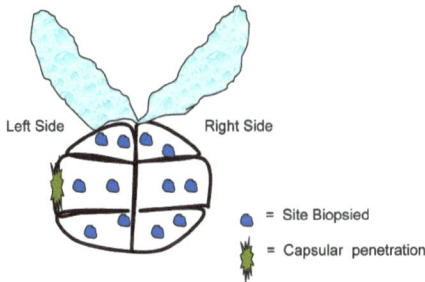

Left Side   Right Side

● = Site Biopsied

✦ = Capsular penetration

Description of gland on DRE and findings at TRUSP:

Example of Text typed here. The DRE revealed a gland estimated at 50 cc. The gland is abnormal on the left side with a hard nodule of about 1 cm present in the region of the midgland. No other nodularity is appreciated. The DRE is consistent with a T2a clinical stage. The TRUSP reveals hypoechoic areas in the R base measuring 4x3 mm and in the L midgland measuring 5x6 mm. Capsular penetration is likely at the L midgland. The TRUSP stage is therefore T3a.

(Report *Courtesy of* The Prostate Cancer Research Institute, Los Angeles, California)

Positron Emission Tomography (PET):

Also called PET Imaging or PET Scan, this diagnostic exami-nation acquires physiologic images based on the detection of radiation from the emission of positrons. Positrons are tiny particles emitted from a radioactive substance injected to the patient and permit to visualize 3-dimensionally a variety of diseases, primarily cancers, for evaluation pre- and post-treatment. It can detect and examine the ef-fects of cancer and cancer therapy by characterizing biochemical

98

changes. The value of PET is enhanced when it is part of a diagnostic program that includes other imaging studies, such as CT or MRI.

Magnetic Resonance Imaging (MRI):
    This technique, high-definition magnetic resonance scanning, is used to obtain high-resolution three-dimensional images of internal organs. But the purpose is much more ambitious: to measure the function of the body, specifically energy metabolism, at the cellular and biochemical levels. Although similar to the CT or the CAT Scans, it works on magnetic field and radio waves and the hydrogen atom is the target of the magnetic resonance. Hydrogen atom is in water H_2O (75% of our body is water) and in most other compounds of our body. The MRI response depends on the environment of the H atom, and is different for cancerous tissue and for normal healthy tissue –i.e., **cancerous lymph nodes appear white, healthy nodes appear black**. Thus, the MRI technique may detect the spread of the cancer beyond the prostate.

    The patient lies on the table that moves slowly to inside a narrow tube or tunnel for about 45 minutes. It is painless but irritating to some because of the "strange" noises heard inside the tunnel of the machine, and especially if the patient suffers from claustrophobia (some clinics pipe soft music inside the tunnel). When this Author had an MRI for the first time, the nurse explained the routine warning about the noises and the possibility of claustrophobic side effects. She was surprised by the report at the end: this Author had enjoyed trying to identify the "symphony", the dancing rhythm or whatever patterns that were giving cohesion to the sounds, and that the time inside the tunnel was actually too short to outline a melody. Newest models of MRI machines are "open", thus, avoiding claustrophobic effects.

Magnetic Resonance Spectroscopic Imaging (MRSI):
    Similar to the MRI, this technique uses magnetic field and radio waves to obtain metabolic images (spectra) based on the relative concentration of cellular chemicals (metabolites). **Dr. Robert Bard**, of the University of San Francisco, California, adopted it in 1976 using pelvic sonograms performed over the lower abdomen, a technique he had initiated on expectant mothers to detect and see the fetus. It detects blood vessels and quantifies the flow of blood in the prostate, a process that is helpful in refining diagnosis and prognosis.

99

ProstaScint Scan:

   Approved by the FDA in 1996 for use as an imaging agent, it is not yet popularized. This sophisticated technique helps to refine prostate cancer diagnoses as well as evaluate recurrent disease after surgery. The images it produces indicate how much the cancer has spread and metastasized –with fine details often missed by other diagnosing modalities.

SUMMARY OF MOST COMMON DIAGNOSING TESTS

Digital Rectal Exam	Computerized Tomography (CT, PET)
P S A	Magnetic Resonance Imaging (MRI)
Urinalysis	Magnetic Resonance Spectroscopic Imaging (MRSI)
Uroflowmetry	Transrectal Ultrasound (TRUS)
Cystoscopy	Chest X-Ray
Biopsy	Intravenous Pyelogram (IVP)
Staging	Bone Scan
	ProstaScint Scan

Prostate Cancer Awareness Poster
(*Courtesy of* Dave Grundy, Canada)

Chapter 5

How to trick the Prostate... gently

By now, our man may ask, *"How did I get into this mess?"* If he looks at the scores of the different tests as he recorded them on the sample spreadsheet suggested in Chapter 1, he will probably see that the trend throughout time was paving the road to a predictable target. The outcome of the prostate misbehavior was feared but also expected. Nothing can be done now to reverse the circumstance: the man is one of the hundreds of thousands of Americans diagnosed every year with cancer of the prostate.

Moreover, since we already have learned that there is no specific answer until scientists advance a little more in their search for causes of prostate cancer, the question *"How did I get into this mess?"* becomes purely rhetorical. The next question however is the most important to the patient, *"How do I get out of this mess?"* And his objective at this point is going to be to avoid becoming one more member of the other group, the unfortunate ~30,000 men who die of this disease in the U.S. every year.

"How bad is my cancer?" The thesis that cancer of the prostate grows so slowly that the man will die *with* but not *of* the disease is, as we have seen, unreliable and unrealistic. Before a decision on treatment, and since each man is an individual case, the patient will want to evaluate several issues when he visits his urologist and/or oncologist:

- **How curable is his cancer?**
- **Who is his HMO's specialist and which treatment center will have to be used?**
- **What are the cure/failure historical records of the specialist at 5 and 10 years after treatment?**
- **Is the physical condition of the patient, aside from his cancer, favorable to forecast a successful treatment?**
- **Which is the "right treatment" for him?**
- **Is the contemplated treatment available within his HMO network and will such clinic or center accept him? Many centers do not accept patients with PSA ≥10 ng/ml or Gleason ≥7 because of statistically poor cure and survival rates. Candidates for surgery and for brachytherapy are normally expected to have gland-localized cancer because it may not be curable if already metastasized.**

Following is a summary of **common initial protocols** that urologists, oncologists and patients consider:

"WATCHFUL WAITING" = DO NOTHING

In the 1990s, 30% of the men diagnosed with prostate cancer were treated with surgery, 30% with some type of radiation, 20% with other therapies, and 20% adopted the *Watchful Waiting* attitude for asymptomatic prostate cancer –meaning, "**Do nothing**".

The decision of *waiting,* with or without the doctor's suggestion, may be caused by one or more circumstances:

* The patient, for whatever reasons, refuses to go through any treatment at all –and chooses to live [and die] with and perhaps of his cancer.

* The specialist advises that, due to advanced metastasis, his age, or the existence of other unfavorable physical conditions, any treatment other than supporting drugs could be fatal, or else unjustifiably damaging. Most specialists advise against surgery when the man is ≥74 years since actuarial tables suggest that his life expectancy is <10 years (the minimum estimated life span to recommend treatment is 10 years according to most experts). However, a good number of men age ≥74 do decide to have some treatment.

* His HMO refuses to pay for the procedure elsewhere and he cannot afford the bill.

* The patient adheres to the attitude of "avoiding all treatments' side effects", a criteria prevalent in some countries.

Many experts strongly oppose waiting to make decisions. Dr. Stephen B. Strum emphatically conveyed to this Author,

"There is NOWHERE in Oncology where waiting for the tumor cell population to increase (and to mutate) is in the better interest of the patient. (...) In my experience, it is the early use of therapy, before the tumor volume increases, that allows for long-term responses.

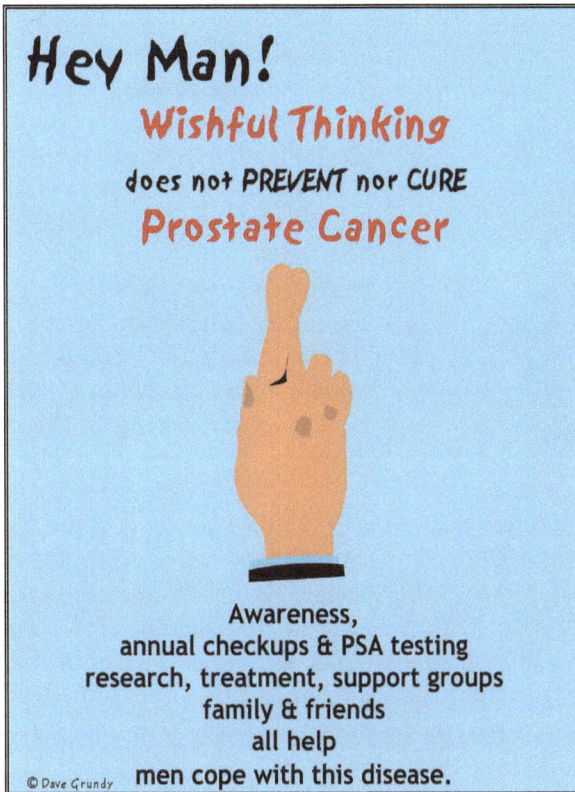

Prostate Cancer Awareness Poster
(Courtesy of **Dave Grundy, Canada)**

ORCHIECTOMY:
HORMONAL and SURGICAL

Hormonal Treatment

American urologist **Dr. Charles B. Huggins** (1901-1997), Professor of Surgery at the University of Chicago, Illinois discovered a landmark in 1941 for which he was awarded the Nobel Prize in 1966: upon removal of the testicles in dogs with enlarged prostate or prostate cancer, the production of testosterone stopped and the tumor and the prostate shrank. If later testosterone was injected to the castrated animals, the gland and tumor promptly recovered their original diseased size. Subsequent studies with men gave the same results.

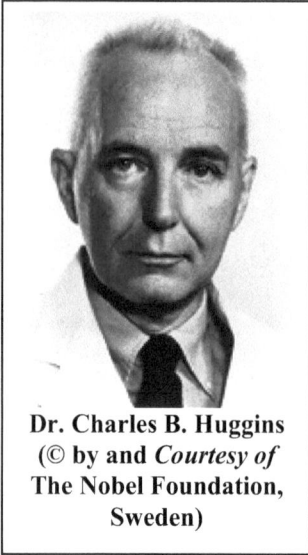

Dr. Charles B. Huggins
(© by and *Courtesy of* The Nobel Foundation, Sweden)

He pursued his research to demonstrate similar targets by using chemicals: (a) that the testicles of men secrete testosterone, the **masculine hormone** *androgen*, and (b) that the production of testosterone stopped when men were given the **female hormone** *estrogen*. That is, **the male hormone androgen controls the growth of the prostate and fuels the growth of the cancerous tumors.**

Therefore, since prostate cancerous cells do not grow without androgen, Dr. Huggins concluded that **we could manipulate the hormones** and eliminate the testosterone. That could be accomplished either by removing the testicles or by administering to the man the female hormone estrogen or other chemicals to retard the growth of even advanced tumors –in fact, by bringing testosterone down to its castrate level.

Dr. Huggins' discovery of hormonal therapy had an enormous impact in Medicine, with later applicability to both men and women.

Hormonal Orchiectomy

Also known as **Androgen-Deprivation Therapy**, it was introduced in the early 1980s. It consists of injections and/or capsules to reduce or eliminate the production of testosterone; levels of 16 to 20 ng/dl testosterone are normally associated with castration. It is mainly used (a) as therapy for prostate cancer patients of advanced age or deficient physical condition who are not candidates for surgery or radiation, (b) to temporarily reduce the volume of the prostate gland from the time of diagnosis to the time of treatment by surgery or radiation, or (c) as a palliative treatment of recurrent cancer after the patient has had surgery and/or radiation. Specialists may prescribe a shot of a medication that provides slow-dispensing effects lasting 1, 3 or 12 months, during which period the drug releases a message to the brain either to instruct the testicles to stop the production of testosterone or to nullify its effects in the prostate, depending on the drug.

105

Frequently, shots are combined with oral anti-androgen blocking capsules.

The effects of most of these drugs start in 7 to 14 days after the first dose. The *agonists* may stimulate the production of testosterone at the beginning (giving the man a false impression of libido renewed) until the production is abruptly shut down.

Studies show that hormonal/pharmacological therapy **does not cure cancer**. It is a **suppressive** or **palliative** therapy. Its effectiveness consists in tricking the body to manipulate or alter the production of certain chemicals to slow down cancer cells growth and to reduce the size of the prostate.

Hormone resistance may occur at 2 to 3 years after the initiation of therapy if the individual has a positive bone scan; otherwise, the average time for hormone resistance is currently about 11 years. Most men are started on hormone blockade before the development of a positive bone scan; afterwards, the hormone-resistant cancerous cells may take over, become *refractive*, and later they may "wake up hungry" and resume growth –perhaps with more aggressiveness. Specialists favor an **"intermittent" hormonal therapy**: to use it until the PSA is controlled down to its lowest, "undetectable" level, say ≤0.2 ng/ml, then suspend it to allow the cells to recover and then resume the hormonal therapy when the PSA starts climbing again.

Side effects of hormonal therapy may include, among others: impotence (and lack of libido), psychological (depression, loss of self-identity due to loss of masculinity, emotional swings), abrupt hot flashes (in more than 62% of patients), pain (35%), tenderness and enlargement of the breast, fatigue, weight increase, dizziness, cardiovascular risks, and osteoporosis (loss of bone mineral density or BMD, thinning of bones making them susceptible to fracture). Statistics show that many men with prostate cancer and under hormone therapy are usually osteopenic or osteoporotic, caused by BMD loss.

Hot Flushes or **Flashes**, experienced also by women during menopause, are unpredictable sudden waves of heat felt in the face, neck, chest, back and arms lasting ≤1 up to 5 minutes or even an hour. They are not painful but embarrassing to the patient. Hot flushes are also felt by >50% of men who have had the testicles removed.

Most of the symptoms disappear several months after discontinuing the treatment.

Surgical Orchiectomy

Bilateral Orchiectomy or **Subcapsular Orchiectomy** consists in the surgical extirpation or removal of the testicles through an incision in the scrotum in order to eliminate the primary source of testosterone, which fuels the cancer of the prostate (and when cancer has attacked the testicles); also known as surgical castration.

During the Subcapsular protocol, the surgeon empties the content of the testes. The emptied shells may be put back in the scrotum for cosmetic or psychological reasons to avoid the appearance of having the bag empty –many surgeons strongly oppose this procedure due to the risk that some cells still making testosterone may be left inside. To disguise the appearance of the empty bag some men opt for an implant or insertion of "prosthesis" with a physical configuration similar to a testicle.

Studies show that neither chemical nor surgical orchiectomy actually **cures** prostate cancer, but rather drastically eliminates its fuel, the testosterone produced by the testicles. They also suggest the fear that, once the testes are removed, the adrenal glands may increase the production of testosterone (from the normal 5%- 15% to as high as 40%), although there is no consensus among specialists.

This surgical procedure is irreversible –the testicles are gone. The prostate begins to shrink rapidly. Side effects are similar to those experienced with hormonal orchiectomy. A high percentage of men become irritable, less aggressive, and gain weight.

Studies show also that 50% of patients who underwent this surgical procedure lived >3 years, 25% lived >5 years; if the cancer was localized, 50% to 60% lived >5 years, and 40% >10 years. However, there are records of patients who lived 20 and 30+ years after surgical removal of the testicles.

The above discussion on orchiectomy therapy, whether hormonal or surgical, completes another cycle of this book. Our man has traveled (a) from the masculinity and machismo as suggested by *Don Juan Tenorio*, (b) through apprehension of having a digital rectal examination, (c) to taking female hormones, (d) to hormonal or surgical castration.

Masculinity and *machismo* are seemingly in jeopardy now that the prostate does not behave due to chemicals or to testicles removal. Exclusively the patient himself can evaluate the significance of the event. Although many, when suggested as cancer treatment, accept it *as a matter of fact*, most resent it. The adverse psychological impact on the patient is not caused just by the loss of capability to perform sexual functions, but rather by his awareness of the loss of masculinity, and hence, of self-identity. The libido or interest in sex and the ability to achieve erection to have sex are gone, thus, he is tormented by memories of desire, which in American culture is associated with the loss of manhood. Such psychological impact extends also to the patient's female partner but perhaps in a dual dimension. Research shows that she is not concerned exclusively by her man's loss of sexual capability, but also by what she perceives as the possibility that her man may have lost interest in her, as a female, therefore being no longer attractive to him.

Chapter 6

How to remove or murder the Prostate...and feel great about it!

Prostate cancer patients are, in our times, quite lucky. Scientists have devised sophisticated strategies to control, remove or even to "murder" the gland and to cure the cancer without killing or handicapping themselves in the process.

We have already commented scientists' search for the **when** and **why** cancer of the prostate begins (the single-cause, the start), as well as their pursuit to discover or to refine **palliatives such as hormonal therapy**. Following is a summary of those who discovered or perfected methods **of attacking the end-result** –the most predominant therapies to eradicate the cancer by removing or killing the gland.

Part 1

TRADITIONAL RADICAL PROSTATECTOMY

Since the early 1880s, surgeons all over the world have attempted to cure prostate cancer by complete, surgical removal of the gland and the adjoining tissues where cancerous cells were assumed to nest. They tried various procedures or protocols, by an incision in the lower section of the abdomen (**Suprapubic**), by an incision in the perineum between the anus and the scrotum (**Perineal**), or by several small incisions in the abdomen (**Laparoscopy**).

German stamp honoring Dr. Theodor Billroth

German **Dr. Theodor Billroth** (1829-1894) performed the first radical perineal prostatectomy for cancer in 1867 in the Medical School of Vienna University (Austria), about two decades after American **Dr. Oliver Wendell Holmes** (1804-1894) had discovered anesthesia. But Dr. Billroth's first two patients died within 14 months. He paved the road however, for the great American urologist **Dr. Hugh Hampton Young** (September 18, 1870-August 23, 1945), of Johns Hopkins University in Baltimore, Maryland, known as the *Father of American Urology*. On April 7, 1904, Dr. Young performed an improved technique to extract the whole prostate through the perineum; this is actually considered **the first radical perineal prostatectomy**.

Radical prostatectomy became the most significant surgical therapy for prostate cancer, refined by others throughout the first half of the twentieth century. However, in spite of his initial success (Dr. Young's patient died six years later of other causes) **the general results were a complete failure** because of devastating side effects and fatalities. The surgeon could hardly see what he was doing when manipulating the organs and tissues submerged in a sea of blood. That is why tissues, nerves and vessels were all cut out *as a matter of fact.*

The tragic results were not evident until shortly after surgery when the patient became incapacitated or died.

Rare photo of Dr. Hugh H. Young while in the Military. (*Courtesy of* **The Museum of Urology of the American Urological Association**)

Actually, not until 1978 when **Dr. Patrick Craig Walsh,** Director of Brady Urological Institute at Johns Hopkins University in Baltimore, Maryland, described his revolutionary technique for control of bleeding from **the dorsal vein complex** were surgeons able "to see" what they were doing. This eminent urologist also culminated in 1981 years of research and scientific curiosity that changed many conceptions and misconceptions about prostate cancer, surgery and the very anatomy of men. While attending a medical convention in The Netherlands, Dr. Walsh visited with the retired famous urologist **Dr. Pieter J. Donker** (Holland March 2, 1914-February 19, 1999) and both agreed to perform together a dissection of an infant male cadaver. It was Friday February 13, 1981 (Dr. Walsh's 43rd birthday) and the date made medical history. Dr. Walsh discovered (actually, proved his theory) and charted **the exact location of the nerve bundles that control urination and sexual erection**, which had never before been charted. Furthermore, it had been assumed that they ran through the prostate, but he demonstrated that they run outside the gland held by a thin tissue sheet called the *pelvic fascia.* In 1990, he charted for the first time the anatomy of the striated sphincter, which controls urination. That is, he re-discovered men's anatomy and made radical prostatectomy safe. Such nerve bundles are since known as *The Walsh Nerves.*

Dr. Walsh had already gained an international reputation for other discoveries: an experimental technique for the **induction of benign prostatic hyperplasia**, demonstration of the influence of **reversible androgen deprivation** on BPH, and for the first time the characterization of **hereditary prostate cancer** or **HPC** demonstrating the link between family history and development of this disease.

111

Back in the United States, Dr. Walsh performed the first *anatomical* or *nerve-sparing* **radical prostatectomy** in April of 1982. The 52-year-old patient survived, regained all of his functions and was doing well years after the operation. Dr. Walsh's new technique immediately became the *"Gold Standard"* for prostate surgery.

With this discovery, Dr. Walsh demonstrated for the first time that **the prostate gland is treatable and disposable**, that it can be removed and that the man can survive, urinate well and continue having sexual intercourse.

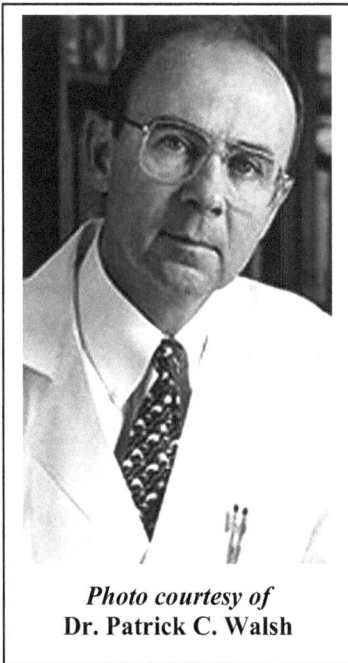

Photo courtesy of
Dr. Patrick C. Walsh

Radical prostatectomy is major surgery lasting 2+ hours. **The most common technique currently performed is the retropubic**, under general anesthesia. The surgeon makes an 8" to 10" incision in the abdomen below the navel. The lymph nodes are first removed and the dorsal vein complex divided. The prostatic urethra is also divided, tissues are separated from rectum and bladder, seminal vesicles are dissected, the entire prostate gland is removed, and then the bladder neck is adjusted and stitched back to the urethral stump around a Foley catheter.

Hospitalization lasts between 4 to 6 days; the healing of the abdominal incision, as with all deep incisions, takes time depending on the patient, and carries the possibility of infection. The catheter is removed within 1 to 2 weeks. The recovery period may last 2-6 months or more depending on side effects and the overall health of the patient.

The alternative to retropubic radical prostatectomy is the **perineal prostatectomy**, less common because of the difficulty in accessing some of the areas surrounding the gland.

Radical Prostatectomy is irreversible –the prostate is gone, irreplaceable. In theory, after removal of the organ where the cancer developed, that is the prostate, the patient should be considered *cured*. Immediately after surgery and within six months at the latest, the PSA

112

of 70% of the patients is expected to fall to a **PSA Nadir level ≤0.2 ng/ml**. This ≤0.2 ng/ml level in medical terms is usually defined as **undetectable** because it is the lowest level that some common laboratory measuring assays are capable of detecting. **PSA Nadir** means, "the lowest PSA level achieved and which must remain at that level at 5 and at 10 years after the operation, that is, indefinitely, in order for the patient to be considered cured".

Since his innovative **Anatomical Approach to Radical Prostatectomy**, Dr. Walsh operated on thousands of patients, of whom 94% and 91% were still cured, at 10 and at 15 years, respectively, as shown by their PSA Nadir of ≤0.2 ng/ml. Continence and potency results for his first series of 593 consecutive patients were remarkable:

Continence:
- 92% achieved complete urinary control
- 8% had "stress" incontinence
- 6% wore one or fewer pads per day
- 2 men (0.3%) had "stress" incontinence sufficient to require surgical placement of an artificial sphincter. (This prostate implant device, approved by the FDA, mimics the function of the natural sphincter: the patient squeezes a pump in the scrotum that causes the urethra to open and the urine to flow. Although highly effective, some need to be replaced surgically.)
- 0 (none) patients suffered total incontinence

In his last series of 700 men, none experienced total urinary incontinence or stress incontinence.

Potency (defined by Dr. Walsh as "*the ability to have an unassisted erection sufficient for vaginal penetration and orgasm on a regular basis*"):

Patient's Age at Surgery	Sexual Function Preserved
< 50 years	91%
50 – 60	75%
60 – 70	58%
> 70	25%

113

Evaluation of 955 men who underwent radical prostatectomy by Dr. Walsh for localized cancer between 1982 and 1991 revealed that, at 10 years, 70% had "undetectable" serum PSA, 23% had an isolated elevation of PSA, 7% developed distant metastases, and only 4% developed local recurrence.

"...And those are the best results on cancer control that have ever been reported", has said Dr. Walsh.

Dr. William J. Catalona reported also impressive statistics of the thousands radical prostatectomy operations he performed: 90% of all patients were alive and only 3% have died of prostate cancer, that is, a 97% cancer-specific survival at 7 years after surgery. Dr. Catalona also reported that bladder control or continence returned to normal in his patients within 6 to 18 months after removal of the catheter.

POTENCY AND CONTINENCE REGAINED 18 MONTHS AFTER A RADICAL PROSTATECTOMY (Dr. Catalona's 1990-2002 series)		
	Regained	
Age	**Potency**	**Continence**
<50-59	94%	95%
60-69	72%	93%
>70	52%	85%

Not all surgeons match those statistics. Studies show significant discrepancies among surgeons regarding survival rates as well as incidence of incontinence and impotence –many said they do not even keep their own records. Assuming proper selectivity of candidates for surgery, and in spite of modern technology, the **success of this surgical procedure depends fundamentally on the skills of the surgeon**, even more so when performed by "low volume" surgeons. Six statistical compilations from prominent centers of excellence in U.S. universities showed an overall median cure rate of 76.67% at 5 years (range 69% to 87%) and of 63.67% at 10 years (range from 47% to 88%). A rise in serum prostate-specific antigen (PSA) after radical prostatectomy occurs in 10-40% of cases (median of 41% within 10 years), suggesting cancer recurrence. It is revealed by palpable digital rectal examination or by PSA levels of >0.02 ng/ml after the operation.

Over 55,000 radical prostatectomy procedures are performed in the U.S. annually.

Recurrence, that is, unsuccessful attempt to eradicate the cancer the first time, may be due to one or more of the following causes:

- **Inadequate competence of the surgeon or oncologist in the chosen treatment.**
- **Error/accident, medical error, during the procedure.**
- **Underrating by the pathologist of the cancer growth, because there was already advanced spread, metastasis.**
- **The physical condition of the patient prior to treatment, aside from his prostate cancer, which may not have been properly evaluated when designing the treatment.**

A life-threatening side effect of radical prostatectomy is the possibility of a blood clot, currently rare due to the advances of pre-operative care. The other two side effects patients fear most are **incontinence** and **impotence/erectile dysfunction**. Both are sensitive issues when patients weigh the pros and cons (=quality of life) of whatever treatments they might choose. The decisions are of a very individual and intimate nature. Of these two side effects, surveys show that men pay first consideration to preserving the capability of being able to void in a toilet when they need.

Incontinence

Dr. Catalona affirms that the most common cause of **incontinence** after nerve-spared radical prostatectomy is **a weak external sphincter muscle**. During the convalescent period, the patient may feel a tightening in the lower stomach when moving or walking, as well as incontinence.

> "Normally", **Dr. Catalona** says, "the bladder wall is thin and very elastic and maintains a low pressure until it has stored 8 to 10 ounces of urine. But after surgery, the swollen bladder does not store much urine at a low pressure and, as soon as it starts to fill, the pressure goes up and the patient feels the need to urinate."

115

A recent general study revealed that almost 30% of radical prostatectomy patients wore pads to keep dry and that 10% became totally or almost totally incontinent. Remedies for urinary incontinence include, among others: drugs, use of small underpants absorbent towels or pads in the underwear, surgical implant of an artificial sphincter, and the easiest, the so-called "**Kegel Exercises**".

Dr. Arnold A. Kegel (1894-1976), a specialist in gynecology who practiced in Los Angeles, California for many years, announced in 1948 unique exercise methods for women to control incontinence following childbirth, uterine or intestinal surgery, or urinary-stress incontinence due to age or menopause. His methods were later also applied to men suffering urinary or fecal incontinence or weakening of the pelvic muscles due to surgery or age. By strengthening the affected muscles, the patient can recover flexibility and continence. A report showed "considerable improvement" after the first month, and a research published in 2003 in Europe found that seven out of ten patients, men and women, **were cured using Kegel exercises**. Nineteen million Americans (80% of them women) suffer urinary incontinence.

Dr. Kegel's original set of exercises has been throughout the years modified by urologists and therapists. The **pelvic floor muscles** (the largest being the so-called **pubococcygeus**) surround and support the bladder, control the opening/closing of the sphincters and affect the muscles of the anus and the pelvis as well. Pelvic floor muscles, traumatized by bladder infection, weakened or injured by surgery (radical prostatectomy) or radiation (brachytherapy, external radiation), may cause what is known as "**stress**" or "**urge**" **incontinence** or **leakage**. This type of incontinence may happen when coughing, laughing, sneezing, or suddenly because of feeling an overwhelming necessity to urinate.

The exercises are recommended for before treatment, if possible, but otherwise as soon as feasible after treatment, regularly, several times a day, at home, at the office, while driving a car or talking on the telephone –anytime, anywhere. If the man is too weak at the start, he may do them lying down on his back on the floor until he can proceed standing up.

Following is a summary of the Kegel Exercises most frequently recommended. The suggested numbers for repetitions, contractions and "hold and rest" patterns are to start. Experts say that the patient should monitor and increase them as he progresses, with a **final ideal target of between 100 and 200 contractions per day**. They also ad-

116

vise working individually on each target muscle (e.g., pelvic, anus) and leaving the others alone for subsequent exercises (thigh, back, abdominal). Specialists also warn to stay away from Vitamin C, citrus-acid drinks and other bladder irritants as well as over-the-counter allergy and cold medications during the program.

THE "*KEGEL EXERCISES*"

Urinary:
1. **While urinating but before finishing the void, contract the pelvic floor muscles to stop or slow down the flow for 10 seconds. This will also allow a man to ascertain that he is using the right muscles (pelvic floor). Do this as many times in a row as possible; rest few seconds between contractions.**
2. **When not urinating, contract the pelvic muscles and hold for 3 seconds x 10 times, resting 5 seconds between contractions.**
3. **Same as 2 above, but hold for 5-10 seconds. Contract and release quickly, abruptly.**
4. **Same as 2 above, but laugh, cough or clear the throat while holding a contraction.**

Repeat the session as many times as possible during the day.

Dr. Frederick E. B. Foley
(Courtesy of The Museum
of Urology, American
Urological Association)

Rectal:
In addition to the above exercises: Tighten and contract the anus 10 times as if trying to avoid passing gas. Maintain the contraction for 5-10 seconds, rest or hold for 5.

Foley.- Throughout centuries, men have designed numerous and ingenious methods to discreetly relieve the effects of incontinence. Even in the 1930s, men still used especially made catheters (Greek *catheter* = let down) with a reservoir hidden in hats, umbrella shafts and walk canes. **Dr. Frederick Eugene Basil Foley** (1891-1966), of the University of Minneapolis, Minnesota invented in 1934 a special **Catheter** to be used during and after surgery to facilitate the voiding of urine. It consisted

117

of a rubber tube with a balloon at the end to be inflated. It became immediately so popular all over the world that even today a catheter is simply called "a **Foley**".

Erectile Dysfunction

Although sometimes used indistinctively, experts say that the terms sexual dysfunction and erectile dysfunction have in strict comparison different causes.

Sexual dysfunction.- It defines difficulties to engage in sexual intercourse. It affects both men and women. It may be the result of physical or psychological factors, or a combination of both, such as anger toward the partner, depression, anxiety (and performance anxiety), fear of pregnancy, guilt, ignorance about sexual behavior, previous sexual trauma (rape, abuse), medications.

Erectile Dysfunction.- In 1993, the Consensus Development Panel of the U.S. National Institutes of Health proposed **replacing the term Impotence for the "less offensive" Erectile Dysfunction (ED)** and defined it as *"The inability to attain and/or maintain penile erection sufficient for satisfactory sexual performance"*. Studies show that conditions conducive to erectile dysfunction include, besides surgery, diabetes, obesity, hypertension, hormonal, chemical abuse (drugs, alcohol), age, and aging of the arteries. It is estimated that 30 million Americans are affected by some kind of erectile dysfunction (25% in their 40s, 25% by age 65). Within the context of this book, we shall refer to **Impotence** or **Erectile Dysfunction** as side effect of prostate surgery or brachytherapy pertaining to men.

Men have tried for centuries to find remedies to their impotence. Greeks and Egyptians suspected that impotence could be caused by spells, and they entrusted witches to device therapies.

To remedy potency anomalies after radical prostatectomy, urologists may suggest, depending on the patient, various drugs (Viagra, etc.) and technical devices to alleviate or reverse general erectile dysfunction (e.g., an injection in the penis shortly before intercourse, inflatable or mechanical accessories such as a vacuum erection pump, a penis implant or prosthesis).

Statistically, **erections may begin to return between 3 and 6 months after radical prostatectomy surgery**. Frequently, they begin as "partial erections", its strength improving for about three years after surgery.

Experts warn that, after surgery, the lack of erections can cause atrophy of structures such as the valves that trap blood in the penis during erection and cause also fibrosis (scarring) of the penile tissue. They strongly recommend **forcing erections**, naturally or artificially, always attempting penetration even if only slightly erect. If this is not done early and regularly, they advise, **atrophy may worsen the elasticity of the muscles and delay recovery**.

A group of surgeons at the Sloan-Kettering Memorial Cancer Center in New York has been experimenting with ***nerve implant*** or ***nerve graft***, a procedure consisting of removing some nerves from a foot or leg of the patient and inserting them to replace [some of] the ones dissected during radical prostatectomy. Tentative results of this complex surgery suggest a 50% recovery of sexual function.

Attitudes regarding potency

Attitudes regarding sexual potency after radical prostatectomy and, in certain degree, after radiation (or any other cause, for that matter) swing like a pendulum. For example, a British author ventured the thesis that, when to become a father is not the purpose of the patient, sexual dysfunction caused by the removal of the prostate "should not be of great concern". Another urologist informed this Author that when he reported to a 40-year-old patient that he had prostate cancer and advised him a prompt radical prostatectomy to remove "everything" (prostate, nerve bundles, etc.) the patient accepted without concern when warned of becoming impotent. Most men, however, disagree, and the preservation, frequency and quality of erections are of high priority when selecting treatment –even at age >70. Erectile function, within U.S. culture, has been defined as "**The mirror of a man's health**". Urologists surveyed by this Author affirmed that, although mental attitude by itself is not a cure, they consider it **being more important than physical condition when designing whichever remedial treatment program.**

To reduce this priority (preservation of the ability to perform sexually) to *objective* statistics is very difficult, as demonstrated by a survey undertaken by a U.S. university: patients refused to answer 25% of the questions because they judged them "too personal". Such results were confirmed by this Author in his survey of over one hundred prostate cancer patients. Questions on sexual issues were answered quite differently if asked to the patient alone, to his wife alone, or to both present at the same time. The quality of the answers was tricky also and frequently in the form of another issue or ques-

119

tion: whether "capability to have an erection conducive to intercourse" meant "spontaneous capability" or "stimulation" by him or by his partner, and whether "partner" meant the wife or someone else. Of the U.S. patients surveyed, 25% of those age >60 declared that they would like to have more frequent sexual activity but that they either (a) lacked a partner (although statistically, 60% of American men age >50 are married and live with their spouse); (b) that the wife had no interest; (c) that one or both were under unrelated medications that also reduced their sex desire, and (d) other issues not associated with the radical prostatectomy side effects −or with any other medical procedure for that matter.

The issue is a universal concern. For most of the American aging population, both men and women, sex remains an important consideration, as found in a recent U.S. survey of sexual encounters per year according to age. Surprisingly to many, **the 60-69 age group scored the third place with 68 times**. Another study revealed in 2006 that patients' wives are frequently the ones who prompt men to go to the urologist to obtain a drug for the relief of erectile dysfunction

OTHER SIDE EFFECTS OF SURGERY

Dry ejaculation-Infertility: Prostate surgery, as well as radiation, frequently remove or damage the internal valve or sphincter that controls, at sexual orgasm, the flow of the sperm from the epididymis to/through the urethra and the penis. When this valve is removed or does not function properly, the result is a **dry ejaculation, and thus, infertility** because the sperm backs up to the bladder instead of flowing to the urethra and out through the penis. This phenomenon however, does not seem to alter the man's feeling of pleasure; in fact, most do not feel any difference (see Anatomy discussion - Chapter 2).

Shrinkage of the penis: After a radical prostatectomy, ~68% of patients have **shrinkage of the penis**, as determined by comparison of the penile length before and three months after surgery. As we have seen in Chapter 2, the median length of the penis (which is the same whether stretched or erect) is 4½ to 5 inches. Most patients are not aware of the change immediately after the operation because of lack of natural erections. Researchers at the University of Miami, in March 2003 confirmed a decrease of ~15% of the length as compared with the measurement before surgery. Dr. William J. Catalona explains that the removal of the prostate *"causes a gap between the bladder neck and the urethra, which has to be bridged. In some men the bladder is very mobile and easily reaches the urethral stump, but in other men there is a* **stretch** *that pulls the bladder and urethra together, and consequently the penis gets* **pulled up** *inside. With time and return of regular erections, this retraction often corrects itself."*

Part 2

RADIOLOGY, RADIATION

Not being transparent, the interior of the human body has been a mystery since the beginning of human life. Insights were gained into the structure of the organs only by the dissection of corpses. The **ability "to see through"** the skin and the tissue, whether by creating images or, later, by "seeing" three-dimensionally and interactively how the interior organs behave, is one of the most important milestones in the history of Medicine.

German scientist **Wilhelm Konrad Röntgen** (1834-1923) in 1895 discovered the short wave rays, first known as the *Röntgen Rays*, for which we won the first Nobel Prize awarded in 1901. He was experimenting how electricity could be conducted in a dilute gas when, to his surprise,

Dr. Wilhelm K. Röntgen (© The Nobel Foundation. *Courtesy of* The Nobel Foundation, Sweden)

he noticed a strange glow (a penetrating ray) irradiating from the darkened lab when he activated a vacuum tube –a "Crookes' Tube". Pursuing his research, he discovered that the impression of the glow passed through different densities, including his wife's hand. Not knowing yet exactly what the phenomenon was, he called it "**X-Rays**" (**X = unknown**). The impact of the discovery was impressive and within a few months, physicians all over the world were using X-Rays "to see" the inside of the body.

One year later, in 1896, French scientist **Dr. Henri Becquerel** (1852-1908) discovered that **Uranium** emits a similar penetrating radiation (X-Rays). On July 18, 1898 his disciple the eminent scientist **Dr. María Sklodowska Curie** (1867-1934), while seeking the cause of the radioactivity of pitchblende, an ore containing uranium, discovered that other elements also produce radiation; one such element was **Polonium** (she named it after Poland, her birthplace). Teaming with her French husband the also eminent scientist **Dr. Pierre Curie** (1859-1906), both discovered and isolated **Radium** (from Latin *radius* = ray) in their laboratory in Paris December 26, 1898. Their discovery was a basis for the **Science of Radioactivity**; they won the Nobel Prize in 1903.

L-R: Dr. Pierre Curie, Dr. Marie S. Curie, Dr. Antoine H. Becquerel. (© by and *Courtesy of* The Nobel Foundation, Sweden)

The discovery of radium marked a turning point in the history of modern Physics. The Curies demonstrated that radiation emitted by radium moves at a speed (16,000 Km. per second) much faster than uranium (10,000 Km. per second) and that it has positive (alpha), negative (beta) and neutral (gamma) radioactive emissions; it led to, among other discoveries, the knowledge of how to release the energy of the **Atom**.

The excitement caused by these discoveries, along with the **Sonography** discovered in 1880 by **Dr. Pierre Curie** and his brother **Dr. Jacques Curie**, triggered research all over the world to perfect methods of better seeing the interior of the human body, to obtain more precise images and higher resolutions, and to treat diseases (cancer) with radiation. American urologist **Dr. Moses Swick** (1900-1985), of Mount Sinai Cancer Center in New York, went to Berlin to work under the famous German surgeon **Dr. Alexander von Lichtenberg** (Budapest 1880-Mexico 1949) to test with injecting into a vein an **iodine contrasting compound** that, while traveling through the urinary system, could be X-Rayed; thus, marking in 1928 another milestone in urological diagnosis. In France, scientists experimented with prostate cancer by placing **radium into the gland** through a tube inserted in the urethra. And Dr. Young brought some radium from

122

Paris to his Urology Department at Johns Hopkins University, improved the French technique and performed about 400 radium procedures in 10 years. Another urologist, **Dr. Benjamin S. Barringer** (1878- ?), of the Sloan-Kettering Memorial Hospital in New York, inserted **radon gas** inside thin glass tubes through the perineum into the prostate, thus initiating in 1915 the technique of **perineal seeding implants**.

Imaging is used for diagnosis and evaluation of diseases, and radiation is used for therapy. Radiotherapy is performed by specialists called **Radiation Therapists** under the direction of **Oncologists**.

A patient may receive radiation in his prostate in three ways: directed from outside, generated inside by irradiating seeds (brachytherapy), or a combination of both.

EXTERNAL RADIATION

A **linear accelerator** machine is connected to a computer, which programs and automatically sets the desired dosimetry according to the patient's tumor condition and the determination by the oncologist.

Dr. Gosta Forsell (March 2, 1876-1950), of the Swedish Defense Research Agency in Sweden, started the use of radiation in 1905. **Dr. Malcolm A. Bagshaw** (Adrian, Michigan June 24, 1925-_____), of Stanford University in San Francisco, California, is recognized as the U.S. pioneer of radiotherapy for the treatment of prostate cancer, the *Father of American Radiation*. His studies constituted a major step toward cancer therapy. Under his leadership, the Stanford University Radiation Department in 1956 started **external beam radiation** for prostatic cancer. In 1962, he demonstrated that high-dose radioactive gold celluloid radiation could be an effective treatment for early-detected prostate cancer, and Stanford built the first linear accelerator for medical use in 1965, the *Electron-Gamma-Shower (EGS),* designed to calculate accurately radiation aiming at the tumor but with minimum damage to adjoining organs or tissues.

Treatment consists of sessions lasting from 20 seconds to 20 minutes usually once a day for several weeks. Radiation destroys cancerous cells –and healthy ones too.

123

Radiation therapy expanded rapidly. In some countries, it became the most popular cancer treatment. Some scientists believed that it could cure cancer without the invasive surgery and its then devastating side effects.

Photo courtesy of
Dr. Malcolm A. Bagshaw

Ideally, the PSA should drop to a ≤0.2 ng/ml within six months after external radiation treatment. It is recommended for post-radical prostatectomy, pre- or post-implants and for those patients who do not want or should not have surgery. As treatment for advanced cancer, oncologists may apply external radiation by itself or with adjuvant hormonal therapy received before, after or simultaneously with radiation.

External radiation may cause cystitis and inflammation of the rectum with or without bleeding, diarrhea, inflammation and bleeding of hemorrhoids (even if they have been inactive for years), urine leakage, inflammation of the bladder, impotence, rectal discharge, and gastro-intestinal problems (to 10%-20% of patients). Generally, these symptoms disappear 4-6 months after finishing treatment, except for about 10%-15% of patients who continue experiencing the symptoms for ≥1 year.

SEED IMPLANT RADIATION: BRACHYTHERAPY

Brachytherapy (Greek *brachy, brachios* = short, close distance to [the prostate]+*therapy*) is the procedure whereby the urologist and the oncologist teaming together plant inside the prostate 60 to 125 or more irradiating seeds of Iodine, Palladium or other radioisotope encased in Titanium –isotopes contain atoms with the same atomic number but different mass number. The radioactive activity is the number of particles emitted in a given length of time –the radioactive decay. **Alexander Graham Bell** (Scotland, March 3, 1847-Nova Scotia, U.S. August 2, 1922), inventor of the telephone, is credited for having suggested in 1903 the insertion of radium "into the heart of the cancer".

The term *Brachytherapy* was coined in 1931 in Sweden by **Dr. Gosta Forsell**.

Scientists made repeated attempts in different countries to find a way to cure cancer of the prostate by means of some kind of **radiation from inside**. All of those attempts were guided by a finger in the rectum to direct the implants, frequently followed by devastating side effects due to the imprecision in placing and seating the seeds.

The great urologist **Dr. Willet F. Whitmore, Jr.** (Long Island, New York, December 13, 1917-May 8, 1995), of Sloan-Kettering Hospital in New York, and **Dr. Basil S. Hilaris** (September 3, 1928-_____), then at the same Sloan-Kettering Hospital and now Chairman of Radiation Medicine at Our Lady of Mercy Medical Center in Bronx, New York, were the first in the U.S. to perform **retropubic brachytherapy** (1972). They used Iodine-125 seeds, a radioisotope or radionuclide that had been developed in 1905 by **Dr. William Myers** (August 7, 1908-June 17, 1988) at Ohio State University. It was open surgery.

Photo courtesy of
Dr. Haakon Ragde

The procedure became common treatment in the following years but was not successful because of the impossibility of being precise in the placement of the implants, the loss of blood, trauma, and even death. To be successful, brachytherapy, as well as radical prostatectomy, requires that the cancer be gland-localized. The lack of diagnosing tests at the time, such as the PSA, advanced radiology and ultrasound caused **patients to be treated after already experiencing symptoms,** and by that time, as we have already discussed, **the cancer is far too advanced.**

Dr. Hans Henrik Holm (Denmark, September 1931-), of the Herlev Hospital in Copenhagen, Denmark, who had developed in 1974 the first ultrasound scanner for bladder tumor staging in 1983, was the first in the world to perform in 1982 a **Transrectal Ultrasound-Guided Brachytherapy**, a revolutionary "non-surgical minimum invasive technique".

But the milestone that solidified brachytherapy as the most promising prostate cancer treatment after radical prostatectomy, but without the side effects of the latter, was produced by **Dr. Haakon**

125

Ragde (July 26, 1927-   ), then with the Pacific Northwest Cancer Foundation in Seattle, Washington. Dr. Ragde traveled in 1984 to do research under two eminent specialists. One was **Dr. Hans Henrik Holm** in Copenhagen, Denmark. The other, also using advanced ultrasonic techniques, was **Dr. Hiroki Watanabe** in Japan.

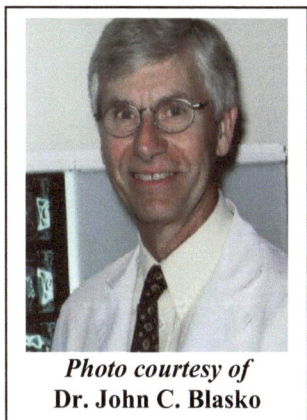

Photo courtesy of
Dr. John C. Blasko

Upon his return to the U.S., Dr. Ragde adapted and improved their techniques, and designed the special ultrasound probe. Teaming with the great oncologist **Dr. John Charles Blasko** (St. Louis, Missouri 1943-   ), then with the Northwest Tumor Institute in Seattle, Washington and now Director of Clinic Research of the Prostate Cancer Institute in Seattle and Professor of Radiology and Oncology at the University of Washington, they accurately calculated the required dose of irradiating seeds and performed the **first transrectal ultrasound-guided brachytherapy in the United States** on November 6, 1985. The success of this innovative technique precipitated the expansion and popularity of brachytherapy. Dr. Ragde and Dr. Blasko also established **the first National Brachytherapy Implant Course in 1987**, where they trained hundreds of physicians and physicists from all over the country.

Dr. John C. Blasko joined in 1998 the Seattle Prostate Cancer Institute, created in 1997 under the direction of **Dr. Peter Grimm**; since then they have performed thousands implants and trained more than 1,000 physicians.

**BIOCHEMICAL (PSA) DISEASE-FREE PATIENTS
OF THE SEATTLE GROUP LED BY DR. JOHN C. BLASKO**

Patient Risk	Gleason Sc.	PSA	TS 1,2	5 - year Pal-103	10 - year I-125 + EBR
Low	3 – 6	≤ 10	Any	94%	87%
Intermediate	7 – 10	> 10	1 – 2	82%	79%
High	7 - 10 +	> 10	Any	65%	47%

CRITERIA: Implant as monotherapy, intention curative. High-risk patients treated with combination of External Beam Radiation plus boost. No hormone treatment.
Failure definition: ASTRO but reducing the raises in serum PSA to 2 instead of 3.
Disease-free: PSA Nadir ≤0.2 ng/ml.

(Courtesy of **Dr. John C. Blasko)**

DISEASE-FREE STATISTICS OF 8,000 BRACHYTHERAPY PROCEDURES BY DR. HAAKON RAGDE, ET AL

Implant Only:	3 years	5 years	10 years	13 years
Palladium-103	87%	82%	80%	80%
Iodine-126	84%	79%	96%	76%
Failure (per ASTRO; Astro is discussed later in this Chapter)				
Positive Bone Scan	0.3%	0.7%	0.7%	0.7%
Positive Biopsy	1.6%	2.5%	2.4%	2.6%
Biochemical PSA	13.3%	17.1%	19.6%	19.7%
Disease-Free by Patient's Risk:	**Risk**	**Therapy**	**12 years**	
Group I	Low	Mono	66%	
Group II	High	" +EBR	79%	
Both Groups: 4,000 Pt			70%	

CRITERIA: Data include, both, pre- and post-PSA era. No hormone treatment. Group II had high risk of extra capsule extension of cancer. **Failure definition:** ASTRO but with 2 raises instead of 3. No patient died of prostate carcinoma. **Continence:** preserved 100%. **Potency:** no change in men <60 age, 20% erectile dysfunction in men 60-70.

(Courtesy of **Dr. Haakon Ragde)**

Clinics that had performed brachytherapy surgically switched then to the ultrasound-guided technique and in recent years to the Intensity-Modulated Radiation Therapy or IMRT (commented below), making the U.S. the world-center of this procedure.

BIOCHEMICAL (PSA) DISEASE-FREE PATIENTS OF THE SEATTLE GROUP LED BY DR. JOHN C. BLASKO

Patient Risk	Gleason Sc.	PSA	TS 1,2	5 - year Pal-103	10 - year I-125 + EBR
Low	3 – 6	≤ 10	Any	94%	87%
Intermediate	7 – 10	> 10	1 – 2	82%	79%
High	7 - 10 +	> 10	Any	65%	47%

CRITERIA: Implant as monotherapy, intention curative. High-risk patients treated with combination of External Beam Radiation plus boost. No hormone treatment. **Failure definition:** ASTRO but reducing the raises in serum PSA to 2 instead of 3. **Disease-free:** PSA Nadir ≤0.2 ng/ml.

(Courtesy of **Dr. John C. Blasko)**

The team Dr. Ragde-Dr. Blasko adopted, according to the case, the protocols of implant only, or of radiation first and then the implant of Palladium-103 seeds. Other specialists, like **Dr. Frank A. Critz**

(1945-   ), Medical Director of Radiotherapy Clinics of Georgia (RCOG), Decatur became pioneers of first implanting Iodine-125 seeds followed 21 days later by 6 to 7 weeks of 3-Dimensional External Conformal Radiation Therapy (3D-CRT); the seventh week was added as a *booster,* aiming the radiation at small fields (apex zone, seminal vesicles) more susceptible to the recurrence of cancer. Most specialists recommend seed implant alone for low risk patients: PSA of <10 ng/ml, Gleason score 2-6, stage T1 and T2. Seeds with external beam radiation before or after the implant are suggested for intermediate and high-risk patients: PSA 10>, Gleason score 7-10, stage T3 cancer.

Contraindications to undergo brachytherapy include a large prostate, previous external radiation, and when the cancer has already metastasized. Statistics show that this treatment is not advisable either for men with a reasonable life expectancy of ≤10 years; and that men with a prostate volume of ≥60cc should first be on a hormonal treatment to shrink the gland. Nevertheless, implants have been made in men ages between 40s and early 90s.

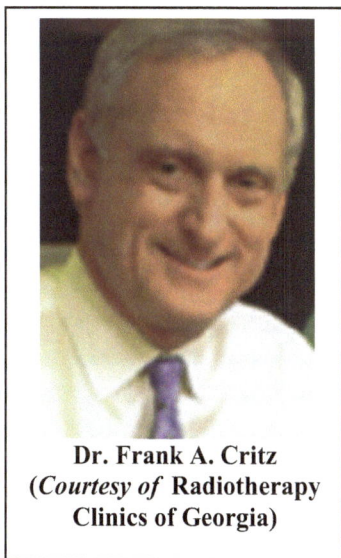

Dr. Frank A. Critz
(*Courtesy of* **Radiotherapy Clinics of Georgia**)

This brachytherapy technique, also known as **Interstitial Brachytherapy**, is performed in outpatient facilities. Under spinal anesthesia, the patient lies on his back on the operating table, knees bent and in holders (stirrups), a position quite similar to that in which a woman delivers a baby. The seeds are loaded in 18-gauge needles, aligned at 5-millimeter intervals in a template or loader held between the anus and the scrotum, through which the seeds will be shot. Two inactive, not irradiating seeds (they used to be of gold) are first implanted in upper and lower pre-determined areas of the prostate as "markers" or guides for later imaging.

The actual brachytherapy procedure lasts less than one hour. After recovery, the patient can leave the clinic. The following day, he is subjected to several tests to verify accurately number and location of each of the seeds (exceptionally, one may have migrated outside of the prostate), flowmetry to evaluate that after removal of the Foley catheter the urinary system is functioning properly, etc. If all tests are satisfactory, the man is dismissed and he can resume his normal activities.

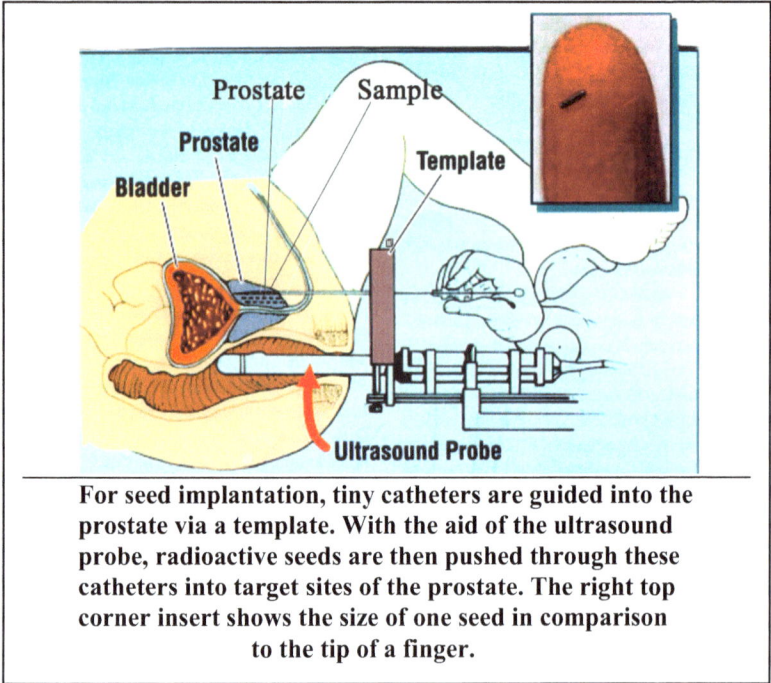

For seed implantation, tiny catheters are guided into the prostate via a template. With the aid of the ultrasound probe, radioactive seeds are then pushed through these catheters into target sites of the prostate. The right top corner insert shows the size of one seed in comparison to the tip of a finger.

Each seed has an overall length of 4.5 mm (0.18") and a diameter of 0.8 mm (0.31"). Iodine-125 seeds have a half-life of 59.4 days, radiation energy of 28keV and they irradiate in some degree for several months up to a year; Palladium-103 seeds have a half-life of 17 days and deplete their 21keV energy radiation more quickly. Both are similar. Neither is intrinsically stronger than the other is. The dose of radiation to the tumor over the time of the treatment depends on the amount of the radioisotope implanted as well as the energy of its radiation and its half-life. For example, Palladium-103 gives more radiation at the beginning but it has a much shorter life. The use of one or the other depends on the technique the medical team prefers and on the evaluation of the prostate condition.

Iodine-125 has become the most popular radioactive seed. Its use was first introduced by **Dr. Whitmore** in 1971. The use of Palladium-103 was introduced by **Dr. Ragde** and **Dr. Blasko** in 1987.

129

When the prostate is enlarged (average size before treatment is 35cc), the patient may be prescribed hormonal drugs two or three months prior to the procedure in an attempt to reduce the size for better implant and efficacy of radiation from the seeds.

If external radiation follows the implant, the patient has daily sessions for 6-7 weeks, beginning 21 days after the implant because that is considered the approximate half-life of the seeds irradiation. The synergistic action comprises the seeds destroying the cancerous cells from inside and the external radiation destroying malignant cells that might have escaped from the prostate and lodged around the gland.

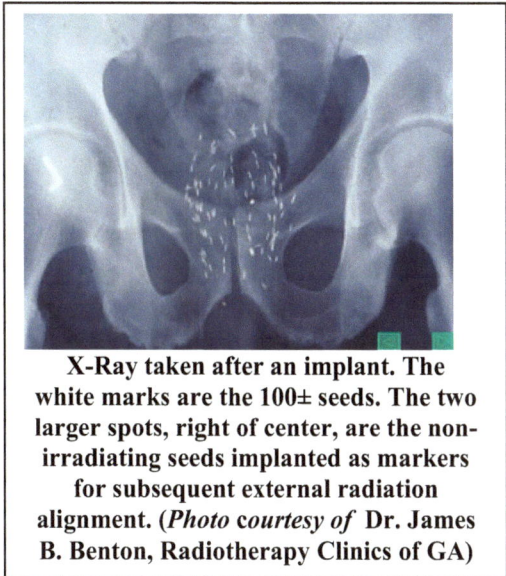

X-Ray taken after an implant. The white marks are the 100± seeds. The two larger spots, right of center, are the non-irradiating seeds implanted as markers for subsequent external radiation alignment. (*Photo courtesy of* Dr. James B. Benton, Radiotherapy Clinics of GA)

COMPARISON OF IODINE & PALLADIUM SEEDS

Seed	Size (mm)	Half-Life	Energy	Half-value layer
Iodine-125	0.8 x 4.5	60 days	28 KeV	2 cm Tissue
Palladium-103	0.8 x 4.5	17 days	21 KeV	1.6 cm Tissue

(*Courtesy of* Dr. Haakon Ragde)

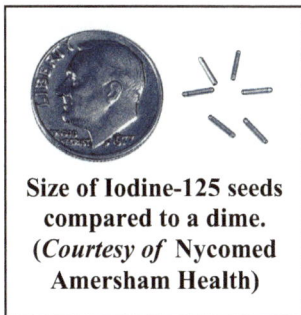

Size of Iodine-125 seeds compared to a dime. (*Courtesy of* Nycomed Amersham Health)

After six months, the seeds are essentially dead or depleted of radiation. **The seeds are implanted permanently.**

• * * * *

Remarkable improvements have been introduced in brachytherapy in the last few years due to a revolutionary new technology: the **Intensity-Modulated Radiation Therapy (IMRT)** equipment, by itself or attached to a **B-Mode Acquisition and Targeting (BAT)**. **External beam radiation**

of the prostate tumor (and of any cancer tumor) **will never be the same**.

IMRT attempts to resolve the two most critical variables in curing the cancer: the exact Gy dosimetry of radiation and the precise target to hit while sparing surrounding healthy tissue and organs.

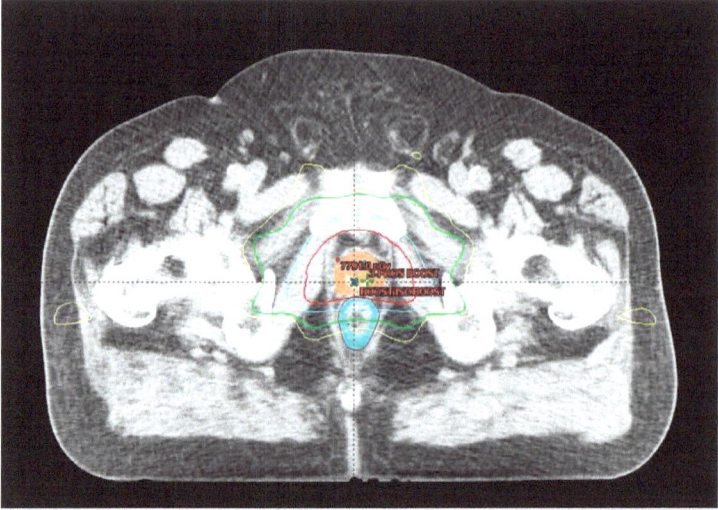

> **In this IMRT treatment plan, the prostate is the exact central structure (almost round); the rectum (oval) appears below. The horizontal lines to the right outline and contain the exact radiation dose to be delivered to the prostate. The first semi-circle (in red on the monitor) shows the radiation dose and designates a generous area to the sides and top of the prostate, while skimming and then curving around the rectum. The additional semi-circles represent regions of decreasing dose.**
>
> (*Courtesy of* **Dr. Hamilton Williams,**
> **Medical Director of Radiation Oncology of Atlanta, GA**

Following are the IMRT technology features that have impressed specialists the most:

* Fully computer-intensive, it reduces to a minimum the oncologist's possible margin of error, therefore, the side effects. For example, when determining the exact distance between the prostate and the bladder (in many men separated by only 8 millimeters) and the prostate and the rectum (by only 5 millimeters). Additionally, since not all targets (prostate, tumor) have the same shape and volume, it can determine the exact Gy dosimetry as per the precise configuration of the target, eliminating the need for the protective block used by the conventional radiation therapy.
* The arm of the machine literally rotates around the body to reach precisely the target.
* It uses photon beams to kill the cancer.
* The BAT technology allows for the ultrasound adjustment of the mobility of the prostate within the body (usually displaced about ½ inch, in whichever direction) just before starting the radiation session –therefore, reducing side effects.
* The so-called "dynamic dosimetry" software allows the oncologist to see the prostate and the seeds in three full-color dimensions, thus, increasing accuracy when delivering the radiation.
* Images generated during the needle/seeds placement are transferred directly into the software, eliminating the need for CT scans.
* While conventional beam radiation therapy dispenses about 65 to 70-Gray doses (with a long-term cure rate of 60%), the new technique can dispense higher intensity radiation of 80 Gy or more directly into the prostate, meaning a higher probability of killing the cancer.
* Depending on the tumor characteristics, Gleason score and PSA, the treatment may last one to six weeks, less than 30 minutes per daily session and it is painless.

SIDE EFFECTS

Generally, brachytherapy does not cause psychological stress or disruption of relationships or of social functions. Its side effects, and those of general radiation, are summarized in the following four categories:

Urinary: (1) Inflammation of the prostate (**Prostatitis**), traumatized and suddenly enlarged about 50% of its size within a few hours after the seed implant; and (2) perhaps the one causing major concern, **Urethritis**, the effects of radiation on the urethra, exposed to the full radiation dose and squeezed by the sudden enlargement of the gland. The symptoms are slow start of urination, weak or slow urine flow, burning, blood in the urine, urgency and frequency of urination (in >40% of patients), disuria (>17%) and stop-and-start –all described in more detail in Chapter 3. These symptoms may last from few months to one or more years in 10%-15% of patients. Very few report need for a catheter >24 hours after the procedure, and only about 1% have urine stream totally blocked for a prolonged period. About 60% of men are prescribed alpha-blocker medication to relax the irritated muscles and improve the urinary flow. Specialists advise patients under radiotherapy treatment to avoid Vitamin C, citrus/acid drinks (orange, grape), fruits that can act like water pills or diuretics

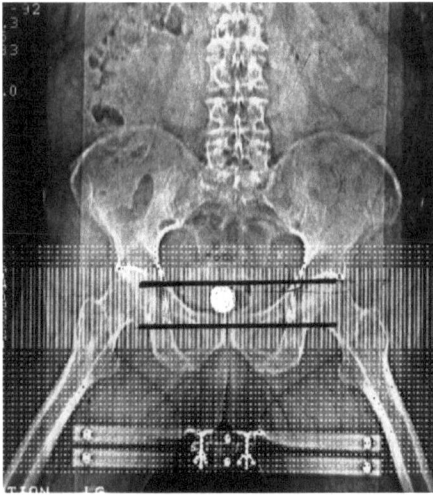

CT scan of a patient's prostate (highlighted in white between black lines). Multiple axial images are reconstructed in 3-dimensions to visualize the entire prostate and normal tissue surrounding it for treatment planning. (*Courtesy of* Dr. Basil S. Hilaris. Teaming with Dr. Whitmore, Dr. Hilaris performed in 1972 the first prostate implant using Iodine-125 seeds)

(melon) and over-the-counter allergy and cold medicines to prevent further displacements of the prostate, the rectum or the bladder. Incontinence is rare and it is attributed mostly to **stress incontinence** (leakage when the man coughs, sneezes, laughs), which may be caused by radiation damage to the bladder sphincter.

Rectal: Cuts or bleeding of the anal tissue, rectal discomfort symptoms, ulcers, inflammation, abrupt hyperactivity of hemorrhoids (even after having been dormant for many years), more frequent bowel movements, and diarrhea, or the opposite, constipation. After ~18 months, when the full effects appear, some patients find blood in the stool, due to small capillaries breaking, as well as in the urine.

133

Statistically, >2% of patients with implant and 10%-15% of patients with implant and external radiation have these symptoms.

Erectile: Studies show that if the patient was potent and sexually active prior to brachytherapy, most probable he will continue experiencing the same erectile functions beginning one or two days after the seed implant, including the production of sperm. Since the target nerves are generally not affected, sexual functions are not interrupted –unless by error the radiation has been misdirected. However, other statistics show 10% impotence in men <60 years, and ≥25% in men >70 years. A 2004 study by the National Cancer Institute found that men who had radiation underwent a decline in sexual function beginning between two and five years later. Radiation frequently damages vascular tissue surrounding the prostate and its progress throughout the years may cause impotence.

Dry ejaculation: Radiation of the prostate, like surgery, tends to damage the sphincter valve that controls, at sexual orgasm, the direction of the flow of the sperm from the epididymis to/through the urethra and the penis. When this valve does not function properly, the result is a **dry ejaculation** because the sperm backs up to the bladder instead of flowing to the urethra and out through the penis. The damage, and thus the infertility, may be permanent (see anatomical discussion in Chapter 2, and above paragraphs under "Radical Prostatectomy-Other Side Effects"). This phenomenon however, does not seem to alter the man's feeling of pleasure; in fact, most men report not feeling any difference.

Other side effects:
* One third of patients complain of tiredness starting two to three weeks into radiation treatment. Radiation in general is known to decrease red and white blood cells as well as platelet counts.
* It is normal to have blackness or dark blueness on the skin of the scrotum, because of the trauma of the activity in the area during the procedure; the discoloration progressively disappears, along with the inflammation, within a few weeks.
* There is no record that patients are themselves radioactive after seed implantation, although as a matter of precaution doctors recommend that the patient refrain from holding small children, pregnant women or pets on his lap for more than 10-15 minutes at a time for three weeks.
* There is no record that patients are themselves radioactive after seed implantation, although as a matter of precaution doctors rec-

ommend that the patient refrain from holding small children, pregnant women or pets on his lap for more than 10-15 minutes at a time for three weeks.

* There is no record either that the implanted seeds have ever set off the screening alarm of security detectors –such as at airports.

* Specialists also affirm, (a) that the radiation from the seeds poses no danger to the patient's sexual partner, (b) that the semen is not radioactive either, (c) that the radiation will not contaminate anyone by shaking hands, kissing, or contacting linen, clothing, tableware, toilet facilities, etc., and (d) that the radiation does not cause falling hair, nausea or sickness as does a chemotherapy treatment.

QUALITY OF LIFE AFTER IMPLANT ALONE
(Survey of patients 6 months after implant <u>alone</u>, conducted by Dr. V. Elayne Arterbery, et al)

Symptoms, Opinions 6 months after Implant	%
Burning with urination	17%
Difficulty controlling urination	3%
Fatigue	15%
Hesitancy in urination	25%
Incontinence	0%
Increased sexual desire	14%
Nocturia >3 times per night	15%
Patients that would choose implant again	98%
Patients that would recommend implant to friends	100%
Psychological distress	0%
Rectal discomfort	0%
Sexual desire decreased	12%
Sexual desire unchanged by implant	74%
Sexual potency	15%
Slower stream of urination	35%
Urination more frequent	40%
Other urological symptoms	30%

CRITERIA: Patients clinically staged T1c or T2a received implant alone with Iodine-125 or Palladium-103 as definitive treatment. Survey completed six months after treatment. The above data are a compilation of selected answers.

(Adapted from a Survey conducted by a group of specialists led by Dr. V. Elayne Arterberry at the Radiation Oncology Department of Wayne State University and the Department of Urology of Sinai Hospital, in Detroit, Michigan.)
(Courtesy of **Dr. V. Elayne Arterbery)**

IMRT vs. 3D Conformal Radiation

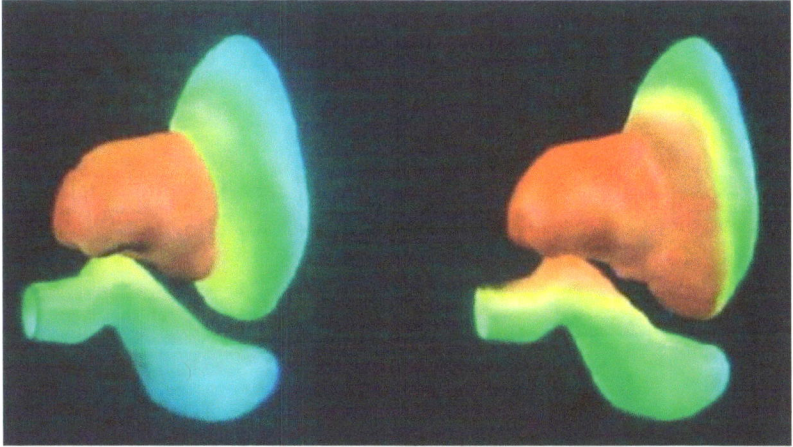

When "bombarding" the prostate, modern IMRT technology allows more precise direction and spread of the radiation (left) than traditional 3D conformal, therefore reducing the risk of affecting surrounding organs and tissues, such as the bladder and the rectum (darken areas on the right). (*Photo courtesy of* Zack D. Smith, Director Radiation Oncology, LA General Cancer Center, Baton Rouge)

HIGH DOSE RADIATION (HDR)

The **High Dose Rate Temporary Implant Radiation** or **High Dose Radiation (HDR)**, also known as just **Temporary Brachytherapy**, has been used in the U.S. since 1980 but by only few specialized clinics. Between 16 and 22 small-diameter needles are inserted into the prostate with high activity Iridium-192 followed by three doses of radiation through the needles while the patient is in the hospital for two days; the needles are then removed. Five weeks of subsequent external beam radiation completes the treatment.

136

CURE/SURVIVAL and FAILURE RATES

HOW TO EVALUATE THEM

Of all available prostate cancer protocols, surgical radical prostatectomy (except robotic, discussed later), brachytherapy and external radiation show the highest cure rates (=Disease-Free Survival or DFS) at 5 and 10 years after treatment. However, there had been no general agreement among medical specialists regarding one single common-denominator formula or **definition** to measure the cure rate of the three treatments. Surgeons many years ago accepted Dr. Patrick C. Walsh's proposal for radical prostatectomy: *"A prostate cancer patient is cured if he has maintained at 5 and 10 years after treatment an undetectable PSA Nadir of ≤0.2 ng/ml."* This became the *Golden Definition*. By having removed surgically the prostate, which is the source of the prostate-specific antigen, it is presumed that the cancer has been eliminated too and that therefore, the patient is free of cancer, cured. However, how are the cure-failure rates of the other treatments to be measured?

The American Society of Therapeutic Radiology Oncology (ASTRO) in 1997 adopted the so-called *ASTRO Definition*. Unlike radical prostatectomy, wherein the gland is completely removed, radiation is not called "radical" because cancerous cells are not killed or removed instantaneously –and additionally, other cells, healthy, die too although they later reproduce again as healthy cells. The ASTRO's definition of biochemical failure is determined by PSA level measurement: *"Three consecutive PSA increases measured six months apart occurring before or after having registered a PSA Nadir of 0.2 ng/ml."* Other specialists have judged that the use of this formula "inflates" the cure results.

The controversy took a new turn when two years later, in 1999, Dr. Frank A. Critz proposed that, irrespective of the prostate cancer therapy used, **the cure-rate definition should be the same for all protocols** and suggested the use of Dr. Walsh's definition mentioned above. Dr. Critz added that the statistics of his RCOG, using that definition, show a cure rate of 92% at 5 years and 72% at 10 years

137

after treatment, *"comparable to those of radical prostatectomy"*, he said.

There are still two other important issues to consider. First, after a radical prostatectomy the PSA level should drop *immediately* to ≤0.2 ng/ml, but after radiation therapy it may take up to 27 months to reach the same PSA Nadir level. And second, about 41% of patients treated with implant and radiation experience the phenomenon called **PSA rebound** or **PSA Bounce** as soon as 12 months and as late as 36 months after treatment (median 18-24 months). PSA Bounce is defined as (a) an initial PSA fall after seed implant and external radiation treatment, (b) followed by a PSA rise and then (c) by a second PSA fall that goes below the first fall. Then, if treatment has been successful, the PSA stabilizes to reach and maintain a ≤0.2 ng/ml Nadir.

Since the prostate gland is left *in situ*, the PSA decreases slowly after a potentially successful brachytherapy but it may fluctuate between an undetectable ≤0.2 ng/ml and 16.0 ng/ml. During the first 18 months, the PSA may rise due to inflammation of the prostate gland and then drop. This **PSA bounce** does not mean **treatment failure**, said Dr. Critz, *"It is rather generated by the prostatitis caused by the radiation, still prevalent, and because of the regrowth of normal good cells"*. If the patient is unaware of this predictable occurrence, he may feel anxiety for fear of cancer recurrence; and doctors other than the ones who performed the brachytherapy, if also unaware, may erroneously advise additional alternative surgical treatment(s) or a biopsy –and either may have serious adverse effects. However, if the PSA does not drop and it remains high, that is considered an indication that the brachytherapy treatment failed and that the patient is not cancer-free. For still unknown reasons, 22% of patients experiencing PSA rebound show slightly **lower cancer recurrence** (78% survival) than patients without PSA rebound (69% survival) at 10 years after treatment. Statistically, cancer recurs in ~20% of patients who underwent brachytherapy, and when it does, most surgeons refuse to perform surgery because radiation may have "fused" tissues (e.g., two become one) and the risk of damaging adjoining tissues or organs with surgery is very high.

Applying the cure definition of PSA ≤0.2 ng/ml, Dr. Critz released the following results of his ProstRcision method since 1992:

PSA GROUP BEFORE TREATMENT	*ProstRcision* CURE-RATE	
	5-YEAR	10-YEAR
0.0 – 4.0 ng/ml	96%	85%
4.1 – 10.0 ng/ml	94%	85%
10.1 – 20.0 ng/ml	79%	67%
≥20.1 ng/ml	71%	34%
Overall	89%	72%

In general, as with all treatments, brachytherapy cure rates vary considerably. **Dr. Anthony V. D'Amico** has shown success rates of 87% to 97% in low-risk patients (PSA <10 ng/ml, Gleason <6) using either brachytherapy, radical prostatectomy, or external radiation. His study, remarkably, **does not reveal an advantage of one treatment over another**. It is also interesting his research showing that **cure results of all treatments are the same irrespective of the race, color, or nationality of the patients**.

The popularity of brachytherapy has increased in the past few years, as summarized in the following statistical chart

TREATMENT OF GLAND-LOCALIZED PROSTATE CANCER		
	1988	2005
Radical Prostatectomy	58%	30%
Brachytherapy	24%	55%
Radiation alone	12%	9.5%

Medical experts predict substantial changes in the future distribution of the number of prostate cancer treatments as Laparoscopic Robotic Prostatectomy becomes more available.

139

Part 3

NEW, REVOLUTIONARY TECHNIQUE: LAPAROSCOPIC ROBOTIC PROSTATECTOMY

Laparoscopic Radical Prostatectomy for locally confined prostate cancer was explored numerous times in the last decades. It reached popularity when it was first developed in France in the 1950s and then after Dr. Young's first trials in the United States. They used a laparoscope, a lighted viewing tube inserted through tiny incisions in the abdomen for direct examination of internal organs and for surgery. Surgeons used one of two techniques: five incisions of ½" each (=1 cm) in the shape of an inverted "V" in the abdomen or, as for the perineal radical prostatectomy, a 2-inch incision in the perineum between the anus and the scrotum. A high-powered "telescope" with a fiber-optic camera connected to a monitor allows the surgeon to see the prostate and other tissue to be dissected. One of the limited studies on this surgical system reported mixed results.

* * * * *

A new technique surged in 1999 that is **revolutionizing the practice of prostate surgery** –and of surgery in general, from cardiac to gynecologic to urologic. It is called **[The] da Vinci Nerve-Sparing Laparoscopic Robotic Prostatectomy**. Surgeons do not move instruments or operate with their hands "physically" on the patient. Instead, they sit at an ergonomic console and perform the procedure from a computer panel and monitors located several feet away from the operating table –by **telemanipulation**. The robotic movements are so precise that the surgeon can dissect nerves using micro-scissors and still maintain control of the bleeders –the surgeon can successfully connect tiny two-millimeter blood vessels. The operation takes two to four hours under general anesthesia. Like in open surgery, specialists do not advise this procedure for men >70 years old, those who have <10-year life expectancy, men whose tests may suggest metastatic disease, or men with other adverse physical condition such as diabetes or high blood pressure.

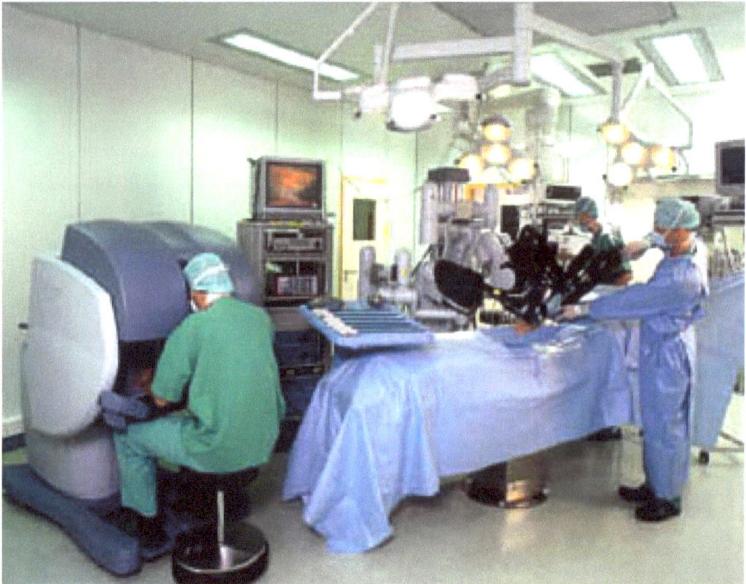

Da Vinci's operating room set up. The surgeon sits at a viewfinder (left) and remotely manipulates the probes and micro-instruments on the robotic arms over the table where the patient is being operated. Standing is the surgeon's assistant, and behind the table is the nurse.
(© 2006 by and Courtesy of Intuitive Surgical, Inc.)

Da Vinci is the result of the merge of visionary medical ideals and sophisticated technology. **Intuitive Surgical, Inc.** was created in 1995 in Sunnyvale, California to design, manufacture and market the revolutionary system. The founders were two physicians, **Dr. Frederic Moll** (professor at Harvard Medical School) and **Dr. John Freund** (MD and MBA, Harvard), and the electrical and mechanical engineer **Robert Younge**. The technology first used had been developed in the 1980s by SRI International, formerly Stanford University Research Institute. Subsequent technological contributors include IBM, the Massachusetts Institute of Technology, Olympus Optical, Ethicon Endo-Surgery (Johnson & Johnson), and Computer Motion, Inc. (the company already specialized in medical robotics that was acquired by Intuitive in 2003). The name is a tribute to the genius Italian scientist, inventor and artist **Leonardo da Vinci** (1452-1519). The word **Robot** had been coined in 1920 by cubist painter, writer

141

and poet **Josef Capek** (Czechoslovakia 1887-1945) during a casual conversation with his brother **Karel Capek** (1890-1938) when suggesting him to call *Robots* the *"artificial workers"* Karel was using as characters in his forthcoming play *"R.U.R.."*, published later the same year.

Da Vinci Robotic Surgical Systems were introduced to the medical world in 1999 and tested successfully in Europe for various procedures, mainly cardiac. It performed the **First Robotic Prostatectomy in the world** in May 2000 in Frankfurt, Germany; the first in the United States was done in November 2000 in Richmond, Virginia. The FDA approved it for prostate surgery in June 2001.

This robot-assisted, minimally invasive surgery requires only five dime-sized incisions in the abdomen (½-1" each = 1-2 cm, versus the 8"-10" incision required by the traditional radical prostatectomy). The incisions or holes are called operating "ports" and are used to introduce into the body a camera (endoscope) and multiple narrow-shafted extremely accurate pencil-sized instruments. They are manipulated by means of *EndoWrist* technology or mechanical micro-wrists that seamlessly replicate the identical movements of the surgeon's hands performed at the ergonomic console by a monitor.

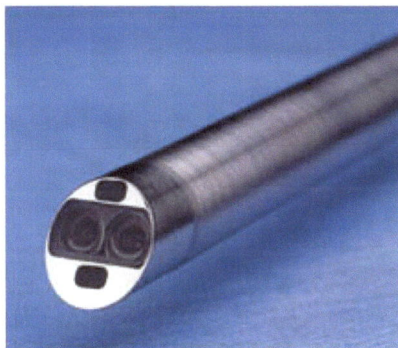

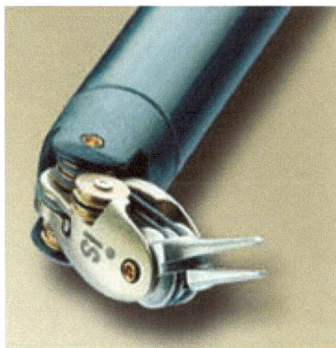

Introduced through incisions or "ports" in the abdomen, an endoscope (left) illuminates and peers inside the patient's body to generate 3-D images amplified 10-15 times, while micro-instruments (right) perform the precise surgical procedures.

(© 2006 by and Courtesy of Intuitive Surgical, Inc.)

A master-slave robot incorporates three-dimensional visualization and scaling of movements. The tiny but powerful camera magnifies images 10-15 times and helps the surgeon see vital anatomical structures considerably more clearly than the naked eye can perceive (*"These robots have superhuman capabilities that make surgery easier"*, said one doctor). It has three multi-joint robotic arms, two finger-controlled handles and one foot pedal control.

The *da Vinci* robot consists of four main sections. The first is the robot itself composed of a cluster of three articulated robotic arms, each with several degrees of freedom and 360° rotating flexibility. The second is the "vision" system, composed of fiber-optic lines that enable surgeons to see precisely what they are doing. The third is a group of hand and foot controls to teleoperate the robot. The fourth is a set of sophisticated control and image processing algorithms to enhance the surgeon's accuracy. For example, an adaptive disturbance rejection scheme cancels a surgeon's natural hand tremors and enables great accuracy in the movements of the micro-instruments.

Da Vinci has a price tag of $1.3-$1.5 million. Every instrument that attaches to one of its robotic arms contains a microchip that allows usage for only ten procedures; the average cost of consumables/disposables is over $1,500 per patient.

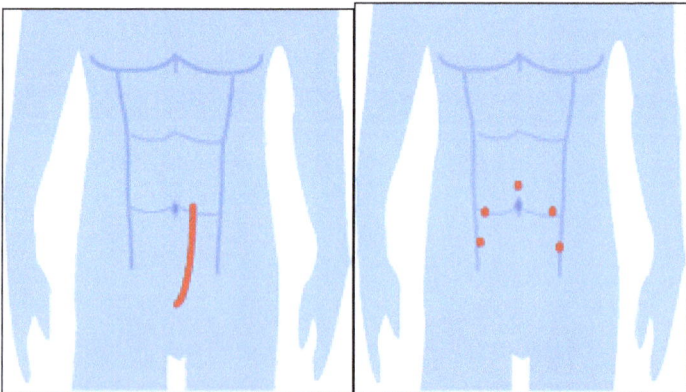

Left: Average 8-10" incision on the lower abdomen made by surgeons to perform traditional Radical Prostatectomy. **Right:** The five dime-sized (½") incisions or "ports" made by micro-instruments to perform the Robotic Prostatectomy; once detached, the prostate is extracted through the "port" at the top of the inverted "V".
(© 2006 by and Courtesy of Intuitive Surgical, Inc.)

Technically, Laparoscopic Robotic Prostatectomy is a very demanding procedure on the doctor. The FDA requires manufacturers of robotic surgical systems to train the surgeon before he can perform *in*

143

solo. Training involves 12-18 patients and 40 hours under supervision at the company's headquarters and specialized hospitals. Many urologists suggest that such "learning curve" is too long; however, the FDA focuses on full "team training": the surgeon, the assistant and the nurses.

This new surgical system does not have yet long enough history to provide meaningful statistics regarding critical aspects such as side effects, PSA Nadir levels, cancer recurrence, etc., as we have from most other prostate cancer therapies. Studies being released predict that this revolutionary technique is transforming the way surgery has been performed for over a century. When comparing *da Vinci* to conventional radical prostatectomy or even to traditional laparoscopy, surgeons praise great advantages: less blood loss, less pain, less risk of infection, fewer complications, shorter hospital stay (2-4 days), and quicker recovery (average of 14 days to resume normal activities).

The robotic system removes the prostate and other tissue while allowing preservation of the Walsh Nerves, thus, lowering the incidence of incontinence and impotence. Nevertheless, some of the side effects of conventional radical prostatectomy surgery are also observed in robotic surgery. For example, some men regain continence in few weeks while others may need protective pads, surgeons recommend the Kegel Exercises (described above) to strengthen muscles in the pelvis area, erectile function is somehow impacted and its partial (between 3 weeks to 18 months) or total recovery is influenced also by the patient's sexual activity before the operation and by his overall physical condition. Robotic surgeons suggest starting therapy with Viagra or other similar drugs a few weeks after the procedure. No mortality has been reported.

Never before now have prostate cancer patients had so many formidable means to cure the disease. Unquestionably, *da Vinci* defines a new era in prostate cancer management that is spreading worldwide. Its success however, like the success of the other surgical therapies we have discussed, depends on the surgeon's training and skills. **The surgeon is not replaceable. Side effects, cancer recurrence, cure, even the patient's life, rest on the hands of the surgeon and not on the arms of the robot**. The medical robot cannot be programmed to make decisions on its own.

LANDMARK DATES OF THE MOST PREDOMINANT
PROSTATE CANCER TREATMENTS

Treatment	1941	1962	1982	1985	2000
Hormonal	Huggins				
Extern. Beam Radiation		Bagshaw			
Retropubic Radical Prostatectomy			Walsh		
Ultrasound-guided Brachytherapy				Ragde/ Blasko	
Robotic Prostatectomy					daVinci

TeleSurgery:

Da Vinci technological advancements are making possible for surgeons to perform also **Robotic Surgery across Long Distances.**

A **robotic telesurgical milestone** was marked in 2001 when surgeons at Mount Sinai Medical Center in New York, working together with the Department of Electrical Engineering at the University of California, removed the gallbladder of a 68-year old woman in Strasbourg, France. The mean time-delay between the surgeon's command in New York and the robot's performance in France was 155 milliseconds, that is, the surgeon could see the result of his commands a little more than one-tenth of a second later. The gallbladder was dissected in 54 minutes without complications, about the same time it would have taken to perform a standard laparoscopic surgery in New York.

MAIN PROSTATE TREATMENTS AVERAGE COST TO UNINSURED PATIENTS		
Procedure	2003	2006
Surgery: Radical Prostatectomy	$27,000	$33,000
" Robotic Radical Prostatectomy		$45,000
External Beam Radiation (EBR)	$20,000	$22,000
Seed Implant + EBR (Brachytherapy)	$30,000	$35,000
Intensity-Modulated Radiation (IMRT) with BAT	$83,000	$85,000

OTHER TREATMENTS

Although not as popular, other prostate cancer treatments are performed and being improved, among them:

CRYOTHERAPY, CRYOSURGERY

Also known as **Targeted Cryoablation of the Prostate (TCAP).** The attempt to eradicate the cancer by freezing the prostate cells was first introduced in the 19th century. It gained some popularity in the 1960s with the use of liquid nitrogen, and then discontinued for thirty years due to its significant side effects. With the introduction of needles and the transrectal ultrasound-guidance, it regained acceptance in recent years because "it is minimally invasive" and "has fewer complications than surgery", specialists say. With the patient under anesthesia, the doctor inserts through the area between the scrotum and the anus several ultra-thin 17-gauge needles. Upon reaching the prostate, they inject liquid nitrogen to freeze tissue like a ball of ice, -40°C (-40°F) –the temperature at which cancerous cells are destroyed is estimated to be -29°C = -20°F. The prostate is not removed. The procedure takes 1-2 hours, the patient may need 1-2 hospitalization days, and a catheter is retained for several days. Although long-term follow-data are not yet available, limited statistical reports suggest a 95% survival rate at 7 years, 7.5% incontinence and 33%-95% impotence.

CHEMOTHERAPY

Combining drugs and radiation, chemotherapy does not seem to be as effective with prostate cancer as it is with other cancers. It is used, when metastasis is advanced, to mitigate pain and help to maintain a certain level of quality of life while artificially extending the patient's survival. **Metastasized prostate cancer is incurable**. Patients survive an average of 6-9 months. Doctors and patients welcomed the FDA approval of new chemotherapy drugs in 2004, "unenthusiastically" however, after studies indicated a "life extension" limited to 2 to 2½ months.

146

HIGHLIGHTS OF PREDOMINANT TREATMENTS

Protocol:	Highlights:
Watchful Waiting	Do nothing
Hormonal	Non-surgical, drugs (shots and/or pills)
" Hormonal & Radiation	Non-surgical, drugs plus external radiation
Surgical Orchiectomy	Surgical removal of testicles
Radical Prostatectomy	Surgical removal of the prostate
Seeds Implant alone	Implant of irradiating seeds into the prostate
Seeds plus Radiation	Implant of irradiating seeds into the prostate plus external radiation before or after the implant
External Radiation alone	Conventional External 3-Dimensional
Radiation alone-IMRT	New Intensity-Modulated Radiation Therapy with B-mode Acquisition and Targeting (IMRT+ BAT), non-surgical, drug-free
Cryotherapy/Cryosurgery	Surgical, freezing of the prostate
Laparoscopy	Surgical dissection of the prostate through small openings in the abdomen or the perineum
Laparoscopic Robotic Da Vinci Prostatectomy	Same as above but robot-assisted
Chemotherapy	Drugs and radiation

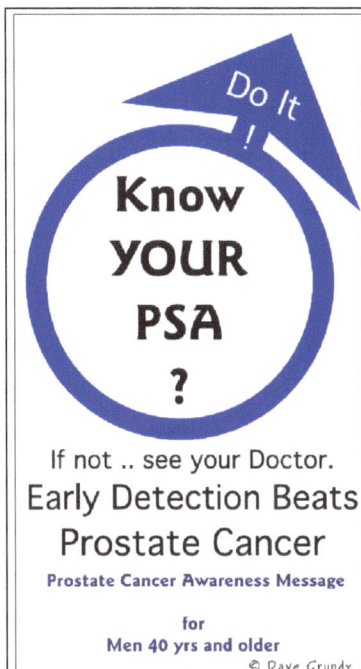

Do It !

Know YOUR PSA ?

If not .. see your Doctor.
Early Detection Beats Prostate Cancer

Prostate Cancer Awareness Message

for
Men 40 yrs and older

© Dave Grundy

The artist behind the posters:

Dave Grundy

IS THERE LIFE AFTER RADICAL PROSTATECTOMY?

Dave Grundy resides on the 60th parallel in the mountains of Fort Smith, North West Territories (Canada) where thermometers frequently seem to forget how to cross the freezing line when returning upward. Diagnosed with prostate cancer at 58, he underwent radical prostatectomy in 1988, radiation in 1991 and further treatment in 2003 when metastatic cancer unrelated to his prostate was suddenly discovered in his neck. To help other men to fight prostate diseases, Dave used his artistic talents to design the *"Hey, Man" Prostate Cancer Awareness Poster* series, which made him famous. All posters herein inserted are Dave's generous contribution to this book. When this Author talked with him in October 2003, Dave was enjoying, under -30°C to -40°C (-22°F to -40°F, respectively), *"life to its fullest as a father, grandfather, husband, teacher, basketball coach, golf club president, photographer, poet, cook, wood hauler, and student recruiter for the local College...but with little time to be a 'professional survivor' since life is wonderful with or without prostate"*, he said.

(Dave died in July 2004)

148

Chapter 7

Complementary & Alternative Medicine, Diet & Obesity... and the Prostate

In spite of the numeric explosion of "over-the-counter" health products of all sorts in the last years, there is no conclusive evidence that herbs, vitamins, minerals or even diet do indeed **prevent** or **cure prostate cancer**. Some of those products are intrinsically good for the health of the individual; in other cases, they do not benefit, and in still other cases, actually they do harm. Patients have favorably taken supplements to reduce cancer treatments side effects and organ toxicity, to stimulate their immune system, to make them feel better, or to recover faster. Statistics show that many people (but not all) have a biochemical-unbalanced body that lacks certain vitamins or minerals or the like, and that the substances they ingest and the natural chemical production by their body may not be complete or perfect. Consequently, the dilemma is centered on **whether we are wise or imprudent taking which supplement and when and how much**.

On the other hand, commercialization, sophisticated marketing psychology, stimuli of feelings of hope, fear, guilt, etc. have induced people and especially "baby boomers" to load ourselves with many untested and unregulated products. We feed a business empire of $20 billion, 1,000 manufacturers, 29,000 products –just in the U.S. Studies indicate that more money is spent annually on over-the-counter uncontrolled health products than on medical and nutritional research. Studies released in 2006 confirmed that "more than half" of Americans take dietary supplements, mostly multivitamins. Although lower than in the U.S., the number of people in Europe who use or have used at one time those products, whether herbs, homeopathy, vitamins or mineral supplements, has increased to about one-third of all cancer patients –they use those compounds for an average of 27 months.

Complementary and Alternative Medicine (CAM)
Current status of alternative medicine is greatly the result of the following events:

1992: The U.S. establishes the Office of Alternative Medicine.
1994: Congress passes the Dietary Supplement and Health and Education Act (DSHEA) –dietary supplement defined as "any product, besides tobacco, that contains a vitamin, mineral, herb, or amino acid and that is intended as a supplement to the normal diet".
1998: The U.S. creates the National Center for Complementary and Alternative Medicine (NCCAM), a division of the National Institutes of Health (NIH) in the area of Alternative Medicine. It started with a budget of $20 million, increased to $100 million in 2002, to $117.7 million in 2004, and to $123.1 million in 2005 for funding primarily research and trials on herbals and other alternative medicines.

The Health and Education Act of 1994 was passed by Congress under strong lobbying pressure and demanding "**consumers want unrestricted access to herbs and dietary supplements**". The Act establishes that **supplements are not considered drugs but foods**. Therefore, the Act shifts full oversight jurisdiction from the Food and Drug Administration (FDA) to the manufacturers, whose responsibil-

150

ity, in turn, has been since to write on the label what is in the bottle. The manufacturers have to adhere only to "good manufacturing processes", such as sanitary mechanical issues: the places where the herbals are treated and packaged are required to be clean. They **do not have to prove safety, quality or effectiveness or to demonstrate that a supplement works for the purpose it purports to treat** prior to its being on the shelves. Supplements do not need approval from the FDA before they are marketed. **The FDA jumps in when it finds, or is informed of, a product to be unsafe once it is on the market.**

Categories of Medicine

When referring to health care, we identify three main categories of therapy, **as defined by the National Center for Complementary and Alternative Medicine**:

* **Conventional Medicine:** Practiced by holders of M.D. (Medical Doctor) or D.O. (Doctor of Osteopathy) degree. After years of scientific studies and professional internship, after obtaining a license and professional liability insurance, they provide medical health care to the population. They must adhere to a Code of Ethics and are ethically and legally liable for their practice.

* **Integrative Medicine** combines mainstream medical therapies and complementary and alternative therapies for which there is some high-quality scientific evidence of safety and effectiveness.

* **Complementary and Alternative Medicine (CAM)** constitutes a group of diverse medical and health care systems, practices, and products that are not considered part of Conventional Medicine. (For simplicity, we shall use the term **Alternative Medicine** when referring to either or both, "alternative" and "complementary" medicine.) For most of these therapies, there are key questions not yet answered through formally-designed scientific studies, such as whether they are safe and work for the diseases or medical conditions for which they are marketed (for example, a diet or herb to treat cancer instead of undergoing surgery, radiation, or chemotherapy that has been prescribed by a conventional doctor). **Dietary supplements**, as defined by the Act of 1994, may include "vitamins, minerals, herbs, amino acids, and sub-

151

stances such as enzymes, organ tissues, and metabolites. They may come in the form of extracts, concentrates, tablets, capsules, gel caps, liquids, and powders". They also include acupuncture, ancient Indian and Chinese therapies, electromagnetic fields, homeopathy, massage, even religion. Manufacturers of alternative medicine are not regulated and their products can be sold to the public over the Internet and in any store, which, like the agents or clerks who sell them, does not need a professional regulatory license or academic credentials or malpractice insurance.

Issue of extraordinary proportions

Alternative medicine (and each of its components) is currently an issue of extraordinary proportions among physicians, manufacturers, marketers, patients and the public in general. Volume, spread, effectiveness, safety, advertising, and the sound of money, all are ingredients of an explosive cocktail. **From informal writings to formal medical abstracts, arguments in favor or against are generally followed by responses defending the opposite side**, irrespective of the side defended by the initial position. With respect to our subject, prostate cancer, we shall see that the decision to use alternative medicine is ultimately the responsibility of the patient.

A recent study conducted by the NCCAM showed the following surprising results on the **"most common alternative medicine" therapies** used by adults 21 years or older:

- **Frequency of use:** Ever 74.6%, in the last 12 months 62.1%.
- **By Race/Ethnicity:** Blacks 71.3%, Asian 61.7%, 61.4% Hispanic, 60.4% Whites.
- **Reasons for use:** 54.9% thought that alternative medicine combined with conventional medicine would help (although **only 4% of them informed their physicians**), 50.1% thought it would be "interesting" to try, 27.7% thought conventional medicine would not help, 25.8% suggested by their doctor, and 13% said that conventional medicine was too expensive.
- **Most common therapies:** 43.0% Prayer by self, 24.4% Prayer with/by others, 18.9% Natural Products, 11.6% Deep Breathing, 7.6% Meditation, 7.5% Chiropractic, 5.1% Yoga, 5.0% Massage, 3.5% Diets.

Patient's Education

Our man must now address some fundamental issues before making decisions:

First: Whether he should consult with a physician specialized in the field to determine if he, and not his neighbor or friend, should take a supplement. Pertinent tests of the biochemistry of his body will identify strengths and deficiencies. Abundant literature on nutrition demonstrates the favorable results of a well-balanced, healthy diet. Numerous books have been published with advices and thousands of recipes on how to condiment and eat healthy foods. However, reality shows that most people run first, instead of to the doctor's office, to the "natural products store" or to the Internet to make a quick decision to purchase whatever they saw promoted. By comparison, we are much more hesitant to pour an additive (supplement) into the gasoline or oil tank of our valuable automobile than ingesting untested alternative medicine compounds –particularly those commercialized as **"miraculous products that cure prostate cancer"**. Such products are generally received with skepticism by professional medical practitioners unless and until the true therapeutic effectiveness has been scientifically (**not commercially***)* demonstrated –and such effectiveness is increasingly being scientifically contested. *"Whether a compound or the announcement of a new treatment"*, a renowned urologist told this Author, *"everything must be taken with a 'grain of salt' and a decade of testing"*. The National Cancer Institute (NCI) urges to be aware of people or companies making claims, particularly over the Internet, that **they have a product that cures prostate cancer** but provide no proof or copy of conclusive scientific studies supporting the evidence –which, thus far, does not exist. The old saying, *"If it sounds too good to be true, it probably is"*…it normally is.

Second: The same doctor that runs the tests must propose what, if anything, the patient should take and its dose based on the man's physical condition and after studying the possible side effects and the interaction with drugs he may be taking. This Author's research found overwhelming responses from men self-convinced that they have "vitamin deficiencies" and that therefore, they do not need to run a biochemical analysis –"natural products are good supplements", they said. But "**a *natural* product**", the NCI warns, "**does not mean a *safe* product.**" It also advises: "**The same scientific evaluation that is used to assess conventional cancer treatments should be used to assess alternative medicine therapies**".

Studies, Warnings

There are numerous studies supporting the thesis that prostate cancer remains "a disease in which **life style and nutritional factors** have important causative roles". Other studies demonstrate the "natural weakness" of many people to adhere to a healthy diet –hence, their vulnerability to absorb supplements instead. **The ambivalence confuses the patient.** The result is that, without medical advice and not knowing what may improve or damage his health, a man may overload himself with some compounds **recklessly**.

There are indeed products with proven healthy enhancement results. For example, recent studies show that **omega-3 fatty acids** found in ocean fish oil (not in "flax seed oil") have some important cardiovascular benefits; however, the same researchers failed to find any strong evidence to suggest that omega-3 reduces the risk of any type of cancer –including prostate cancer.

History, scientific research and governmental agencies frequently offer data to better educate people. For example: **Free radicals**, known as "unstable molecules", smash through cell walls and tear up DNA molecules. **Antioxidants** build up a defense against those damaging free radicals. Many studies suggested that antioxidants such as **Vitamins A, C, E and D, the mineral selenium, and lycopene found in tomatoes** can help the severity of side-effects of prostate cancer treatments (radical prostatectomy, brachytherapy), but radiation oncologists strongly advise against taking vitamin C, citrus and other **substances known to increase urinary side-effects**. Some men with prostate cancer have shown a deficiency of **vitamin D**, but without his physician's supervision, a man may take excessive doses or simultaneously with more than 1,000 mg/day of **calcium**, and the latter will interfere with the body's natural production of vitamin D. A recent study on **vitamin E** conducted in Great Britain with the participation of 50,000 persons concluded with an ironic one-phrase statement: *"It does not work"*. Another major study published in a medical journal in 2003 revealed that, *"Neither **vitamin E nor beta-carotene** pills provide any protection"* against prostate cancer. Worse: vitamin E actually may damage the prostate: the American Heart Association's 2004 Scientific Session emphasized, *"**Don't take**"* **vitamin E supplements**.

Additionally, another study revealed that men consuming ≥600 mg/day of calcium had a 32% higher risk of prostate cancer compared to men consuming <160 mg/day, and that those consuming ≥1,200

154

mg/day had 112% higher risk of developing the disease. Other researches have found **"no favorable effect" of saw palmetto on prostate cancer** in spite of proposals for its use, but they did confirm that it could artificially lower PSA levels, which generally makes it difficult to monitor accurately the development of prostatic anomalies. **Chandroitin**, commonly taken along with **glucosamine sulfate** to protect or *shell* bone joints, has been found to "protect" and *shell* also the cancerous cells in the prostate; in fact, one of the predictors of metastatic spread of prostate cancer is the presence of Chandroitin sulfate around the cancerous cells. Men taking **testosterone** to enhance their athletic performance run also a serious risk of increasing the probabilities of prostate cancer because testosterone, as we have discussed, is precisely the fuel that feeds this cancer.

It has been suggested that other foods and drinks (**broccoli, cauliflower, Brussels sprouts, soy products, soja, Swiss "chard"**, **green tea**, to name a few) may reduce the risk of prostate cancer (indeed, of "many kinds of cancer"), but no study has been conclusive. What happens, some experts emphasize, is that soy products contain also phytoestrogens, **estrogen** –which is known to reduce the production of testosterone. This process is said to lower artificially the PSA level but **not to cure prostate cancer**. Research revealed that, interestingly, monks living in a monastery and who followed a vegetarian diet found soy products "very desirable" because they lower the libido as well.

The FDA, in a lengthy ruling released in June 2005 concluded that, **"it is highly unlikely that green tea reduces the risk of prostate cancer, of breast cancer, or of any other type of cancer"**. The FDA warned also that consumers who purchased **Actra-Rx** (known as Yilishen) should immediately stop taking it because it can be dangerous to their health, and even life threatening. Actra-Rx has been promoted as "all natural" and sold over the Internet as a "dietary supplement" for treating erectile dysfunction and enhancing sexual performance for men. The supplement contains prescription-strength quantities of **sildenafil**, an ingredient of Viagra. Other recent recommendations include the following:

- The U.S. Preventive Services Task Force (USPSTF) concluded that there is insufficient evidence to recommend the use of **vitamins A, C, or E, multivitamins with folic acid, or antioxidant combinations** for the prevention of cancer or cardiovascular disease.
- The same agency recommends against the use of **beta-carotene** supplements, either alone or in combination, for the prevention of cancer or cardiovascular disease.
- The National Cancer Institute warned (a) that the herb **St. John's Wart**, which some people with cancer use for depression, may cause certain anticancer drugs not to work properly.

PC-SPES (*PC=prostate cancer*, *SPES*=Latin for *hope*) is another example of profound confusion created by the marketing of "miracle" products purported **to cure prostate cancer**. Eight different *known* herbals and other *unknown* ingredients composed its formula. Marketing began September 9, 1997 and, at a cost of about $500 for one-month supply, it quickly became one of the fastest high-profile selling products among men suffering of untreated prostate cancer. The product was shut down by the Food and Drug Administration in February 2002. It had been improperly mixed with pharmaceuticals and it contained, among other adverse ingredients, an anti-inflammatory drug, an **artificial estrogen (DES)** considered so dangerous that it had been taken off the market 26 years before (1971). PC-SPES artificially lowered the PSA levels, as hormonal therapy does –and such side effects require close medical supervision. In another case, a few years ago, a company was selling a comparable high-profile, high-priced ($300 one-month supply) "miraculous" drug for cancer, *but exclusively and directly* **to medical doctors** who had to send in a copy of their medical license to be able to purchase it for their patients. Less than two years later, this Author found the product at a considerably lower price through vitamin catalogs mailed to the public and with incentives such as "a watch or other gift" with a purchase of $25 or more. A class lawsuit filed against the manufacturer was settled to the tune of millions of dollars and the production was shut down.

Studies have documented numerous **false claims to cure prostate cancer** promoted by over-commercialization, among them, **apricot pits (laetrile), coffee enemas, mineral oil, grapes, shark carti-**

lage (uncovered after a lengthy study by the FDA), "**anti-neoplastons**" (that may cause brain damage); even **transcendental meditation** has been proposed to cure the disease. Interestingly, there are now several "magic" **products sold by untreated prostate cancer patients who became agents of "pyramid"** distributing and marketing programs.

A Federal science panel concluded in May 2006: "**There is no evidence for recommending certain vitamin supplements for cancer prevention**", "**There is no vitamin or mineral supplement proven to reduce the risk of cancer**" and, on the contrary, "**beta-carotene actually increases lung cancer incidence in smokers by 18%**".

Physicians express surprise that some patients are hesitant to take tested prescription medicines while at the same time they jump into taking supplements of unknown composition, side effects and interactions. Doctors advise that, irrespective of the pros and cons of alternative medicine compounds, the prostate patient should research and resolve by himself the dilemma of the risk he takes by using certain products, or large quantities of them, **without first having his doctor run a complete analysis** to establish his body's deficiencies and the recommended therapy and its doses.

Obesity

Notwithstanding the above, it has been demonstrated that a well-balanced diet and physical exercise decisively contribute to better health, and that excessive and uncontrolled eating cause **obesity** – and, **as a result, contributing to up to 30% of cancers**. Obesity in the U.S. increased by 60% in the last 10 years, and over 300,000 new cases are reported every year: 127 million people are overweight, 60 million of them are obese, 9 million are severely obese. Interestingly, the age group 65-74 registers the highest incidence of obesity (76%) and that is precisely the age group with the highest percentage of prostate cancer as well. Obesity is a major cause of diabetes, of impotence (in 50% of patients) and **it is known to increase the production of testosterone**, which fuels the cancer in the prostate.

Two logical patterns are identified to reduce weight:

(a) To ingest less food, less energy than our activity consumes, or

(b) To increase our energetic consumption with more activity.

The Pennington Biomedical Research Center in Baton Rouge, Louisiana recently completed a formidable program evaluating 900,000 persons over a 16-year period. The results show that excess weight may account for 14% of all cancer deaths in men and for 20% of all cancer deaths in women. The study was based on the **Body Mass Index (BMI)** that divides weight in pounds by height in inches.

BODY MASS INDEX TABLE

Find your appropriate height in inches in the left-hand column labeled **Height**. Move across to find your **Weight in pounds**. The number at the top of that column is your BMI. Pounds have been rounded off. The result:

Below 18: Underweight   **19-24.9: Normal**
25-29.9: Overweight   **30 and above: Obese**

BMI	19	20	21	22	23	24	25	26	27	28	29	30	31	32	33	34	35
Height (inches)	Body Weight (pounds)																
58	91	96	100	105	110	115	119	124	129	134	138	143	148	153	158	162	167
59	94	99	104	109	114	119	124	128	133	138	143	148	153	158	163	168	173
60	97	102	107	112	118	123	128	133	138	143	148	153	158	163	168	174	179
61	100	106	111	116	122	127	132	137	143	148	153	158	164	169	174	180	185
62	104	109	115	120	126	131	136	142	147	153	158	164	169	175	180	186	191
63	107	113	118	124	130	135	141	146	152	158	163	169	175	180	186	191	197
64	110	116	122	128	134	140	145	151	157	163	169	174	180	186	192	197	204
65	114	120	126	132	138	144	150	156	162	168	174	180	186	192	198	204	210
66	118	124	130	136	142	148	155	161	167	173	179	186	192	198	204	210	216
67	121	127	134	140	146	153	159	166	172	178	185	191	198	204	211	217	223
68	125	131	138	144	151	158	164	171	177	184	190	197	203	210	216	223	230
69	128	135	142	149	155	162	169	176	182	189	196	203	209	216	223	230	236
70	132	139	146	153	160	167	174	181	188	195	202	209	216	222	229	236	243
71	136	143	150	157	165	172	179	186	193	200	208	215	222	229	236	243	250
72	140	147	154	162	169	177	184	191	199	206	213	221	228	235	242	250	258
73	144	151	159	166	174	182	189	197	204	212	219	227	235	242	250	257	265
74	148	155	163	171	179	186	194	202	210	218	225	233	241	249	256	264	272
75	152	160	168	176	184	192	200	208	216	224	232	240	248	256	264	272	279
76	156	164	172	180	189	197	205	213	221	230	238	246	254	263	271	279	287

Thanks!

Seldom does an author find an opportunity to be so authentic when thanking others for help received as this Author finds right now. There is no way for this book to have been written without patients and physicians and drug manufacturers and HMOs and governments from several countries, and without the creators of remarkable educational websites. The uniqueness in the writing of this book has been the spontaneous kindness, warmth and willingness to cooperate that I received from practically all of the sources from which I requested help. Hopefully, patients-to-be and patients have found here enough data (a) to defuse the myth and fear of prostate cancer, (b) to make better treatment decisions, (c) to monitor the disease, and (d) to identify and appreciate the work of the mentioned giants of Medicine.

Gratitude is hereby emphasized to all of those already named in the text by "thanking" captions such as "*Courtesy of...*", or else, included in the list of *Selected Reference Sources* inserted in the *Appendix* - **Section A**. However, the name of others does not appear in the text and I wish to include it in this *Thanks!* Additionally, gratitude follows again to those physicians who, taking one more step forward, graciously compiled for me data or illustrations in an effort to further contribute to this book, and to those physicians no longer in practice who became essential in my research for the reconstruction of historical data or for information on other colleagues, not found anywhere else. The good wishes of all of them in the preparation of this book through personal, telephone or correspondence contacts gratified my efforts to complete the five-year project to help patients and patients-to-be. By alphabetical order:

In the United States:

159

Dr. Richard J. Ablin
Dr. V. Elayne Arterberry
Dr. Malcolm A. Bagshaw
Mr. Bobby Barnett, Director of Quality Control, Radiotherapy Clinics
    of Georgia, Decatur
Dr. John C. Blasko
Dr. William J. Catalona
Dr. T. Ming Chu
Data Collection Department, American Medical Association
Rev. William & Margaret Frisbee, Georgia, founders of a unique
    mission that I named *"The Prostate Cancer Survivors Inter-*
    national Exchange Oasis"
Dr. Donald F. Gleason
Dr. Judd W. Moul
Dr. George Prout, winner of the first *"Dr. Willet F. Whitmore, Jr.*
    Fellowship" to specialize in Urology, renowned pioneer of
    kidney surgery, retired Chief of Urology of Massachusetts
    General Hospital, Boston
Dr. Haakon Ragde
Dr. Mark Scholz, Prostate Oncology Specialist, California, Co-
    Founder of the Prostate Cancer Research Institute, California
Dr. Stephen B. Strum, Prostate Oncology Specialist, Oregon, Co-
    Founder of the Prostate Cancer Research Institute, California
Dr. Patrick C. Walsh
Dr. Willet F. Whitmore, III, urologist, Sarasota, FL, and his sister
    Ms. Polly Whitmore, Marblehead, MA
In Canada:
Mr. Dave Grundy, Fort Smith, Northwest Territories
The University of Toronto
In Denmark:
Dr. Hans Henrik Holm, Copenhagen
In Mexico:
Dr. Homero Decanini, urologist, Monterrey
In Japan:
Dr. Hiroki Watanabe, Kyoto
In Spain:
Dr. Rafael Arráns Lara, Head, RT Physics, Hospital Virgen de la
    Macarena, Sevilla
Dr. Tomás S. Crespo Rincón, Internal Medicine, Vigo
Dr. Alejandro Fernández-Larrañaga, urologist, Vigo

Thanks go also to the over one hundred prostate cancer patients and survivors from seven countries (U.S., Great Britain, Canada, New Zealand, Poland, Spain and China) who kindly shared with me their experiences, their anxieties and hopes, their intimacies and frustrations, their *ups-and-downs* when facing a disease that changed their lives, their partners' lives, and their philosophy of living. And my profound desire that the diagnostic helped them to discover or reinforce the inner strength of their own identity. Patients are to be recognized as the central point upon which all health care systems gravitate. This book is, with admiration, dedicated to them.

This book is dedicated also to the many eminent physicians who generously shared with me a galaxy of scientific data and experiences and who agreed to supply personal and professional information and photos –the latter, at my request, to allow patients to "visualize" those brave personalities who carried the torch a step farther for the benefit of humankind. Thanks to them, predictably, future generations may enjoy a cancer-free prostate. When on a hospital bed after surgery or elsewhere under treatment, frequently patients wonder who were or are the great researchers that made it possible for them to be alive, hopefully cured. Generally, they cannot find answers or data. And I believe that when one of those doctors breaks the mold by discovering or perfecting advances, no restraint should obstruct the spontaneous recognition in whichever way by peers and by related institutions –and consequently, by the patients in general.

Thanks also to Doris M. Thompson, Ph.D., of Baton Rouge, Louisiana, for her editing of the English version.

Particular gratitude goes to Dr. Andrew T. Zaruski, Head of the Urology Department, Ochsner Clinic of Baton Rouge, Louisiana, for his remarkable reviews and critique of some medical sections of the manuscript.

And special thanks to my wife Diane, not just for being a wife (a formality easily obtainable through rituals) but for her unconditional support on every step in the five-year-long making of this book and on every aspect of my life.

Santiago Vilas, Ph.D.

The Author

Santiago **Vilas y Gil** was born August 15, 1931 in the Northwest region of Spain, Galicia, in the city of Vigo. Here, he says, "*is where the Atlantic Ocean displays its indomitable fury, where the eucalyptus perfumes the salty air and shutters with its thin verticality the horizontal line of the enigmatic sea*".

He grew up among writers, poets, physicians, painters and church hierarchy. After a first degree in Business Administration, he completed Journalism in Madrid and was a professional journalist for over ten years. In his mid-twenties, he became one of the youngest journalists to substitute editing a daily newspaper and to anchor the newscast of a radio station. He was a correspondent of dailies and literary magazines of Madrid and Barcelona, edited the professional magazine of the association of corporate managers, and reported news to Reuters and Associated Press. He authored numerous articles, and interviewed and published studies on prominent personalities of Literature, Medicine, Philosophy, and Art.

Still under the dictatorship and censorship of Franco, he left Spain for the U.S.A., initially as a press correspondent; he then completed a Master's and a Doctor of Philosophy degrees, and he was on the faculty of universities in North Carolina and Louisiana, and he lectured at universities in Georgia, Tennessee and Texas. He has also lectured and directed Summer Schools in Mexico and Madrid, and he was invited Special Lecturer by the University of Mediterranean Studies, Rome, Italy. He has served as Advisor to and Panelist of the National Endowment for the Humanities, in Washington, D.C. In

1997, he was invited to lead a delegation of American educators to China to meet with top administrators and faculty of the main universities and make recommendations for curriculum and procedural improvements.

Among others, he has authored the books *El Humor y la Novela Española Contemporánea (Humor and the Spanish Contemporary Novel)*, where he formulates "*Humorism*" as a philosophy of living (Editorial Guadarrama, Madrid, Spain); *España: Cultura y Civilización (Spain: Culture and Civilization),* a college textbook (Prentice Hall, New Jersey); and *Tres Sombreros de Copa (Three Top Hats)*, a college edition of Spain's masterpiece of the "Theater of the Absurd" written by Miguel Mihura. He has also contributed to the book *La Medicina Mágica en Galicia (Magic Medicine in Galicia),* investigating the unknown, edited by physician Dr. José Zunzunegui (Tipografía Faro, Spain).

Elected a member of the academic honor societies *Phi Kappa Phi, Sigma Delta Pi* and *Phi Sigma Iota*, he was voted International President of the 31,000-member *Phi Sigma Iota* (1978-1980) and he was later appointed its Executive Director (1986-2000); he founded its magazine *The Forum*, which he edited for several years.

Two years after he underwent left nephrectomy surgery due to a kidney tumor, in 2002 he was diagnosed with prostate cancer: Gleason 4+4=8, PSA 14.6. Treatment selected: brachytherapy, implantation of 123 seeds Iodine-125 followed by a seven-week external beam radiation treatment. Four days after the implant he found the opportunity to test his condition by enjoying his favorite pastime and physical exercise, ballroom dance. He emphasized the fast *Viennese Waltz* (the speed of which is 60 measures per minute x 3 beats per measure=180 steps per minute) followed by the agile *Cha-Cha* (31 measures x 4 beats=124 steps per minute). After the three-hour event, he concluded that, "systems were in very good working order" –what, he added, reaffirmed his contention that, "other than for the *conditions* described above, his health has been and is excellent"…and still "clocking" in 2006 a PSA of 0.01 ng/ml.

C. D. C.

Appendix

A

Selected
Reference Sources
relevant to the
Prostate

Modern technology has affected the content of the ***Bibliography*** or ***Further Research Sources*** sections traditionally inserted in books. Now, at the click of the computer mouse, the Internet offers an unlimited wealth of sources of data tailored to the will of the *navigator*. By entering in the *Search* box of the main engines a word or a theme, the name of an author or a renowned specialist, a clinic or institution, a drug manufacturer or a book title a whole databank pops up on the monitor almost instantaneously. One search engine alone provides, literally, millions of pages on prostate and prostate cancer – in half a second. An online bookseller offers six hundred books on prostate. The Internet has become the most comprehensive and used data research vehicle for prostate-concerned men.

Following is a list of websites relevant to the prostate, operational at the time of this writing, selected for their excellence in design and/or content. Several of these websites have each over one million pages of data plus additional hundreds of links to direct the *navigator* to any conceivable related sources.

Main general engines:
http://www.google.com
http://www.yahoo.com

Websites beginning with: http://
seer.cancer.gov –Statistics

Websites beginning with: http://www.
acor.org –Association of Cancer Online Resources
afud.org –American Foundation for Urologic Disease
ama-assn.org –American Medical Association, Doctors Directory
ameripros.org –American Prostate Society
auanet.com –American Urological Association
boodrow.com -Educ., Web publisher of Man to Man Newsletters
bostwicklaboratories.com –Pathology, Prostate
cancer.org & **cancercare.org** –American Cancer Society
cancerlinksusa.com/prostate –Interactive data and calculations
cancernet.nci.nih.gov –National Cancer Institute
cancertrialshelp.org –Coalition of Nat Cancer Cooperative Groups
capcure.org –Association for the Cure of Prostate Cancer
cityofhope.org –Cancer Patients Support
drcatalona.com –Urological Research Foundation, Dr. W. Catalona
fda.gov –Food & Drug Administration
ftc.gov –To report health frauds
helpingpatients.com –Drug Assistance to needy Patients
herbalgram.org –American Botanical Council
hopkinsprostate.com –Johns Hopkins University Urologic Center
icare.org –Cancer Alliance for Research
ingenta.com –Medical Journals
malecare.com –PCa Support for Gay Men and their Families
manderson.org –M D Anderson Cancer Center
med.umich.edu/umim –University of Michigan Integrative Medicine
megasystemsusa.com –Interactive Anatomy Atlas
mskcc.org –Memorial Sloan-Kettering Cancer Center
mwsearch.com –Medical Word Search
nafc.org –National Association for Continence
nccam.nih.gov/health –Cancer & Complimentary-Alternative Medic.
needymeds.com –Drug Assistance to needy Patients
nih.gov –National Institutes of Health
nlm.nih.gov –National Library of Medicine
oncology.com –Up-to-date source of online cancer news

pathguy.com –Dr. Ed Friedlander's Pathology Educational site
pcacoalition.org –National Prostate Cancer Coalition
pcref.org –Prostate Cancer Research and Education
pcri.org –PCa Research Institute
pdr.net –Pharmaceutical Information
phoenix5.org –Prostate Cancer Information
phrma.org/patients –Drug Assistance to needy Patients
prostate.org –Prostatitis, BPH, Cancer Foundation
prostatecalculator.org –Interactive data and calculations
prostatecancer.com –PCa Research & Education, Cryosurgery
prostatecancerfoundation.org –Prostate Cancer Foundation
prostate-cancer.org –PCa Research Institute
prostateforum.com –Prostate Forum
prostate-online.com –The Prostate Net
prostatepointers.org –Prostate Pointers, *US Too!*
quackwatch.org –Guide to Quackery & Health Fraud
radoncatlanta.com –Cancer Education and Radiation Clinic
rcog.com –Educational and Radiation Center
seattleprostateinst.com –Seattle Prostate Institute
themedicineprogram.com –Drug Assistance to needy Patients
togetherrx.com –Drug Assistance to needy Patients
ustoo.com *–US TOO!* PCa Education & Support Organization

B

Selected Glossary relevant to the Prostate

A

abdomen: the part of the body below the ribs and above the pelvic bone that houses the intestines, liver, kidneys, stomach, bladder, prostate

adenocarcinoma (adenoma + carcinoma): cancer that develops from malignant cells in organs such as the prostate

adenoma (of the prostate): enlargement of the prostate; also Benign Prostatic Hyperplasia (BPH) and Prostatic Hypertrophy, benign tumor of glandular origin and structure

adjuvant: additional treatment sometimes used immediately after surgery or radiation to compliment the effectiveness of the primary therapy

adrenal androgen: male hormone produced by the adrenal glands situated on top of each kidney

adrenal glands: the two adrenal glands on top of each kidney; produce adrenal androgens, small amount of sex hormone testosterone, and hormones that help control blood pressure, heart rate and other vital functions

alpha-blockers: drugs to relax prostate muscle tissue often in treatment of BPH

167

androgen: any of the hormones responsible for certain male characteristics (skin, facial hair, deepening of the voice), testosterone being the main androgen hormone

Androgen Deprivation Therapy (ADT): prostate cancer treatment consisting of blocking the amount of androgen to the prostate cancer cells by means of drugs

anterior: the front of the prostate

anus: the opening of the rectum to the outside of the body

apex: the bottom of the prostate, the part farthest away from the bladder

ASTRO: American Society for Therapeutic Radiology and Oncology

asymptomatic: without recognizable symptoms

B

base: the wide part at the top of the prostate closest to the bladder

BAT: normally used along with IMRT, ultrasound evaluation of the prostate prior to radiotherapy treatment

benign: not cancerous or malignant; does not invade or spread to other tissues or organs; does not threaten the person's life

Benign Prostatic Hyperplasia or Hypertrophy (BPH): non-cancerous overgrowth of cells in the prostate, enlargement of the prostate that may block the flow of urine

biopsy: sampling of tissue from the prostate to be examined microscopically by a pathologist for the presence of cancer

bladder: the organ where urine is collected and stored until it exits through the urethra and the penis

bone marrow: soft tissue in bone cavities that produces blood cells

bone scan: more sensitive than X-Rays, used to identify cancerous growth or metastases of cells that migrated from the prostate gland

BPH: see Benign Prostatic Hyperplasia

brachytherapy: implantation of radioactive isotopes (seeds, pellets) in the prostate; the procedure may be preceded or followed by external radiation

C

cancer: growth of abnormal or mutated cells in some part of the body in an uncontrolled manner

capsule: outer lining of the prostate made of fibrous tissue

carcinoma: (see **Adenocarcinoma**)

castrate: (see **castration**)

castration: to stop or reduce production of testosterone by means of chemical (hormonal) or anatomical (surgical removal of the testicles); men registering testosterone levels of <20 ng/dl are considered **castrate**

catheter: a hollow flexible plastic tube inserted through the penis and the urethra into the bladder to drain urine during surgery or brachytherapy

chemotherapy: use of chemicals to destroy cancer cells; frequently, it kills cancerous cells and healthy cells too

chromosome: a linear strand of DNA in the nucleus of cells that carries the genes and hereditary data

clinical trial: research to evaluate a treatment, a medication or a test

Conformal External Radiation Therapy: technique to beam external radiation specifically to the areas of the prostate affected by cancer tumor and while protecting the surrounding areas

Cryosurgery, cryoablation: the technique of using liquid nitrogen to freeze and destroy the prostate affected by cancerous tumor

CT (Computerized Tomography scan), CAT (Computerized Axial Tomography scan): technology to obtain rotating images from multiple X-Rays "slices" to produce a picture to determine abnormalities (e.g., of the prostate) not found with conventional radiography

cystitis: inflammation and possible infection of the bladder that may be caused by infection or radiation

cystoscope: lighted instrument (like a telescope) inserted through the penis and the urethra used to look and examine the bladder and the urethra (Cystoscopy)

D

Digital Rectal Examination (DRE): a physician's examination of the prostate by inserting a gloved, lubricated finger into the rectum of the patient to feel abnormalities of the gland

DNA (Deoxyribonucleic Acid): basic biological active chemical that defines the physical development and growth of nearly all living organisms; carrier of genetic data

dosimetry: measurement of the doses of radiation to treat a tumor

disuria: painful urination

E

EBRT (External Beam Radiation Therapy): (see **Conformal Radiation**)

ejaculation: the sudden release of sperm and seminal fluid, especially semen, through the penis during orgasm. **Dry Ejaculation** or **Dry Orgasm**: when no fluid or semen is released at orgasm through the penis (it goes to the bladder) due to surgical removal or radiation injury of the valve that controls the direction of the flow

enzyme: chemical substances produced by living cells that cause particular chemical reactions

epididymis: coiled tube that stores and conducts sperm from the testes to the vas deferens

erectile dysfunction: (see **impotence**)

estrogen: a female sex hormone, used in the treatment of prostate cancer

F

false negative: a negative biopsy when, in fact, there is cancer in the prostate, an erroneous negative test result

false positive: a positive test result when, in fact, the malignant condition does not exist, an erroneous positive test result

frequency: the need to urinate more frequently than normal

G

gene: piece or segment of DNA, unit of heredity passed from parent to off-spring; the major functional unit of DNA

Genital System (male): the organs characteristic of males: testicles, vas deferens, prostate, penis

Genome: the entire DNA in an organism, the complete genetic inherence data

gland: organ that produces substances used by another part of the body

gland volume: the size of the prostate measured in cubic centimeters or grams

Gleason: name of pathologist Dr. Donald F. Gleason who developed the **Gleason Grading System** used to grade prostate cancer; the **Gleason Score** is used to classify the glandular cancer of the prostate by evaluating the patterns of glandular differentiation

Gy (Gray): (see **Rad**)

H

hematuria: when blood is found in the urine

histology: investigation of appearance and behavior of tissue as studied under a microscope by a pathologist

hormone: biologically active chemicals responsible for the development of certain sexual characteristics

Hormone (or **Hormonal) Therapy**: use of hormones to treat prostate cancer; chemical orchiectomy

hot flash (or **flush**): sudden sensation of warmth in the face, neck and upper body, one of the side effects of Hormonal Therapy

hyperplasia: enlargement of the prostate or other organ due to the increase in the number of cells

hyperthermia: treatment of prostate cancer by using heat, such as by internal microwave radiation

I

imaging: radiology technique to allow a physician to see inside the body

Immune System: the person's biological system that protects against invasion of bacteria, viruses, cancer cells, etc.

implant: the technique of inserting, for example, radioactive seeds into the prostate or of a device for treatment of Erectile Dysfunction

impotence: inability to have and maintain an erection for sexual intercourse, also known as Erectile Dysfunction

incontinence: result of the inability or impossibility to control urination due to a number of causes

inflammation: swelling or irritation

Informed Consent: a legal document whereby a patient gives permission to his doctor to proceed with whichever testing or treatment after having been informed of its pros and cons

Intensity Modulated Radiation Therapy (IMRT): a radiation therapy technique that combines the expertise of the oncologist with sophisticated technological equipment to deliver carefully measured dose to a tumor while isolating the surrounding tissues and organs

interstitial radiation therapy: radiation applied within the prostate using implanted radioactive seeds; brachytherapy

intravenous: into a vein

invasive: treatment that "invades" a part of the body, such as a surgical incision or the insertion of an instrument or substance

K

Kegel Exercises: exercises designed to strengthen the pelvic muscles

L

laparoscopy: technique that allows the doctor to observe internal organs, such as in the abdominal cavity, through optical cylindral tubes or trocars inserted into the body through a surgical incision; essential for the modern surgical technique Laparoscopic Robotic Prostatectomy

LH (Luteinizing Hormone): hormone secreted by the pituitary gland that stimulates the secretion of sex hormones (testosterone in men)

LHRH (Luteinizing Hormone-Releasing Hormone): hormone secreted by the hypothalamus in the brain that interacts with the LHRH receptor in the pituitary to release LH

LHRH Analogs (or Agonists): synthetic compounds that are chemically similar to luteinizing hormone releasing hormone (LHRH), but that suppress testicular production of testosterone

LHRH Antagonist: an agent that blocks the LHRH receptor without the initial release of LH

libido: interest or desire in sexual activity

linear accelerator: high energy X-Ray machine that revolves around the treatment bed, generates radiation fields for external beam radiation therapy

lobe: one of the two sides of the prostate

localized: restricted to a defined area or organ, such as the prostate

lymph nodes: small glands existing throughout the body that filter out the clear lymphatic fluid or remove waste, bacteria, and cancerous cells traveling through the lymphatic system

lymph, lymphatic fluid: fluid in which all of the cells in the body are constantly bathed and that contains cells that help fight infection

Lymphatic System: tissue and organs that produce, store and carry cells that fight infection

M

Magnetic Resonance Imaging (**MRI**): machine that uses magnetic resonance of atoms in body tissues to produce detailed three-dimensional images of inside the body

malignancy (malignant): a growth or tumor composed of cancerous cells

metastasis, plural **metastases**; **metastatic**: spread of cancerous cells (like from tumor in the prostate) to outside areas, such as the lymphatic nodes, to form new tumors

microwave radiation: electromagnetic radiation whose wavelength is between radio and infrared

N

Nadir: the lowest possible point or level; **PSA Nadir**: the lowest level the PSA in the blood that remains at that level, or lower; used to evaluate cure after a treatment

Nanogram per milliliter (ng/ml): (nanogram=1/billionth of a gram; a gram=1/40 of an ounce; milliliter of fluid volume=1/1000 of a liter; a liter=1+quart). Unit of measurement of PSA in the blood

nephrectomy: surgical removal of a kidney

neoadjuvant: the use of another therapy, such as Androgen Deprivation Therapy (ADT), prior to radiation or surgery to improve the outcome of the procedure

neoplasia: growth of cells, such as cancerous ones, under conditions that would prevent the development of normal tissue

nerve-sparing: a radical prostatectomy technique whereby the surgeon saves the nerves that affect sexual and continence functions

nocturia: the need to urinate frequently at night

nomogram (nomograph): a table or spreadsheet consisting of formulas of coplanar curves resulting from different variables with one straight line that, when intersecting the curves, suggest a value of each variable (see **Partin Tables**)

O

oncologist: physician specialized in diagnosing and treating cancer; **Radiation Oncologist**: physician specialized in cancer radiation treatment

oncology: the branch of medicine studying cancerous tumors

orchiectomy: surgical removal of one or both testicles; castration

organ: grouping of tissues that perform independently specific functions such as the heart, the prostate, the lungs

organ-confined or **organ-localized disease**: tumor growth limited or confined to the prostate and not spread beyond the capsule, not metastasized

osteopenia, osteopororis: reduction in the bone density reaching T score of -2.5; risk of bone fractures; affects many prostate cancer patients

P

palliative: therapy that may relieve a problem or disease without necessarily solving or curing it

Partin Tables: formulas in a Nomogram (see) that, based on PSA, Clinical Stage and Gleason Score may predict the probability of spread of cancer beyond the prostate

pathologist: medical doctor specialized in identifying diseases by studying cells and tissues under a microscope

PCa: common abbreviation for Prostate Cancer

perineal: of the perineum, the area between the scrotum and the anus

PIN (Prostatic Intraepithelial Neoplasia): condition discovered by pathological exam of prostate tissue, considered precursor of cancer; high grade (PIN3) suggests presence of cancer

proctitis: inflammation of the rectum, possibly a side effect of Radiation Therapy

prognosis: evaluation of the clinical outlook or probability of cure of a disease

ProstaScint Scan: imaging using an antibody focused on androgen-independent tumor tissue that may detect early spread of prostate cancer

prostate: male gland that surrounds the urethra and located below the bladder; among other functions, it produces a fluid that is part of the semen

prostatectomy: surgical removal of all or part of the prostate

Prostate-Specific Antigen (PSA): protein secreted by both normal and cancerous cells of the prostate gland and whose elevated level in the blood may flag the development of diseases of the prostate

Prostate-Specific Antigen Test (PSA Test): test to measure the amount of prostate-specific antigen that escaped from the prostate into the blood; used to evaluate abnormal prostate conditions

Prostatic Acid Phosphatase (PAP): enzyme or biomarker secreted by prostate cells and associated, in increased amounts, with a probability of cancer; use of the PAP Test declined since the discovery of the PSA Test

prostatitis: infection or inflammation of the prostate gland

protocol: a treatment, procedure, or therapy to attack a disease

PSA Baseline: the PSA level before starting a treatment; PSA levels considered "normal" according to age and other factors before arising suspicion of disease

PSA-Free (freePSA): one of the PSA tests family, shows the percentage of Free PSA in the blood; Free PSA divided by Total PSA x 100 shows low risk prostate cancer if the result is >25%, while <10% suggests prostate cancer developing

PSA Nadir: the lowest level the PSA in the blood that remains at that level, or lower, so many years after treatment; used to evaluate cure rates

173

PSA: (see **Prostate-Specific Antigen-PSA**)

R

rad: measured unit of absorbed radiation dose; 100 rads = 1 Gray (Gy), 1Gy = 1joule/kg = 100 rads

Radiation Therapy (Conformal, 3-Dimensional): if externally administered, high energy radiation from X-Rays, neutrons or other sources directed to a tumor to kill the cells and shrink the tumor while sparing the surrounding normal tissues; if internally or interstitial, radiation emitted by radioisotopes that have been implanted in the prostate, such as in brachytherapy

radical prostatectomy (RP): surgical removal of the entire prostate and seminal vesicles

radioisotope: metal or chemical made of an atom that emits ionizing radiation

rectum: the last eight to ten inches of the large intestine leading to the outside of the body

refractory: cells resistant to Hormonal Therapy

robot, robotic: programmable electronic machine or device capable of manipulating objects or perform tasks ordinarily adscribed to humans only; in Medicine, revolutionary surgical technique that allows a surgeon to operate on a patient from a console located several feet distant (as in Laparoscopic Robotic Prostatectomy)

S

screening: evaluation of large number of men to diagnose possible prostate anomalies at an early stage

scrotum: the external pouch or bag of skin that contains the testicles

semen: white fluid released by a male through his penis during sexual climax; composed of sperm from the testicles and fluid from the prostate and other sex glands

seminal vesicles: glands below the bladder and connected to the prostate that supply nutrients for the semen

seminal: regarding semen

side-effect: undesirable consequence of a medication or treatment

sphincter: a muscle that, under certain conditions and stimuli, naturally contracts and extends, for example to allow urine to come out of the bladder or to direct the flow of sperm to the urethra

staging (clinical and pathologic): methods based on the results of certain exploratory tests (DRE, biopsy) that stabilize the size and extent or spread of cancer; used to devise adequate treatment and prognosis

stricture: frequently, a side effect of surgical injury or radiation that constricts the flow of urine out of the bladder and through the urethra

systemic: affecting the whole body (e.g., metastasis)

T

testis (plural **testes**) or **testicle**: one of the two egg-shaped male reproductive glands located inside the scrotum that produce sperm and secrete male hormones

testosterone: the male hormone or androgen produced mainly by the testicles, essential for his fertility and the stimulation of sexual activity and the growth of other organs such as the prostate

tissue: an organized group of cells to perform specialized functions

transperineal: through the perineum

Transrectal Ultrasound (TRUS): technique that uses ultrasound waves to image the prostate by inserting a probe into the rectum for biopsy or similar procedures

transrectal: through the rectum

Transurethral Resection of the Prostate (TURP): surgical procedure inserting an instrument through the penis and urethra to remove prostate tissue that was obstructing the passage of urine from the bladder through the urethra

transurethral: through the urethra

tumor: whether benign or cancerous, a mass or abnormal growth of tissue that could be caused by uncontrolled cell division

U

ultrasound (ultrasonogram, sonogram): the use of sound waves whose echoes produce on a computer monitor images of internal organs; used for diagnosing

ureter: each of the two anatomical tubes that drain urine from the kidneys to the bladder

urethra: tube that drains urine from the bladder, and semen from the sex glands, through the prostate to exit through the penis

urethritis: inflammation of the urethra, frequently after radiation of the prostate

urgency: the feeling of sudden need to urinate

urologist: physician specialized in diseases of the urinary and sex organs

W

watchful waiting: a man's decision, on his own or by his physician's recommendation, not to undergo cancer treatment at the time and to wait until symptoms appear or other condition develops

X

X-Rays: electromagnetic radiation whose wavelength is between ultraviolet and gamma rays; used to see and to picture the inside of the body

C
Index

urination:
- -burning, 46
- -disuria, 46
- -dribbling, 46
- -frequency, 46
- -hematuria, 46
- -hesitancy, 46
- -incomplete emptying, 46
- -intermittency, 46
- -nocturia, 46
- -self-test, 47
- -voiding, 28, 60

uroflowmetry, 60

V

vas deferens, 39

W

Walsh Nerves, 111
Watchful Waiting, 102
Where is the patient?, 70
Why me?, 8, 20, 75

X

X-Rays, 121

Z

Zorrilla, José, 37

www.ingramcontent.com/pod-product-compliance
Lightning Source LLC
Chambersburg PA
CBHW041146210326
41519CB00046B/133